Turas 2

Gaeilge na Sraithe Sóisearaí
GNÁTHLEIBHÉAL
An Dara Bliain & An Tríú Bliain

An Dara hEagrán

Mo Leabhar Gníomhaíochta

Ainm: ....
Rang: ....

educate.ie

Risteard Mac Liam

FOILSITHE AG:
Educate.ie
Walsh Educational Books Ltd
Oileán Ciarraí
Co. Chiarraí
www.educate.ie

ARNA CHLÓ AGUS ARNA CHEANGAL AG:
Walsh Colour Print
Oileán Ciarraí
Co. Chiarraí

© Risteard Mac Liam 2022

Gach ceart ar cosaint. Ní ceadmhach aon chuid den fhoilseachán seo a chóipeáil, a atáirgeadh ná a tharchur in aon mhodh ná slí, bíodh sin leictreonach, meicniúil, bunaithe ar fhótachóipeáil, ar thaifeadadh nó eile gan cead scríofa a fháil ón bhfoilsitheoir roimh ré.

Tá na foilsitheoirí faoi chomaoin acu siúd a thug cead dúinn grianghraif a atáirgeadh: Gary Mather / Alamy Stock Photo; Shutterstock; Tsuni / USA / Alamy Stock Photo.

Cé go ndearnadh gach iarracht dul i dteagmháil leo siúd ar leo an cóipcheart ar ábhair sa téacs seo, theip orainn teacht ar dhaoine áirithe. Is féidir leis na daoine sin dul i dteagmháil le Educate.ie, agus beimid sásta na gnáthshocruithe a dhéanamh leo.

ISBN: 978-1-913698-69-0

Mo Leabhar Gníomhaíochta

Clár Ábhair

Réamhrá iv

Caibidil 1: Mé Féin 1

Caibidil 2: Mo Theaghlach 10

Caibidil 3: Mo Theach 18

Caibidil 4: Mo Cheantar 28

Caibidil 5: Mo Scoil 38

Caibidil 6: Mo Chaithimh Aimsire 50

Caibidil 7: Ceol 60

Caibidil 8: Spórt 70

Caibidil 9: Laethanta Saoire 80

Caibidil 10: Tinneas agus Sláinte 90

Trialacha Cluastuisceana 100
Script Éisteachta: An Téacsleabhar 120
Script Éisteachta: Mo Leabhar Gníomhaíochta 132

Fáilte chuig do Leabhar Gníomhaíochta. Feicfidh tú sa Leabhar Gníomhaíochta rudaí a d'fhoghlaim tú in *Turas 2*. Tá na caibidlí sa Leabhar Gníomhaíochta bunaithe ar Chaibidil 1 go Caibidil 10 de do théacsleabhar. Sa Leabhar Gníomhaíochta seo:

- Déanfaidh tú réimse leathan cleachtaí foclóra agus gramadaí. / You will do a wide range of vocabulary and grammar exercises.
- Comhlánóidh tú seicliosta chun measúnú a dhéanamh ar do chuid foghlama. Féach an sampla thíos. / You will complete a checklist in which you assess your learning. Look at the example below.

	Go maith 🙂	Measartha 😐	Go dona ☹
An Ghaeilge sa Rang	✔		

- Déanfaidh tú nóta de na príomhscileanna a mbaineann tú úsáid astu. / You will make a note of the key skills that you use.
- Forbróidh tú plean gníomhaíochta ar an bhféinmheasúnú a dhéanann tú. / You will develop a plan of action based on your self-assessment.
- Cleachtfaidh tú do scileanna éisteachta i dtrialacha cluaistuisceana atá bunaithe ar gach topaic. / You will practise your listening skills in listening comprehensions based on each topic.
- Beidh fáil agat ar na scripteanna chun cabhrú leat leis na trialacha cluastuisceana. / You will have access to the scripts to help you with the listening comprehensions.

Go n-éirí leat ar do thuras!

Clár Ábhair

Cuid 1–2	An Ghaeilge sa Rang 1
Cuid 3–6	Ag Cur Síos Orm Féin 2
Cuid 7	Uimhreacha 4
Cuid 8	Aoiseanna 4
Gramadach	Na Focail 'ar' agus 'ag' 5
Cuid 9–11	Cleachtaí Athbhreithnithe 6
Measúnú chun Foghlama	Féinmheasúnú 8
Measúnú chun Foghlama	Plean Gníomhaíochta 9

Cuid 1

Líon na bearnaí.

> conas atá tú   go raibh maith agat   Dia duit   táim go maith

Máirín _____.

Eoin Dia 's Muire duit.

Máirín _____?

Eoin Táim go maith, _____. Agus tusa?

Máirín _____ freisin, go raibh maith agat.

Cuid 2

Líon na bearnaí.

> conas atá tú   céard fútsa   táim go maith freisin   a Órla

Ciarán Dia duit, _____.

Órla Dia 's Muire duit, a Chiaráin. _____?

Ciarán Go maith, go raibh maith agat. _____?

Órla _____, go raibh maith agat.

Turas 2: Mo Leabhar Gníomhaíochta

Cuid 3

Scríobh an dath ceart. (*Write the correct colour*).

> dubh   donn   liath   bán   buí   oráiste   dearg   bándearg   corcra   gorm   glas

1 = _____

2 = _____

3 = _____

4 = _____

5 = _____

6 = _____

7 = _____

8 = _____

9 = _____

10 = _____

11 = _____

Cuid 4

Cén dath súl atá acu? Líon na bearnaí.

| súile donna | súile gorma | súile glasa | súile cnódhonna |

1. Tá _____ _____ aige.

2. Tá _____ _____ aici.

3. Tá _____ _____ aige.

4. Tá _____ _____ aici.

Cuid 5

Cén sórt gruaige atá orthu? Líon na bearnaí.

| gruaig ghearr fhionn | gruaig chatach dhubh | gruaig fhada liath | gruaig dhíreach rua |

1. Tá _____ _____ _____ uirthi.

2. Tá _____ _____ _____ air.

3. Tá _____ _____ _____ air.

4. Tá _____ _____ _____ uirthi.

Cuid 6

Líon na bearnaí. Is féidir leat níos mó ná focal amháin a úsáid.

> fial   cliste   greannmhar   cabhrach   foighneach
> dílis   spórtúil   cairdiúil   fuinniúil   cneasta

Sampla: Seasann mo chairde liom. Tá siad <u>dílis agus cneasta</u>.

1. Imríonn siad peil. Tá siad _____.
2. Bíonn siad i gcónaí ag rith. Tá siad _____.
3. Insíonn siad scéalta grinn. Tá siad _____.
4. Fanann siad go ciúin. Tá siad _____.
5. Tugann siad bronntanais dom. Tá siad _____.
6. Cabhraíonn siad liom. Tá siad _____.
7. Tá siad go maith ag an Mata. Tá siad _____.
8. Labhraíonn siad le gach duine. Tá siad _____.

Cuid 7

Déan na suimeanna seo. Tá an chéad cheann déanta duit.

1	a dó **móide** a dó	a ceathair
2	a trí **móide** a trí	
3	a ceathair **móide** a dó	
4	a ceathair **lúide** a dó	
5	a dó **lúide** a haon	
6	a trí **faoina** haon	
7	a dó **faoina** trí	
8	a hocht **roinnte ar** a dó	
9	a deich **roinnte ar** a cúig	
10	a haon **roinnte ar** a haon	

Cuid 8

Scríobh na haoiseanna i bhfocail. Tá an chéad cheann déanta duit.

12	dhá bhliain déag d'aois	9	
14		11	
5		19	
8		1	
10		20	

GRAMADACH

Na Focail 'ar' agus 'ag'

Gramadach 1

Tá na liostaí seo san ord mícheart. Athscríobh san ord ceart iad.

1. orm, ort, uirthi, air, orainn, orthu, oraibh

   _____

2. agam, acu, agat, agaibh, againn, aige, aici

   _____

Gramadach 2

Aistrigh na habairtí seo.

1. Tá gruaig ghearr dhubh air.

   _____

2. Níl gruaig dhualach dhonn orm.

   _____

3. An bhfuil tuirse ort?

   _____

4. Tá súile donna agam.

   _____

5. Níl deartháireacha aici.

   _____

6. An bhfuil a lán cairde acu?

   _____

Gramadach 3

Athscríobh na focail idir lúibíní.

1. Tá gruaig ghearr [ar: é] _____.
2. An bhfuil tuirse [ar: tú] _____?
3. Níl ocras [ar: tú] _____.
4. Tá súile móra donna [ag: í] _____.
5. Tá súile geala gorma [ag: muid] _____.
6. An bhfuil deirfiúracha [ag: é] _____?

Caibidil 1

Mé Féin

Turas 2: Mo Leabhar Gníomhaíochta

Cuid 9

Léamhthuiscint

Léigh an píosa seo faoi Chiara agus freagair na ceisteanna a ghabhann leis.

Haigh, is mise Ciara. Táim beagnach cúig bliana déag d'aois. Tá gruaig fhada fhionn orm agus tá súile gorma agam. Táim spórtúil, cabhrach agus dílis.

1. Cén aois í Ciara?

   _____

2. Cén sórt gruaige atá uirthi?

   _____

3. Cén dath súl atá aici?

   _____

4. Cén sórt duine í?

   _____

Cuid 10

Freagair na ceisteanna seo.

1. Cad is ainm duit?

   _____

2. Cén sórt gruaige atá ort?

   _____

3. Cén dath súl atá agat?

   _____

4. Cén sórt duine thú?

   _____

Cuid 11

Cuardach focal

Déan an cuardach focal.

Mé Féin

C	X	J	C	Z	S	L	T	E	S	E	B	R	W	X	Y	R	C	O	M
H	F	W	B	I	Q	Ú	W	B	C	A	B	H	R	A	C	H	U	Y	S
G	O	R	M	U	B	I	I	B	N	B	V	D	D	E	U	C	E	C	A
D	H	Y	D	H	Á	G	K	L	W	G	I	O	F	F	A	T	Y	H	O
X	S	G	P	M	N	A	T	U	E	W	W	N	I	R	T	L	G	H	I
D	B	M	F	A	K	R	J	H	M	I	D	J	Y	L	C	H	Z	Y	S
I	T	Q	Z	H	W	R	U	Q	G	E	T	Q	D	R	A	E	F	V	W
I	B	B	T	S	Y	W	U	U	X	Z	G	Y	S	Y	I	Q	L	Y	D
T	Z	F	B	A	G	G	D	A	W	Y	L	C	G	U	R	U	V	H	A
U	N	S	Q	A	L	L	G	A	Y	P	M	S	X	P	D	E	E	Q	A
R	U	N	A	B	P	P	Q	E	N	B	U	K	O	M	I	A	I	V	W
T	Y	Y	E	F	G	A	Q	R	U	K	F	U	Q	Y	Ú	W	S	Y	C
H	R	P	T	Z	D	G	U	I	V	Y	M	J	C	V	I	I	S	B	E
H	O	F	P	J	Y	G	R	M	J	K	V	Y	O	X	L	H	Z	E	A
N	Z	B	F	B	U	K	N	O	J	R	A	N	H	B	T	Z
G	S	I	K	A	E	J	U	N	A	M	G	P	C	Z	R	F	S	X	H
B	J	A	X	M	N	J	V	O	X	I	D	C	R	W	N	A	N	F	Q
R	H	E	C	I	T	K	M	G	R	N	G	U	A	E	E	Z	P	X	Y
D	D	E	K	N	K	I	I	K	V	Y	F	X	B	N	V	F	D	A	M
O	T	R	V	Q	N	X	M	G	J	A	V	B	C	H	U	D	C	G	E

dubh	súile
bán	gruaig
gorm	cabhrach
aois	cairdiúil
corcra	cneasta

Féinmheasúnú

Léigh gach topaic sa chéad cholún. An bhfuil tú ag déanamh dul chun cinn? Cuir tic (✓) sa cholún cuí. Tá uimhir an leathanaigh chuí in aice leis an topaic.

Stór focal

féinmheasúnú	self-assessment	dul chun cinn	progress
topaic	topic	sa cholún cuí	in the appropriate column

TOPAIC	Lch	Go maith 🙂	Measartha 😐	Go dona ☹
FOCLÓIR				
An Ghaeilge sa Rang	4			
Ag Cur Síos Orm Féin 1	6			
Ag Cur Síos Orm Féin 2	8			
Uimhreacha	10			
Aoiseanna	11			
GRAMADACH				
Na Focail 'ar' agus 'ag'	16			
SCRÍOBH				
Iarratas ar Phost	19			

Na príomhscileanna

Le cabhair ó do mhúinteoir, cuir tic in aice leis na príomhscileanna ar bhain tú úsáid astu i gCaibidil 1.

Na príomhscileanna	Bhain mé úsáid as
A bheith liteartha	
A bheith uimheartha	
Cumarsáid	
A bheith cruthaitheach	
Mé féin a bhainistiú	
Fanacht folláin	
Obair le daoine eile	
Eolas agus smaointeoireacht a bhainistiú	

Plean Gníomhaíochta

Déan machnamh ar do chuid foghlama! Féach ar an bhféinmheasúnú a rinne tú ar leathanach 8. Bunaithe ar an eolas seo, déan plean gníomhaíochta. Líon isteach na míreanna thíos.

Mír 1: Tá eolas maith agam ar na topaicí seo

Mír 2: Tá cleachtadh le déanamh agam ar na topaicí seo

Mír 3: Plean gníomhaíochta

Mar shampla: 'Scríobhfaidh mé focail agus nathanna nua i mo phunann ar leathanach 2.'

Mo Theaghlach

Clár Ábhair

Cuid 1–2	Mo Theaghlach	10
Cuid 3	Ag Comhaireamh Daoine	11
Cuid 4	Dátaí Breithe	11
Gramadach	An Aidiacht Shealbhach	12
Cuid 5–7	Cleachtaí Athbhreithnithe	13
Measúnú chun Foghlama	Féinmheasúnú	16
Measúnú chun Foghlama	Plean Gníomhaíochta	17

Cuid 1

Líon na bearnaí.

> beirt   mo dhearthaireacha   is ainm do   deirfiúr amháin   go han-mhaith

Colm Cé mhéad siblín atá agat, a Irena?

Irena Tá _____ siblíní agam. Tá deartháir amháin agam. Pavel is ainm dó. Tá _____ agam freisin. Petra is ainm di. Céard fútsa?

Colm Tá ceathrar siblíní agam. Yvonne agus Siobhán _____ mo dheirfiúracha agus Éamonn agus Réamann is ainm do _____.

Irena An réitíonn sibh le chéile?

Colm Réitímid _____ le chéile.

Cuid 2

Líon na bearnaí.

> an réitíonn sibh   céard fútsa   is ainm dóibh   deirfiúracha nó dearthaireacha

Dara A Olwen, an bhfuil aon _____ agat?

Olwen Tá beirt deirfiúracha agam, Maria agus Clare. Níl aon deartháireacha agam. _____?

Dara Tá deartháir amháin agus deirfiúr amháin agam. Éanna agus Etain _____.

Olwen _____ le chéile?

Dara Réitímid go hiontach le chéile.

Cuid 3

Cé mhéad duine atá sna pictiúir seo? Tá an chéad cheann déanta duit.

Tá triúr sa phictiúr seo.

Cuid 4

Cathain a rugadh na daoine seo? Tá an chéad cheann déanta duit.

Rugadh mé ar an [23/05]

tríú lá is fiche de mhí na Bealtaine

Rugadh mé ar an [31/01]

Rugadh mé ar an [02/12]

Rugadh mé ar an [15/08]

GRAMADACH

An Aidiacht Shealbhach

Gramadach 1

Athscríobh na focail idir lúibíní. Tá an chéad cheann déanta duit.

1. [mo: deartháir] my brother _____ mo dheartháir _____
2. [a: máthair] his mother _____
3. [a: teaghlach] their family _____
4. [ár: seanathair] our grandfather _____
5. [a: garmhac] their grandson _____
6. [do: cairde] your friends _____

Gramadach 2

Athscríobh na focail idir lúibíní. Tá an chéad cheann déanta duit.

1. [ár: athair] our father _____ ár n-athair _____
2. [mo: aintín] my aunt _____
3. [a: athair] her father _____
4. [a: uncail] his uncle _____
5. [bhur: iníon] your (pl) daughter _____
6. [do: uncail] your uncle _____

Gramadach 3

Athscríobh na focail idir lúibíní. Tá an chéad cheann déanta duit.

Haigh, is mise Aoife. Tá cúigear i [mo: teaghlach] **mo theaghlach**. Tá deartháir amháin agus deirfiúr amháin agam. Aindreas agus Caoimhe is ainm dóibh.

Tá [mo: deartháir] _____ dhá bhliain déag d'aois. Tá [mo: deirfiúr] _____ deich mbliana d'aois.

Tá [mo: tuismitheoirí] _____ an-chineálta agus an-chabhrach.

Tá [mo: aintín] _____, [mo: uncail] _____ agus [a: páistí] _____ ina gcónaí síos an bóthar uainn.

Cuid 5

Fógra

Léigh an fógra seo agus freagair na ceisteanna a ghabhann leis.

TEAGHLAIGH Á LORG AG GAEILGE 24!

Ar mhaith leat páirt a ghlacadh i gclár réaltachta?

Sa chlár nua, *Mo Lá, Do Lá*, leanfaidh na ceamaraí trí theaghlach ar feadh ceithre seachtaine.

Fiosróimid:
- Cén sórt daoine iad
- Cén sórt rudaí a thaitníonn leo
- Cén sórt rudaí nach dtaitníonn leo
- Cad a dhéanann siad gach lá
- Cén chaoi a réitíonn siad le chéile

Chun cur isteach ar an gclár:
1. Líon isteach an fhoirm iarratais ar www.g24/ie/mo-la-do-la.
2. Taifead físeán gearr faoi do theaghlach.

Ní mór do theaghlaigh a bheith ar fáil don taifeadadh i mí Dheireadh Fómhair agus i mí na Samhna.

Tuilleadh eolais ar www.g24/ie/mo-la-do-la.

1. Cuir in iúl cé acu **fíor** nó **bréagach** atá na habairtí seo a leanas. Cuir **tic** (✔) sa bhosca ceart.

	Fíor	Bréagach
(i) Tá ranganna scoile á lorg ag Gaeilge 24.	☐	☐
(ii) Clár réaltachta a bheidh ar siúl.	☐	☐
(iii) Leanfaidh na ceamaraí na teaghlaigh ar feadh dhá sheachtain.	☐	☐
(iv) Fiosróidh siad cén sórt daoine iad.	☐	☐
(v) Fiosróidh siad cén sórt bia a itheann siad.	☐	☐

2. Conas a chuireann tú isteach ar an gclár?
   _____
   _____

3. Cathain a dhéanfar an taifeadadh?
   _____

Cuid 6

Léamhthuiscint

Léigh an píosa seo faoi Jason agus freagair na ceisteanna a ghabhann leis.

Haigh. Is mise Jason. Is as Ceatharlach mé ach táim i mo chónaí i gCill Dara. Táim ceithre bliana déag d'aois. Rugadh mé ar an gcéad lá de mhí na Bealtaine.

Tá seisear i mo theaghlach: mé féin, mo mháthair, m'athair, mo bheirt deartháireacha agus mo dheirfiúr. Tá go leor uncailí agus aintíní agam freisin. Tá tríocha col ceathrar (*cousins*) agam, creid é nó ná creid.

Tá gruaig ghearr fhionn orm agus tá súile glasa agam. Tá gruaig ghearr fhionn ar mo dheartháireacha freisin ach tá súile gorma acu. Tá gruaig fhada dhíreach fhionn ar mo dheirfiúr agus tá súile donna aici. Tá siad go léir fuinniúil agus fial.

Tá gruaig fhionn ar mo mháthair agus tá súile glasa aici. Tá sí an-spórtúil. Tá gruaig dhubh ar m'athair agus tá súile donna aige. Tá sé an-chineálta.

Réitímid go léir go han-mhaith le chéile.

1. Cá bhfuil Jason ina chónaí?
   _____

2. Cén aois é?
   _____

3. Cathain a rugadh é?
   _____

4. Cé mhéad duine atá ina theaghlach?
   _____

5. Cé mhéad col ceathrar atá aige?
   _____

6. Cén sórt gruaige atá ar a dheartháireacha?
   _____

7. Cén dath súl atá ag a dheirfiúr?
   _____

8. Cén sórt daoine iad a mháthair agus a athair?
   _____
   _____

9. An réitíonn siad go léir le chéile?
   _____

10. Buaileann tú le Jason. Scríobh síos **dhá** cheist ar mhaith leat a chur air.
    _____
    _____

Caibidil 2

Cuid 7

Cuardach focal

Déan an cuardach focal.

Mo Theaghlach

D	E	A	R	T	H	Á	I	R	U	Y	Z	A	Q	Y	G	D	N	Q	M
I	E	L	A	O	B	U	W	A	B	J	E	I	T	Z	X	B	U	Q	Á
I	R	I	L	L	E	A	N	Á	I	R	L	D	J	B	N	U	T	B	T
D	R	K	R	A	D	V	U	W	D	J	A	C	G	K	I	X	K	V	H
I	N	I	X	F	T	R	N	R	D	P	V	W	J	Z	U	E	M	A
R	F	M	D	F	I	I	H	S	F	U	D	C	B	K	G	I	I	M	I
P	E	Á	F	T	K	Ú	J	W	R	L	D	P	D	T	L	F	N	Q	R
X	A	R	D	F	H	A	R	S	M	P	I	R	Z	I	D	S	Q	Q	Y
W	B	T	W	E	F	Z	O	T	O	I	B	R	K	D	S	S	T	Z	H
W	H	A	E	A	W	N	R	A	I	G	N	J	M	Z	X	X	A	E	R
G	R	F	Y	X	B	I	E	K	U	Z	F	K	A	D	O	O	M	R	C
F	A	U	I	L	E	C	H	S	S	P	G	V	C	V	R	G	Z	V	S
J	F	Z	D	B	R	Y	I	K	B	S	F	G	I	L	F	T	K	I	Q
N	H	G	R	I	G	V	D	W	J	K	K	R	V	S	S	G	W	D	Y
J	T	U	M	T	P	P	L	N	P	I	D	E	U	E	C	M	O	W	R
B	Z	P	K	R	X	X	M	B	W	B	J	X	B	M	B	L	X	D	M
L	H	V	Ú	M	K	B	M	F	S	X	I	B	N	P	L	N	X	U	P
L	D	I	D	R	O	E	W	G	K	C	D	N	E	B	N	A	H	C	L
T	R	V	P	F	J	P	S	Z	B	A	J	R	Y	F	F	I	W	E	Y
T	E	A	G	H	L	A	C	H	R	Z	T	T	A	T	H	A	I	R	H

teaghlach

máthair

athair

deartháir

deirfiúr

beirt

triúr

Eanáir

Feabhra

Márta

Turas 2: Mo Leabhar Gníomhaíochta

Féinmheasúnú

Léigh gach topaic sa chéad cholún. An bhfuil tú ag déanamh dul chun cinn? Cuir tic (✓) sa cholún cuí. Tá uimhir an leathanaigh chuí in aice leis an topaic.

TOPAIC	Lch	Go maith 🙂	Measartha 😐	Go dona ☹
FOCLÓIR				
Mo Theaghlach	26			
Ag Comhaireamh Daoine	28			
Dátaí Breithe	30			
GRAMADACH				
An Aidiacht Shealbhach	32			
SCRÍOBH				
Alt	38			

Na príomhscileanna

Le cabhair ó do mhúinteoir, cuir tic in aice leis na príomhscileanna ar bhain tú úsáid astu i gCaibidil 2.

Na príomhscileanna	Bhain mé úsáid as
A bheith liteartha	
A bheith uimheartha	
Cumarsáid	
A bheith cruthaitheach	
Mé féin a bhainistiú	
Fanacht folláin	
Obair le daoine eile	
Eolas agus smaointeoireacht a bhainistiú	

Plean Gníomhaíochta

Déan machnamh ar do chuid foghlama! Féach ar an bhféinmheasúnú a rinne tú ar leathanach 16. Bunaithe ar an eolas seo, déan plean gníomhaíochta. Líon isteach na míreanna thíos.

Mír 1: Tá eolas maith agam ar na topaicí seo

Mír 2: Tá cleachtadh le déanamh agam ar na topaicí seo

Mír 3: Plean gníomhaíochta

Mar shampla: 'Úsáidfidh mé trí nath nua gach seachtain.'

Clár Ábhair

Cuid 1	An Bloc Árasán	18
Cuid 2–4	An Áit a Bhfuil Cónaí Orm	18
Cuid 5–6	An Seomra is Fearr Liom	20
Gramadach	An Aimsir Chaite	21
Cuid 7–10	Cleachtaí Athbhreithnithe	22
Measúnú chun Foghlama	Féinmheasúnú	26
Measúnú chun Foghlama	Plean Gníomhaíochta	27

Cuid 1

Líon na bearnaí.

> i m'árasán   dhá   is fearr   folctha   cé mhéad seomra

Leona   _____ atá i d'árasán, a Phóil?

Pól   Tá cúig sheomra _____.

Leona   Céard iad?

Pól   An chistin, an seomra suí, _____ sheomra leapa agus an seomra _____.

Leona   Cén seomra _____ leat?

Pól   Is fearr liom an chistin, gan dabht ar bith!

Cuid 2

Líon na bearnaí.

> cathrach   i dteach sraithe   aoibhinn   i do chónaí   suite

Daithí   Cén sórt tí ina bhfuil tú _____, a Ursula?

Ursula   Táim i mo chónaí _____.

Daithí   Cá bhfuil an teach _____?

Ursula   Tá sé suite i lár na _____.

Daithí   An maith leat é?

Ursula   Ó, is _____ liom é.

Cuid 3

Scríobh an téarma Gaeilge faoi na pictiúir. Tá an chéad cheann déanta duit.

~~teach feirme~~   teach leathscoite   teach sraithe   teach scoite

teach feirme

Cuid 4

Scríobh an téarma Gaeilge faoi na pictiúir. Tá an chéad cheann déanta duit.

~~cois farraige~~   sna bruachbhailte   faoin tuath   i lár na cathrach

cois farraige

Cuid 5

Meaitseáil na pictiúir leis na focail.

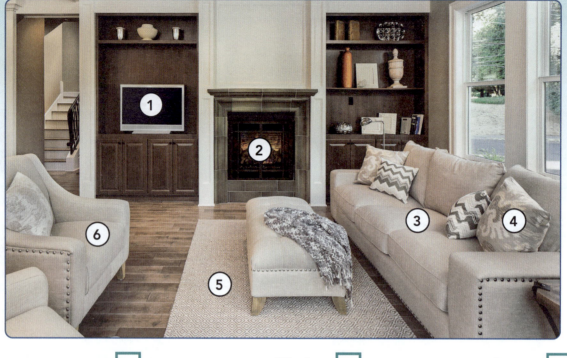

| ruga ☐ | teilifíseán ☐ | tolg ☐ |
| cathaoir uilleach ☐ | cúisín ☐ | tinteán ☐ |

Cuid 6

Meaitseáil na pictiúir leis na focail.

| miasniteoir ☐ | cócaireán ☐ | reoiteoir ☐ |
| doirteal ☐ | tarraiceán ☐ | cuisneoir ☐ |

GRAMADACH

An Aimsir Chaite

Gramadach 1

Scríobh an cheist (an fhoirm 'tú'), an freagra dearfach (an fhoirm 'mé') agus an freagra diúltach (an fhoirm 'mé'). Tá an chéad cheann déanta duit.

	An briathar	An cheist (?)	An freagra dearfach (+)	An freagra diúltach (–)
1	dún	ar dhún tú?	dhún mé	níor dhún mé
2	fan			
3	ól			
4	bris			
5	seinn			

Gramadach 2

Scríobh an cheist (an fhoirm 'tú'), an freagra dearfach (an fhoirm 'mé') agus an freagra diúltach (an fhoirm 'mé'). Tá an chéad cheann déanta duit.

	An briathar	An cheist (?)	An freagra dearfach (+)	An freagra diúltach (–)
1	ceannaigh	ar cheannaigh tú?	cheannaigh mé	níor cheannaigh mé
2	tosaigh			
3	liostaigh			
4	sínigh			
5	fáiltigh			

Gramadach 3

Athscríobh na focail idir lúibíní san Aimsir Chaite.

1. Ar [dún: tú] _____ an doras?
2. Níor [fan: sibh] _____ sa teach.
3. [Ól: mé] _____ trí chupán tae.
4. [Bris: siad] _____ an fhuinneog.
5. [Seinn: muid] _____ ceol le chéile.
6. Ar [ceannaigh: tú] _____ arán?
7. Ar [tosaigh: sé] _____ ag siúl ón gclub?
8. Níor [liostaigh: muid] _____ na pointí.
9. Ar [sínigh: sí] _____ a hainm?
10. [Fáiltigh: mé] _____ roimh na scoláirí.

Cuid 7

Fógra

Léigh an fógra seo agus freagair na ceisteanna a ghabhann leis.

CEANT TROSCÁIN!

Déardaoin, 15 Samhain • Caisleán Bhaile Átha Cliath

Beidh na nithe seo a leanas ar ceant

- leapacha
- taisceadáin taobh leapa
- cathaoireacha uilleacha
- toilg
- vardrúis
- tinteáin
- matail
- uirlisí cistine
- miasa
- sceanra
- ornáidí
- pictiúir

Tosóidh an ceant ag 10.00 • Cláraigh ag www.ceant123.ie

1. Cuir in iúl cé acu **fíor** nó **bréagach** atá na habairtí seo a leanas. Cuir **tic** (✔) sa bhosca ceart.

   Fíor   Bréagach

   (i) Beidh an ceant ar siúl ar an 15 Samhain. ☐ ☐
   (ii) Beidh sé ar siúl i gCaisleán Chorcaí. ☐ ☐
   (iii) Beidh leapacha ar ceant. ☐ ☐
   (iv) Beidh toilg, cófraí agus matail ar ceant. ☐ ☐
   (v) Beidh troscán gairdín ar ceant. ☐ ☐

2. Cén t-am a thosóidh an ceant?

   _____

3. Cén áit ar féidir clárú don cheant?

   _____

Cuid 8

Léamhthuiscint

Léigh an píosa seo faoi Ellen agus freagair na ceisteanna a ghabhann leis.

Haigh. Ellen is ainm dom. Táim i mo chónaí faoin tuath. Teach scoite is ea é. Tá leaba agus bricfeasta (*B&B*) againn agus tá seacht seomra codlata ann. Tá cistin mhór thíos staighre agus tá seomra suí agus seomra bia mór ann freisin. Tá gairdín mór os comhair an tí freisin.

Ar ndóigh, déanaimid go leor cúraimí tí gach lá. Bímid ag ní na ngréithe, ag cócaráil an bhricfeasta, ag dustáil, ag mapáil, ag scuabadh, ag glanadh, ag ní éadaí leapa agus ag iarnáil. Is fuath liom an iarnáil! Déanaim an iarnáil gach Satharn.

1. Cá bhfuil Ellen ina cónaí?
   _____

2. Cén sórt tí é?
   _____

3. Cé mhéad seomra codlata atá ann?
   _____

4. Céard atá os comhair an tí?
   _____

5. Luaigh **ceithre** chúram tí a dhéanann siad gach lá.
   _____
   _____

6. Cén cúram a dhéanann Ellen gach Satharn?
   _____

Turas 2: Mo Leabhar Gníomhaíochta

Cuid 9

Freagair na ceisteanna seo.

1. Cén sórt tí nó árasáin atá agat?
   _____

2. Cá bhfuil sé suite?
   _____

3. Cé mhéad seomra atá ann? Céard iad?
   _____
   _____
   _____
   _____

4. Déan cur síos ar do sheomra codlata. Scríobh **trí** abairt.
   _____
   _____
   _____
   _____

5. Cén sórt troscáin atá agat (i) sa seomra suí agus (ii) sa chistin?
   _____
   _____
   _____
   _____
   _____
   _____

Cuid 10

Cuardach focal

Déan an cuardach focal.

Mo Theach

```
L O F N X N M P M D C W K I Z X P V X J
V C R C E K I Y H Q T L P T L A S P U B
J R C A O W U R A E B L D T J N P E V N
W L V Y T J Y C U I S N E O I R W A M X
A Q W A I H N J E Y H R Y F X V Z S B I
N P C V J P U W T X R F Y J G V X T O V
Y G O X Z E B A S G A N G G O E T Á W E
H X J L O K G L A N A D H F L C D T G L
F F Y O O S P Q V B S Y Q E Y W I I C E
B J B Q D J W S O W I L W Z O G A R I K
V G A Z O H J Y R P U R P O T R H Q A P
L E A T H S C O I T E R V L R S L T R E
I X Q R Y X Z V X B I Z I A X T P N W
K Q B O U Y H X M O L H F B N O V W Á J
J G H S P B O E E Z C B S D H L H C I Z
J C J C C B L T P U J C Z G O G G E L P
C R M Á E W I U H H U T I Q V Z P L K A
C U U N F O O A Á R A S Á N H Z Q F Y P
K W I F E Z U F D I H D F T V K Y D K Q
P H W R U E V D H X D B M Z A F J X F J
```

leathscoite   iarnáil

árasán   cuisneoir

farraige   reoiteoir

eastát   tolg

glanadh   troscán

Féinmheasúnú

Léigh gach topaic sa chéad cholún. An bhfuil tú ag déanamh dul chun cinn? Cuir tic (✓) sa cholún cuí. Tá uimhir an leathanaigh chuí in aice leis an topaic.

TOPAIC	Lch	Go maith 🙂	Measartha 😐	Go dona ☹
FOCLÓIR				
An Teach	52			
An Bloc Árasán	53			
An Áit a Bhfuil Cónaí Orm	54			
An Seomra is Fearr Liom 1	56			
An Seomra is Fearr Liom 2	60			
An Seomra is Fearr Liom 3	61			
Cúraimí an Tí	68			
GRAMADACH				
An Aimsir Chaite	64			
SCRÍOBH				
Ríomhphost	74			

Na príomhscileanna

Le cabhair ó do mhúinteoir, cuir tic in aice leis na príomhscileanna ar bhain tú úsáid astu i gCaibidil 3.

Na príomhscileanna	Bhain mé úsáid as
A bheith liteartha	
A bheith uimheartha	
Cumarsáid	
A bheith cruthaitheach	
Mé féin a bhainistiú	
Fanacht folláin	
Obair le daoine eile	
Eolas agus smaointeoireacht a bhainistiú	

Plean Gníomhaíochta

Déan machnamh ar do chuid foghlama! Féach ar an bhféinmheasúnú a rinne tú ar leathanach 26. Bunaithe ar an eolas seo, déan plean gníomhaíochta. Líon isteach na míreanna thíos.

Mír 1: Tá eolas maith agam ar na topaicí seo

Mír 2: Tá cleachtadh le déanamh agam ar na topaicí seo

Mír 3: Plean gníomhaíochta

Mar shampla: 'Déanfaidh mé liosta de na rudaí atá sa seomra is fearr liom.'

Clár Ábhair

Cuid 1–3	An Baile Mór	28
Cuid 4	Treoracha sa Bhaile Mór	29
Cuid 5–6	Cineálacha Siopaí	30
Gramadach	Na Focail 'do' agus 'le'	31
Cuid 7–11	Cleachtaí Athbhreithnithe	32
Measúnú chun Foghlama	Féinmheasúnú	36
Measúnú chun Foghlama	Plean Gníomhaíochta	37

Cuid 1

Líon na bearnaí.

> i nDún na nGall   fútsa   i do chónaí   go hálainn   aoibhinn

Eithne Cá bhfuil tú _____, a Chormaic?

Cormac Táim i mo chónaí i gCorcaigh, a Eithne.

Céard _____?

Eithne Tá mise i mo chónaí _____.

Cormac An maith leat é?

Eithne Is _____ liom é.

Tá an ceantar _____!

Cuid 2

Líon na bearnaí.

> sa cheantar   áiseanna   linn snámha   i mo chónaí   is fearr

Ultan Cá bhfuil tú i do chónaí, a Chaoimhe?

Caoimhe Táim _____ i gCeanannas Mór.

Ultan An bhfuil a lán áiseanna _____?

Caoimhe Tá go leor _____ sa cheantar. Is ceantar bríomhar é.

Ultan Cén áis _____ leat?

Caoimhe Is é an _____ an áis is fearr liom.

Cuid 3

Scríobh an áit cheart faoi na pictiúir.

> oifig an phoist   stáisiún traenach   linn snámha   banc

Cuid 4

Scríobh an treo (*direction*) ceart faoi na pictiúir.

> téigh díreach ar aghaidh   cas ar chlé   téigh trasna na sráide   cas ar dheis

Turas 2: Mo Leabhar Gníomhaíochta

Cuid 5

Scríobh an áit cheart faoi na pictiúir.

> siopa bréagán   siopa guthán   siopa ceoil   bácús   siopa spóirt   siopa éadaí

1.

2.

3.

_____

4.

5.

6.

_____

Cuid 6

Cén áit ar féidir leat na hearraí seo a cheannach? Tá an chéad cheann déanta duit.

> ~~siopa bréagán~~   siopa bróg   siopa peataí   siopa guthán
> siopa búistéara   bácús   siopa caife   siopa spóirt

	Earra (*Item*)	Áit
1	Lego	siopa bréagán
2	arán	
3	feoil	
4	fóin phóca	
5	cupán caife	
6	éisc órga	
7	geansaithe peile	
8	bróga scoile	

GRAMADACH

Na Focail 'do' agus 'le'

Gramadach 1
Tá na liostaí seo san ord mícheart. Athscríobh san ord ceart iad.

1. dom, dó, di, dúinn, dóibh, daoibh, duit

   _____

2. leat, liom, léi, leis, libh, linn, leo

   _____

Gramadach 2
Aistrigh na habairtí seo.

1. Pádraigín is ainm di.

   _____

2. Séamus is ainm dó.

   _____

3. Thug sí obair bhaile dúinn.

   _____

4. An maith libh seacláid?

   _____

5. Is aoibhinn liom ceol.

   _____

6. Cén seomra is fearr leat?

   _____

Gramadach 3
Athscríobh na focail idir lúibíní.

1. Thug siad bronntanas [do: mé] _____.
2. Níor thug mé bronntanas [do: í] _____.
3. Dia [do: sibh] _____!
4. An dtiocfaidh sibh [le: mé] _____?
5. Cén seomra is fearr [le: í] _____?
6. Míle buíochas [le: sibh] _____ go léir!

Cuid 7

Léamhthuiscint

Léigh an píosa seo faoi Pheadar agus a cheantar agus freagair na ceisteanna a ghabhann leis.

Haigh, is mise Peadar. Táim i mo chónaí i Sord Cholmcille i mBaile Átha Cliath. Is breá liom mo cheantar. Tá go leor le déanamh ann.

Tá a lán áiseanna i Sord Cholmcille. Mar shampla, tá cúpla club óige, go leor siopaí, bialanna deasa agus an t-ionad siopadóireachta Swords Pavilions anseo. Tá caisleán againn freisin. Is iad na páirceanna imeartha an áis is fearr liom.

1. Cá bhfuil Peadar ina chónaí?

   _____

2. Luaigh **trí** áis atá sa cheantar.

   _____

3. Cad is ainm don ionad siopadóireachta?

   _____

4. Buaileann tú le Peadar. Scríobh síos **dhá** cheist ar mhaith leat a chur air.

   _____

   _____

Cuid 8

Léamhthuiscint

Léigh an píosa seo faoi Jane agus a ceantar agus freagair na ceisteanna a ghabhann leis.

Dia daoibh, is mise Jane. Táim i mo chónaí i nGleann Cholm Cille i nDún na nGall. Is breá liom an ceantar seo. Tá sé go hálainn anseo.

Tá a lán áiseanna i nGleann Cholm Cille. Tá club óige agus halla pobail anseo. Tá bialanna, siopaí deasa, clubanna spóirt agus páirceanna imeartha anseo freisin. Tá trá álainn againn cúpla míle suas an bóthar. Téim ag snámh san fharraige sa samhradh.

1. Cá bhfuil Jane ina cónaí?

   _____

2. Luaigh **trí** áis atá sa cheantar.

   _____

3. Cá bhfuil an trá álainn?

   _____

4. Buaileann tú le Jane. Scríobh síos **dhá** cheist ar mhaith leat a chur uirthi.

   _____

   _____

Cuid 9

Fógra

A. Léigh an fógra seo agus freagair na ceisteanna a ghabhann leis.

1. Cuir in iúl cé acu **fíor** nó **bréagach** atá na habairtí seo a leanas. Cuir **tic** (✔) sa bhosca ceart.

                                                                                      Fíor   Bréagach

   (i) Club Óige na Mara is ainm don chlub óige seo.

   (ii) Beidh an oscailt mhór ar siúl tar éis na Nollag.

   (iii) Beidh Daidí na Nollag ann.

   (iv) Beidh comórtas péintéireachta ar siúl.

   (v) Ní bheidh aon bhia ná deochanna ar fáil.

2. Ainmnigh an bheirt aíonna a bheidh ann.

   _____

3. An bhfuil an ócáid saor in aisce?

   _____

B. Scríobh teachtaireacht chuig do chara ag tabhairt cuireadh dó/di teacht leat chuig an ócáid seo. (Bain úsáid as an teimpléad ar leathanach 108 de do théacsleabhar.)

_____

_____

_____

_____

_____

Cuid 10

Freagair na ceisteanna seo.

1. Cá bhfuil tú i do chónaí?
   _____

2. An maith leat do cheantar?
   _____

3. An bhfuil a lán áiseanna i do cheantar? Cad iad?
   _____
   _____
   _____

4. Cén áis is fearr leat? Cén fáth?
   _____
   _____

5. Cad iad na siopaí atá sa cheantar?
   _____
   _____
   _____

Cuid 11

Cuardach focal

Déan an cuardach focal.

Mo Cheantar

O	S	C	A	I	R	D	E	Á	N	H	V	U	D	A	A	R	T	X	C
L	L	A	D	B	H	M	K	E	L	S	G	P	G	S	F	I	O	N	R
L	X	Z	D	U	U	C	V	H	B	S	Y	Y	Z	D	T	W	O	F	O
M	Q	J	H	F	E	T	U	I	M	M	C	P	I	V	N	I	S	K	S
H	T	A	O	X	D	N	Z	S	B	Y	G	B	N	F	V	O	T	M	B
A	C	L	U	I	C	H	Í	J	J	N	J	P	Q	N	Q	R	L	U	H
R	Z	V	S	T	T	V	N	B	T	Q	L	H	Y	R	H	N	M	V	Ó
G	Á	B	M	E	I	I	L	O	G	X	B	U	F	S	V	L	S	F	T
A	L	D	H	H	S	S	M	T	A	D	O	O	Y	Y	Q	H	I	C	H
D	A	S	F	L	U	S	O	P	B	Q	H	A	K	C	S	V	F	X	A
H	I	D	Z	F	X	T	U	W	E	R	D	T	Y	Z	M	H	G	H	R
H	N	F	V	W	V	Z	S	W	F	A	C	A	F	A	X	R	U	I	G
Q	N	N	P	U	P	G	R	L	A	Z	L	N	O	B	W	T	P	H	D
F	L	I	Z	J	O	A	Y	A	T	Q	S	L	P	W	N	P	C	F	M
G	V	D	E	M	H	W	T	U	L	V	I	F	Á	H	V	M	J	P	J
B	O	Y	K	M	T	Q	S	N	N	A	Z	V	K	N	Q	G	E	Y	B
E	M	W	O	L	Y	W	Q	B	O	L	K	N	A	Y	T	B	J	W	I
T	R	Í	M	O	G	T	K	X	M	O	U	S	É	I	P	É	A	L	N
W	R	O	O	C	F	V	R	K	S	C	U	S	Y	F	M	F	H	Y	S
B	R	O	N	N	T	A	N	A	I	S	J	B	L	P	Y	V	G	A	E

scairdeán

binse

ollmhargadh

séipéal

cluichí

bronntanais

timpeallán

crosbhóthar

bríomhar

álainn

Féinmheasúnú

Léigh gach topaic sa chéad cholún. An bhfuil tú ag déanamh dul chun cinn? Cuir tic (✓) sa cholún cuí. Tá uimhir an leathanaigh chuí in aice leis an topaic.

TOPAIC	Lch	Go maith 😊	Measartha 😐	Go dona ☹
FOCLÓIR				
An Baile Mór	92			
Treoracha sa Bhaile Mór	94			
Cineálacha Siopaí	96			
Comharsana Callánacha	106			
GRAMADACH				
Na Focail 'do' agus 'le'	102			
SCRÍOBH				
Teachtaireacht	108			

Na príomhscileanna

Le cabhair ó do mhúinteoir, cuir tic in aice leis na príomhscileanna ar bhain tú úsáid astu i gCaibidil 4.

Na príomhscileanna	Bhain mé úsáid as
A bheith liteartha	
A bheith uimheartha	
Cumarsáid	
A bheith cruthaitheach	
Mé féin a bhainistiú	
Fanacht folláin	
Obair le daoine eile	
Eolas agus smaointeoireacht a bhainistiú	

Plean Gníomhaíochta

Déan machnamh ar do chuid foghlama! Féach ar an bhféinmheasúnú a rinne tú ar leathanach 36. Bunaithe ar an eolas seo, déan plean gníomhaíochta. Líon isteach na míreanna thíos.

Mír 1: Tá eolas maith agam ar na topaicí seo

Mír 2: Tá cleachtadh le déanamh agam ar na topaicí seo

Mír 3: Plean gníomhaíochta

Mar shampla: 'Déanfaidh mé liosta de na háiseanna i mo cheantar.'

Clár Ábhair

Cuid 1	Mo Scoil	38
Cuid 2–3	Na hÁbhair Scoile	38
Cuid 4	An Lá Scoile	39
Cuid 5–7	Áiseanna na Scoile	40
Cuid 8	Éide Scoile	41
Gramadach	An Aimsir Láithreach	42
Gramadach	An Focal 'Bíonn'	43
Cuid 9–11	Cleachtaí Athbhreithnithe	44
Measúnú chun Foghlama	Féinmheasúnú	48
Measúnú chun Foghlama	Plean Gníomhaíochta	49

Cuid 1

Líon na bearnaí.

> ag freastal   cá bhfuil   áis   ríomhaireachta   deasa

Liam _____ tú ag dul ar scoil, a Órla?

Órla Táim _____ ar Phobalscoil na Farraige, a Liam.

Liam An maith leat an scoil?

Órla Is maith. Tá go leor áiseanna _____ ann.

Liam Cén _____ is fearr leat?

Órla An seomra _____, déarfainn. Is aoibhinn liom ríomhairí.

Cuid 2

Líon na bearnaí.

> an-phraiticiúil   seachtain   teangacha   cén t-ábhar   ceithre

Deirdre _____ is fearr leat, a Mhíchíl?

Mícheál Is breá liom Gaeilge, Gearmáinis agus Fraincis.

Is breá liom _____. Céard fútsa?

Deirdre Ó, is aoibhinn liom Mata agus Ríomhairí mar tá siad

_____.

Mícheál Cé mhéad rang ríomhaireachta a bhíonn agat gach

_____?

Deirdre _____ cinn.

Cuid 3

Scríobh an teanga cheart faoi na pictiúir. Tá an chéad cheann déanta duit.

 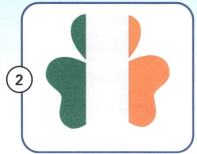 

Gearmáinis

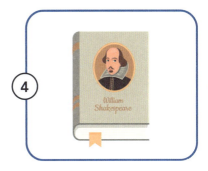  

Cuid 4

Scríobh an t-am i bhfocail. Tá an chéad cheann déanta duit.

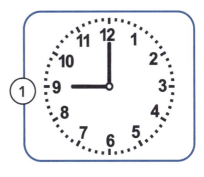  

a naoi a chlog

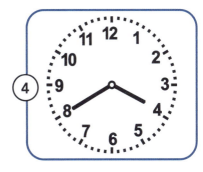  

Cuid 5

Scríobh an téarma Gaeilge faoi na pictiúir.

póstaer   cathaoir   ríomhaire   leabhragán   deasc   clár bán

1. _____
2. _____
3. _____

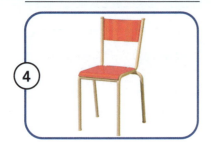

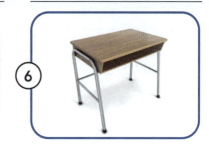

4. _____
5. _____
6. _____

Cuid 6

Meaitseáil an Ghaeilge leis an mBéarla.

1	ceaintín	A	art room
2	seomra ríomhaireachta	B	staffroom
3	seomra foirne	C	secretary's office
4	halla spóirt	D	canteen
5	seomra ealaíne	E	sports hall
6	oifig an rúnaí	F	computer room

1 = ___   2 = ___   3 = ___   4 = ___   5 = ___   6 = ___

Cuid 7

Aistrigh go Gaeilge.

1. one poster
2. ten chairs
3. two canteens
4. eight rooms
5. six halls
6. seven offices

Cuid 8
Fógra

Léigh an fógra seo agus freagair na ceisteanna a ghabhann leis.

Cruinniú Scoile le Tuismitheoirí faoi Éide Scoile Nua

Beidh an cruinniú ar siúl ar an 30 Aibreán ag 7pm.

Rogha 1
- Geansaí gorm le suaitheantas
- Bríste liath / Sciorta liath (rogha an scoláire)
- Léine bhán / Blús bán (rogha an scoláire)
- Bróga dubha

Ní bheidh carbhat ag teastáil a thuilleadh

Rogha 2
- Geansaí 'muineál cruinn' nó geansaí 'V-mhuiníl'
- Léine fhoirmeálta (dath ar bith)
- Bríste (dath ar bith ach cosc ar jíons)
- Bróga

Caithfear vóta le linn an chruinnithe.

1. Cuir in iúl cé acu **fíor** nó **bréagach** atá na habairtí seo a leanas. Cuir **tic** (✔) sa bhosca ceart.

                                 Fíor   Bréagach
   - (i) Cruinniú faoi rialacha na scoile a bheidh ann. ☐ ☐
   - (ii) Beidh an cruinniú ar siúl ag 7pm. ☐ ☐
   - (iii) Tá trí rogha ann. ☐ ☐
   - (iv) Ní mór (*one must*) carbhat a chaitheamh i rogha 1. ☐ ☐
   - (v) Tá dhá rogha geansaí i rogha 2. ☐ ☐

2. Ainmnigh **dhá** rogha a bheidh ag scoláirí i rogha 1.

   _____

3. Cathain a chaithfear an vóta?

   _____

GRAMADACH

An Aimsir Láithreach

Gramadach 1

Scríobh an cheist (an fhoirm 'tú'), an freagra dearfach (an fhoirm 'mé') agus an freagra diúltach (an fhoirm 'mé'). Tá an chéad cheann déanta duit.

	An briathar	An cheist (?)	An freagra dearfach (+)	An freagra diúltach (–)
1	dún	an ndúnann tú?	dúnaim	ní dhúnaim
2	fan			
3	ól			
4	bris			
5	seinn			

Gramadach 2

Scríobh an cheist (an fhoirm 'tú'), an freagra dearfach (an fhoirm 'mé') agus an freagra diúltach (an fhoirm 'mé'). Tá an chéad cheann déanta duit.

	An briathar	An cheist (?)	An freagra dearfach (+)	An freagra diúltach (–)
1	ceannaigh	an gceannaíonn tú?	ceannaím	ní cheannaím
2	tosaigh			
3	liostaigh			
4	sínigh			
5	fáiltigh			

Gramadach 3

Athscríobh na focail idir lúibíní san Aimsir Láithreach.

1. An [dún: sibh] _____ na fuinneoga tar éis an ranga?
2. [Fan: siad] _____ linn am lóin.
3. [Ól: mé] _____ buidéal uisce ag an sos.
4. Ní [bris: muid] _____ na rialacha.
5. [Seinn: mé] _____ an giotár sa rang ceoil.
6. An [ceannaigh: tú] _____ cóipleabhar do gach ábhar?
7. An [tosaigh: muid] _____ traenáil tar éis na scoile?
8. Ní [liostaigh: sé] _____ gach ceist sa scrúdú.
9. An [sínigh: tú] _____ an rolla gach maidin?
10. [Fáiltigh: muid] _____ roimh na múinteoirí nua.

An Focal 'Bíonn'

Gramadach 4

Athscríobh na habairtí seo leis an bhfocal 'Bíonn'. Tá an chéad cheann déanta duit.

1. Tá an aimsir go deas anois.
   _____Bíonn an aimsir go deas_____ go minic.

2. Tá mo thuismitheoirí as baile anois.
   _____ go minic.

3. An bhfuil tuirse ort anois?
   _____ go minic?

4. Níl an t-am agam anois.
   _____ go minic.

5. Tá na scoláirí ar saoire anois.
   _____ go minic.

Gramadach 5

Scríobh 'Tá' nó 'Bíonn' sa bhearna. Tá an chéad cheann déanta duit.

1. _____Tá_____ Seán anseo anois.
2. _____ mo thuismitheoirí in Éirinn faoi láthair.
3. _____ saoire againn gach samhradh.
4. _____ lón againn ag a haon chlog gach lá.
5. _____ sé fliuch in Éirinn go minic.
6. _____ an príomhoide san oifig anois.

Cuid 9

Léamhthuiscint

Léigh an píosa seo agus freagair na ceisteanna.

Dia daoibh, is mise Ciarán. Táim ag freastal ar scoil mhór i gcathair na Gaillimhe. Is maith liom an scoil.

Tá go leor áiseanna anseo. Mar shampla, tá ceaintín, trí leabharlann, dhá chlós, go leor páirceanna imeartha, seomra urnaí, dhá sheomra ealaíne, seomra foirne, seomra ceoil, trí shaotharlann, dhá sheomra ríomhaireachta agus go leor leor eile ann. Is é an seomra ceoil an seomra is fearr liom.

Caithimid éide scoile anseo, faraor. Caithim bléasar dúghorm, léine ghorm, carbhat gorm agus dúghorm, bríste liath agus bróga dubha. Ní maith liom é ar chor ar bith!

Ar an dea-uair, beidh cruinniú agus vóta mór ar siúl an tseachtain seo chugainn. Vótálfaidh tuismitheoirí ar son éide scoile nua nó in aghaidh na héide scoile ar fad. Tá súil agam go vótálfaidh siad in aghaidh na héide scoile, ar ndóigh.

Tá go leor rialacha eile inár scoil freisin. Aontaím le roinnt de na rialacha agus ní aontaím le roinnt rialacha eile. Mar shampla, tá cosc ar chaint sa rang, tá cosc ar mhilseáin agus tá cosc ar an mbulaíocht. Aontaím leis na rialacha sin.

Faraor, tá cosc ar bhróga spóirt, níl fón ceadaithe agus níl fáinní cluaise ná smideadh ceadaithe. Ní aontaím leis na rialacha sin.

Is é an rud is fearr faoi mo scoil ná na cairde atá agam anseo. Buailimid le chéile ar maidin roimh an scoil, ag na sosanna agus am lóin, agus tar éis na scoile. Bíonn an-chraic agus an-spórt againn.

Caibidil 5

1. Cén chathair ina bhfuil an scoil ar a bhfreastalaíonn Ciarán?
   _____

2. Cé mhéad seomra ealaíne atá sa scoil?
   _____

3. Déan cur síos ar an éide scoile atá ag na scoláirí.
   _____
   _____

4. Céard a bheidh ar siúl an tseachtain seo chugainn?
   _____

5. Luaigh **dhá** riail a n-aontaíonn sé leo.
   _____
   _____

6. Luaigh **dhá** riail nach n-aontaíonn sé leo.
   _____
   _____

7. Tabhair sampla **amháin** a thugann le fios go mbíonn craic agus spórt aige lena chairde.
   _____
   _____

8. Buaileann tú le Ciarán. Scríobh síos **dhá** cheist ar mhaith leat a chur air.
   _____
   _____
   _____
   _____

Mo Scoil

Cuid 10

Freagair na ceisteanna seo.

1. Cá bhfuil tú ag dul ar scoil?
   _____

2. An maith leat do scoil?
   _____

3. Céard iad na hábhair a dhéanann tú?
   _____
   _____
   _____
   _____

4. Cén t-ábhar is fearr leat? Cén fáth?
   _____
   _____

5. Luaigh **trí** riail atá sa scoil.
   _____
   _____
   _____
   _____

Cuid 11

Cuardach focal

Déan an cuardach focal.

Mo Scoil

E	L	W	B	G	Y	C	L	S	W	V	X	K	P	R	R	H	U	J	G
A	E	Y	K	O	H	O	Z	G	R	D	N	S	D	P	L	Ú	T	R	L
U	S	E	L	K	S	C	H	K	K	T	S	C	Q	I	I	N	J	K
A	V	M	J	R	G	O	K	U	Q	Z	S	T	Ú	X	Z	F	M	A	G
P	Y	F	R	L	Y	E	J	N	O	F	Q	I	H	R	R	R	O	J	Í
R	I	E	N	S	D	X	F	B	V	K	M	K	L	É	I	N	E	W	Y
A	L	R	V	N	Y	U	L	A	O	I	Z	G	N	Y	Q	L	X	I	S
I	M	S	Y	H	L	G	A	T	U	R	G	K	G	A	B	P	V	B	N
T	C	Y	W	U	R	D	P	S	R	B	F	C	P	E	G	F	T	M	S
I	B	H	H	N	Z	R	P	G	P	R	Í	O	M	H	O	I	D	E	A
C	S	K	K	X	Z	B	M	W	N	K	V	U	G	S	G	T	C	V	O
I	F	Z	A	D	H	M	A	D	Ó	I	R	E	A	C	H	T	H	H	T
Ú	J	K	E	T	M	R	F	G	X	C	E	A	D	A	I	T	H	E	H
I	E	O	L	A	Í	O	C	H	T	T	T	I	A	V	Y	F	V	V	A
L	E	C	A	D	P	Y	I	I	A	B	W	F	D	C	X	C	G	W	R
V	Q	W	Q	Y	K	B	D	H	C	S	H	O	E	T	S	F	E	Y	L
K	A	O	Q	K	L	Z	J	W	Y	J	M	U	N	Q	D	Q	E	S	A
Y	G	U	Y	G	R	M	A	T	A	U	X	Q	W	A	R	H	E	B	N
R	J	R	K	V	O	K	P	Y	Z	O	Q	V	S	V	S	F	P	H	N
L	F	Q	J	E	Z	B	G	E	X	G	O	G	A	L	T	R	W	T	H

Adhmadóireacht   saotharlann

Mata   rúnaí

Eolaíocht   príomhoide

suimiúil   léine

praiticiúil   ceadaithe

Turas 2: Mo Leabhar Gníomhaíochta

Féinmheasúnú

Léigh gach topaic sa chéad cholún. An bhfuil tú ag déanamh dul chun cinn? Cuir tic (✓) sa cholún cuí. Tá uimhir an leathanaigh chuí in aice leis an topaic.

TOPAIC	Lch	Go maith 🙂	Measartha 😐	Go dona ☹
FOCLÓIR				
Na hÁbhair Scoile	134			
An Lá Scoile	136			
An Seomra Ranga	146			
Áiseanna na Scoile	148			
Éide Scoile	150			
GRAMADACH				
An Aimsir Láithreach	140			
An Focal 'Bíonn'	145			
SCRÍOBH				
Aiste	152			

Na príomhscileanna

Le cabhair ó do mhúinteoir, cuir tic in aice leis na príomhscileanna ar bhain tú úsáid astu i gCaibidil 5.

Na príomhscileanna	Bhain mé úsáid as
A bheith liteartha	
A bheith uimheartha	
Cumarsáid	
A bheith cruthaitheach	
Mé féin a bhainistiú	
Fanacht folláin	
Obair le daoine eile	
Eolas agus smaointeoireacht a bhainistiú	

Caibidil 5

Plean Gníomhaíochta

Déan machnamh ar do chuid foghlama! Féach ar an bhféinmheasúnú a rinne tú ar leathanach 48. Bunaithe ar an eolas seo, déan plean gníomhaíochta. Líon isteach na míreanna thíos.

Mír 1: Tá eolas maith agam ar na topaicí seo

Mír 2: Tá cleachtadh le déanamh agam ar na topaicí seo

Mír 3: Plean gníomhaíochta

Mar shampla: 'Scríobhfaidh mé mo chlár ama i nGaeilge agus cuirfidh mé i mo dhialann scoile é.'

Mo Scoil

Clár Ábhair

Cuid 1–3	Caithimh Aimsire	50
Cuid 4	Ag Féachaint ar an Teilifís	51
Cuid 5	Ag Dul go dtí an Phictiúrlann	52
Cuid 6	Cluichí Ríomhaire	52
Gramadach	An Aimsir Fháistineach	53
Cuid 7–10	Cleachtaí Athbhreithnithe	54
Measúnú chun Foghlama	Féinmheasúnú	58
Measúnú chun Foghlama	Plean Gníomhaíochta	59

Cuid 1

Líon na bearnaí.

> ag léamh   an dtaitníonn   fuath   caithimh aimsire   fútsa

Caoimhín Cad iad na _____ is fearr leat?

Martina Is breá liom a bheith _____ agus ag snámh.

Céard _____?

Caoimhín Is breá liom an iascaireacht agus an ceol. An dtaitníonn spórt leat?

Martina Taitníonn. _____ spórt leatsa?

Caoimhín Ó, ní thaitníonn. Is _____ liom é!

Cuid 2

Líon na bearnaí.

> is aoibhinn liom   sobaldrámaí   cineál   is fearr leat   tá suim agam

Colm Cén _____ clár teilifíse is fearr leat?

Aoibhe _____ cláir faisin.

Colm Cláir faisin? Cén fáth?

Aoibhe Mar _____ san fhaisean! Céard fútsa?

Colm Is fearr liom _____.

Aoibhe I ndáiríre? Cén clár teilifíse _____?

Colm *Corrie*, ar ndóigh.

Aoibhe Dia ár sábhála!

Cuid 3

Scríobh an téarma Gaeilge faoi na pictiúir.

> ag péinteáil   ag dul ar líne   ag cócaráil   ag campáil   ag siúl   ag iascaireacht

Cuid 4

Meaitseáil an cineál clár teilifíse leis an gclár teilifíse féin.
Téigh ar líne chun do fhreagraí a sheiceáil.

1	clár thráth na gceist	A	Soccer Saturday
2	clár faisin	B	Home and Away
3	clár spóirt	C	Say Yes to the Dress
4	cartún	D	The Voice
5	sobaldráma	E	The Chase
6	clár ceoil	F	The Simpsons

1 = ___   2 = ___   3 = ___   4 = ___   5 = ___   6 = ___

Cuid 5

Meaitseáil an Ghaeilge leis an mBéarla.

1	scannán grinn	A	thriller
2	scannán aicsin	B	horror film
3	coiméide rómánsúil	C	action film
4	scéinséir	D	fantasy film
5	scannán ficsean eolaíochta	E	comedy film
6	scannán fantaisíochta	F	science fiction film
7	scannán beochana	G	animated film
8	scannán uafáis	H	romantic comedy

1 = ___   2 = ___   3 = ___   4 = ___   5 = ___   6 = ___   7 = ___   8 = ___

Cuid 6

Scríobh an téarma Gaeilge faoi na pictiúir.

> scáileán   méarchlár   consól cluichí
> rialtán   ríomhaire glúine   fón cliste

GRAMADACH

An Aimsir Fháistineach

Gramadach 1

Scríobh an cheist (an fhoirm 'tú'), an freagra dearfach (an fhoirm 'mé') agus an freagra diúltach (an fhoirm 'mé'). Tá an chéad cheann déanta duit.

	An briathar	An cheist (?)	An freagra dearfach (+)	An freagra diúltach (–)
1	dún	an ndúnfaidh tú?	dúnfaidh mé	ní dhúnfaidh mé
2	fan			
3	ól			
4	bris			
5	seinn			

Gramadach 2

Scríobh an cheist (an fhoirm 'tú'), an freagra dearfach (an fhoirm 'mé') agus an freagra diúltach (an fhoirm 'mé'). Tá an chéad cheann déanta duit.

	An briathar	An cheist (?)	An freagra dearfach (+)	An freagra diúltach (–)
1	ceannaigh	an gceannóidh tú?	ceannóidh mé	ní cheannóidh mé
2	tosaigh			
3	liostaigh			
4	sínigh			
5	fáiltigh			

Gramadach 3

Athscríobh na focail idir lúibíní san Aimsir Fháistineach.

1. An [dún: tú] _____ an doras, le do thoil?
2. [Fan: mé] _____ leat taobh amuigh den phictiúrlann.
3. Ní [ól: muid] _____ uisce as buidéal plaisteach.
4. Ní [bris: mé] _____ an fón.
5. [Seinn: muid] _____ ag an gceolchoirm amárach.
6. An [ceannaigh: tú] _____ slat iascaireachta?
7. An [tosaigh: muid] _____ ag féachaint ar an scannán?
8. [Liostaigh: siad] _____ na cláir sa pháipéar nuachta.
9. An [sínigh] _____ an t-údar mo leabhar?
10. [Fáiltigh: muid] _____ roimh aisteoirí nua.

Turas 2: Mo Leabhar Gníomhaíochta

Cuid 7

Léamhthuiscint

Léigh an píosa seo faoi Carisa agus freagair na ceisteanna a ghabhann leis.

Haigh, is mise Carisa. Is í an iascaireacht an caitheamh aimsire is fearr liom mar tá sí síochánta agus suaimhneach.

Tá bád beag ag mo Dhaid agus téimid amach ag iascaireacht go minic. Dé Sathairn, éireoimid go moch ar maidin. Ansin, rachaimid síos go dtí an ché (*pier*). Seolfaimid amach cúpla míle agus ansin, cuirfimid na heangacha (*nets*) amach. Dar liom, béarfaimid ar go leor maicréal.

Tabharfaimid na maicréil chuig an óstán sa bhaile mór. Beidh lón breá againn nuair a thiocfaimid abhaile.

1. Cén fáth a dtaitníonn an iascaireacht le Carisa?
   _____
   _____

2. Cá rachaidh siad nuair a éireoidh siad ar maidin?
   _____

3. Cé mhéad míle a sheolfaidh siad amach?
   _____

4. Cén sórt éisc a mbéarfaidh siad orthu, dar léi?
   _____

5. Cá dtabharfaidh siad na maicréil?
   _____

6. Buaileann tú le Carisa. Scríobh síos **dhá** cheist ar mhaith leat a chur uirthi.
   _____
   _____

Cuid 8
Fógra

Léigh an fógra seo agus freagair na ceisteanna a ghabhann leis.

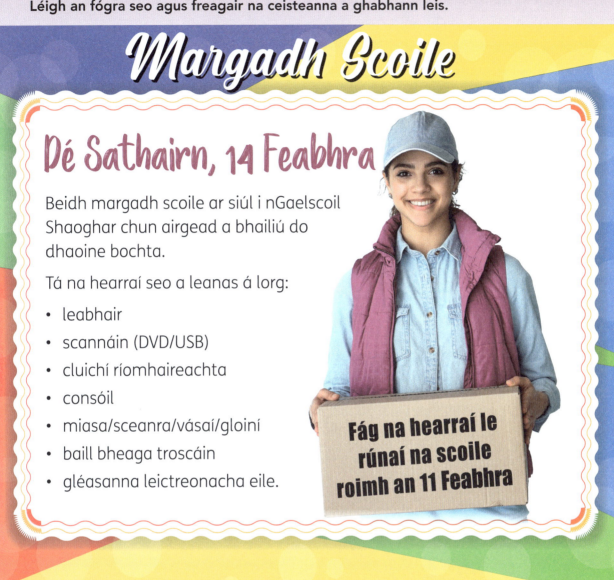

Margadh Scoile

Dé Sathairn, 14 Feabhra

Beidh margadh scoile ar siúl i nGaelscoil Shaoghar chun airgead a bhailiú do dhaoine bochta.

Tá na hearraí seo a leanas á lorg:
- leabhair
- scannáin (DVD/USB)
- cluichí ríomhaireachta
- consóil
- miasa/sceanra/vásaí/gloiní
- baill bheaga troscáin
- gléasanna leictreonacha eile.

Fág na hearraí le rúnaí na scoile roimh an 11 Feabhra

1. Cuir in iúl cé acu **fíor** nó **bréagach** atá na habairtí seo a leanas. Cuir **tic** (✔) sa bhosca ceart.

    Fíor   Bréagach
    (i) Beidh an margadh ar siúl ar an 11 Feabhra.
    (ii) Beidh sé ar siúl i nGaelscoil Shaoghar.
    (iii) Tá leabhair á lorg.
    (iv) Tá earraí cistine á lorg.
    (v) Tá carranna á lorg.

2. Cé leis ar cheart earraí a fhágáil?
   _____

3. Cén dáta ar cheart earraí a fhágáil roimhe?
   _____

Cuid 9

Freagair na ceisteanna seo.

1. Cad iad na caithimh aimsire is fearr leat?
   _____
   _____
   _____

2. Cén cineál clár teilifíse a thaitníonn leat?
   _____
   _____
   _____

3. Cé chomh minic is a fhéachann tú ar an teilifís?
   _____
   _____

4. Cad é an scannán deireanach a chonaic tú?
   _____

5. Cé chomh minic is a théann tú ar líne?
   _____
   _____

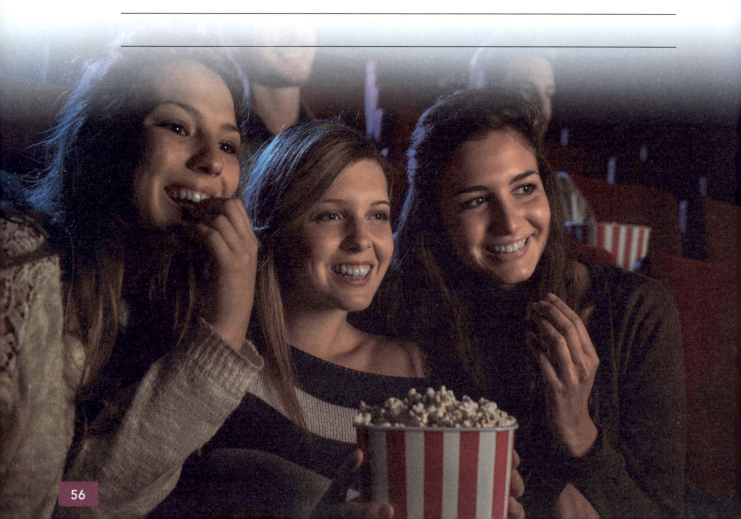

Cuid 10

Cuardach focal

Déan an cuardach focal.

Mo Chaithimh Aimsire

M	E	X	R	Y	E	T	K	J	J	K	L	P	O	V	I	X	Z	S	H
K	T	H	C	E	P	F	O	J	W	G	T	Y	I	N	Q	J	T	C	H
X	D	G	T	Z	H	J	Z	J	Q	C	I	D	A	M	H	S	A	A	V
B	T	E	Z	P	S	F	W	F	B	A	K	R	D	X	E	V	T	N	C
D	P	T	T	E	A	C	H	T	A	I	R	E	A	C	H	T	F	N	L
D	G	Y	T	D	E	I	O	F	A	N	K	W	M	O	L	E	Z	Á	Á
E	Y	E	J	I	S	V	O	M	C	É	A	M	V	A	U	R	Y	N	R
R	O	W	P	Z	L	S	Á	I	Q	A	W	P	T	U	B	H	I	P	S
B	X	B	B	Y	T	R	C	A	A	L	G	X	O	A	B	Á	F	N	C
D	N	M	K	M	D	O	O	T	L	Z	B	I	G	M	E	H	D	A	Á
U	R	B	T	L	J	A	L	L	P	L	H	A	S	M	E	C	F	D	T
C	F	P	A	T	F	I	O	K	F	T	H	O	O	K	T	U	R	E	Á
A	P	B	L	E	R	S	T	X	B	S	H	A	Q	F	B	Y	D	V	I
V	O	F	E	K	S	S	V	J	L	M	C	W	G	N	N	X	N	C	L
S	K	P	I	C	T	I	Ú	R	L	A	N	N	L	U	Ó	Y	A	I	I
S	X	C	H	E	Q	N	L	P	F	J	C	X	S	M	F	L	Y	N	E
L	K	V	X	M	A	Z	F	E	M	R	Y	W	O	U	L	U	L	A	C
X	S	G	G	Y	I	O	O	P	U	F	Y	D	H	S	X	J	L	D	M
Q	N	K	U	W	M	X	D	U	K	L	M	I	W	E	R	K	I	H	W
V	V	J	U	S	N	F	N	C	K	X	V	U	C	W	P	H	A	L	T

damhsa

clárscátáil

canadh

sobaldráma

cainéal

pictiúrlann

scannán

meáin

fón

teachtaireacht

Turas 2: Mo Leabhar Gníomhaíochta

Féinmheasúnú

Léigh gach topaic sa chéad cholún. An bhfuil tú ag déanamh dul chun cinn? Cuir tic (✓) sa cholún cuí. Tá uimhir an leathanaigh chuí in aice leis an topaic.

TOPAIC	Lch	Go maith 😊	Measartha 😐	Go dona ☹
FOCLÓIR				
Caithimh Aimsire	166			
Ag Féachaint ar an Teilifís	168			
Ag Dul go dtí an Phictiúrlann	174			
Cluichí Ríomhaire	178			
An Fón Cliste	180			
GRAMADACH				
An Aimsir Fháistineach	172			
SCRÍOBH				
Litir	182			

Na príomhscileanna

Le cabhair ó do mhúinteoir, cuir tic in aice leis na príomhscileanna ar bhain tú úsáid astu i gCaibidil 6.

Na príomhscileanna	Bhain mé úsáid as
A bheith liteartha	
A bheith uimheartha	
Cumarsáid	
A bheith cruthaitheach	
Mé féin a bhainistiú	
Fanacht folláin	
Obair le daoine eile	
Eolas agus smaointeoireacht a bhainistiú	

Caibidil 6

Plean Gníomhaíochta

Déan machnamh ar do chuid foghlama! Féach ar an bhféinmheasúnú a rinne tú ar leathanach 58. Bunaithe ar an eolas seo, déan plean gníomhaíochta. Líon isteach na míreanna thíos.

Mír 1: Tá eolas maith agam ar na topaicí seo

Mír 2: Tá cleachtadh le déanamh agam ar na topaicí seo

Mír 3: Plean gníomhaíochta

Mar shampla: 'Déanfaidh mé liosta de na caithimh aimsire atá ag gach duine i mo theaghlach.'

Mo Chaithimh Aimsire

Clár Ábhair

Cuid 1–3	Cén Sórt Ceoil a Thaitníonn Leat?	60
Cuid 4	An Ceol Gaelach	61
Cuid 5	An Cheolfhoireann	61
Gramadach	Na Focail 'faoi' agus 'ó'	62
Cuid 6–9	Cleachtaí Athbhreithnithe	63
Measúnú chun Foghlama	Féinmheasúnú	68
Measúnú chun Foghlama	Plean Gníomhaíochta	69

Cuid 1

Líon na bearnaí.

> seinnim   beoga   ceol traidisiúnta   a thaitníonn   uirlis

Jeaic Cén sórt ceoil _____ leat, a Lúsaí?

Lúsaí Taitníonn popcheol liom mar tá sé fuinniúil agus _____. Céard fútsa?

Jeaic Is maith liom _____.

Lúsaí An seinneann tú aon _____ cheoil?

Jeaic _____ an giotár agus an bodhrán.

Cuid 2

Líon na bearnaí.

> a sheinneann   miotal trom   go hiontach   ceolchoirm   is fearr leat

Dara Cén banna ceoil _____?

Fiona Is é Metallica an banna ceoil is fearr liom.

Dara Cén sórt ceoil _____ siad?

Fiona Seinneann siad _____.

Dara An raibh tú riamh ag _____ Metallica?

Fiona Bhí. Bhí sé _____.

Cuid 3

Aistrigh go Béarla.

1. Tá rac-cheol fuinniúil.
   _____

2. Tá popcheol beoga.
   _____

3. Tá snagcheol leadránach.
   _____

4. Tá ceol tíre corraitheach.
   _____

5. Tá rapcheol cruthaitheach.
   _____

6. Tá miotal trom suaimhneach.
   _____

Cuid 4

Scríobh an téarma Gaeilge faoi na pictiúir.

| bainseó | fidil | cláirseach | feadóg stáin |

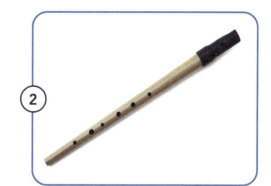

Cuid 5

Liostaigh dhá uirlis i ngach catagóir. Tá an chéad cheann déanta duit.

1. Na cnaguirlisí   _____xileafón_____   _____ciombail_____
2. Na prásuirlisí   _____   _____
3. Na gaothuirlisí   _____   _____
4. Na téaduirlisí   _____   _____

Turas 2: Mo Leabhar Gníomhaíochta

GRAMADACH

Na Focail 'faoi' agus 'ó'

Gramadach 1

Tá na liostaí seo san ord mícheart. Athscríobh san ord ceart iad.

1. fút, fúm, fúithi, faoi, fúthu, fúinn, fúibh

   _____

2. uaim, uait, uainn, uaithi, uaidh, uaibh, uathu

   _____

Gramadach 2

Aistrigh na habairtí seo.

1. Chuala an ceoltóir faoi.

   _____

2. Bhí an banna ag canadh fúm.

   _____

3. An bhfuil tú ag caint fúthu?

   _____

4. Tá fidil uaim.

   _____

5. An bhfuil giotár nua uait?

   _____

6. An bhfaca tú an téacs ó Phádraig?

   _____

Gramadach 3

Athscríobh na focail idir lúibíní.

1. Ní raibh siad ag caint [faoi: muid] _____.
2. An raibh tú ag magadh [faoi: iad] _____?
3. Ar chuala tú [faoi: é] _____?
4. Tá olldord nua [ó: í] _____.
5. Ghoid siad mo phianó [ó: mé] _____!
6. Cad atá [ó: sibh] _____ anois?

Cuid 6

Léamhthuiscint

Léigh an píosa seo faoi Eibhlín agus freagair na ceisteanna a ghabhann leis.

Haigh, is mise Eibhlín. Is é an ceol traidisiúnta an ceol is fearr liom.

Seinnim an fheadóg mhór, an fheadóg stáin agus an bosca ceoil. Thosaigh mé ag seinm ceoil nuair a bhí mé cúig bliana d'aois. Faighim ceachtanna dhá uair sa tseachtain – Dé Luain agus Dé Céadaoin.

Uaireanta, téim ag buscáil ar Shráid Grafton le mo chairde. Bíonn an-chraic againn.

1. Cén sórt ceoil is fearr le hEibhlín?
   _____

2. Luaigh **dhá** uirlis cheoil a sheinneann sí.
   _____

3. Cathain a thosaigh sí ag seinm ceoil?
   _____

4. Cathain a fhaigheann sí ceachtanna?
   _____

5. Cá dtéann sí ag buscáil lena cairde?
   _____

Cuid 7

Léamhthuiscint

Léigh an píosa seo faoi Mhairéad agus freagair na ceisteanna a ghabhann leis.

Haigh, is mise Mairéad. Chuaigh mé chuig ceolchoirm Ed Sheeran Dé hAoine seo caite. Bhí an cheolchoirm ar siúl i bPáirc an Chrócaigh.

Cheannaigh mé mo thicéad ar líne. Bhí na ticéid díolta amach tar éis deich nóiméad! Bhí siad costasach go leor – chosain siad €65.

Bhí an cheolchoirm thar barr. Chuaigh mé ann le mo chara, mo dheartháir agus a chairde. Fuaireamar síob go dtí stáisiún Mhic Dhiarmada i Sligeach agus ansin fuaireamar an traein go Stáisiún Uí Chonghaile i mBaile Átha Cliath. Shiúlamar go dtí an staidiam ansin.

Bhí an staidiam plódaithe (*packed*). Bhí Griff ann mar amhránaí tacaíochta. Is amhránaí as Sasana í. Bhí sí ar fheabhas. Tháinig Ed Sheeran ar stáitse timpeall 20.30. Sheinn sé ceol ar feadh dhá uair an chloig. Bhí gach duine ag damhsa agus ag canadh in éineacht leis. Bhí an t-atmaisféar go hiontach.

Nuair a chríochnaigh an cheolchoirm, d'fhágamar Páirc an Chrócaigh. Fuaireamar burgar agus sceallóga ar an mbealach go dtí an stáisiún. Shroicheamar Sligeach arís tar éis meán oíche. Oíche iontach a bhí ann. Ní dhéanfaidh mé dearmad uirthi go deo na ndeor.

1. Cathain a bhí ceolchoirm Ed Sheeran ar siúl?
   _____

2. Cá raibh an cheolchoirm ar siúl?
   _____

3. Cé mhéad a chosain na ticéid?
   _____

4. Cé a bhí ag seinm mar amhránaí tacaíochta?
   _____

5. Tabhair sampla **amháin** a thugann le fios gur bhain gach duine sult as an gceolchoirm.
   _____
   _____

6. Cathain a tháinig siad ar ais go Sligeach?
   _____

7. Tá Griff agus Ed Sheeran ag teacht chuig do scoil. Scríobh **dhá** cheist ar mhaith leat a chur orthu.
   _____
   _____
   _____
   _____

Turas 2: Mo Leabhar Gníomhaíochta

Cuid 8

Freagair na ceisteanna seo.

1. Cén sórt ceoil a thaitníonn leat? Cén fáth?

   _____
   _____
   _____

2. Cén ceoltóir nó banna ceoil is fearr leat?

   _____
   _____

3. Cén t-amhrán is fearr leat?

   _____
   _____

4. An seinneann tú aon uirlis cheoil?

   _____
   _____

5. An raibh tú riamh ag cheolchoirm? Déan cur síos uirthi.

   _____
   _____
   _____
   _____

Cuid 9

Cuardach focal

Déan an cuardach focal.

Ceol

E	L	W	B	G	Y	A	M	H	R	Á	I	N	P	R	R	H	U	J	G
A	E	Y	K	O	H	O	Z	G	R	D	N	S	D	P	F	X	T	R	L
U	S	E	L	K	S	C	H	K	K	T	S	C	Q	Z	I	I	P	J	K
A	V	M	T	R	O	M	B	Ó	N	Z	S	T	C	X	Z	F	P	C	G
N	Y	F	R	L	Y	E	J	N	O	F	Q	O	H	R	R	R	J	O
I	I	E	N	S	D	X	F	B	V	K	P	K	B	Ó	B	Ó	Á	W	Y
V	L	R	V	N	Y	U	L	A	O	X	Z	G	N	Y	Q	L	S	I	Í
G	M	S	Y	H	L	T	É	A	D	U	I	R	L	I	S	Í	U	S	N
K	C	X	I	L	E	A	F	Ó	N	B	F	C	P	E	G	F	I	M	T
F	B	H	H	N	Z	R	P	G	E	G	D	N	W	U	K	L	R	Z	D
N	S	K	K	X	Z	B	M	W	N	K	V	U	G	S	R	T	L	V	G
P	F	Z	H	T	S	B	M	C	M	X	K	U	G	I	W	C	I	H	D
M	J	K	E	T	M	R	F	G	X	L	M	E	U	U	F	Q	S	W	W
K	Y	D	I	T	S	J	E	G	J	T	T	G	A	V	Y	F	Í	V	Q
K	E	C	A	D	P	Y	I	I	A	B	A	F	D	C	X	C	G	W	Z
V	Q	W	Q	Y	K	B	D	H	C	N	H	O	E	T	S	F	E	Y	G
K	A	O	Q	K	L	Z	J	W	C	J	M	U	N	Q	D	Q	E	S	E
Y	G	U	Y	G	A	O	T	H	U	I	R	L	I	S	Í	H	E	B	E
R	V	E	I	D	H	L	Í	N	C	E	O	L	T	Ó	I	R	P	H	O
L	F	Q	J	E	Z	B	G	E	X	G	O	G	A	L	T	R	W	T	H

cnaguirlisí

prásuirlisí

gaothuirlisí

téaduirlisí

óbó

xileafón

trombón

veidhlín

amhráin

ceoltóir

Turas 2: Mo Leabhar Gníomhaíochta

Féinmheasúnú

Léigh gach topaic sa chéad cholún. An bhfuil tú ag déanamh dul chun cinn? Cuir tic (✓) sa cholún cuí. Tá uimhir an leathanaigh chuí in aice leis an topaic.

TOPAIC	Lch	Go maith 😊	Measartha 😐	Go dona ☹
FOCLÓIR				
Cén Sórt Ceoil a Thaitníonn Leat?	194			
An Ceol Gaelach	196			
An Cheolfhoireann	198			
GRAMADACH				
Na Focail 'faoi' agus 'ó'	200			
SCRÍOBH				
Postáil Bhlag	206			

Na príomhscileanna

Le cabhair ó do mhúinteoir, cuir tic in aice leis na príomhscileanna ar bhain tú úsáid astu i gCaibidil 7.

Na príomhscileanna	Bhain mé úsáid as
A bheith liteartha	
A bheith uimheartha	
Cumarsáid	
A bheith cruthaitheach	
Mé féin a bhainistiú	
Fanacht folláin	
Obair le daoine eile	
Eolas agus smaointeoireacht a bhainistiú	

Plean Gníomhaíochta

Déan machnamh ar do chuid foghlama! Féach ar an bhféinmheasúnú a rinne tú ar leathanach 68. Bunaithe ar an eolas seo, déan plean gníomhaíochta. Líon isteach na míreanna thíos.

Mír 1: Tá eolas maith agam ar na topaicí seo

Mír 2: Tá cleachtadh le déanamh agam ar na topaicí seo

Mír 3: Plean gníomhaíochta

Mar shampla: 'Scríobhfaidh mé blag gearr faoi cheolchoirm a chonaic mé.'

Spórt

Clár Ábhair

Cuid 1–3	Cén Spórt is Fearr Leat?...	70
Cuid 4	Sladmhargadh Spóirt	71
Cuid 5	Ag Cur Síos ar Phearsana Spóirt	72
Cuid 6	Áiseanna Spóirt	72
Gramadach	Céimeanna Comparáide na hAidiachta	73
Cuid 7–10	Cleachtaí Athbhreithnithe	74
Measúnú chun Foghlama	Féinmheasúnú	78
Measúnú chun Foghlama	Plean Gníomhaíochta	79

Cuid 1

Líon na bearnaí.

> iománaíocht   imrím   go rialta   ag snámh   imríonn

Ciara   An _____ tú aon spórt, a Thomaí?

Tomaí   _____, go deimhin. Imrím spórt _____.

Ciara   Cad iad na spóirt a imríonn tú?

Tomaí   Imrím peil Ghaelach, _____ agus sacar. Téim _____ go minic freisin.

Cuid 2

Líon na bearnaí.

> phearsa spóirt   a imríonn   Átha   as   is fearr

Criostóir   Cén spórt _____ tú, a Ailbhe?

Ailbhe   Imrím sacar. Is aoibhinn liom é.

Criostóir   Agus cén _____ is fearr leat?

Ailbhe   Is í Katie McCabe an phearsa spóirt _____ liom. Imríonn sí sacar.

Criostóir   Cárb _____ di?

Ailbhe   Is as Cill na Manach i mBaile _____ Cliath di.

Cuid 3

Scríobh an téarma Gaeilge faoi na pictiúir.

| rámhaíocht | cispheil | iománaíocht | leadóg | sacar | rothaíocht |

Cuid 4

Scríobh an téarma Gaeilge faoi na pictiúir.

| camán | lámhainní | bróga peile | sliotar | rothar | liathróid sacair |

Turas 2: Mo Leabhar Gníomhaíochta

Cuid 5

Déan cur síos ar na pearsana spóirt seo. Bain úsáid as na focail thíos.

> ard   tapa   sciliúil   solúbtha   láidir   crua   cróga   diongbháilte

Tá sé _____   Tá sí _____

agus _____.   agus _____.

Tá sí _____   Tá sé _____

agus _____.   agus _____.

Cuid 6

Scríobh an téarma Gaeilge faoi na pictiúir.

> cúirt leadóige   balla dreapadóireachta   raon reatha   rinc haca oighir

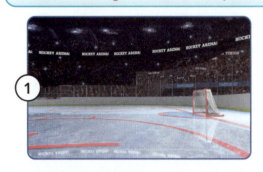

_____   _____

_____   _____

GRAMADACH

Céimeanna Comparáide na hAidiachta

Gramadach 1

Athraigh foirm na haidiachta más gá. Tá an chéad cheann déanta duit.

1	ard	tall	níos _____airde_____
2	láidir	strong	níos _____
3	foighneach	patient	níos _____
4	sciliúil	skilful	níos _____
5	cróga	brave	níos _____
6	deacair	difficult	níos _____
7	maith	good	níos _____
8	mór	big	níos _____
9	beag	small	níos _____
10	tapa	fast	níos _____

Gramadach 2

Athraigh na focail idir lúibíní.

1. Tá Sorcha níos [tapa] _____ ná Aoife.

2. Níl Árón níos [foighneach] _____ ná Éamonn.

3. An bhfuil Colm níos [láidir] _____ ná Mánas?

4. Tá Greta níos [cróga] _____ ná Jeaic.

5. Tá Olivia níos [maith] _____ ná Eleanor.

6. Tá Aindriú níos [láidir] _____ ná Eric.

7. Tá an luch níos [beag] _____ ná an cat.

8. Tá an coinín níos [tapa] _____ ná an madra rua.

Cuid 7

Léamhthuiscint

Léigh an píosa seo faoi Dheirdre agus freagair na ceisteanna a ghabhann leis.

Dia daoibh, is mise Deirdre. Is breá liom go leor spóirt dhifriúla ach is é an sacar an spórt is fearr liom.

Imrím sacar le mo chlub Salthill Devon i nGaillimh. Imrím ar an mbóthar nó sa pháirc le mo chairde freisin. Bíonn traenáil againn trí huaire sa tseachtain agus bíonn cluiche againn gach Satharn. Uaireanta bíonn cluiche againn ar an gCéadaoin. Tá na háiseanna i mo chlub thar barr. Tá go leor páirceanna sacair againn.

Is é Galway United an fhoireann is fearr liom. Téim go dtí a gcuid cluichí go minic.

1. Cén spórt is fearr le Deirdre?
   _____

2. Cén club a n-imríonn sí leis?
   _____

3. Cá n-imríonn sí sacar?
   _____

4. Cé chomh minic is a bhíonn traenáil acu?
   _____

5. An mbíonn cluiche acu ar an gCéadaoin?
   _____

6. Cén fhoireann is fearr léi?
   _____

Cuid 8

Léamhthuiscint

Léigh an blag seo agus freagair na ceisteanna a ghabhann leis.

http://www.camanagussliotar.com

Haigh, is mise Dara. Chuaigh mé chuig cluiche iománaíochta iontach Dé Domhnaigh seo caite. Bhí an Clár ag imirt in aghaidh Loch Garman. Bhí an cluiche ar siúl i Loch Garman.

Cheannaigh mé mo thicéad ag an ngeata. Chosain sé €10. Bhí go leor daoine ann. Chuaigh mé ann le mo thuismitheoirí agus beirt chairde.

Bhí an cluiche go hiontach. Thosaigh an dá fhoireann go maith agus ag leath ama, comhscór a bhí ann. D'imir siad go maith sa dara leath freisin, ach sa nóiméad deireanach, fuair Loch Garman cúl iontach. Bhuaigh siad an cluiche 3–15 in aghaidh 2–15.

Nuair a chríochnaigh an cluiche, d'fhágamar an staid agus shiúlamar go dtí an carrchlós. Fuaireamar an bus ar ais go Contae an Chláir. Beidh lá eile ag an bPaorach!

1. Cathain a bhí an cluiche iománaíochta ar siúl?

2. Cá raibh an cluiche ar siúl?

3. Cár cheannaigh Dara an ticéad?

4. Cé mhéad a chosain an ticéad?

5. Cé a chuaigh in éineacht leis?

6. Cad a tharla sa nóiméad deireanach?

7. Cé a bhuaigh an cluiche?

8. Conas a chuaigh Dara ar ais go Contae an Chláir?

Turas 2: Mo Leabhar Gníomhaíochta

Cuid 9

Freagair na ceisteanna seo.

1. Céard iad na spóirt a thaitníonn leat?
   _____
   _____

2. An imríonn tú spórt? Cén spórt?
   _____
   _____

3. An bhféachann tú ar spórt ar an teilifís?
   _____
   _____

4. An imríonn aon duine i do theaghlach spórt? Cén spórt?
   _____
   _____

5. An raibh tú riamh ag cluiche spóirt? Ar thaitin sé leat?
   _____
   _____

Cuid 10

Cuardach focal

Déan an cuardach focal.

Spórt

K	C	G	S	W	C	D	G	N	D	V	E	G	O	O	Z	S	J	N	D
C	H	I	X	D	P	L	C	Q	B	J	S	Y	S	E	M	G	G	O	R
I	N	H	N	H	E	K	B	L	F	F	I	V	G	I	W	U	R	I	R
F	R	G	B	U	I	C	Y	Ú	T	S	O	F	X	B	U	A	A	N	S
E	J	K	G	N	L	A	T	T	X	V	G	S	Q	I	V	L	I	D	G
W	D	T	R	E	C	S	R	H	O	A	H	Y	M	A	E	A	C	W	N
B	U	W	F	T	V	R	E	C	Q	V	F	S	Q	C	F	E	É	I	S
I	D	X	Á	X	V	G	A	H	J	U	L	T	I	R	G	X	A	O	Z
U	I	G	I	I	D	L	L	L	X	P	Q	L	N	F	T	T	D	V	G
P	O	L	S	D	L	P	A	E	H	I	R	F	Á	Q	C	D	K	T	A
O	N	E	E	X	B	U	M	A	V	H	Q	I	W	I	S	H	P	C	H
E	G	A	A	R	E	V	H	S	T	N	A	Z	J	Z	D	Q	G	B	V
K	B	C	N	I	E	W	P	A	S	U	I	C	X	Z	Y	I	H	X	D
K	H	A	N	P	J	V	F	Í	V	G	L	X	A	H	G	E	R	A	I
H	Á	Í	A	V	H	N	X	O	L	O	Y	B	P	Y	G	Z	G	P	Q
T	I	O	A	S	F	O	H	C	I	V	N	B	Y	P	B	O	B	C	S
O	L	C	T	L	J	A	K	H	V	M	N	T	K	K	L	W	K	I	K
H	T	H	L	B	A	P	Y	T	H	R	I	A	O	C	D	M	G	G	F
V	E	T	K	N	U	X	P	N	Y	L	M	L	G	Z	Q	R	V	F	Q
X	N	V	S	X	N	J	Y	I	N	K	P	M	H	B	M	Z	W	Q	O

peil

haca

lúthchleasaíocht

gleacaíocht

trealamh

áiseanna

clogad

raicéad

láidir

diongbháilte

Féinmheasúnú

Léigh gach topaic sa chéad cholún. An bhfuil tú ag déanamh dul chun cinn? Cuir tic (✓) sa cholún cuí. Tá uimhir an leathanaigh chuí in aice leis an topaic.

TOPAIC	Lch	Go maith 🙂	Measartha 😐	Go dona ☹
FOCLÓIR				
Cén Spórt is Fearr Leat?	222			
Sladmhargadh Spóirt	224			
Ag Cur Síos ar Phearsana Spóirt	228			
Áiseanna Spóirt	230			
GRAMADACH				
Céimeanna Comparáide na hAidiachta	229			
SCRÍOBH				
Postáil Bhlag	234			

Na príomhscileanna

Le cabhair ó do mhúinteoir, cuir tic in aice leis na príomhscileanna ar bhain tú úsáid astu i gCaibidil 8.

Na príomhscileanna	Bhain mé úsáid as
A bheith liteartha	
A bheith uimheartha	
Cumarsáid	
A bheith cruthaitheach	
Mé féin a bhainistiú	
Fanacht folláin	
Obair le daoine eile	
Eolas agus smaointeoireacht a bhainistiú	

Plean Gníomhaíochta

Déan machnamh ar do chuid foghlama! Féach ar an bhféinmheasúnú a rinne tú ar leathanach 78. Bunaithe ar an eolas seo, déan plean gníomhaíochta. Líon isteach na míreanna thíos.

Mír 1: Tá eolas maith agam ar na topaicí seo

Mír 2: Tá cleachtadh le déanamh agam ar na topaicí seo

Mír 3: Plean gníomhaíochta

Mar shampla: 'Scríobhfaidh mé blag gearr faoi chluiche/rás/throid a chonaic mé.'

CAIBIDIL 9 — Laethanta Saoire

Clár Ábhair

Cuid 1–2	Cineálacha Saoire	80
Cuid 3	Saoire Ghréine Thar Lear	81
Cuid 4	Saoire Sciála	81
Cuid 5–6	Tíreolaíocht na hÉireann	82
Gramadach	An Aidiacht agus an Dobhriathar	83
Cuid 7–10	Cleachtaí Athbhreithnithe	84
Measúnú chun Foghlama	Féinmheasúnú	88
Measúnú chun Foghlama	Plean Gníomhaíochta	89

Cuid 1

Líon na bearnaí.

> an ndeachaigh   an Airgintín   saoire   gach cineál   thaitin

Bláthnaid Cén sórt _____ a thaitníonn leat, a Hector?

Hector Is aoibhinn liom _____ saoire, a Bhláthnaid. Ach is iad saoirí gníomhaíochta na saoirí is fearr liom.

Bláthnaid _____ tú ar saoire i mbliana?

Hector Chuaigh, go deimhin. Chuaigh mé go dtí _____ agus an Bhrasaíl.

Bláthnaid Ar thaitin an tsaoire leat?

Hector Ó, _____ an tsaoire go mór liom.

Cuid 2

Líon na bearnaí.

> ag snámh   le déanaí   an-taitneamh   ar bhain   thar barr

Piaras An ndeachaigh tú ar saoire _____, a Iwa?

Iwa Chuaigh. Chuaigh mé go dtí an Chróit.

Piaras _____ tú taitneamh as?

Iwa Bhain mé _____ as.

Piaras Céard a rinne tú?

Iwa Chuaigh mé _____ agus ag siúl gach lá. Chuaigh mé ag sciáil ar uisce freisin. Bhí sé _____.

Cuid 3

Scríobh an téarma Gaeilge faoi na pictiúir.

> ag snámh   ag sciáil ar uisce   ag lapadaíl   ag scríobh cárta poist

Cuid 4

Scríobh an téarma Gaeilge faoi na pictiúir.

> ag sciáil síos le fána   ag clársciáil   ag dreapadh sléibhte   ag léim

Cuid 5

Scríobh na cúigí ar an léarscáil. Tá an chéad cheann déanta duit.

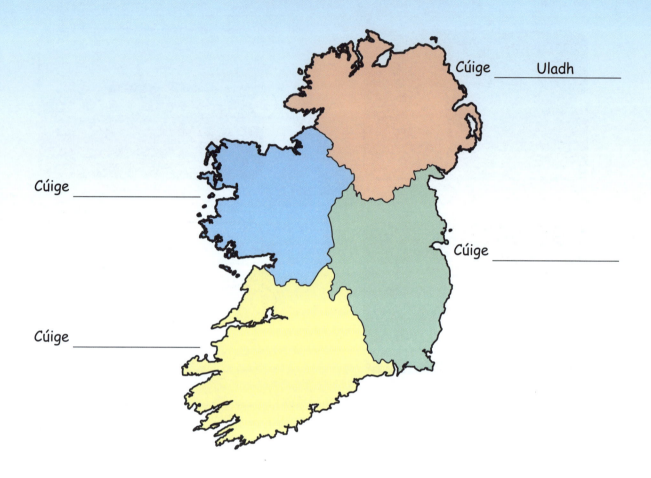

Cúige ____Uladh____

Cúige _____

Cúige _____

Cúige _____

Cuid 6

Cén cúige ina bhfuil na contaetha seo?

	Contae	Cúige
1	Lú	
2	Ard Mhacha	
3	Liatroim	
4	Luimneach	
5	Doire	
6	Cill Dara	
7	Gaillimh	
8	Port Láirge	

GRAMADACH

An Aidiacht agus an Dobhriathar

Gramadach 1

Cuir an réimír 'an-' roimh na haidiachtaí seo. Tá an chéad cheann déanta duit.

1	beag	an-bheag
2	cairdiúil	
3	ard	
4	lách	
5	grianmhar	
6	blasta	
7	mór	
8	óg	
9	láidir	
10	fuar	

Gramadach 2

Cuir an réimír 'ró' roimh na haidiachtaí seo. Tá an chéad cheann déanta duit.

1	beag	róbheag
2	cairdiúil	
3	ard	
4	lách	
5	grianmhar	
6	blasta	
7	mór	
8	óg	
9	láidir	
10	fuar	

Gramadach 3

Cuir ciorcal thart ar an bhfreagra ceart.

1. Chuaigh mé ag sciáil inné. Bhí sé **iontach** / **go hiontach**!
2. Tá an ghrian ag taitneamh **ard** / **go hard** sa spéir.
3. Tá an trá sin **álainn** / **go hálainn**.
4. Rith mé go dtí an trá **tapa** / **go tapa**.
5. An raibh an cluiche **leadránach** / **go leadránach**?

Cuid 7

Léamhthuiscint

Léigh an cárta poist seo agus freagair na ceisteanna a ghabhann leis.

A Emmet, a chara,

Conas atá tú? Tá súil agam go bhfuil tú i mbarr na sláinte!

Táim ar shaoire ghréine in Lanzarote. Is aoibhinn liom é. Tá an aimsir go hálainn. Bíonn sé te agus grianmhar gach lá.

Tá go leor rudaí le déanamh anseo. Téimid go dtí an trá gach lá. Chuaigh mé ag surfáil inné agus rachaidh mé ag sciáil ar uisce níos déanaí inniu.

Rachaimid ag siopadóireacht agus ag fámaireacht amárach. Tá an baile mór go han-deas. Tá go leor siopaí agus bialanna deasa ann.

Beidh mé ar ais in Éirinn Dé Domhnaigh. Feicfidh mé Dé Luain thú!

Slán!

Étain

Emmet de Barra

An tSráid Mhór

An Cabhán

Éire

1. Cá bhfuil Étain ar saoire?

2. Conas a bhíonn an aimsir gach lá?

3. Cad a dhéanann siad gach lá?

4. Cad a rinne sí inné?

5. Cad a dhéanfaidh siad amárach?

6. Cathain a bheidh sí ar ais in Éirinn?

Cuid 8

Léamhthuiscint

Léigh an cárta poist seo agus freagair na ceisteanna a ghabhann leis.

A Ghráinne, a chara,

Conas atá cúrsaí? Tá súil agam go bhfuil gach rud go maith.

Táimid ar saoire i nDún na nGall le mo theaghlach. Tá sé ar fheabhas anseo. Ar an dea-uair, tá an aimsir go hálainn. Bíonn an ghrian ag taitneamh go hard sa spéir gach lá.

Táim ag freastal ar scoil surfála. Déanaim ceachtanna gach maidin. Sa tráthnóna, siúlaimid timpeall an bhaile mhóir. Tá go leor bialann agus siopaí deasa anseo.

Rachaimid ar thuras báid amárach. Ba bhreá liom dul ag iascaireacht freisin.

Beimid ar ais Dé Sathairn. Buailfidh mé aníos chugat Dé Domhnaigh.

Slán tamall!

Fionn

Gráinne Ní Mháille
Bóthar na Móna
Bré
Cill Mhantáin

1. Cé leis a bhfuil Fionn ar saoire i nDún na nGall?

2. Conas a bhíonn an aimsir gach lá?

3. Cad a dhéanann Fionn gach maidin?

4. Cén sórt áiseanna atá sa bhaile mór?

5. Cad a dhéanfaidh siad amárach?

6. Cathain a bheidh siad ar ais?

Cuid 9

Freagair na ceisteanna seo.

1. Cén sórt saoirí a thaitníonn leat?
   _____
   _____

2. Cad is féidir leat a dhéanamh ar na saoirí sin?
   _____
   _____
   _____

3. An raibh tú ar saoire anuraidh? Cá ndeachaigh tú?
   _____
   _____

4. An rachaidh tú ar saoire i mbliana? Cá rachaidh tú?
   _____
   _____

5. Cad é an áit is fearr leat in Éirinn?
   _____
   _____

Cuid 10

Cuardach focal

Déan an cuardach focal.

Laethanta Saoire

G	N	Í	O	M	H	A	Í	O	C	H	T	A	Í	L	L	X	D	P	T
G	R	J	D	Z	Z	Q	R	G	C	H	R	V	L	Z	K	N	E	S	U
O	S	I	O	R	K	K	P	I	D	O	Á	H	D	W	X	I	D	X	R
U	P	K	A	E	P	S	Y	J	D	X	K	E	D	Y	E	R	D	J	A
M	U	D	Z	N	G	R	N	K	B	E	G	G	F	T	E	Z	J	B	S
S	N	U	C	V	T	Z	R	L	K	P	E	D	K	H	N	D	J	F	Ó
B	B	N	H	I	X	Z	R	J	D	F	N	Q	P	K	A	S	O	V	I
F	T	O	P	T	S	C	D	E	C	A	M	P	Á	I	L	P	I	T	R
P	D	R	J	U	O	G	R	E	L	W	L	H	K	D	I	I	W	I	Í
D	G	E	E	B	J	E	C	I	O	V	Z	O	S	L	W	M	K	M	F
S	C	E	C	W	N	T	Á	G	C	K	I	C	I	R	M	Z	I	R	B
R	N	S	E	Y	Q	F	V	W	A	R	A	K	H	M	V	E	U	Q	I
Q	U	K	W	O	R	B	E	B	M	I	V	D	W	P	R	E	K	I	L
E	Y	X	H	U	Q	G	P	I	A	R	X	Q	R	B	Y	K	Z	W	D
X	K	R	S	C	I	Á	I	L	Z	A	L	H	T	R	B	I	S	S	B
K	K	Y	W	A	M	H	V	I	G	Y	W	C	R	D	V	I	W	A	Y
U	I	U	R	F	W	S	D	L	X	X	M	V	S	N	D	E	X	F	H
I	C	R	B	R	K	C	B	F	I	D	J	J	R	U	U	B	K	A	R
W	A	P	W	N	G	E	F	E	Y	P	S	Q	K	X	J	S	P	R	G
F	Á	M	A	I	R	E	A	C	H	T	N	O	J	R	B	D	H	I	W

sciáil

grian

safari

campáil

gníomhaíochtaí

surfáil

turasóirí

farraige

trá

fámaireacht

Féinmheasúnú

Léigh gach topaic sa chéad cholún. An bhfuil tú ag déanamh dul chun cinn? Cuir tic (✓) sa cholún cuí. Tá uimhir an leathanaigh chuí in aice leis an topaic.

TOPAIC	Lch	Go maith 🙂	Measartha 😐	Go dona ☹
FOCLÓIR				
Cineálacha Saoire	246			
Saoire Ghréine Thar Lear	248			
Saoire Sciála	250			
Tíreolaíocht na hÉireann	256			
GRAMADACH				
An Aidiacht agus an Dobhriathar	252			
SCRÍOBH				
Cárta Poist	262			

Na príomhscileanna

Le cabhair ó do mhúinteoir, cuir tic in aice leis na príomhscileanna ar bhain tú úsáid astu i gCaibidil 9.

Na príomhscileanna	Bhain mé úsáid as
A bheith liteartha	
A bheith uimheartha	
Cumarsáid	
A bheith cruthaitheach	
Mé féin a bhainistiú	
Fanacht folláin	
Obair le daoine eile	
Eolas agus smaointeoireacht a bhainistiú	

Plean Gníomhaíochta

Déan machnamh ar do chuid foghlama! Féach ar an bhféinmheasúnú a rinne tú ar leathanach 88. Bunaithe ar an eolas seo, déan plean gníomhaíochta. Líon isteach na míreanna thíos.

Mír 1: Tá eolas maith agam ar na topaicí seo

Mír 2: Tá cleachtadh le déanamh agam ar na topaicí seo

Mír 3: Plean gníomhaíochta

Mar shampla: 'Seolfaidh mé cárta poist i nGaeilge chuig cara liom.'

CAIBIDIL 10: Tinneas agus Sláinte

Clár Ábhair

Cuid 1	Lá san Ospidéal	90
Cuid 2	Bia	90
Cuid 3	An Corp	91
Cuid 4	An Ceann	91
Gramadach	Freagraí Gearra	92
Cuid 5–9	Cleachtaí Athbhreithnithe	93
Measúnú chun Foghlama	Féinmheasúnú	98
Measúnú chun Foghlama	Plean Gníomhaíochta	99

Cuid 1

Líon na bearnaí.

> mo rúitín   san ospidéal   níor fhan   am dinnéir   an-phianmhar

Niall   An raibh tú _____ riamh?

Sophie   Bhí, faraor!

Niall   Céard a tharla?

Sophie   Bhris mé _____ nuair a bhí mé ag imirt peile.

Bhí sé _____.

Niall   Ar fhan tú thar oíche?

Sophie   _____. Tharla an timpiste ar maidin agus bhí

mé ar ais sa bhaile faoi _____.

Cuid 2

Líon na bearnaí.

> céard fútsa   is breá liom   an-bhlasta   a itheann tú   bia Iodálach

Marta   Cén sórt bia a thaitníonn leat, a Evan?

Evan   Is aoibhinn liom _____. Céard fútsa?

Marta   _____ bia Indiach, go háirithe curaí.

Evan   Cén sórt bia _____ ag am lóin?

Marta   Ithim ceapaire agus úll nó oráiste. _____?

Evan   Is aoibhinn liom rollaí 4 in a 1. Sicín, sceallóga, rís fhriochta, anlann curaí.

Bíonn siad _____.

Marta   Uch! Déistineach!

Cuid 3

Scríobh an téarma Gaeilge faoi na pictiúir.

> droim　　　cos　　　gualainn　　　lámh　　　glúin　　　rúitín

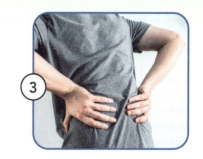

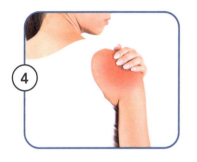

Cuid 4

Scríobh an téarma Gaeilge faoi na pictiúir.

> beola　　　muineál　　　cluas　　　smig　　　súil　　　fiacla

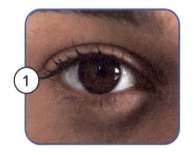
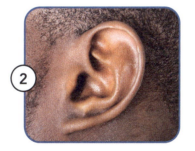
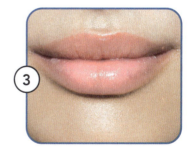

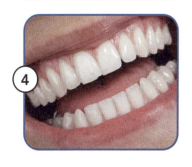

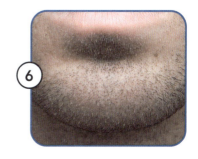

GRAMADACH

Freagraí Gearra

Gramadach 1

Scríobh freagra gearr dearfach (+) agus freagra gearr diúltach (–) ar na ceisteanna seo. Tá an chéad cheann déanta duit.

	An cheist	An freagra dearfach	An freagra diúltach
1	Ar dhún tú?	Dhún	Níor dhún
2	Ar fhan sé?		
3	Ar sheinn sí?		
4	Ar cheannaigh tú?		
5	Ar ith siad?		

Gramadach 2

Scríobh freagra gearr dearfach (+) agus freagra gearr diúltach (–) ar na ceisteanna seo. Tá an chéad cheann déanta duit.

	An cheist	An freagra dearfach	An freagra diúltach
1	An gceannaíonn sé?	Ceannaíonn	Ní cheannaíonn
2	An dtosaíonn sí?		
3	An liostaíonn siad?		
4	An gcuireann sé?		
5	An éiríonn sí?		

Gramadach 3

Scríobh freagra gearr dearfach (+) agus freagra gearr diúltach (–) ar na ceisteanna seo. Tá an chéad cheann déanta duit.

	An cheist	An freagra dearfach	An freagra diúltach
1	An osclóidh siad?	Osclóidh	Ní osclóidh
2	An rithfidh sí?		
3	An dtuigfidh siad?		
4	An imreoidh siad?		
5	An nglanfaidh sé?		

Cuid 5

Léamhthuiscint

Léigh an píosa seo faoi Zara agus a tinneas agus freagair na ceisteanna a ghabhann leis.

Haigh, is mise Zara. Faraor, bhí mé tinn an tseachtain seo caite. Bhí an fliú orm. Ar dtús, bhí tinneas cinn orm. Ansin, bhí pian i mo scornach. Ansin, bhí mo shrón blocáilte.

D'fhan mé trí lá sa leaba. Mhothaigh mé pianta i mo mhuineál, i mo chosa agus i mo dhroim! Níor chreid mé é. D'ól mé go leor uisce agus d'ith mé beagán tósta. D'fhéach mé ar go leor scannán freisin!

1. Céard a bhí cearr (*wrong*) le Zara an tseachtain seo caite?

   _____

2. Luaigh **dhá** shiomptóm (*symptoms*) a bhí aici.

   _____
   _____

3. Cé mhéad lá ar fhan sí sa leaba?

   _____

4. Cár mhothaigh sí pianta?

   _____

5. Cad a d'ól sí agus cad a d'ith sí?

   _____

Cuid 6

Léamhthuiscint

Léigh an píosa seo faoi Fhiachra agus freagair na ceisteanna a ghabhann leis.

Bail ó Dhia oraibh. Is mise Fiachra. Is aoibhinn liom sacar. Imrím le club áitiúil. Faraor, an tseachtain seo caite, nuair a bhí mé ag imirt cluiche, thit mé agus bhris mé mo ghualainn. Bhí sé an-phianmhar.

Thug mo Dhaid síob go dtí an t-ospidéal dom. Rinne an dochtúir x-gha agus chuir sí guailleán (*sling*) air.

Tá an guailleán fós air. Dúirt an dochtúir go mbeidh orm fanacht trí seachtaine eile!

1. Cén spórt a thaitníonn le Fiachra?

   _____

2. Cad a tharla an tseachtain seo caite?

   _____
   _____

3. Conas a chuaigh sé go dtí an t-ospidéal?

   _____

4. Cad a chuir an dochtúir ar a ghualainn?

   _____

5. An bhfuil an guailleán fós ar a ghualainn?

   _____

Cuid 7

Léamhthuiscint

Léigh an biachlár seo agus freagair na ceisteanna a ghabhann leis.

Caifé ar an gCoirnéal

Bricfeasta
Babhla leite	€3.50
Babhla gránóla	€3.50
Iógart	€1.00

Lón
Anraith an lae	€3.00
Ceapairí/Rollaí	€3.00
Sailéid	€4.00

Deochanna
Pota tae	€1.50
Cupán caife	€2.00
Deochanna súilíneacha	€2.00

Sneaiceanna
Barra seacláide	€1.00
Torthaí	€1.00
Paicéad criospaí	€1.00

1. Cé mhéad atá ar bhabhla leite? _____
2. Cé mhéad atá ar bhabhla gránóla? _____
3. Cé mhéad atá ar anraith an lae? _____
4. Cé mhéad atá ar shailéid? _____
5. Cé mhéad atá ar phota tae? _____
6. Cé mhéad atá ar chupán caife? _____
7. Cé mhéad atá ar bharra seacláide? _____
8. Cé mhéad atá ar phaicéad criospaí? _____

Turas 2: Mo Leabhar Gníomhaíochta

Cuid 8

Freagair na ceisteanna seo.

1. Cén sórt bia a thaitníonn leat?

   _____
   _____
   _____

2. Cad a itheann tú ag am bricfeasta, de ghnáth?

   _____
   _____
   _____

3. Cad a itheann tú ag am lóin ar scoil, de ghnáth?

   _____
   _____
   _____

4. Cad is ainm don bhialann is fearr leat?

   _____

5. Cad a d'ith tú ag am dinnéir inné?

   _____
   _____

Cuid 9

Cuardach focal

Déan an cuardach focal.

Tinneas agus Sláinte

R	Ú	I	T	Í	N	G	Z	T	V	J	B	T	F	L	D	W	C	S	Q
K	J	T	S	S	J	S	Y	J	M	C	M	I	A	C	A	N	O	A	N
T	N	R	L	K	S	B	K	G	O	Y	B	E	V	N	O	G	V	I	J
W	X	M	E	U	N	T	I	J	Y	T	Q	H	Z	Ó	S	U	Q	L	Q
C	Y	S	T	O	H	G	Y	Z	G	G	J	T	X	N	H	A	B	É	G
V	B	I	U	S	U	P	L	T	N	O	R	B	Y	N	Y	L	C	A	Y
U	A	N	R	A	I	T	H	Y	N	V	M	A	O	A	Y	A	U	D	P
X	L	Y	O	Z	O	G	S	E	H	X	M	V	V	I	Y	I	Q	S	X
O	W	F	V	B	V	D	W	H	X	V	S	S	U	U	X	N	R	G	A
C	D	I	K	C	V	N	A	C	I	S	W	O	I	O	I	N	H	M	J
X	K	Q	B	T	Y	D	Q	T	Z	L	M	T	F	S	E	Z	S	J	I
C	P	Y	R	P	O	X	A	A	H	A	P	P	U	T	H	Í	M	E	R
I	M	S	P	B	G	J	F	A	I	G	F	M	T	A	R	G	Y	W	I
T	P	M	T	V	J	I	K	R	K	H	K	U	V	W	Z	H	P	U	F
I	W	F	S	H	J	M	K	H	L	D	Y	I	D	L	H	P	Q	A	J
U	K	Y	A	E	U	C	D	W	E	Á	U	N	R	G	A	R	C	Q	T
P	F	T	G	G	D	X	G	O	M	N	R	E	V	C	L	T	S	Y	N
D	W	I	S	N	T	I	N	N	E	A	S	Á	C	Q	Y	V	A	I	D
F	U	F	J	C	Q	I	Q	T	H	C	I	L	R	J	A	X	P	V	B
X	U	X	R	Q	T	Z	M	R	A	V	Q	X	T	U	X	Z	D	U	J

rúitín

gualainn

muineál

sailéad

anraith

cnónna

rís

tinneas

slaghdán

ata

Féinmheasúnú

Léigh gach topaic sa chéad cholún. An bhfuil tú ag déanamh dul chun cinn? Cuir tic (✓) sa cholún cuí. Tá uimhir an leathanaigh chuí in aice leis an topaic.

TOPAIC	Lch	Go maith 🙂	Measartha 😐	Go dona ☹
FOCLÓIR				
An Corp	288			
An Ceann	292			
Tinneas agus Leigheas	294			
Biachlár: Caifé na Cathrach	300			
GRAMADACH				
Freagraí Gearra	298			
SCRÍOBH				
Scéal	304			

Na príomhscileanna

Le cabhair ó do mhúinteoir, cuir tic in aice leis na príomhscileanna ar bhain tú úsáid astu i gCaibidil 10.

Na príomhscileanna	Bhain mé úsáid as
A bheith liteartha	
A bheith uimheartha	
Cumarsáid	
A bheith cruthaitheach	
Mé féin a bhainistiú	
Fanacht folláin	
Obair le daoine eile	
Eolas agus smaointeoireacht a bhainistiú	

Plean Gníomhaíochta

Déan machnamh ar do chuid foghlama! Féach ar an bhféinmheasúnú a rinne tú ar leathanach 98. Bunaithe ar an eolas seo, déan plean gníomhaíochta. Líon isteach na míreanna thíos.

Mír 1: Tá eolas maith agam ar na topaicí seo

Mír 2: Tá cleachtadh le déanamh agam ar na topaicí seo

Mír 3: Plean gníomhaíochta

Mar shampla: 'Dearfaidh mé biachlár do mo scoil nó do bhialann áitiúil.'

Trialacha Cluastuisceana

Tagraíonn uimhreacha na leathanach don leabhar gníomhaíochta sa mhír seo.

Caibidil 1: Mé Féin

Traic 2 — A. Píosa Cainte

Cloisfidh tú píosa cainte sa cheist seo. Cloisfidh tú an píosa cainte faoi dhó. Beidh sos ann leis na freagraí a scríobh tar éis na chéad éisteachta agus tar éis an dara héisteacht.

1. Cén pictiúr a théann leis an bpíosa cainte seo?

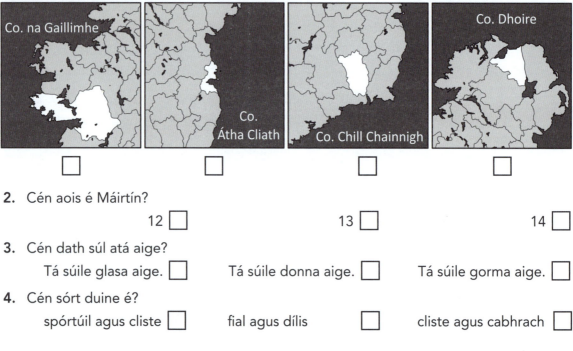

2. Cén aois é Máirtín?
   - 12 ☐
   - 13 ☐
   - 14 ☐

3. Cén dath súl atá aige?
   - Tá súile glasa aige. ☐
   - Tá súile donna aige. ☐
   - Tá súile gorma aige. ☐

4. Cén sórt duine é?
   - spórtúil agus cliste ☐
   - fial agus dílis ☐
   - cliste agus cabhrach ☐

Traic 3 — B. Fógra

Cloisfidh tú fógra sa cheist seo. Cloisfidh tú an fógra faoi dhó. Beidh sos ann leis na freagraí a scríobh tar éis na chéad éisteachta agus tar éis an dara héisteacht.

1. Céard atá á lorg ag G24?
   _____

2. Cén cineál gruaige a bheidh ar na haisteoirí óga?
   _____

3. Cá bhfuil tuilleadh eolais ar fáil?
   - www.TeilifisVikings.ie ☐
   - www.AisteoiriVikings.ie ☐
   - www.SeoVikings.ie ☐

Trialacha Cluastuisceana

C. Píosa Nuachta

Cloisfidh tú píosa nuachta sa cheist seo. Cloisfidh tú an píosa nuachta faoi dhó. Beidh sos ann leis na freagraí a scríobh tar éis na chéad éisteachta agus tar éis an dara héisteacht.

1. Cén pictiúr a théann leis an bpíosa nuachta seo?

☐ ☐ ☐ ☐

2. Cá bhfuil tuilleadh eolais ar fáil?

www.siopatanya.ie ☐ www.turastanya.ie ☐

www.rangtanya.ie ☐ www.faiseantanya.ie ☐

D. Comhrá

Cloisfidh tú comhrá sa cheist seo. Cloisfidh tú an comhrá faoi dhó. Cloisfidh tú an comhrá ó thosach deireadh an chéad uair. Ansin cloisfidh tú ina dhá mhír é. Beidh sos ann leis na freagraí a scríobh tar éis gach míre díobh.

Mír 1

1. Cén t-aisteoir mór le rá a bheidh sa scannán nua?

☐ ☐ ☐ ☐

2. Scríobh síos **dhá** thréith faoin aisteoir seo a luann Liam.

_____

Mír 2

3. Cad a admhálann (*admit*) Liam faoin eolas atá aige?

   Admhálann sé nach bhfuil sé suas chun dáta le réaltaí ceoil. ☐

   Admhálann sé nach bhfuil sé suas chun dáta le réaltaí scannán. ☐

   Admhálann sé nach bhfuil a lán eolais aige faoi scannáin. ☐

   Admhálann sé nach bhfuil a lán eolais aige faoi chúrsaí ceoil. ☐

4. An aontaíonn Emma le tuairim Liam faoin eolas atá aige?

_____

Caibidil 2: Mo Theaghlach

Script: leathanach 133

A. Píosa Cainte

Cloisfidh tú píosa cainte sa cheist seo. Cloisfidh tú an píosa cainte faoi dhó. Beidh sos ann leis na freagraí a scríobh tar éis na chéad éisteachta agus tar éis an dara héisteacht.

1. Cén pictiúr a théann leis an bpíosa cainte seo?

   | Eanáir 8 ☐ | Samhain 18 ☐ | Samhain 8 ☐ | Eanáir 18 ☐ |

2. Cé mhéad deartháir atá ag Labhaoise?
   1 ☐   2 ☐   3 ☐

3. Cé mhéad deirfiúr atá aici?
   1 ☐   2 ☐   3 ☐

4. Cad is ainm don pháiste is óige?
   _____

B. Fógra

Cloisfidh tú fógra sa cheist seo. Cloisfidh tú an fógra faoi dhó. Beidh sos ann leis na freagraí a scríobh tar éis na chéad éisteachta agus tar éis an dara héisteacht.

1. Cén pictiúr a théann leis an bhfógra seo?

   ☐   ☐   ☐   ☐

2. Céard atá á lorg ag G24?
   _____

3. Cén contae ina mbeidh an clár ar siúl?
   _____

C. Píosa Nuachta

Cloisfidh tú píosa nuachta sa cheist seo. Cloisfidh tú an píosa nuachta faoi dhó. Beidh sos ann leis na freagraí a scríobh tar éis na chéad éisteachta agus tar éis an dara héisteacht.

1. Cén duais a bhuaigh clann Uí Ríordáin?

    seic do €3,000,000 agus corn mór ☐
    seic do €2,000,000 agus corn mór ☐
    seic do €3,000 agus corn mór ☐
    seic do €2,000 agus corn mór ☐

2. Cé hí Deirdre Uí Ríordáin?

    _____

D. Comhrá

Cloisfidh tú comhrá sa cheist seo. Cloisfidh tú an comhrá faoi dhó. Cloisfidh tú an comhrá ó thosach deireadh an chéad uair. Ansin cloisfidh tú ina dhá mhír é. Beidh sos ann leis na freagraí a scríobh tar éis gach míre díobh.

Mír 1

1. Cén post a fuair Áine?

Comhfhreagraí nuachta	Comhfhreagraí ceoil	Comhfhreagraí faisin	Comhfhreagraí leantóirí

☐	☐	☐	☐

2. Scríobh síos **dhá** dhualgas (*duties*) a bheidh i gceist leis an bpost sin.

    _____

    _____

Mír 2

3. Cathain a thosóidh sí?

    ar an 3 Aibreán ☐
    ar an 6 Bealtaine ☐
    ar an 10 Meitheamh ☐
    ar an 20 Iúil ☐

4. Cad iad na huaireanta oibre a bheidh aici?

    _____

Caibidil 3: Mo Theach

Script: leathanach 134

A. Píosa Cainte

Cloisfidh tú píosa cainte sa cheist seo. Cloisfidh tú an píosa cainte faoi dhó. Beidh sos ann leis na freagraí a scríobh tar éis na chéad éisteachta agus tar éis an dara héisteacht.

1. Cén pictiúr a théann leis an bpíosa cainte seo?

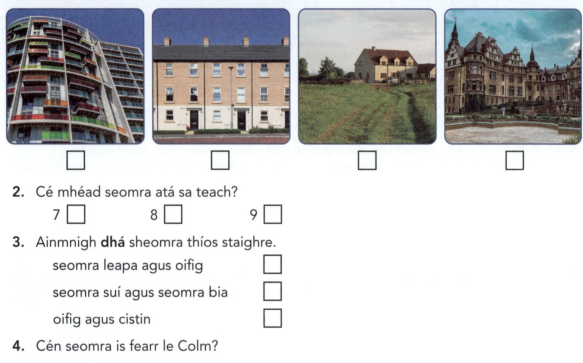

2. Cé mhéad seomra atá sa teach?
   7 ☐   8 ☐   9 ☐

3. Ainmnigh **dhá** sheomra thíos staighre.
   seomra leapa agus oifig ☐
   seomra suí agus seomra bia ☐
   oifig agus cistin ☐

4. Cén seomra is fearr le Colm?
   _____

B. Fógra

Cloisfidh tú fógra sa cheist seo. Cloisfidh tú an fógra faoi dhó. Beidh sos ann leis na freagraí a scríobh tar éis na chéad éisteachta agus tar éis an dara héisteacht.

1. Cé mhéad teach a bheidh ar díol amárach?
   _____

2. Cé mhéad a bheidh ar gach teach?
   €300,000 ☐   €350,000 ☐   €400,000 ☐

3. Cá bhfuil tuilleadh eolais ar fáil?
   _____

Trialacha Cluastuisceana

C. Píosa Nuachta

Cloisfidh tú píosa nuachta sa cheist seo. Cloisfidh tú an píosa nuachta faoi dhó. Beidh sos ann leis na freagraí a scríobh tar éis na chéad éisteachta agus tar éis an dara héisteacht.

1. Cén foirgneamh ar briseadh isteach ann?

  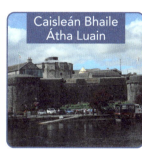 

Caisleán na Blarnan ☐   Caisleán Bhaile Átha Cliath ☐   Caisleán Bhaile Átha Luain ☐   Caisleán Chill Chainnigh ☐

2. Cén **dá** rud a bhí á gcaitheamh ag na buirgléirí?

   spéaclaí gréine ☐   éadaí dubha ☐   balaclávaí ☐   lámhainní ☐

D. Comhrá

Cloisfidh tú comhrá sa cheist seo. Cloisfidh tú an comhrá faoi dhó. Cloisfidh tú an comhrá ó thosach deireadh an chéad uair. Ansin cloisfidh tú ina dhá mhír é. Beidh sos ann leis na freagraí a scríobh tar éis gach míre díobh.

Mír 1

1. Cá bhfuil Damien ar saoire faoi láthair?

An Fhrainc ☐   An Spáinn ☐   An Iodáil ☐   An Ghréig ☐

2. Luaigh **dhá** rud a deir Damien faoin teach saoire ina bhfuil sé ag fanacht.

   _____

   _____

Mír 2

3. Cathain a bheidh Damien ar ais?

   Dé hAoine ☐   Dé Sathairn ☐   Dé Domhnaigh ☐   Dé Luain ☐

4. Cad a thabharfaidh Damien ar ais do Chóra?

   _____

Caibidil 4: Mo Cheantar

Script: leathanach 135

A. Píosa Cainte

Cloisfidh tú píosa cainte sa cheist seo. Cloisfidh tú an píosa cainte faoi dhó. Beidh sos ann leis na freagraí a scríobh tar éis na chéad éisteachta agus tar éis an dara héisteacht.

1. Cén pictiúr a théann leis an bpíosa cainte seo?

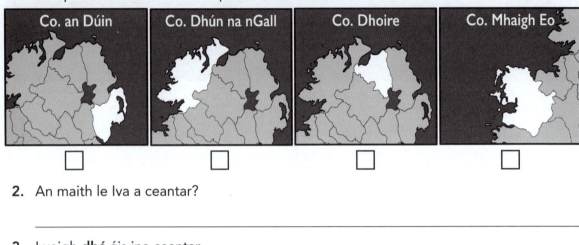

Co. an Dúin ☐   Co. Dhún na nGall ☐   Co. Dhoire ☐   Co. Mhaigh Eo ☐

2. An maith le Iva a ceantar?

   _____

3. Luaigh **dhá** áis ina ceantar.
   - siopaí agus amharclann ☐
   - club óige agus amharclann ☐
   - pictiúrlann agus club óige ☐

4. Cá dtéann sí go minic?
   siopaí ☐   club óige ☐   pictiúrlann ☐

B. Fógra

Cloisfidh tú fógra sa cheist seo. Cloisfidh tú an fógra faoi dhó. Beidh sos ann leis na freagraí a scríobh tar éis na chéad éisteachta agus tar éis an dara héisteacht.

1. Cén rud nua a osclófar i dTulach Mhór Dé Sathairn seo chugainn?

Ionad Sláinte ☐   Ionad Spóirt ☐   Ionad Campála ☐   Ionad Siopadóireachta ☐

2. Cé mhéad euro atá le buachan sa raifil mhór?
   €100 ☐   €1,000 ☐   €10,000 ☐   €100,000 ☐

C. Píosa Nuachta

Cloisfidh tú píosa nuachta sa cheist seo. Cloisfidh tú an píosa nuachta faoi dhó. Beidh sos ann leis na freagraí a scríobh tar éis na chéad éisteachta agus tar éis an dara héisteacht.

1. Cén spórt a bheidh á imirt ag Éirinn agus an tSeapáin amárach?

   _____

2. Cén cineál áite é Shizuoka?
   - cathair mhór ☐
   - cathair bheag ☐
   - sráidbhaile ☐

3. Ainmnigh áis **amháin** i gceantar Shizuoka.

   _____

D. Comhrá

Cloisfidh tú comhrá sa cheist seo. Cloisfidh tú an comhrá faoi dhó. Cloisfidh tú an comhrá ó thosach deireadh an chéad uair. Ansin cloisfidh tú ina dhá mhír é. Beidh sos ann leis na freagraí a scríobh tar éis gach míre díobh.

Mír 1

1. Conas atá Amy ag mothú ar maidin?

   ☐   ☐   ☐   ☐

2. Céard a bhí á dhéanamh ag comharsana Amy aréir? Luaigh **dhá** rud.

   _____
   _____

Mír 2

3. Cén t-am a tháinig na Gardaí?
   - 00.00 ☐
   - 01.00 ☐
   - 12.00 ☐
   - 13.00 ☐

4. Cén t-am a bheidh Amy sa bhaile tráthnóna?

   _____

Caibidil 5: Mo Scoil

Script: leathanach 136

A. Píosa Cainte

Cloisfidh tú píosa cainte sa cheist seo. Cloisfidh tú an píosa cainte faoi dhó. Beidh sos ann leis na freagraí a scríobh tar éis na chéad éisteachta agus tar éis an dara héisteacht.

1. Cén pictiúr a théann leis an bpíosa cainte seo?

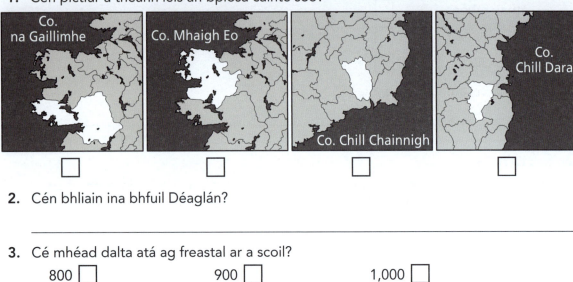

   Co. na Gaillimhe ☐   Co. Mhaigh Eo ☐   Co. Chill Chainnigh ☐   Co. Chill Dara ☐

2. Cén bhliain ina bhfuil Déaglán?

   _____

3. Cé mhéad dalta atá ag freastal ar a scoil?
   800 ☐   900 ☐   1,000 ☐

4. Cén t-ábhar is fearr leis?
   Mata ☐   Adhmadóireacht ☐   Béarla ☐

B. Fógra

Cloisfidh tú fógra sa cheist seo. Cloisfidh tú an fógra faoi dhó. Beidh sos ann leis na freagraí a scríobh tar éis na chéad éisteachta agus tar éis an dara héisteacht.

1. Cé mhéad fógra a dhéanfaidh an cainteoir ar maidin?

   _____

2. Cén cineál foirne lena ngabhann an cainteoir comhghairdeas?
   foireann sacair ☐
   foireann díospóireachta ☐
   foireann pheile ☐

3. Cén bhliain ina bhfuil an fhoireann?

   _____

C. Píosa Nuachta

Cloisfidh tú píosa nuachta sa cheist seo. Cloisfidh tú an píosa nuachta faoi dhó. Beidh sos ann leis na freagraí a scríobh tar éis na chéad éisteachta agus tar éis an dara héisteacht.

1. Cén cineál scoile atá á tógáil i gContae na Mí?

  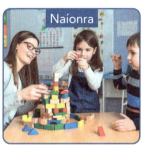 

Meánscoil ☐   Bunscoil ☐   Naíonra ☐   Ollscoil ☐

2. Cathain a osclóidh an scoil nua?

   i mí Mheán Fómhair ☐   i mí Lúnasa ☐

   i mí Iúil ☐   i mí an Mheithimh ☐

D. Comhrá

Cloisfidh tú comhrá sa cheist seo. Cloisfidh tú an comhrá faoi dhó. Cloisfidh tú an comhrá ó thosach deireadh an chéad uair. Ansin cloisfidh tú ina dhá mhír é. Beidh sos ann leis na freagraí a scríobh tar éis gach míre díobh.

Mír 1

1. Cén leabhar atá á lorg ag an múinteoir?

Stair ☐   Eolaíocht ☐   Tíreolaíocht ☐   Mata ☐

2. Cá bhfuil an leabhar anois?

   _____

Mír 2

3. Cén áit a dtabharfaidh Caitríona an leabhar?

   go dtí an seomra ealaíne ☐   go dtí an seomra foirne ☐

   go dtí an seomra eolaíochta ☐   go dtí an seomra urnaí ☐

4. Cé a bheidh ag fanacht leis an leabhar?

   _____

Turas 2: Mo Leabhar Gníomhaíochta

Caibidil 6: Mo Chaithimh Aimsire

Script: leathanach 137

 A. Píosa Cainte

Cloisfidh tú píosa cainte sa cheist seo. Cloisfidh tú an píosa cainte faoi dhó. Beidh sos ann leis na freagraí a scríobh tar éis na chéad éisteachta agus tar éis an dara héisteacht.

1. Cén pictiúr a théann leis an bpíosa cainte seo?

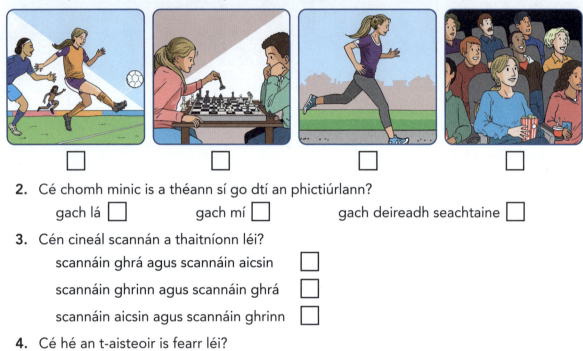

2. Cé chomh minic is a théann sí go dtí an phictiúrlann?

   gach lá ☐   gach mí ☐   gach deireadh seachtaine ☐

3. Cén cineál scannán a thaitníonn léi?

   scannáin ghrá agus scannáin aicsin ☐

   scannáin ghrinn agus scannáin ghrá ☐

   scannáin aicsin agus scannáin ghrinn ☐

4. Cé hé an t-aisteoir is fearr léi?

   _____

B. Fógra

Cloisfidh tú fógra sa cheist seo. Cloisfidh tú an fógra faoi dhó. Beidh sos ann leis na freagraí a scríobh tar éis na chéad éisteachta agus tar éis an dara héisteacht.

1. Cén pictiúr a théann leis an bhfógra seo?

☐ ☐ ☐ ☐

2. Cathain a bheidh searmanas bronnta na nOscar ar siúl?

   ar an dara Domhnach deireanach de mhí Feabhra ☐

   ar an Domhnach deireanach de mhí Feabhra ☐

   ar an gcéad Domhnach de mhí Feabhra ☐

   ar an dara Domhnach de mhí Feabhra ☐

C. Píosa Nuachta

Cloisfidh tú píosa nuachta sa cheist seo. Cloisfidh tú an píosa nuachta faoi dhó. Beidh sos ann leis na freagraí a scríobh tar éis na chéad éisteachta agus tar éis an dara héisteacht.

1. Cén aois í Caireann Ní Chléirigh?

   _____

2. Cad a bhuaigh sí?

   duais €300 ☐   duais €3,000 ☐   duais €30,000 ☐

3. Cén gléas leictreonach ar dhear sí an cluiche air?

   _____

D. Comhrá

Cloisfidh tú comhrá sa cheist seo. Cloisfidh tú an comhrá faoi dhó. Cloisfidh tú an comhrá ó thosach deireadh an chéad uair. Ansin cloisfidh tú ina dhá mhír é. Beidh sos ann leis na freagraí a scríobh tar éis gach míre díobh.

Mír 1

1. Cén lá a mbeidh Aodh ag iarraidh dul go dtí an phictiúrlann?

Dé Luain	Dé Céadaoin	Dé hAoine	Dé Sathairn
☐	☐	☐	☐

2. Cén **dá** chineál scannáin ar mhaith leat a fheiceáil?

   _____

   _____

Mír 2

3. Cathain a bheidh *Star Wars* ag tosú?

   8.00 ☐   8.30 ☐
   8.15 ☐   8.45 ☐

4. Cén áit a mbuailfidh siad le chéile?

   _____

Caibidil 7: Ceol

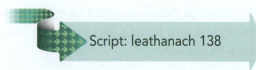

A. Píosa Cainte

Cloisfidh tú píosa cainte sa cheist seo. Cloisfidh tú an píosa cainte faoi dhó. Beidh sos ann leis na freagraí a scríobh tar éis na chéad éisteachta agus tar éis an dara héisteacht.

1. Cén pictiúr a théann leis an bpíosa cainte seo?

   ☐   ☐   ☐   ☐

2. Cén sórt ceoil is fearr le Garbhán?
   snagcheol ☐   punc-cheol ☐   rac-cheol ☐

3. Cé chomh minic is a chleachtann sé lena bhanna ceoil?
   gach Aoine ☐   gach Satharn ☐   gach Domhnach ☐

4. Cathain a thosaigh sé ag seinm ceoil?
   _____

B. Fógra

Cloisfidh tú fógra sa cheist seo. Cloisfidh tú an fógra faoi dhó. Beidh sos ann leis na freagraí a scríobh tar éis na chéad éisteachta agus tar éis an dara héisteacht.

1. Cén áit a mbeidh an cheolchoirm ar siúl?
   _____

2. Cé mhéad a bheidh ar na ticéid?
   €30 ☐   €40 ☐   €50 ☐

3. Cathain a bheidh na ticéid ar díol?
   _____

C. Píosa Nuachta

Cloisfidh tú píosa nuachta sa cheist seo. Cloisfidh tú an píosa nuachta faoi dhó. Beidh sos ann leis na freagraí a scríobh tar éis na chéad éisteachta agus tar éis an dara héisteacht.

1. Céard a bhí á ndíol ag an bhfear agus ag an mbean taobh amuigh den cheolchoirm?

| T-léinte ☐ | Deochanna ☐ | Ticéid bhréige ☐ | Grán rósta ☐ |

2. Cé mhéad a bhí an fear agus an bhean ag lorg ar gach ticéad bréige?

   €320 ☐   €310 ☐   €300 ☐   €290 ☐

D. Comhrá

Cloisfidh tú comhrá sa cheist seo. Cloisfidh tú an comhrá faoi dhó. Cloisfidh tú an comhrá ó thosach deireadh an chéad uair. Ansin cloisfidh tú ina dhá mhír é. Beidh sos ann leis na freagraí a scríobh tar éis gach míre díobh.

Mír 1

1. Conas atá Olivia ag mothú?

☐ ☐ ☐ ☐

2. Luaigh **dhá** rud faoin duine a bheidh ag seinm ag an gceolchoirm.

   _____

   _____

Mír 2

3. Cé a bheidh ag dul in éineacht léi?

   a deirfiúr mhór ☐   a deartháir mór ☐

   a deirfiúr óg ☐   a deartháir óg ☐

4. Cé a cheannaigh na ticéid di?

   _____

Turas 2: Mo Leabhar Gníomhaíochta

Caibidil 8: Spórt

Script: leathanach 139

A. Píosa Cainte

Cloisfidh tú píosa cainte sa cheist seo. Cloisfidh tú an píosa cainte faoi dhó. Beidh sos ann leis na freagraí a scríobh tar éis na chéad éisteachta agus tar éis an dara héisteacht.

1. Cén pictiúr a théann leis an bpíosa cainte seo?

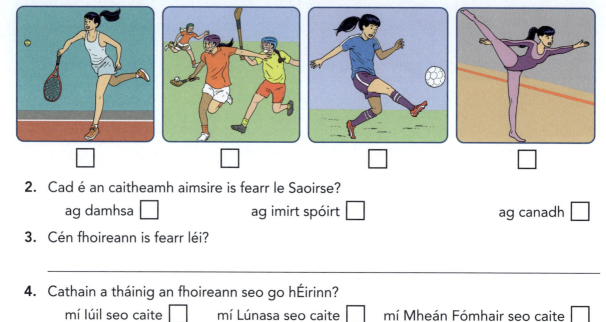

2. Cad é an caitheamh aimsire is fearr le Saoirse?

   ag damhsa ☐   ag imirt spóirt ☐   ag canadh ☐

3. Cén fhoireann is fearr léi?

   _____

4. Cathain a tháinig an fhoireann seo go hÉirinn?

   mí Iúil seo caite ☐   mí Lúnasa seo caite ☐   mí Mheán Fómhair seo caite ☐

B. Fógra

Cloisfidh tú fógra sa cheist seo. Cloisfidh tú an fógra faoi dhó. Beidh sos ann leis na freagraí a scríobh tar éis na chéad éisteachta agus tar éis an dara héisteacht.

1. Cén tír a mbeidh Éire ag imirt ina haghaidh?

2. Cé mhéad atá ar thicéid do dhaoine fásta agus do dhaoine óga?

   €80 agus €40 ☐   €70 agus €50 ☐

   €70 agus €40 ☐   €80 agus €50 ☐

C. Píosa Nuachta

Cloisfidh tú píosa nuachta sa cheist seo. Cloisfidh tú an píosa nuachta faoi dhó. Beidh sos ann leis na freagraí a scríobh tar éis na chéad éisteachta agus tar éis an dara héisteachta.

1. Cén fhoireann spóirt a bhuaigh cúig bhonn óir sna Cluichí Oilimpeacha?

    foireann rugbaí ☐   foireann dornálaíochta ☐   foireann sacair ☐

2. Cé air a raibh bród as na himreoirí?

    _____

3. Cá n-eagrófar searmanas speisialta don fhoireann?

    _____

D. Comhrá

Cloisfidh tú comhrá sa cheist seo. Cloisfidh tú an comhrá faoi dhó. Cloisfidh tú an comhrá ó thosach deireadh an chéad uair. Ansin cloisfidh tú ina dhá mhír é. Beidh sos ann leis na freagraí a scríobh tar éis gach míre díobh.

Mír 1

1. Cén cluiche a bhí á imirt ag Tomás?

   ☐   ☐   ☐   ☐

2. Luaigh **dhá** phointe eolais faoinar tharla sa chluiche, dar le Tomás.

    _____
    _____

Mír 2

3. Cén scór a bhí ann ag leath ama?

    0-09 – 0-09 ☐   1-08 – 1-08 ☐
    0-09 – 0-08 ☐   0-01 – 1-10 ☐

4. Cé mhéad cúl a fuair an fhoireann eile?

    _____

Caibidil 9: Laethanta Saoire

A. Píosa Cainte

Script: leathanach 140

Cloisfidh tú píosa cainte sa cheist seo. Cloisfidh tú an píosa cainte faoi dhó. Beidh sos ann leis na freagraí a scríobh tar éis na chéad éisteachta agus tar éis an dara héisteacht.

1. Cén pictiúr a théann leis an bpíosa cainte seo?

   ☐   ☐   ☐   ☐

2. Cá dtéann Breandán gach samhradh?
   an Ghréig ☐   an Spáinn ☐   an Iodáil ☐

3. Luaigh rud **amháin** faoin tír sin a thaitníonn leis.
   _____

4. Cathain a bheidh sé ag dul ar ais?
   mí Aibreáin ☐   mí na Bealtaine ☐   mí an Mheithimh ☐

B. Fógra

Cloisfidh tú fógra sa cheist seo. Cloisfidh tú an fógra faoi dhó. Beidh sos ann leis na freagraí a scríobh tar éis na chéad éisteachta agus tar éis an dara héisteacht.

1. Cén cineál saoire atá á fógairt?
   _____

2. Cén praghas atá ar phacáistí Turais Spóirt Uisce go dtí an Phortaingéil?
   €279 ☐   €289 ☐   €299 ☐

3. Cá bhfuil tuilleadh eolais ar fáil?
   _____

C. Píosa Nuachta

Cloisfidh tú píosa nuachta sa cheist seo. Cloisfidh tú an píosa nuachta faoi dhó. Beidh sos ann leis na freagraí a scríobh tar éis na chéad éisteachta agus tar éis an dara héisteacht.

1. Cé mhéad airgid a bhuaigh an teaghlach ar *Winning Streak*?

   €150,000 ☐   €200,000 ☐   €250,000 ☐   €300,000 ☐

2. Cén cineál saoire ar mhaith leo a thógáil?

   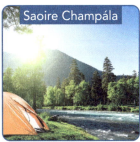

Saoire Ghréine ☐   Saoire Sciála ☐   Saoire Safari ☐   Saoire Champála ☐

D. Comhrá

Cloisfidh tú comhrá sa cheist seo. Cloisfidh tú an comhrá faoi dhó. Cloisfidh tú an comhrá ó thosach deireadh an chéad uair. Ansin cloisfidh tú ina dhá mhír é. Beidh sos ann leis na freagraí a scríobh tar éis gach míre díobh.

Mír 1

1. Cén fáth a bhfuil Eoin chomh dearg le tráta?

☐   ☐   ☐   ☐

2. Cathain a tháinig Eoin ar ais?

   _____

Mír 2

3. Cá bhfuair Eoin post?

   Ospidéal ☐   Siopa spóirt ☐   Siopa a Mham ☐   Óstán ☐

4. Cén post atá ag a Mham?

   _____

Caibidil 10: Tinneas agus Sláinte

Script: leathanach 141

A. Píosa Cainte

Cloisfidh tú píosa cainte sa cheist seo. Cloisfidh tú an píosa cainte faoi dhó. Beidh sos ann leis na freagraí a scríobh tar éis na chéad éisteachta agus tar éis an dara héisteacht.

1. Cén pictiúr a théann leis an bpíosa cainte seo?

☐ ☐ ☐ ☐

2. Cén sórt bricfeasta a thaitníonn le hAoibh?

    iógart agus mil ☐   gránóla agus bainne ☐   gránóla agus iógart ☐

3. Luaigh sneaic **amháin** atá ar fáil sa siopa caife.

    _____

4. Cad é seoladh gréasáin an tsiopa caife?

    www.caifeanbhaile.ie ☐   www.caifenacathrach.ie ☐   www.caifefaointuath.ie ☐

B. Fógra

Cloisfidh tú fógra sa cheist seo. Cloisfidh tú an fógra faoi dhó. Beidh sos ann leis na freagraí a scríobh tar éis na chéad éisteachta agus tar éis an dara héisteacht.

1. Cén pictiúr a théann leis an bhfógra seo?

☐ ☐ ☐ ☐

2. Cén uimhir do na Gardaí a thugtar leis an bhfógra?

    (043) 999 4488 ☐   (043) 999 5588 ☐
    (043) 999 6688 ☐   (043) 999 7788 ☐

C. Píosa Nuachta

Cloisfidh tú píosa nuachta sa cheist seo. Cloisfidh tú an píosa nuachta faoi dhó. Beidh sos ann leis na freagraí a scríobh tar éis na chéad éisteachta agus tar éis an dara héisteacht.

1. Céard a bhí dúnta i mBaile Átha Cliath?

   _____

2. Cad a dúirt na cigirí faoi na bialanna?

   go raibh na cistineacha salach agus go raibh an bia as dáta ☐

   go raibh an bia go hálainn ☐

   go raibh an tseirbhís uafásach ☐

3. I gceann cé mhéad seachtain a thiocfaidh na cigirí ar ais?

   _____

D. Comhrá

Cloisfidh tú comhrá sa cheist seo. Cloisfidh tú an comhrá faoi dhó. Cloisfidh tú an comhrá ó thosach deireadh an chéad uair. Ansin cloisfidh tú ina dhá mhír é. Beidh sos ann leis na freagraí a scríobh tar éis gach míre díobh.

Mír 1

1. Céard atá cearr le Jeaic?

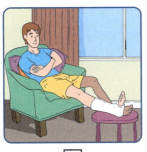   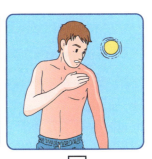

   ☐   ☐   ☐   ☐

2. Cad a mholann a Mham dó? Luaigh **dhá** rud.

   _____
   _____

Mír 2

3. Cá rachaidh siad tar éis an lae scoile?

   _____

4. Cad a ordaíonn a Mham dó a dhéanamh ag an deireadh?

   _____

Script Éisteachta: An Téacsleabhar

Tagraíonn uimhreacha na leathanach don téacsleabhar sa script éisteachta seo.

Caibidil 1: Mé Féin

 Leathanach 11

Aoiseanna

Jacob Tremblay
Rugadh an réalta scannán Jacob Tremblay in 2006. Is minic a ghlacann sé páirt sna scannáin is mó. Rinne sé guth Luca sa scannán *Luca* freisin.

Blue Ivy Carter
Is iníon leis na réaltaí móra Beyoncé agus JayZ í Blue Ivy Carter. Rugadh sa bhliain 2012 í. Bhuaigh sí gradam Grammy in 2021.

Celine Tam
Is as Hong Cong í Celine Tam. Thosaigh sí ag canadh nuair a bhí sí trí bliana d'aois. Ghlac sí páirt in *America's Got Talent* agus *Britain's Got Talent*. Rugadh in 2007 í.

JD McCrary
Rugadh JD McCrary in California in 2007. Tá cáil air mar aisteoir ar an teilifís agus i scannáin.

 Leathanach 18

Iarratas ar Phost

Haigh, is mise Barra de Barra, bainisteoir an stáisiúin teilifíse G24. An bhfuil suim agat sa cheol? An maith leat scannáin? Ar mhaith leat réaltaí ceoil agus réaltaí scannán a chur faoi agallamh do G24? Bhuel, seo an jab duit!

Tá G24 ag lorg duine óg, fuinniúil agus cairdiúil chun post mar chomhfhreagraí leantóirí a dhéanamh. Tá foirm iarratais ar fáil ar www.comortasG24.ie. Líon isteach an fhoirm iarratais agus cliceáil 'Seol'. Go n-éirí leat!

 Leathanach 18

Iarratas ar Phost

Haigh, is mise Franc. Táim ceithre bliana déag d'aois. Tá gruaig fhada dhonn orm. Tá súile glasa agam. Táim cabhrach agus spórtúil.

M'uimhir fóin ná (088) 031 4101 agus mo sheoladh ríomhphoist ná franc777@gaeilgemail.com.

 Leathanach 21

Cluastuiscint

Cainteoir
Haigh. Is mise Katie Nic Cába. Is as Baile Átha Cliath mé. Tá gruaig fhada dhonn orm. Tá súile gorma agam. Táim fuinniúil agus spórtúil.

Caibidil 2: Mo Theaghlach

 **Leathanach 34**

Cur Síos ar Mo Theaghlach

Éilis:	Haigh. Is mise Éilis. Tá cúigear i mo theaghlach: mo Mham, mo Dhaid, mo bheirt deirfiúracha agus mé féin.
Seán:	Haigh. Seán is ainm dom. Tá cúigear i mo theaghlach: mo Mham, mo dheartháir Liam, mo bheirt deirfiúracha Siobhán agus Caoimhe agus mé féin.
Tomás:	Bail ó Dhia oraibh. Tomás is ainm dom. Tá seisear i mo theaghlach: mo thuismitheoirí agus mo thriúr deartháireacha.

 **Leathanach 34**

Comhrá

Mír 1

Dan:	Haigh, a Eva. Deas a bheith amuigh sa chlós.
Eva:	Cinnte, a Dan. Deas go bhfuil an lá scoile thart. An bhfuil tú ag dul abhaile?
Dan:	Tá. Céard fútsa?
Eva:	Níl. Caithfidh mé bualadh le mo dheartháir anois.

Mír 2

Dan:	Ó, cén fáth?
Eva:	Táimid ag dul go teach m'uncail. A bhreithlá atá ann.
Dan:	Cén aois é?
Eva:	Caoga bliain d'aois inniu.
Dan:	M'anam, tá sé sin an-sean ar fad!

 **Leathanach 47**

Cluastuiscint

Fógra

Tá teaghlach aclaí do sheó spóirt á lorg ag G24. Tá tuilleadh eolais ar fáil ar an suíomh gréasáin www.g24.ie.

 **Leathanach 47**

Píosa Nuachta

Bhuaigh teaghlach Uí Laoi as Ros Comáin Gradam Cheoil inné. Roinneann siad físeáin cheoil ar a gcainéal YouTube gach lá. Bhuaigh siad €1,000 freisin.

Turas 2: Mo Leabhar Gníomhaíochta

Caibidil 3: Mo Theach

 Leathanach 55

An Áit a Bhfuil Cónaí Orm

Aodhán: A Ghráinne, arbh fhearr leat a bheith i do chónaí faoin tuath nó i lár na cathrach?

Gráinne: Hm, a Aodháin, sin ceist dheacair. Le bheith macánta, ba bhreá liom bogadh amach faoin tuath. Bheadh sé an-chiúin. Céard fútsa?

Aodhán: Ó, b'fhuath liom a bheith i mo chónaí faoin tuath. Bheadh sé an-leadránach.

Gráinne: Hm, nílim cinnte. Tá buntáistí agus míbhuntáistí leis an gcathair. Bheinn buartha sa chathair faoi na carranna go léir agus faoin torann agus faoin mbruscar.

Aodhán: Á, b'fhearr liom a bheith i mó chónaí i lár na cathrach. Bheadh go leor le déanamh ann – spórt, ceol, cairde, go leor stuif.

 Leathanach 71

Fógra

Dia daoibh. Seo Cathaoirleach an Bhoird Contae, Síle Nic Stiofáin, ag caint. Beidh raifil mhór ar siúl ag deireadh na míosa, díreach in am don Nollaig. Teach atá le buachan. Tá trí sheomra sa teach agus tá sé suite in eastát tithíochta ciúin gar do lár an bhaile mhóir. Ar mhaith leat ticéad a cheannach? Téigh chuig www.teachlebuachan.com chun tuilleadh eolais a fháil.

 Leathanach 71

Píosa Nuachta

Bhuaigh Órlaith Nic Stiofáin teach nua i raifil mhór de chuid an chlub spóirt áitiúil. Teach leathscoite atá ann agus tá ceithre sheomra codlata ann. Chomh maith leis sin, tá gairdín mór ar chúl an tí agus garáiste ina aice leis. Dúirt Órlaith go bhfuil áthas an domhain uirthi agus go bhfuil sí ag súil le bogadh isteach go luath.

 Leathanach 87

Cluastuiscint

Comhrá

Mír 1

Seosaimhín: Hi, a Sheoirse, conas atá an teach nua?

Seoirse: Hi, a Sheosaimhín, ó tá sé go hiontach. Is aoibhinn liom é. Agus an bhfuil a fhios agat cad é an rud is fearr faoi?

Seosaimhín: Céard?

Seoirse: Tá an scoil ar leac an dorais againn. Seasca soicind ar shiúl uainn.

Mír 2

Seosaimhín: Hmm, níor mhaith liom é sin. Níor mhaith liom a bheith chomh gar sin don scoil!

Seoirse: Ó, níl. Tá sé foirfe. Críochnaíonn an scoil ag a trí agus táim sa bhaile ag ligean mo scíthe ag nóiméad amháin tar éis a trí. Ní chaithfidh mé aon bhus ná aon turas sa charr a dhéanamh. Tá sé foirfe!

Caibidil 4: Mo Cheantar

 Leathanach 107

Comharsana Callánacha

Mír 1

Marta: Haigh, a Dhonnacha, cad é mar atá tú?

Donncha: Ó, tuirseach, a Mharta. Tá tuirse an domhain orm.

Marta: Cén fáth?

Donncha: Bhí na comharsana an-challánach aréir. Ní dhearna mé néal codlata!

Mír 2

Marta: Cad a bhí ar siúl acu?

Donncha: Bhuel, creid é nó ná creid, chuala mé na leanaí ag caoineadh agus ag béicíl. Bhí na madraí ag tafann freisin. Agus bhí an teilifís an-ard. Agus creid é nó ná creid, thosaigh duine éigin ag folúsghlanadh ag meán oíche!

Marta: Ó, tá sin uafásach!

Donncha: Tá a fhios agam, tá a fhios agam.

 Leathanach 129

Cluastuiscint

Cainteoir

Haigh. Is mise Seán Maitiú Ó Cearúill. Táim i mo chónaí i gCeanannas Mór i gContae na Mí. Is aoibhinn liom anseo é mar tá go leor le déanamh. Tá líon mór áiseanna anseo. Mar shampla, tá linn snámha, bialanna agus páirceanna deasa anseo. Gach Satharn, téim ag snámh sa linn snámha.

Caibidil 5: Mo Scoil

🎧 **Leathanach 151**

Éide Scoile

Comhrá a hAon

Mír 1

Sarah:	Dia dhuit.
Siopadóir:	Dia is Muire dhuit. An féidir liom cabhrú leat?
Sarah:	Is féidir. Cé mhéad a chosnaíonn an geansaí dubh?
Siopadóir:	€20.
Sarah:	Ceart go leor. Tógfaidh mé an geansaí dubh. Agus cé mhéad a chosnaíonn an bléasar dubh?
Siopadóir:	€30.
Sarah:	Hmm. Ceart go leor. Tógfaidh mé an bléasar dubh chomh maith.

Mír 2

Siopadóir:	Ar mhaith leat aon rud eile?
Sarah:	Níor mhaith. Cé mhéad a chosnaíonn sin san iomlán?
Siopadóir:	€50, más é do thoil é.
Sarah:	Seo dhuit.
Siopadóir:	Go raibh maith agat.
Sarah:	Go raibh maith agat. Slán.
Siopadóir:	Slán leat.

🎧 **Leathanach 151**

Comhrá a Dó

Mír 1

Damien:	Maidin mhaith. Cad é mar atá tú?
Siopadóir:	Tá mé go breá, go raibh maith agat. An féidir liom cabhrú leat?
Damien:	Is féidir. Táim ag lorg cúpla rud. Léine bhán, geansaí dúghorm, bríste liath agus bróga dubha.
Siopadóir:	Bhuel, tá tú sa siopa ceart. Seo an léine bhán. Cosnaíonn an léine seo €5.50.
Damien:	Go maith. Tógfaidh mé an léine bhán, mar sin.

Mír 2

Siopadóir:	Agus seo an geansaí dúghorm. Cosnaíonn an geansaí dúghorm €20.
Damien:	Tógfaidh mé an geansaí dúghorm freisin.
Siopadóir:	Agus seo an bríste liath. Tá €15 ar an mbríste liath.
Damien:	Tógfaidh mé an bríste freisin.
Siopadóir:	Agus ar deireadh, seo na bróga. Tá €20 ar an bpéire bróg seo agus tá €30 ar an bpéire bróg sin.
Damien:	Hmm. Tógfaidh mé na bróga ar €30, más é do thoil é. Cé mhéad a chosnaíonn gach rud san iomlán?
Siopadóir:	Ceart go leor. Mar sin, €5.50 ar an léine, €20 ar an ngeansaí, €15 ar an mbríste, €30 ar na bróga. Sin … €70.50.
Damien:	Seo dhuit.
Siopadóir:	Go raibh maith agat.
Damien:	Go raibh míle maith agat. Slán.
Siopadóir:	Slán leat.

 Leathanach 161

Cluastuiscint

Comhrá

Mír 1

Príomhoide:	A Sheáin! Cén dath é sin i do chuid gruaige?
Seán:	Á, corcra.
Príomhoide:	Nach bhfuil a fhios agat go bhfuil sin go hiomlán in aghaidh na rialacha?
Seán:	Tá. Tá brón orm.
Príomhoide:	Agus, agus, céard iad sin i do chluas?
Seán:	Á, fáinní cluaise.
Príomhoide:	Fáinní cluaise. Ní chreidim é. A haon, a dó, a trí, a ceathair, a cúig! Cúig cinn! Tá sé sin go hiomlán in aghaidh na rialacha freisin.
Seán:	Tá. Tá brón orm.

Mír 2

Príomhoide:	Sin tús uafásach leis an mbliain, a Sheáin. Beidh orm smaoineamh ar phionós oiriúnach.
Seán:	Dul abhaile, b'fhéidir?
Príomhoide:	Ha! Ní dóigh liom é, a Sheáin. Ní bheidh tú ag dul abhaile go ceann tamaill. Idir an dá linn, téigh go dtí m'oifig agus fan liom ansin.
Seán:	Ceart go leor. Brón orm.
Príomhoide:	Beidh tú brónach!

Caibidil 6: Mo Chaithimh Aimsire

 Leathanach 175

Fógra

Dia daoibh, a dhaoine uaisle. Fáilte romhaibh chuig Pictiúrlann Retro. Is mise Julia Nic Roibeaird, bainisteoir na pictiúrlainne.

Faraor, tá fadhb leis an trealamh agus beidh moill ar na scannáin seo a leanas:

- Tosóidh an scannán uafáis *Dracula* ar a deich a chlog, ní a hocht a chlog.
- Tosóidh an scannán fantaisíochta *Avatar* ar a hocht a chlog, seachas a seacht a chlog.
- Faraor, ní bheidh an scannán beochana *Snow White* ar siúl anocht. Beidh aisíocaíochtaí ar fáil ag an deasc ticéad.

Gabhaigí ár leithscéal as aon mhíchaoithiúlacht. Go raibh maith agaibh.

 Leathanach 175

Píosa Nuachta

Tá sé fógartha go mbeidh premiere an scannáin nua le Tomás Ó Súilleabháin ar siúl ag Féile Scannán na Gaillimhe ar an 1ú Meán Fómhair ag 8.00. *Arracht Eile* an t-ainm atá ar an scannán agus beidh sé ar siúl i bPictiúrlann Retro.

Beidh ticéid ar díol ar líne ón 12ú de mhí Iúil. €30 an praghas a bheidh ar thicéid don seó agus don dinnéar ceiliúrtha ina dhiaidh.

Tá tuilleadh eolais le fáil ar ár suíomh gréasáin www.scunscannan.ie.

 Leathanach 189

Cluastuiscint

Comhrá

Mír 1

Anne:	A Anraí, conas atá tú? Ar mhaith leat dul go dtí an phictiúrlann?
Anraí:	Ó, ba bhreá liom dul ann. Cén phictiúrlann?
Anne:	Tá Pictiúrlann Retro go deas. Bhí mé ann cúpla mí ó shin.
Anraí:	Ó, is aoibhinn liom an phictiúrlann sin.
Anne:	Go hiontach! Céard faoi scannán grá nó scannán grinn?
Anraí:	Ó ní féidir. Nach bhfuil a fhios agat, go bhfuil *Origin of Evil* ar taispeáint ann!

Mír 2

Anne:	*Origin of Evil*? Cén sórt scannáin é sin?
Anraí:	Scannán uafáis, ar ndóigh!
Anne:	Scannán uafáis? Hmm. Níl a fhios agam.
Anraí:	Ó, ba bhreá liom an scannán seo a fheiceáil.
Anne:	Bhuel, níor mhaith liomsa é a fheiceáil.
Anraí:	Goitse, beidh sé go breá. Beidh sé ar siúl ag meán oíche.
Anne:	Meán oíche? *Origin of Evil*? Ag magadh atá tú!
Anraí:	Ag magadh? Mise? Nílim. Beidh tú ceart go leor. Buailfidh mé leat ag leathuair tar éis a haon déag ar Shráid Scanraidh. Slán!

Caibidil 7: Ceol

 **Leathanach 196**

An Ceol Gaelach

Éist leis na huirlisí Gaelacha seo.

Seo an chláirseach; seo an bodhrán; seo an fheadóg mhór; seo an consairtín; seo an phíb uilleann; seo an fhidil; seo an bainseó; seo an bosca ceoil; seo an giotár; seo an fheadóg stáin.

Anois, tomhais céard iad na huirlisí ceoil atá á seinm ag Pilib, Bríd, Seoirse agus Lenka.

Pilib: [fidil]; Bríd: [bodhrán]; Seoirse: [cláirseach]; Lenka: [feadóg stáin]

 **Leathanach 199**

An Cheolfhoireann

Conchúr: Haigh, is mise Conchúr. Seinnim an chláirseach. Is aoibhinn liom í. Táim á seinm le trí bliana anuas.

Adrienne: Adrienne is ainm dom. Seinnim an t-olldord. Cé go bhfuil sé an-trom, is breá liom é. Thosaigh mé á sheinm ceithre bliana ó shin.

Esther: Esther an t-ainm atá orm. Seinnim an trombón. Is aoibhinn liom a fhuaim. Thosaigh mé á sheinm nuair a bhí mé seacht mbliana d'aois – sin ocht mbliana ó shin anois!

Fabio: Bail ó Dhia oraibh. Is mise Fabio. Seinnim an corn Francach. Tá sé thar a bheith deacair é a sheinm go maith. Thosaigh mé á fhoghlaim trí mhí ó shin.

 **Leathanach 199**

An Cheolfhoireann

Na gaothuirlisí

Éist leis na gaothuirlisí seo.

Seo an t-óbó; seo an basún; seo an clairinéad; seo an fhliúit.

Anois, tomhais cén uirlis cheoil atá á seinm ag Colm.

Colm: [basún]

 **Leathanach 199**

Na téaduirlisí

Éist leis na téaduirlisí seo.

Seo an chláirseach; seo an veidhlín; seo an t-olldord; seo an dordveidhil.

Anois, tomhais cén uirlis cheoil atá á seinm ag Úna.

Úna: [veidhlín]

Turas 2: Mo Leabhar Gníomhaíochta

 Leathanach 199

Na prásuirlisí

Éist leis na prásuirlisí seo.

Seo an trumpa; seo an trombón; seo an tiúba; seo an corn Francach.

Anois, tomhais cén uirlis cheoil atá á seinm ag Josh.

Josh: [trombón]

 Leathanach 199

Na cnaguirlisí

Éist leis na cnaguirlisí seo.

Seo an pianó; seo an xileafón; seo na ciombail; seo na drumaí.

Anois, tomhais cén uirlis cheoil atá á seinm ag Zainab.

Zainab: [ciombail]

 Leathanach 217

Cluastuiscint

Fógra

A chairde Gael, Póilín Ní Chóilín anseo, bainisteoir na carthanachta Croí an Cheoil. Beidh ceolchoirm mhór ar son na carthanachta ar siúl i bPáirc Thuamhan ar an 20ú lá de mhí Lúnasa. Tá ticéid agus tuilleadh eolais ar fáil ar an suíomh gréasáin, www.croi.ie. Go raibh míle maith agaibh.

 Leathanach 217

Píosa Nuachta

Bhuaigh Liam Ó Gallchóir an chéad duais san amhránaíocht i bhFeis Cheoil Mhaigh Eo inné. Bhuaigh sé corn agus seic €300.

Caibidil 8: Spórt

 Leathanach 230

Áiseanna Spóirt

Club na Páirce

Seo fógra ó Chlub na Páirce. Beidh na cúirteanna leadóige ar oscailt óna deich a chlog ar maidin go dtí a deich a chlog san oíche. Más maith leat cúirt leadóige a chur in áirithe, téigh chuig www.clubnapairce.ie.

 Leathanach 230

Cispheil BI

Seo fógra ó Chispheil BI. Ní bheidh na cúirteanna cispheile ar oscailt ar maidin an tseachtain seo. Beidh siad ar oscailt, áfach, gach tráthnóna idir a trí a chlog agus a deich a chlog. Más mian leat cúirt chispheile a chur in áirithe, téigh chuig www.cispheilbi.ie.

 **Leathanach 230**

Ballaí Inse Cóir

Seo fógra ó Bhallaí Inse Chór. Beidh na ballaí dreapadóireachta in Inse Cóir ar oscailt óna deich a chlog ar maidin go dtí a hocht a chlog tráthnóna. Más mian leat áit a chur in áirithe, téigh chuig www.agdreapadh.ie.

 **Leathanach 241**

Cluastuiscint

Cainteoir

Haigh. Is mise Chloe Ní Laoi. Is as Cill Dara mé. Is aoibhinn liom spórt. Imrím haca agus sacar. Táim ard agus tapa. Is é Séamus Coleman an phearsa spóirt is fearr liom.

Caibidil 9: Laethanta Saoire

 **Leathanach 257**

Tíreolaíocht na hÉireann

Cúige Laighean: Baile Átha Cliath; Lú; An Mhí; An Iarmhí; An Longfort; Uíbh Fhailí; Laois; Cill Chainnigh; Ceatharlach; Loch Garman; Cill Mhantáin; Cill Dara

Cúige Uladh: Fear Manach; Aontroim; Tír Eoghain; Doire; Ard Mhacha; An Dún; Dún na nGall; Muineachán; An Cabhán

Cúige Chonnacht: Gaillimh; Maigh Eo; Liatroim; Sligeach; Ros Comáin

Cúige Mumhan: Corcaigh; Ciarraí; An Clár; Luimneach; Port Láirge; Tiobraid Árann

 **Leathanach 258**

Saoirí in Éirinn

Cruach Phádraig, Co. Mhaigh Eo – a haon; Clochán an Aifir, Co. Aontroma – a trí;
Brú na Bóinne, Co. na Mí – a ceathair; Cloch na Blarnan, Co. Chorcaí – a seacht;
Mórchuaird Chiarraí, Co. Chiarraí – a hocht; Teach Solais Fhánada, Co. Dhún na nGall – a dó;
Gleann Dá Loch, Co. Chill Mhantáin – a sé;
Coláiste na Tríonóide, Co. Bhaile Átha Cliath – a cúig;
Dún Aonghasa, Inis Mór, Co. na Gaillimhe – a deich;
Aillte an Mhothair, Co. an Chláir – a naoi

 **Leathanach 259**

Cainteoirí

Keith

Haigh, is mise Keith. Chuaigh mé go Clochán an Aifir an samhradh seo caite. Bhí sé go hálainn. Thaitin sé go mór liom. Faraor, ní raibh mé riamh i nDún Aonghusa. Ba bhreá liom dul ann.

Leathanach 259

Nuala

Haigh, is mise Nuala. Chuaigh mé go Cloch na Blarnan an samhradh seo caite. Ar ndóigh, phóg mé an Chloch. Faraor, ní raibh mé riamh i gColáiste na Tríonóide. Ba bhreá liom dul ann lá éigin.

Leathanach 283

Cluastuiscint

Cainteoir

Haigh, is mise Cormac Mac Giolla Chearra. Is as Dún na nGall mé. Is aoibhinn liom saoirí sa bhaile. Chuaigh mé go Contae an Chláir an samhradh seo caite. Bhí sé go hálainn. Beagnach chomh hálainn le mo chontae féin, Dún na nGall.

An áit is fearr sa Chlár, gan aon dabht, ná Aillte an Mhothair. Tá radharc álainn ó na haillte sin – an fharraige, na hOileáin Árann, na báid mhóra i bhfad i gcéin agus na deilfeanna ag léim amach as an uisce agus ag tumadh isteach arís. Tá siad beagnach chomh hard agus chomh deas leis na haillte i nDún na nGall.

Is aoibhinn leo an ceol sa Chlár freisin. Tá an ceol traidisiúnta le cloisteáil fud fad an chontae.

Molaim daoibh dul chuig an gClár am éigin. Ní bheidh aiféala oraibh!

Caibidil 10: Tinneas agus Sláinte

Leathanach 303

Comhrá i mBialann

Mír 1

Freastalaí:	Dia daoibh. Fáilte romhaibh chuig Joey's. Seo an biachlár.
Selena:	Go raibh maith agat.
Chris:	Go raibh maith agat.
Selena:	Mmm. Tá sé seo go deas, nach bhfuil?
Freastalaí:	An bhfuil sibh réidh? Cad a bheidh agaibh?
Chris:	Tá mise réidh. Cad fútsa, a Selena?
Selena:	Táimse réidh. Ba mhaith liom sicín agus sceallóga, le do thoil.
Chris:	Agus ba mhaith liom burgar agus sceallóga, le do thoil.
Freastalaí:	Go breá. Agus le hól?
Selena:	Sú oráiste, le do thoil.
Chris:	Buidéal uisce, le do thoil.
Freastalaí:	Fadhb ar bith. Go raibh maith agaibh.

Mír 2

Freastalaí:	Bhuel, an raibh an béile go deas?
Hailey:	Go hálainn, go raibh maith agat.
Justin:	Sárbhlasta. An féidir linn an bille a fháil, le do thoil?
Freastalaí:	Cinnte … Seo dhaoibh. Ocht euro is fiche.
Hailey:	Seo dhuit. Go raibh míle maith agat. Slán!
Justin:	Go raibh míle maith agat. Slán!

 Leathanach 307

Cluastuiscint

Comhrá

Mír 1

Múinteoir:	A Bhairbre, cad é a tharla duit?
Bairbre:	Ó, bhris mé mo ghualainn i gcluiche camógaíochta.
Múinteoir:	Ó, is dóigh go bhfuil sé pianmhar.
Bairbre:	Bhí ag an am, cinnte. Fuair mé buille de chamáin agus leagadh chun talaimh mé.
Múinteoir:	Ó, ní chreidim é sin.

Mír 2

Bairbre:	'Sea, fuair an t-imreoir eile cárta buí ach níor leor sin.
Múinteoir:	Ba cheart cárta dearg a bheith tugtha di. Agus conas atá an ghualainn anois?
Bairbre:	Tá sí ag éirí níos fearr, buíochas le Dia.
Múinteoir:	Cathain a bheidh tú ábalta spórt a imirt arís?
Bairbre:	I mí Lúnasa, ceapaim.
Múinteoir:	Bhuel, nára fada go mbeidh tú ar ais ar do sheanléim!

Caibidil 11: Éire agus Thar Lear

 Leathanach 315

Scéal na hAimsire

Píosa a haon

Fáilte romhaibh chuig scéal na haimsire. Lá fuar fliuch a bheidh ann inniu. Beidh sé ag cur báistí ar fud na tíre. Beidh an teocht is airde idir naoi gcéim agus deich gcéim Celsius.

 Leathanach 315

Píosa a dó

Fáilte romhaibh chuig réamhaisnéis na haimsire. Lá breá brothallach a bheidh ann inniu. Beidh sé te agus grianmhar ar fud na tíre. Beidh an teocht is airde idir seacht gcéim déag agus naoi gcéim déag Celsius.

Script Éisteachta: Mo Leabhar Gníomhaíochta

Tagraíonn uimhreacha na leathanach don leabhar gníomhaíochta sa script éisteachta seo.

Caibidil 1: Mé Féin

 Leathanach 100

A. Píosa Cainte

Haigh. Is mise Máirtín Mac an tSaoi. Is as Baile Átha Cliath mé. Táim ceithre bliana déag d'aois. Tá gruaig ghearr rua orm agus tá súile gorma agam. Táim spórtúil agus cliste.

 Leathanach 100

B. Fógra

Tá an cainéal teilifíse G24 ag lorg aisteoirí óga chun páirt a ghlacadh sa chlár teilifíse *Vikings*. Caithfidh gruaig fhada a bheith ar gach aisteoir óg. Caithfidh gach aisteoir óg a bheith fuinniúil. Tá tuilleadh eolais ar fáil ar www.aisteoirivikings.ie.

 Leathanach 101

C. Píosa Nuachta

Beidh an réalta faisin, Tanya Burr, ag teacht go hÉirinn ar 5 Bealtaine. Beidh sí ag síniú cóipeanna dá leabhar nua in ionaid siopadóireachta ar fud na hÉireann. Tá tuilleadh eolais ar fáil ar www.turastanya.ie.

 Leathanach 101

D. Comhrá

Mír 1

Emma: Haigh, a Liam. An bhfaca tú an scannán nua le Saoirse Ronan?

Liam: Saoirse Ronan? Cé hí sin?

Emma: Cé hí Saoirse Ronan? An bhfuil tú ag magadh? Is réalta scannáin í as Éirinn!

Liam: Áá, is cuimhin liom anois. Tá gruaig dhubh uirthi, nach bhfuil? Agus súile donna aici?

Mír 2

Emma: Níl! Tá gruaig fhada fhionn uirthi agus tá súile gorma aici.

Liam: Hmm, tá brón orm, is léir nach bhfuil mé suas chun dáta le réaltaí scannáin.

Emma: Ní haon bhréag é sin!

Caibidil 2: Mo Theaghlach

 Leathanach 102

A. Píosa Cainte

Haigh, is mise Labhaoise Ní Éilí. Rugadh mé ar 8 Samhain. Tá seisear i mo theaghlach. Is iad sin mo Mham, mo Dhaid, mo bheirt deartháireacha agus mo dheirfiúr. Is mise an páiste is sine. Is é mo dhearthár David an páiste is óige. Réitímid go han-mhaith le chéile.

 Leathanach 102

B. Fógra

Tá an cainéal teilifíse G24 ag lorg teaghlach chun páirt a ghlacadh sa chlár cócaireachta *An Bhialann*. Beidh ar na teaghlaigh dinnéar speisialta a ithe i mbialann i nGaillimh. Beidh duine cáiliúil ag cócaráil agus beidh ar na custaiméirí marcanna a bhronnadh ar an dinnéar.

 Leathanach 103

C. Píosa Nuachta

Bhuaigh clann Uí Ríordáin an chéad duais i gComórtas Ceoil na hÉireann. Bhuaigh siad seic €3,000 agus corn mór. Dúirt Deirdre Uí Ríordáin, máthair an teaghlaigh, go raibh áthas an domhain orthu. Dúirt a mac agus a hiníon, Dónall agus Rita, gur mhaith leo dul go Disneyland.

 Leathanach 103

D. Comhrá

Mír 1

Áine:	Haigh, a Dhaithí. Ar chuala tú faoi mo phost nua?
Daithí:	Níor chuala! Cén post é seo?
Áine:	Fuair mé post mar chomhfhreagraí leantóirí le G24!
Daithí:	Comhfhreagraí leantóirí? Cad é sin?
Áine:	Beidh mé ag bualadh le agus ag caint le réaltaí teilifíse, réaltaí scannán, réaltaí ceoil – gach sórt réalta!

Mír 2

Daithí:	Sin iontach! Cathain a thosóidh tú?
Áine:	Tosóidh mé ar an 10 Meitheamh.
Daithí:	Cén sórt uaireanta a bheidh á ndéanamh agat?
Áine:	Dé Máirt go Dé Sathairn, óna cúig an chloig tráthnóna go dtí a deich an chloig tráthnóna.
Daithí:	Bhuel, maith thú féin!

Caibidil 3: Mo Theach

 Leathanach 104

A. Píosa Cainte

Is mise Colm Mac Ruairí. Tá cónaí orm i dteach feirme faoin tuath. Tá naoi seomra sa teach. Thuas staighre, tá trí sheomra leapa, seomra folctha agus oifig. Thíos staighre, tá seomra suí, seomra bia, cistin agus seomra folctha eile. Is é an seomra suí an seomra is fearr liom mar tá sé mór agus compordach.

 Leathanach 104

B. Fógra

Cuirfear 20 teach ar díol amárach in eastát tithíochta i gCaisleán an Bharraigh, Co. Mhaigh Eo. Beidh praghas €300,000 ar gach teach. Tá ocht seomra i ngach teach. Thuas staighre tá trí sheomra leapa agus seomra folctha. Thíos staighre, tá seomra suí, seomra bia, cistin agus seomra folctha eile. Tá gairdín mór ar chúl an tí freisin. Tá tuilleadh eolais ar fáil ag www.ficheteach.ie.

 Leathanach 105

C. Píosa Nuachta

Bhris triúr buirgléirí isteach i gCaisleán Bhaile Átha Cliath. Goideadh deich bpictiúr. Bhí na buirgléirí ag caitheamh éadaí dubha agus balaclávaí. D'éalaigh siad i veain dubh. Má chonaic tú nó má chuala tú aon rud, cuir glaoch ar na Gardaí ag (01) 666 7584.

 Leathanach 105

D. Comhrá

Mír 1

Damien:	Heileo?
Córa:	Haigh, a Damien? Conas atá cúrsaí?
Damien:	A Chóra, haigh. Deas cloisteáil uait. Tá gach rud thar barr. Táim ar saoire sa Spáinn!
Córa:	Sa Spáinn? Go haoibhinn. Cá bhfuil tú ag fanacht?
Damien:	Teach saoire díreach cois trá. Tá sé go hálainn. Tá balcóin mhór ann agus tá radharc álainn amach ar an bhfarraige.

Mír 2

Córa:	Á, táim in éad leat. Cathain a bheidh tú ar ais?
Damien:	Dé Domhnaigh. Feicfidh mé ar scoil Dé Luain thú.
Córa:	Iontach. Bain sult as an gcuid eile den tsaoire. Agus tabhair ar ais rud éigin deas, le do thoil!
Damien:	Tá milseáin áitiúla acu anseo - tá siad an-bhlasta. Déanfaidh mé iarracht iad a fháil! Slán!

Caibidil 4: Mo Cheantar

 Leathanach 106

A. Píosa Cainte

Dia daoibh, is mise Iva Smith. Tá cónaí orm i Leitir Ceanainn i gContae Dhún na nGall. Is aoibhinn liom an ceantar seo. Tá go leor áiseanna sa cheantar seo. Tá páirceanna imeartha, pictiúrlann, club óige agus go leor leor siopaí anseo. Téim go dtí an club óige go minic. Is aoibhinn liom é. Taitníonn an margadh feirmeoirí liom freisin. Bíonn go leor bia folláin ar díol ann.

 Leathanach 106

B. Fógra

Osclófar ionad siopadóireachta nua i dTulach Mhór Dé Sathairn seo chugainn. Beidh 20 siopa ann. Ina measc beidh dhá ollmhargadh, trí shiopa bróg, dhá shiopa spóirt, go leor siopaí éadaí agus siopa seodra. Eagrófar raifil mhór freisin agus beidh €1,000 le buachan! Scaip an scéal!

 Leathanach 107

C. Píosa Nuachta

Beidh Éire ag imirt in aghaidh na Seapáine sa rugbaí amárach. Beidh an cluiche ar siúl in Shizuoka. Is cathair mhór é Shizuoka. Tá 3.75 milliún duine ina gcónaí ann. Tá Mount Fuji, an sliabh is airde sa tSeapáin, gar don chathair. Tá go leor tránna agus áiteanna áille eile sa cheantar freisin.

 Leathanach 107

D. Comhrá

Mír 1

Caoimhín: A Amy, cad é mar atá tú?

Amy: Ó, tá tuirse an domhain orm! Bhí na comharsana callánacha agamsa ag seinm ceoil go hard aréir. Bhí siad ag béicíl agus ag canadh agus ag damhsa. Ní bhfuair mé néal codlata!

Mír 2

Caoimhín: Ó, mo thrua thú. Cén t-am a stop siad an ceol?

Amy: Meán oíche. Tháinig na Gardaí ansin agus chuir siad stop leis an gceol.

Caoimhín: Bhuel, is rud maith é sin.

Amy: Is rud maith é an codladh fosta.

Caoimhín: Aontaím leat! Gheobhaidh tú néal codlata tar éis am lóin – leathlá atá againn, buíochas le Dia!

Amy: Rinne mé dearmad! 'Sea, beidh mé sa bhaile ag a dó mar sin. Táim ag súil leis sin.

Caibidil 5: Mo Scoil

 Leathanach 108

A. Píosa Cainte

Dia dhaoibh, a chairde. Déaglán de Búrca is ainm dom. Is as Cill Dara mé. Tá mé ag freastal ar Phobalscoil Chill Dara. Táim sa tríú bliain anois. Is scoil mhór í mo scoil. Tá 1,000 dalta ag freastal uirthi. Is í Adhmadóireacht an t-ábhar is fearr liom agus is é an seomra adhmadóireachta an seomra is fearr liom. Ní maith liom Mata ar chor ar bith.

 Leathanach 108

B. Fógra

A mhúinteoirí agus a scoláirí, tá fógra amháin agam daoibh ar maidin. Ba mhaith liom comhghairdeas a dhéanamh le foireann díospóireachta na tríú bliana. Bhuaigh an fhoireann Comórtas Díospóireachta na hÉireann. An rún a bhí ann ná 'Faigheann scoláirí an iomarca obair bhaile.' Go raibh míle maith agaibh.

 Leathanach 109

C. Píosa Nuachta

Tá meánscoil nua á tógáil i gContae na Mí faoi láthair. Coláiste an Rátha an t-ainm a bheidh uirthi. Beidh go leor áiseanna iontacha sa scoil nua. Mar shampla, beidh trí shaotharlann eolaíochta, trí pháirc imeartha agus trí sheomra ríomhaireachta ann. Osclóidh an scoil i mí Lúnasa.

 Leathanach 109

D. Comhrá

Mír 1

Múinteoir:	A Chaitríona, an ndéanfaidh tú gar dom, le do thoil?
Caitríona:	Cinnte. Cad é?
Múinteoir:	Tá mo leabhar tíreolaíochta ar an deasc sa leabharlann.

Mír 2

Múinteoir:	An féidir leat é a thabhairt go dtí an seomra foirne, le do thoil?
Caitríona:	Is féidir. Déanfaidh mé anois é.
Múinteoir:	Go raibh míle maith agat. Is féidir leat an leabhar a fhágáil leis an Uasal Ó Murchú. Tá sé ag fanacht ag an doras.

Caibidil 6: Mo Chaithimh Aimsire

 Leathanach 110

A. Píosa Cainte

Dia dhaoibh. Is mise Nuala Nic Pháidín. Tá go leor caitheamh aimsire agam. Is breá liom a bheith ag imirt cluichí ríomhaire agus ag seinm ceoil. Thar aon rud eile, áfach, is aoibhinn liom dul go dtí an phictiúrlann. Téim go dtí an phictiúrlann gach deireadh seachtaine. Taitníonn scannáin ghrinn agus scannáin ghrá go mór liom. Is é Dylan O'Brien an t-aisteoir is fearr liom.

 Leathanach 110

B. Fógra

Fógraíodh inniu gur ainmníodh Evanna Lynch agus Barry Keoghan i gcomhair Oscar. Beidh searmanas bronnta na nOscar ar siúl ar an Domhnach deireanach de mhí Feabhra.

 Leathanach 111

C. Píosa Nuachta

Bhuaigh Caireann Ní Chléirigh, cailín ceithre bliana déag d'aois, duais €3,000 as cluiche ríomhaire nua a dhearadh do chonsóil chluichí. Cluiche rásaíocht chairr atá ann. Dhear sí an cluiche ar a ríomhaire glúine.

 Leathanach 111

D. Comhrá

Mír 1

Ciara: Haigh, a Aoidh! Conas atá tú?

Aodh: Táim go breá, a Chiara, go raibh maith agat. Cogar, ar mhaith leat dul go dtí an phictiúrlann tráthnóna Dé hAoine?

Ciara: An phictiúrlann? Cén scannán?

Aodh: Bhuel, bhí mé ag smaoineamh ar scannán aicsin nó scéinséir. *Star Wars*, b'fhéidir?

Mír 2

Ciara: Ó, ba bhreá liom é sin a fheiceáil. Cén t-am?

Aodh: Bhuel, beidh sé ar siúl ag a hocht a chlog. An mbuailfimid le chéile ag leathuair tar éis a seacht taobh amuigh den phictiúrlann?

Ciara: Go breá. Feicfidh mé ansin thú. Slán.

Caibidil 7: Ceol

 Leathanach 112

A. Píosa Cainte

Is mise Garbhán Ó Baoill. Is as Doire mé. Is aoibhinn liom popcheol, ceol Gaelach agus rapcheol. Thar aon rud eile, áfach, is breá liom an rac-cheol. Seinnim dhá uirlis cheoil. Seinnim an giotár agus an pianó. Táim i mbanna ceoil agus cleachtaimid le chéile gach Satharn. Thosaigh mé ag seinm ceoil nuair a bhí mé deich mbliana d'aois. Thosaigh mé leis an ngiotár agus cúpla bliain ina dhiaidh sin, thosaigh mé ag seinm an phianó.

 Leathanach 112

B. Fógra

Fógraíodh inniu go mbeidh Niall Horan agus Julia Michaels ag tabhairt ceolchoirm mhór san RDS i mí na Bealtaine. Caoga euro atá ar na ticéid agus beidh siad ar díol Dé hAoine ag www.ticeid.ie. Scaip an scéal!

 Leathanach 113

C. Píosa Nuachta

Gabhadh fear agus bean i mBaile Átha Cliath aréir taobh amuigh de cheolchoirm Katy Perry. Dúirt na Gardaí go raibh siad ag díol ticéid bhréige. Bhí siad ag lorg €300 an ticéad. Dúirt an Garda Ó Síocháin go bhfuil an fear agus an bhean 'i dtrioblóid mhór'.

 Leathanach 113

D. Comhrá

Mír 1

Mícheál: Bail ó Dhia ort, a Olivia. Conas atá cúrsaí?

Olivia: Go hiontach, a Mhíchíl. Tá sceitimíní orm, chun an fhírinne a rá. Beidh mé ag dul chuig ceolchoirm anocht in Amharclann an Olympia.

Mícheál: I ndáiríre? Cé a bheidh ag seinm?

Olivia: Lorde. Ar chuala tú fúithi?

Mícheál: Níor chuala. Cárb as í?

Olivia: Is as an Nua-Shéalainn í.

Mícheál: Agus cén sórt ceoil a sheinneann sí?

Olivia: Popcheol agus popcheol leictreo. Taitníonn sé go mór liom.

Mír 2

Mícheál: Cé a bheidh ag dul in éineacht leat?

Olivia: Mo dheirfiúr mhór. Cheannaigh sí an ticéad dom.

Mícheál: Nach bhfuil sin go hiontach. Bain súp as an gceolchoirm.

Caibidil 8: Spórt

 Leathanach 114

A. Píosa Cainte

Dia daoibh. Is mise Saoirse Nic Cárthaigh. Tá go leor caitheamh aimsire agam ach is é an spórt an caitheamh aimsire is fearr liom. Is é sacar an spórt is fearr liom. Imrím ar fhoireann na scoile agus le mo chlub. Is é Celtic an fhoireann is fearr liom. Chonaic mé iad ag imirt nuair a tháinig siad go hÉirinn i mí Iúil seo caite.

 Leathanach 114

B. Fógra

Beidh Éire ag imirt in aghaidh Shasana i gComórtas na Sé Náisiún ar Lá Fhéile Pádraig. Beidh an cluiche ar siúl sa Staid Aviva. Tá €80 ar thicéid do dhaoine fásta agus €40 ar thicéid do dhaoine óga. Beidh siad ar díol ag www.cluiche.ie Dé hAoine. Scaip an scéal!

 Leathanach 115

C. Píosa Nuachta

Tá foireann dornálaíochta na hÉireann tar éis cúig bhonn óra a bhuachan sna Cluichí Oilimpeacha. Dúirt bainisteoir na foirne go raibh bród an domhain air as gach dornálaí. Dúirt Uachtarán na hÉireann go n-eagrófar searmanas speisialta dóibh in Áras an Uachtaráin nuair a fhillfidh siad ar Éirinn.

 Leathanach 115

D. Comhrá

Mír 1

Sorcha: Haigh, a Thomáis. Conas ar éirigh libh inné sa chluiche iománaíochta?

Tomás: Á, a Shorcha, d'imríomar go huafásach agus chailleamar, faraor.

Sorcha: Á, is trua é sin. Cén scór a bhí ann?

Mír 2

Tomás: Ag leath ama bhíomar chun tosaigh, naoi bpointe in aghaidh a hocht. Ach ansin, tugadh dhá chárta dhearga dúinn agus scóráil an fhoireann eile sé chúl. Sé chúl agus fiche pointe in aghaidh naoi bpointe an scór deiridh.

Turas 2: Mo Leabhar Gníomhaíochta

Caibidil 9: Laethanta Saoire

Leathanach 116

A. Píosa Cainte

Haigh, is mise Breandán Ó Coinn. Is aoibhinn liom dul ar laethanta saoire. Taitníonn saoirí sciála agus saoirí gníomhaíochta liom. Thar aon rud eile, áfach, is breá liom saoirí gréine. Téim go dtí an Ghréig gach samhradh. Taitníonn tránna, bia agus muintir na Gréige go mór liom. Beidh mé ag dul ar ais le mo theaghlach i mí an Mheithimh, nuair a chríochnóidh mé an Teastas Sóisearach. Táim ag tnúth go mór leis.

Leathanach 116

B. Fógra

An maith leat a bheith ag snámh san fharraige, ag surfáil nó ag sciáil ar uisce? Bhuel, téigh ar saoire spóirt uisce le Turais Spóirt Uisce. Tá margadh speisialta ar siúl againn faoi láthair. Tá pacáistí saoire go dtí an Phortaingéil againn ar €299. Tá tuilleadh eolais ar www.turaisspoirtuisce.ie. Scaip an scéal!

Leathanach 117

C. Píosa Nuachta

Bhuaigh clann Uí Fhearraigh as Gaoth Dobhair €250,000 ar an gclár *Winning Streak* aréir. Bhuaigh siad é nuair a chas siad an roth agus thit an liathróid ar an duais speisialta. Dúirt siad go léir gur mhaith leo dul ar shaoire safari san Afraic.

Leathanach 117

D. Comhrá

Mír 1

Eoin: Haigh, a Marie, cad é mar atá tú?

Marie: Go breá – ach cad é a tharla duit? Tá tú chomh dearg le tráta!

Eoin: Ó, bhí mé ar shaoire ghréine sa Spáinn agus thit mé i mo chodladh ar an trá!

Marie: Bhuel, ní raibh sin cliste ar chor ar bith, an raibh?

Eoin: Ní raibh. Ní tharlóidh sé arís, mise á rá leat!

Marie: Cathain a tháinig tú ar ais?

Eoin: Dhá lá ó shin. Bhí an tsaoire go maith ach is deas a bheith ar ais in Éirinn.

Mír 2

Marie: An bhfuil aon phleananna eile agat don samhradh?

Eoin: Tá. Fuair mé post i siopa mo Mham. Is gníomhaire taistil í.

Marie: Ó, go deas. Bhuel is fógra maith thú leis an aghaidh sin, is dócha!

Caibidil 10: Tinneas agus Sláinte

 **Leathanach 118**

A. Píosa Cainte

Dia dhaoibh. Is mise Aoibh Nic Craith. Tá post páirtaimseartha agam i siopa caife áitiúil. Caife na Cathrach is ainm dó. Is aoibhinn liom an bia folláin a dhíolaimid. Déanaimid bricfeasta agus lón sa chaife. Am bricfeasta, taitníonn gránóla agus iógart go mór liom. Ag am lóin, ithim sailéad nó ceapaire, de ghnáth. Tá sneaiceanna deasa againn freisin. Mar shampla, tá torthaí, barraí gránacha agus cnónna ar díol anseo. Féach ár ar mbiachlár ar www.caifenacathrach.ie!

 **Leathanach 118**

B. Fógra

Seo fógra ó na Gardaí. Tá na Gardaí sa tóir ar bhuirgléir a bhris isteach i dteach i gContae Longfort aréir. Bhí an fear gléasta in éadaí dubha. Bhí gruaig fhada dhubh air. Bhí srón cham air agus bhí colm aige ar a mhuineál. Má tá aithne agat ar an duine seo, cuir glaoch ar na Gardaí ag (043) 999 7788.

 **Leathanach 119**

C. Píosa Nuachta

Dúnadh dhá bhialann i mBaile Átha Cliath inné. Dúirt cigirí ó Údarás Sábháilteachta Bia na hÉireann, nó an Food Safety Authority of Ireland, go raibh na cistineacha salach agus go raibh an bia as dáta. Tiocfaidh na cigirí ar ais go dtí na bialanna i gceann trí seachtaine.

 **Leathanach 119**

D. Comhrá

Mír 1

Jeaic: A Mham, táim an-tinn. An féidir liom fanacht sa bhaile inniu?

Mam: Cad atá cearr leat, a Jeaic?

Jeaic: Bhuel, tá scornach thinn orm agus tá pian i mo bholg.

Mam: Hmm, bhuel níl cuma thinn ort. Cogar, ith slisín tósta agus ól cupán tae agus beidh tú ar ais ar do sheanléim sula i bhfad.

Jeaic: Ceart go leor. Ach ní dóigh liom go n-oibreoidh sé.

Mír 2

Mam: Rachaimid go dtí an dochtúir tar éis na scoile má bhíonn tú fós tinn.

Jeaic: Ach, a Mham!

Mam: Níl aon ach-anna uaim! Anois, éirigh amach as an leaba!

Turas 2

Gaeilge na Sraithe Sóisearaí
GNÁTHLEIBHÉAL
An Dara Bliain & An Tríú Bliain

An Dara hEagrán

Mo Phunann

Ainm: _____
Rang: _____

Risteard Mac Liam

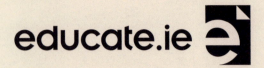

FOILSITHE AG:
Educate.ie
Walsh Educational Books Ltd
Oileán Ciarraí
Co. Chiarraí
www.educate.ie

ARNA CHLÓ AGUS ARNA CHEANGAL AG:
Walsh Colour Print
Oileán Ciarraí
Co. Chiarraí

© Risteard Mac Liam 2022

Gach ceart ar cosaint. Ní ceadmhach aon chuid den fhoilseachán seo a chóipeáil, a atáirgeadh ná a tharchur in aon mhodh ná slí, bíodh sin leictreonach, meicniúil, bunaithe ar fhótachóipeáil, ar thaifeadadh nó eile gan cead scríofa a fháil ón bhfoilsitheoir roimh ré.

Tá na foilsitheoirí faoi chomaoin acu siúd a thug cead dúinn grianghraif a atáirgeadh: RTC FOTO / Alamy Stock Photo; Shutterstock.

Cé go ndearnadh gach iarracht dul i dteagmháil leo siúd ar leo an cóipcheart ar ábhair sa téacs seo, theip orainn teacht ar dhaoine áirithe. Is féidir leis na daoine sin dul i dteagmháil le Educate.ie, agus beimid sásta na gnáthshocruithe a dhéanamh leo.

ISBN: 978-1-913698-69-0

Mo Phunann

Clár Ábhair

Réamhrá iv

Caibidil 1: Mé Féin 1

Caibidil 2: Mo Theaghlach 4

Caibidil 3: Mo Theach 12

Caibidil 4: Mo Cheantar 22

Caibidil 5: Mo Scoil 30

Caibidil 6: Mo Chaithimh Aimsire 37

Caibidil 7: Ceol 48

Caibidil 8: Spórt 58

Caibidil 9: Laethanta Saoire 68

Caibidil 10: Tinneas agus Sláinte 76

Réamhrá

Fáilte chuig do Phunann. Taifeadfar sa phunann seo na rudaí a fhoghlaimíonn tú in *Turas 2*.

Sa phunann seo:

- Déanfaidh tú nóta de na focail is tábhachtaí duitse. / You will make a note of the words that are most important for you.
- Ullmhóidh tú giotaí scríbhneoireachta agus cuir i láthair le haghaidh na measúnuithe rangbhunaithe. / You will prepare written pieces and presentations for the classroom-based assessments.
- Cruthóidh tú sárshamplaí de do chuid oibre. / You will create high-quality examples of your work.
- Déanfaidh tú machnamh ar do chuid foghlama. / You will reflect on your learning.
- Cuirfidh tú le do thuiscint ar phríomhscileanna na Sraithe Sóisearaí a úsáideann tú agus tú ag déanamh na ngníomhaíochtaí. / You will become more aware of the Junior Cycle key skills that you use while completing the activities.
- Foghlaimeoidh tú conas dréachtú, athléamh agus athdhréachtú a dhéanamh ar phíosa oibre. / You will learn how to draft, read over and redraft a piece of work.

Príomhscileanna na Sraithe Sóisearaí

- A bheith liteartha / Being literate
- A bheith uimheartha / Being numerate
- Cumarsáid / Communicating
- A bheith cruthaitheach / Being creative
- Mé féin a bhainistiú / Managing myself
- Fanacht folláin / Staying well
- Obair le daoine eile / Working with others
- Eolas agus smaointeoireacht a bhainistiú / Managing information and thinking

Beidh tú ábalta na samplaí oibre a chruthaigh tú a úsáid agus tú ag déanamh staidéir do scrúduithe agus ag ullmhú do mheasúnuithe rangbhunaithe.

You will be able to use the samples of work that you create while studying for exams and preparing for classroom-based assessments.

Go n-éirí leat ar do thuras!

Caibidil 1: Mé Féin

Punann 1.1 – Próifíl a Dhearadh

A. Dear próifíl díot féin:
- Dear abhatár! Téigh chuig www.avachara.com/avatar nó www.cartoonify.de
- Roghnaigh aghaidh, gruaig, súile, srón, béal agus fiacla duit féin
- Roghnaigh éadaí duit féin
- Priontáil amach an íomhá
- Scríobh **cúig** abairt fút féin (ainm, aois, gruaig, súile agus dhá thréith).

B. Greamaigh (*Stick*) d'abhatár anseo.

C. Scríobh cúig abairt fút féin anseo.

_____
_____
_____
_____
_____
_____

D. Déan an cur síos os comhair an ranga. Bain úsáid as an sampla seo.

Dia daoibh. Seo na cúig abairt a scríobh mé fúm féin:
1. Gráinne is ainm dom, mar is eol daoibh.
2. Táim ceithre bliana déag d'aois.
3. Tá gruaig fhada dhonn orm, mar a fheiceann sibh.
4. Tá súile donna agam.
5. Táim cairdiúil agus cabhrach.

Sin a bhfuil uaim. Go raibh maith agaibh as éisteacht liom.

✓ Seicliosta

Scríobh mé m'ainm agus m'aois.	☐
Luaigh mé mo stíl gruaige.	☐
Luaigh mé dath mo shúl.	☐
Luaigh mé an sórt duine mé.	☐
Rinne mé seiceáil litrithe.	☐

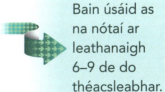

Bain úsáid as na nótaí ar leathanaigh 6–9 de do théacsleabhar.

🗝 Príomhscileanna

Bhain mé an-úsáid as an bpríomhscil seo: _____

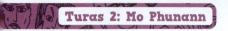

Focail agus Nathanna Tábhachtacha ó Chaibidil 1

Céard iad na focail agus na nathanna is tábhachtaí a d'fhoghlaim tú i gCaibidil 1? Déan liosta anseo. Déan comparáid le daoine eile sa rang.

Gaeilge	Béarla

Gaeilge	Béarla
Gaeilge	Béarla

Caibidil 2: Mo Theaghlach

Punann 2.1 – Fógra le haghaidh Seó Teilifíse

Dear fógra le haghaidh seó teilifíse darb ainm *Teaghlaigh Cheoil*. Luaigh na pointí seo a leanas:

- Ainm an tseó / The name of the show
- Na cineálacha teaghlach atá á lorg / The kind of families being looked for
- An duais / The prize
- An seoladh ríomhphoist / The email address
- Na rudaí atá le déanamh chun cur isteach air / What has to be done to enter
- Cá bhfuil tuilleadh eolais ar fáil. / Where to get more information.

> Malartaigh do chuid oibre leis an duine atá in aice leat. Tabhair aiseolas. Luaigh éacht amháin ✓ agus moladh amháin 💡.
>
> Swap your work with the person beside you. Give feedback. Mention one achievement and one recommendation.

✓ Seicliosta

- Dhear mé fógra cruthaitheach. ☐
- D'úsáid mé dathanna éagsúla. ☐
- Luaigh mé na rudaí ar fad. ☐
- Rinne mé seiceáil litrithe. ☐

➡ Bain úsáid as na nótaí ar leathanach 35 de do théacsleabhar.

🔑 Príomhscileanna

Bhain mé an-úsáid as an bpríomhscil seo: _____

Punann 2.2 – Alt Fúm Féin agus faoi Mo Theaghlach

A. Scríobh alt fút féin agus faoi do theaghlach.

_____

B. Cuir an t-alt i láthair an ranga mar chuid den MRB. Bain úsáid as an gcur i láthair samplach seo (bunaithe ar alt Ji-ho ar leathanach 38 de do théacsleabhar).

> Dia dhaoibh. Is mise Jason, mar is eol daoibh. Is as Baile Átha Cliath ó dhúchas mé agus táim beagnach ceithre bliana déag d'aois.
>
> Tá cúigear i mo theaghlach. Sin iad mé féin ar ndóigh, agus ansin mo mháthair, Fiadh, m'athair, Hong, mo dheartháir mór Eric agus mo dheirfiúr óg Liadh.
>
> Tá gruaig dhubh orm féin, mar a fheiceann sibh, agus ar Eric agus ar Liadh. Tá súile donna agam, tá súile glasa ag Eric agus tá súile cnódhonna ag Liadh. Tá siad cabhrach, cneasta agus cliste.
>
> Tá gruaig liath ar m'athair agus tá súile donna aige. Tá sé fuinniúil agus foighneach. Tá gruaig fhada fhionn ar mo mháthair. Tá sí fial agus greannmhar.
>
> Ar an iomlán, réitímid go han-mhaith le chéile.
>
> Sin a bhfuil uaim. Tá súil agam gur bhain sibh taitneamh as an gcur i láthair seo.

✓ Seicliosta

Rinne mé cur síos ar mo theaghlach.	☐
Luaigh mé ainm agus aois gach duine.	☐
Luaigh mé tréithe gach duine.	☐
D'úsáid mé go leor focail nua.	☐
Rinne mé an cur i láthair.	☐

➡ Bain úsáid as na nótaí ar leathanaigh 38 agus 39 de do théacsleabhar.

🔑 Príomhscileanna

Bhain mé an-úsáid as an bpríomhscil seo: _____

Punann 2.3 – Ríomhphost chuig File faoi Dhán

Tá an chéad dréacht den ríomhphost chuig an bhfile scríofa agat. Scríobh an leagan deiridh den ríomhphost anseo. Ar léigh tú an seicliosta ar leathanach 9?

Ó:
Chuig:
Ábhar:
Seolta:

Caibidil 2

Mo Theaghlach

✓ Seicliosta

Scríobh mé mo sheoladh ríomhphoist féin agus seoladh ríomhphoist an fhile. ☐

Luaigh mé an t-ábhar. ☐

Scríobh mé cúpla rud faoi gach pointe. ☐

Scríobh mé tús agus críoch oiriúnach (*suitable*). ☐

Shínigh mé m'ainm. ☐

Bain úsáid as na nótaí ar leathanach 45 de do théacsleabhar.

Príomhscileanna

Bhain mé an-úsáid as an bpríomhscil seo: _____

Turas 2: Mo Phunann

Focail agus Nathanna Tábhachtacha ó Chaibidil 2

Céard iad na focail agus na nathanna is tábhachtaí a d'fhoghlaim tú i gCaibidil 2? Déan liosta anseo. Déan comparáid le daoine eile sa rang.

Gaeilge	Béarla

Gaeilge	Béarla
Gaeilge	Béarla

Caibidil 3: Mo Theach

Punann 3.1 - Seomra Idéalach in Óstán

Dear seomra idéalach in óstán.
Cuir lipéad ar gach píosa troscáin.

✓ Seicliosta

Tharraing mé pictiúr den seomra.
nó
Dhear mé seomra in
https://planner.roomsketcher.com. ☐

Chuir mé lipéad ar gach píosa troscáin. ☐

D'úsáid mé go leor focail nua. ☐

Rinne mé seiceáil litrithe. ☐

> Bain úsáid as na nótaí ar leathanaigh 56–59 de do théacsleabhar.

🔑 Príomhscileanna

Bhain mé an-úsáid as an bpríomhscil seo: _____

Mo Theach

Punann 3.2 – An Seomra is Fearr Liom

A. Cruthaigh ceithre shleamhnán faoin seomra is fearr leat ar PowerPoint nó Prezi. Bain úsáid as https://planner.roomsketcher.com chun seomra 3D a dhearadh. Cuir lipéad ar gach rud.

B. Déan an cur i láthair os comhair an ranga mar chuid den MRB. Lean na treoracha seo:

1. Léigh an cur i láthair samplach seo.

Sleamhnán 1

Dia dhaoibh, a chairde. Ar dtús, seo pictiúr de m'árasán. Tá sé suite i lár na cathrach. Is aoibhinn liom é mar tá sé mór, geal agus compordach.

Sleamhnán 2

Is é mo sheomra codlata an seomra is fearr liom. Seo pictiúr de. Is breá liom mo scíth a ligean ann.

Sleamhnán 3

Tá leaba shingil agam agus tá sé an-chompordach. Tá deasc bheag agam freisin. Déanaim mo chuid obair bhaile ag an deasc seo. Tá taisceadán in aice le mo leaba. Tá trí tharraiceán sa taisceadán. Tá lampa amháin ar an taisceadán agus lampa eile ar an deasc. Tá vardrús mór sa chúinne. Coimeádaim mo chuid éadaí ann. Coimeádaim mo chuid leabhar ar na seilfeanna.

Sleamhnán 4

Tá *en suite* beag agam freisin. Tá scáthán, doirteal, cithfholcadán agus leithreas ann. Tá dhá tharraiceán faoin doirteal. Coimeádaim smideadh agus earraí níocháin eile sna tarraiceáin.

Focal scoir

Mar fhocal scoir, táim an-sásta anseo. Níor mhaith liom a bheith i mo chónaí faoin tuath. Bheadh sé an-leadránach. Anseo sa chathair, tá gach rud ar leac an dorais againn.

2. Scríobh dréacht-script chur i láthair i do chóipleabhar. Bain úsáid as an gcur i láthair samplach thuas agus as an teimpléad thíos.

3. Seiceáil an dréacht-script. Scríobh an leagan deiridh den script anseo.

Sleamhnán 1
Sleamhnán 2
Sleamhnán 3
Sleamhnán 4
Focal scoir

4. Déan an cur i láthair. Bain úsáid as an script ach ná léigh í focal ar fhocal.

✓ Seicliosta

- Dhear mé seomra 3D. ☐
- Scríobh mé abairtí faoin seomra seo. ☐
- Dhear mé cur i láthair samplach. ☐
- Rinne mé an cur i láthair. ☐

➡ Bain úsáid as na nótaí ar leathanaigh 56–63 de do théacsleabhar.

🔑 Príomhscileanna

Bhain mé an-úsáid as an bpríomhscil seo: _____

Mo Theach

Caibidil 3

Punann 3.3 – Ríomhphost faoi Mo Theach Nua

Samhlaigh go raibh tú ar an seó *Teach Nua*. Tá teach nua agat anois ach faraor, tá sé gránna! Scríobh ríomhphost chuig cara leat faoi na rudaí a tharla sna pictiúir 1–4. Bain úsáid as an teimpléad thíos.

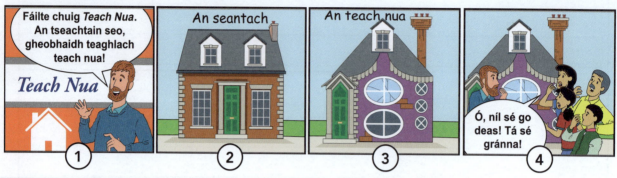

Ó: Ábhar:
Chuig: Seolta:

A _____, a chara,

Conas atá tú? Tá súil agam go bhfuil tú i mbarr na sláinte. Ar chuala tú an scéala? Bhíomar ar an seó *Teach Nua*! Creid é nó ná creid, tá teach nua againn anois! Ach faraor, tá sé gránna.

> Déan cur síos ar an seanteach anseo. Is féidir leat cur síos ar do theach nó d'árasán féin.

Sa seanteach, bhí _____ seomra againn. Bhí _____

_____

_____

_____

_____

_____.

> Déan cur síos ar an teach nua anseo. Luaigh na fadhbanna a bhaineann le gach rud, mar shampla na ballaí, na hurláir, an troscán. Úsáid focail ar nós: gránna (*ugly*), salach (*dirty*), trí chéile (*messy*), míchothrom (*uneven*), briste (*broken*), scoilte (*cracked*), uafásach (*horrible*), bunoscionn (*upside down*), droim ar ais (*back to front*), dorcha (*dark*).

Faraor, scrios siad an seanteach! / Faraor, rinne siad praiseach den seanteach! Anois, tá gach rud ina chíor tuathail (*now everything is in a shambles*). Mar shampla: _____

_____

_____

_____

_____.

Luaigh bhur dtuairimí anseo.

(Ar ndóigh nílim sásta … / ní thaitníonn an/na _____ linn / tá díomá orainn faoi …)

Luaigh bhur réiteach anseo freisin.

(Ba mhaith linn …)

_____
_____
_____
_____
_____
_____
_____.

Bhuel, sin a bhfuil uaim. Tá súil agam go mbeidh dea-scéala agam an chéad uair eile (*I hope I will have better news next time*).

Abair heileo le _____.

Slán tamall,

_____

✓ Seicliosta

Bheannaigh mé do mo chara. ☐

Chuir mé síos ar an seanteach. ☐

Chuir mé síos ar an teach nua. ☐

Luaigh mé ár dtuairimí agus ár réiteach. ☐

Shínigh mé m'ainm. ☐

 Bain úsáid as na nótaí ar leathanaigh 74–75 de do théacsleabhar.

🔑 Príomhscileanna

Bhain mé an-úsáid as an bpríomhscil seo: _____

Punann 3.4 – Ríomhphost chuig Pádraigín

Tá an chéad dréacht den ríomhphost chuig Pádraigín scríofa agat. Scríobh an leagan deiridh den ríomhphost anseo. Ar léigh tú an seicliosta ar leathanach 19?

Ó:
Chuig:
Ábhar:
Seolta:

Seicliosta

- Scríobh mé mo sheoladh ríomhphoist féin agus seoladh ríomhphoist Phádraigín. ☐
- Luaigh mé an t-ábhar. ☐
- Luaigh mé trí rud ba cheart do Phádraigín a dhéanamh. ☐
- Scríobh mé tús agus críoch oiriúnach (*suitable*). ☐
- Shínigh mé m'ainm. ☐

Bain úsáid as na nótaí ar leathanaigh 74, 75 agus 85 de do théacsleabhar.

Príomhscileanna

Bhain mé an-úsáid as an bpríomhscil seo: _____

Focail agus Nathanna Tábhachtacha ó Chaibidil 3

Céard iad na focail agus na nathanna is tábhachtaí a d'fhoghlaim tú i gCaibidil 3? Déan liosta anseo. Déan comparáid le daoine eile sa rang.

Gaeilge	Béarla

Gaeilge	Béarla

Caibidil 4: Mo Cheantar

Punann 4.1 – Léarscáil de Mo Cheantar a Tharraingt

Bí ag caint!

> Cá bhfuil tú i do chónaí?

> Táim i mo chónaí i gCill Chainnigh.

Tarraing léarscáil (*map*) de do cheantar. Liostaigh na siopaí agus na háiseanna. Bain úsáid as Google Maps chun cabhrú leat.

Siopaí agus áiseanna i mo cheantar

✓ Seicliosta

D'aimsigh mé mo cheantar ar Google Maps.
nó
Shiúil mé timpeall mo cheantair. ☐

Scríobh mé liosta de na háiseanna agus na siopaí i mo cheantar. ☐

Tharraing mé léarscáil de mo cheantar. ☐

➡ Bain úsáid as na nótaí ar leathanaigh 92, 93, 96 agus 97 de do théacsleabhar.

🔑 Príomhscileanna

Bhain mé an-úsáid as an bpríomhscil seo: _____

Mo Cheantar

Turas 2: Mo Phunann

Punann 4.2 – Léirmheas faoi Ionad Siopadóireachta

A. Smaoinigh ar ionad siopadóireachta a thaitníonn leat. Scríobh léirmheas gearr.

_____
_____
_____
_____
_____
_____
_____
_____
_____
_____
_____
_____

Cé mhéad réalta?
Dathaigh na réalta atá tuillte.   ☆ ☆ ☆ ☆ ☆

B. Mar chuid den MRB, déan cur i láthair ar shiopa amháin atá san ionad siopadóireachta. Lean na treoracha seo:

1. Léigh an cur i láthair samplach seo.

Réamhrá: Sa chur i láthair seo, déanfaidh mé cur síos ar shiopa amháin san ionad siopadóireachta.

Eolas ginearálta: Cogs the Brain Shop is ainm don siopa seo. Tá sé lonnaithe i lár Bhaile Átha Cliath. Siopa bréagán atá ann.

Cineál earraí: Tá réimse leathan earraí ar díol ann. Mar shampla, tá cluichí cláir, míreanna mearaí, cluichí cártaí, bréagáin adhmaid, puzail agus leabhair ar díol ann.

Custaiméirí: Tagann daoine ó gach cearn den tír go dtí an siopa. Is aoibhinn leo siúl timpeall agus féachaint thart. Ar ndóigh, tá an suíomh gréasáin gnóthach freisin. Seolann siad bréagáin chuig gach cearn den domhan.

Na húinéirí: Gnó teaghlaigh atá ann. Bhunaigh siad an siopa in 2013.

Focal scoir: Ar an iomlán, is aoibhinn liom féin an siopa seo, mar is féidir liom bronntanais speisialta a cheannach ann.

2. Scríobh dréacht-script chur i láthair i do chóipleabhar. Bain úsáid as an gcur i láthair samplach thuas agus as an teimpléad thíos.

3. Seiceáil an dréacht-script. Scríobh an leagan deiridh den script anseo.

Réamhrá

Eolas ginearálta

Cineál earraí

Custaiméirí

Na húinéirí

Focal scoir

4. Déan an cur i láthair. Bain úsáid as an script ach ná léigh í focal ar fhocal.

✓ Seicliosta

- Luaigh mé ainm an tsiopa. ☐
- Liostaigh mé cúpla pointe faoin siopa. ☐
- Scríobh mé faoi na custaiméirí agus na húinéirí. ☐
- Rinne mé an cur i láthair. ☐

➡ Bain úsáid as na nótaí ar leathanaigh 100 agus 101 do théacsleabhar.

Príomhscileanna

Bhain mé an-úsáid as an bpríomhscil seo: _____

Caibidil 4

Mo Cheantar

Punann 4.3 - Póstaer faoi Dhumpáil a Dhearadh

Tá an chéad dréacht den phóstaer deartha agat. Dear an leagan deiridh den phóstaer anseo. Ar léigh tú an seicliosta ar leathanach 27?

✓ Seicliosta

Scríobh mé teachtaireacht shoiléir. ☐
Bhain mé úsáid as focail agus nathanna nua. ☐
Luaigh mé na sonraí teagmhála (*contact details*). ☐

 Bain úsáid as na nótaí ar leathanach 127 de do théacsleabhar.

Príomhscileanna

Bhain mé an-úsáid as an bpríomhscil seo: _____

Turas 2: Mo Phunann

Focail agus Nathanna Tábhachtacha ó Chaibidil 4

Céard iad na focail agus na nathanna is tábhachtaí a d'fhoghlaim tú i gCaibidil 4? Déan liosta anseo. Déan comparáid le daoine eile sa rang.

Gaeilge	Béarla

Gaeilge	Béarla
Gaeilge	Béarla

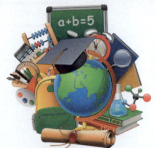

Caibidil 5: Mo Scoil

Punann 5.1 – Ceistneoir faoi Do Scoil

A. Déan an ceistneoir mar rang iomlán. Cé mhéad duine i do rang a aontaíonn nó nach n-aontaíonn leis na ráitis (*statements*)? Ríomh (*calculate*) an céatadán (%) freisin, más mian leat.

	Aontaím go hiomlán.	Aontaím.	Tá mé idir dhá chomhairle.	Ní aontaím.	Ní aontaím ar chor ar bith.
Tá na rialacha cothrom.					
%					
Tá an scoil nua-aimseartha.					
%					
Taitníonn na hábhair scoile liom.					
%					
Tugann na múinteoirí an iomarca obair bhaile dúinn.					
%					
Críochnaíonn an lá scoile ródhéanach.					
%					
Tosaíonn an lá scoile róluath.					
%					

B. Cuir na torthaí i láthair an ranga mar chuid den MRB. Lean na treoracha seo:

1. Léigh an cur i láthair samplach seo.

> Sa chur i láthair seo, chuir mé ceisteanna ar mo chomhscoláirí faoin lá scoile. Bhí na freagraí an-suimiúil ar fad.
>
> Bhain an chéad cheist leis an am a thosaíonn an lá scoile. Cheap formhór (*majority*) na scoláirí go dtosaíonn sé i bhfad róluath (*far too early*). Mheas cúpla scoláire go raibh sé ceart go leor.
>
> Bhain an dara ceist leis an am a chríochnaíonn an lá scoile. Cheap formhór na scoláirí go gcríochnaíonn sé ag am oiriúnach (*suitable*).
>
> Bhain an tríú ceist leis an obair bhaile. Bhí na scoláirí ar aon ghuth (*in full agreement*) faoin gceist seo: tugann na múinteoirí i bhfad an iomarca obair bhaile dúinn!
>
> Bhain an ceathrú ceist leis na hábhair scoile. Bhí meascán cothrom (*even mix*) de thuairimí anseo. Bhí roinnt scoláirí sásta leis na hábhair scoile agus bhí roinnt scoláirí eile míshásta leo.
>
> Bhain an cúigiú ceist leis an scoil féin. Bhí na scoláirí ar aon ghuth faoin gceist seo freisin. Tá scoil an-nua-aimseartha againn.
>
> Bhain an séú ceist le rialacha na scoile. Bhí meascán cothrom (*even mix*) de thuairimí anseo. Cheap roinnt scoláirí go raibh na rialacha cothrom agus cheap roinnt scoláirí eile go raibh siad dian.
>
> Mar fhocal scoir, is léir go bhfuil go leor tuairimí éagsúla ann faoin scoil seo. Mar a deir an seanfhocal, ní lia duine ná tuairim (*different strokes for different folks*).

2. Scríobh dréacht-script chur i láthair i do chóipleabhar. Bain úsáid as an gcur i láthair samplach thuas.

3. Seiceáil an dréacht-script. Scríobh an leagan deiridh den script anseo.

_____
_____
_____
_____
_____
_____
_____
_____
_____
_____
_____
_____
_____
_____
_____
_____
_____
_____
_____
_____

4. Déan cur i láthair. Bain úsáid as an script ach ná léigh í focal ar fhocal.

✓ Seicliosta

- Rinne mé an suirbhé leis an rang. ☐
- Chomhair mé na torthaí. ☐
- Líon mé isteach na torthaí sa tábla thuas. ☐
- Ríomh mé na céatadáin (roghnach (*optional*)). ☐
- Rinne mé an cur i láthair. ☐

➡ Bain úsáid as na nótaí ar leathanach 142 de do théacsleabhar.

🔑 Príomhscileanna

Bhain mé an-úsáid as an bpríomhscil seo: _____

Punann 5.2 – Aiste Ghearr faoi Mo Shaol ar Scoil

Scríobh aiste ghearr nó alt faoi do shaol ar scoil. Bain úsáid as plean Chaoimhe:

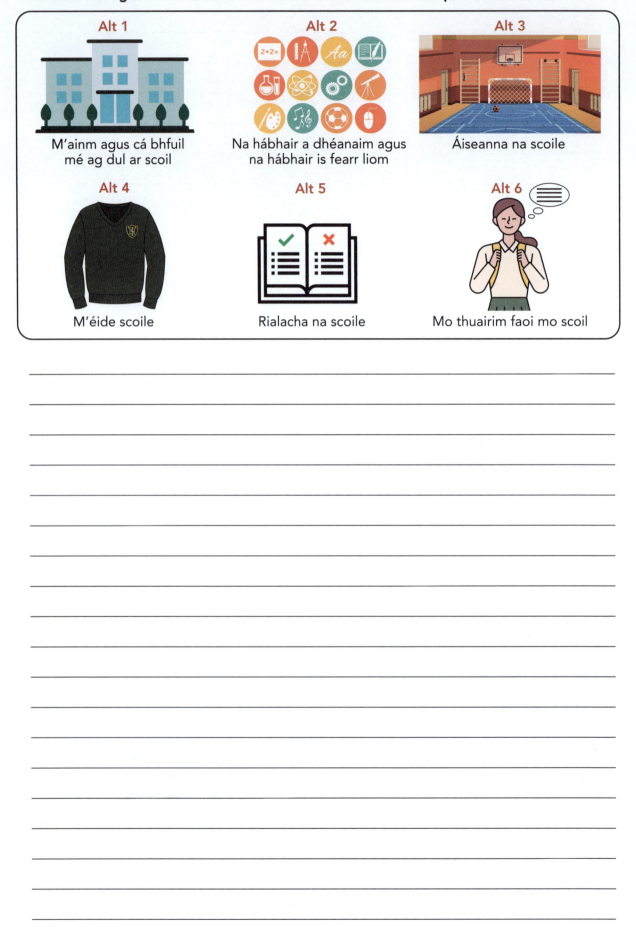

> Malartaigh do chuid oibre leis an duine atá in aice leat. Tabhair aiseolas. Luaigh éacht amháin ✓ agus moladh amháin.
>
> Swap your work with the person beside you. Give feedback. Mention one achievement and one recommendation.

✓ Seicliosta

- Chuir mé mé féin in aithne agus luaigh mé ainm mo scoile. ☐
- Rinne mé cur síos ar na hábhair a dhéanaim. ☐
- Rinne mé cur síos ar mo scoil agus ar m'éide scoile. ☐
- Scríobh mé faoi rialacha na scoile. ☐
- Thug mé mo thuairim faoin scoil. ☐
- Rinne mé seiceáil litrithe. ☐

➡ Bain úsáid as na nótaí ar leathanaigh 152 agus 153 de do théacsleabhar.

Príomhscileanna

Bhain mé an-úsáid as an bpríomhscil seo: _____

Punann 5.3 – Comhrá le Jeaic

Tá an chéad dréacht den chomhrá scríofa agat. Scríobh an leagan deiridh den chomhrá anseo.

Caibidil 5

Mo Scoil

✓ Seicliosta

Scríobh mé an dréacht-chomhrá. ☐

Chinntigh mé gur áirigh (*included*) mé mioneolas as an dán. ☐

Léigh mé siar an méid a scríobh mé. ☐

Scríobh mé an dréacht deireanach. ☐

Rinne mé seiceáil litrithe. ☐

Bain úsáid as na nótaí ar leathanaigh 159 de do théacsleabhar.

🔑 Príomhscileanna

Bhain mé an-úsáid as an bpríomhscil seo: _____

Focail agus Nathanna Tábhachtacha ó Chaibidil 5

Céard iad na focail agus na nathanna is tábhachtaí a d'fhoghlaim tú i gCaibidil 5? Déan liosta anseo. Déan comparáid le daoine eile sa rang.

Gaeilge	Béarla

Caibidil 6: Mo Chaithimh Aimsire

Punann 6.1 – Sceideal Teilifíse a Dhearadh

Dear sceideal teilifíse. Roghnaigh ceithre chainéal agus liostaigh na cláir a bheidh ar siúl oíche Dé Céadaoin. Luaigh an cineál cláir é gach clár freisin. Bain úsáid as an bpáipéar nuachta nó www.entertainment.ie/tv/.

Dé Céadaoin	Sceideal			
19.00				
19.30				
20.00				
20.30				
21.00				
21.30				

✓ Seicliosta

D'fhéach mé ar an sceideal i bpáipéar nuachta.
nó
D'fhéach mé ar an sceideal ar líne. ☐

Liostaigh mé na cláir ar fad. ☐

Luaigh mé an cineál cláir é gach clár. ☐

Bain úsáid as na nótaí ar leathanaigh 168 agus 169 de do théacsleabhar.

Príomhscileanna

Bhain mé an-úsáid as an bpríomhscil seo: _____

Punann 6.2 – Suirbhé faoin bhFón Cliste a Úsáid

A. Déan suirbhé faoin méid ama a chaitheann tú ar d'fhón cliste. Cuir Ceist 1 agus Ceist 2 ar gach duine sa rang. Ar dtús, féach ar an suirbhé a rinne Ciara. Ansin, déan do shuirbhé féin ar leathanach 40.

An suirbhé a rinne Ciara

Céim 1: Chuir sí ceisteanna ar gach duine sa rang (26 scoláire).

Ceist 1: Cad é an fáth is mó a n-úsáideann tú an fón cliste? (Roghnaigh fáth amháin.)

Cúis	Cluichí	Meáin shóisialta	Nuacht/ Spórt	Obair scoile	Eile
	✓✓✓✓ ✓✓✓✓	✓✓✓✓ ✓✓✓✓ ✓✓	✓✓✓✓ ✓✓	✓	✓
Iomlán	8	10	6	1	1

Ceist 2: Cé mhéad ama a chaitheann tú ar d'fhón cliste gach seachtain?

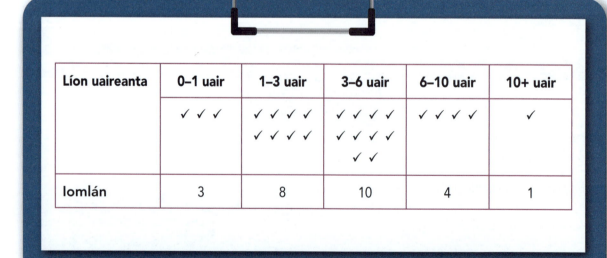

Líon uaireanta	0–1 uair	1–3 uair	3–6 uair	6–10 uair	10+ uair
	✓✓✓	✓✓✓✓ ✓✓✓✓	✓✓✓✓ ✓✓✓✓ ✓✓	✓✓✓✓	✓
Iomlán	3	8	10	4	1

B. Dear dhá phíchairt chun tuairimí an ranga a léiriú. Ar dtús, clóscríobh na torthaí (*type the results*) in MS Excel. Ansin, cruthaigh dhá phíchairt agus greamaigh iad sa bhosca ar leathanach 41. Chun cabhrú leat, féach ar an gcaoi a ndearna Ciara a dá phíchairt féin.

An dá phíchairt a chruthaigh Ciara

Céim 1: Chlóscríobh sí na torthaí in MS Excel.

Ceist 1 (Cad é an fáth is mó a n-úsáideann tú an fón cliste?)

Cluichí	Meáin shóisialta	Nuacht/Spórt	Obair scoile	Eile
8	10	6	1	1

Ceist 2 (Cé mhéad ama a chaitheann tú ar d'fhón cliste gach seachtain?)

0–1 uair	1–3 uair	3–6 uair	6–10 uair	10+ uair
3	8	10	4	1

Céim 2: Chruthaigh sí dhá phíchairt. Conas? D'aibhsigh sí na ceannteidil agus na figiúirí (*She highlighted the headings and the figures*) agus chliceáil sí ar **Insert**. Ansin, chliceáil sí ar an lipéad nó **Pie Chart**. Dheaschliceáil (*right-clicked*) sí ar an bpíchairt chun tuilleadh roghanna a fheiceáil.

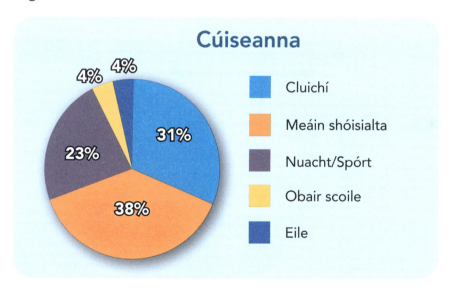

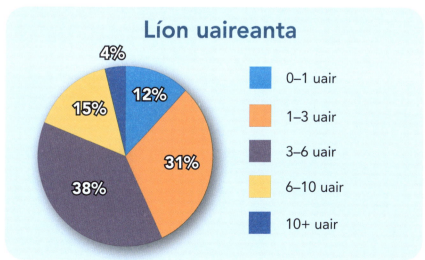

A. Déan do shuirbhé anseo.

Ceist 1: Cad é an fáth is mó a n-úsáideann tú an fón cliste? (Roghnaigh fáth amháin.)

Cúis	Cluichí	Meáin shóisialta	Nuacht/ Spórt	Obair scoile	Eile
Iomlán					

Ceist 2: Cé mhéad ama a chaitheann tú ar d'fhón cliste gach seachtain?

Líon uaireanta	0–1 uair	1–3 uair	3–6 uair	6–10 uair	10+ uair
Iomlán					

B. Greamaigh an dá phíchairt anseo.

✓ Seicliosta

Chuir mé Ceist 1 agus Ceist 2 ar gach duine sa rang. ☐

Rinne mé nóta de na torthaí. ☐

Chlóscríobh mé na torthaí in MS Excel. ☐

Dhear mé dhá phíchairt.

Bain úsáid as na nótaí ar leathanach 180 de do théacsleabhar.

Príomhscileanna

Bhain mé an-úsáid as an bpríomhscil seo: _____

Punann 6.3 – Litir Chuig Do Chara

Scríobh litir chuig cara leat atá ina c(h)ónaí i gcontae eile faoi na rudaí a dhéanfaidh tú féin ag an deireadh seachtaine. Bain úsáid as an tsraith pictiúr seo chun cabhrú leat.

| 1 Maidin Dé Sathairn | 2 Tráthnóna Dé Sathairn | 3 Maidin Dé Domhnaigh | 4 Tráthnóna Dé Domhnaigh |

Do sheoladh _____
_____
_____
_____

Dáta _____

_____,

Mo Chaithimh Aimsire

> Malartaigh do chuid oibre leis an duine atá in aice leat. Tabhair aiseolas. Luaigh éacht amháin ✓ agus moladh amháin 💡.
>
> Swap your work with the person beside you. Give feedback. Mention one achievement and one recommendation.

✓ Seicliosta

Scríobh mé mo sheoladh agus an dáta. ☐
Bheannaigh mé do mo chara. ☐
Scríobh mé faoin deireadh seachtaine seo chugainn. ☐
Rinne mé seiceáil litrithe. ☐

Bain úsáid as na nótaí ar leathanaigh 182 agus 183 de do théacsleabhar.

Príomhscileanna

Bhain mé an-úsáid as an bpríomhscil seo: _____

Punann 6.4 - Teachtaireacht chuig Cara Leat

Tá an chéad dréacht den teachtaireacht ghearr chuig do chara scríofa agat. Scríobh an leagan deiridh den teachtaireacht anseo. Ar léigh tú an seicliosta ar leathanach 45?

✓ Seicliosta

Bheannaigh mé do mo chara (Haigh, conas atá tú?). ☐

Ghabh mé leithscéal le mo chara. ☐

Luaigh mé gach pointe. ☐

Shínigh mé m'ainm. ☐

Rinne mé seiceáil litrithe. ☐

Bain úsáid as na nótaí ar leathanach 187 de do théacsleabhar.

Príomhscileanna

Bhain mé an-úsáid as an bpríomhscil seo: _____

Mo Chaithimh Aimsire

Focail agus Nathanna Tábhachtacha ó Chaibidil 6

Céard iad na focail agus na nathanna is tábhachtaí a d'fhoghlaim tú i gCaibidil 6? Déan liosta anseo. Déan comparáid le daoine eile sa rang.

Gaeilge	Béarla

Gaeilge	Béarla
Gaeilge	Béarla

Caibidil 7: Ceol

Punann 7.1 – Próifíl de Cheoltóir a Dhearadh

Smaoinigh ar cheoltóir a thaitníonn leat. Dear a p(h)róifíl.

Ainm	
Ainm stáitse	
Áit bhreithe	
Dáta breithe	
Oidhreacht	
Teaghlach	
Uirlisí ceoil	
An cineál ceoil a sheinneann sé/sí	
An cineál ceoil a thaitníonn leis/léi	
Gradaim	
Na hamhráin is cáiliúla	
A s(h)uíomh gréasáin	

> Malartaigh do chuid oibre leis an duine atá in aice leat. Tabhair aiseolas. Luaigh éacht amháin ✓ agus moladh amháin .
>
> Swap your work with the person beside you. Give feedback. Mention one achievement and one recommendation.

✓ Seicliosta

- Chuaigh mé ar líne agus rinne mé taighde ar cheoltóir a thaitníonn liom. ☐
- Liostaigh mé go leor eolais faoin gceoltóir. ☐
- D'fhoghlaim mé go leor rudaí faoi/fúithi. ☐
- D'fhoghlaim mé go leor focail nua. ☐

➡ Bain úsáid as na nótaí ar leathanach 203 de do théacsleabhar.

🎤 Príomhscileanna

Bhain mé an-úsáid as an bpríomhscil seo: _____

Punann 7.2 – Póstaer do Cheolchoirm a Dhearadh

Beidh banna ceoil cáiliúil ag teacht go hÉirinn chun ceolchoirm a thabhairt. Dear póstaer don cheolchoirm. Bain úsáid as an teimpléad thíos.

Ceolchoirm Mhór na Bliana

- Áit
- Ainm an bhanna ceoil
- Lá, dáta, am
- Ticéid ar fáil (áit agus praghas)
- Pictiúr
- Críoch mhealltach, mar shampla: 'Ná caill í!'/'Bí ann!'
- Tuilleadh eolais (suíomh gréasáin)

✓ Seicliosta

Luaigh mé eolas faoin láthair (*venue*) agus faoin mbanna ceoil. ☐

Luaigh mé lá, dáta agus am na ceolchoirme. ☐

Luaigh mé eolas faoi na ticéid agus an praghas a bhí orthu. ☐

Scríobh mé críoch mhealltach. ☐

Luaigh mé an áit a raibh tuilleadh eolais ar fáil. ☐

 Bain úsáid as na nótaí ar leathanaigh 204 agus 205 de do théacsleabhar.

Príomhscileanna

Bhain mé an-úsáid as an bpríomhscil seo: _____

Punann 7.3 – Postáil Bhlag faoi Cheolchoirm

D'fhreastail tú ar cheolchoirm mhór. Scríobh postáil bhlag faoin gceolchoirm. Luaigh na pointí seo a leanas:

- Eolas faoin gceolchoirm
- An áit a bhfuair tú na ticéid
- Roimh an gceolchoirm
- An cheolchoirm féin
- Tar éis na ceolchoirme.

https://www.ceolchoirmeacha247.ie

✓ Seicliosta

Luaigh mé eolas faoin gceolchoirm agus an áit a bhfuair mé na ticéid. ☐

Luaigh mé an méid a rinne mé roimh an gceolchoirm. ☐

Scríobh mé faoin gceolchoirm féin. ☐

Luaigh mé an méid a rinne mé tar éis na ceolchoirme. ☐

Bain úsáid as na nótaí ar leathanaigh 206 agus 207 de do théacsleabhar.

🔑 Príomhscileanna

Bhain mé an-úsáid as an bpríomhscil seo: _____

Punann 7.4 – Cur Síos ar Fhíseán Ceoil

Tá an chéad dréacht den chur síos ar fhíseán scríofa agat. Scríobh an leagan deiridh den chur síos anseo. Ar léigh tú an seicliosta ar leathanach 55?

Seicliosta

Rinne mé plean. ☐

Rinne mé nasc idir (*a link between*) scéal an amhráin agus an físeán. ☐

Rinne mé cur síos ar scéal an fhíseáin. ☐

Rinne mé cur síos ar an suíomh (*setting*) agus ar na carachtair. ☐

Bhí mé cruthaitheach (*creative*). ☐

Bain úsáid as na nótaí ar leathanach 215 de do théacsleabhar.

Príomhscileanna

Bhain mé an-úsáid as an bpríomhscil seo: _____

Focail agus Nathanna Tábhachtacha ó Chaibidil 7

Céard iad na focail agus na nathanna is tábhachtaí a d'fhoghlaim tú i gCaibidil 7? Déan liosta anseo. Déan comparáid le daoine eile sa rang.

Gaeilge	Béarla

Gaeilge	Béarla
Gaeilge	Béarla

Caibidil 8: Spórt

Punann 8.1 – Teachtaireacht Chuig Do Chara

Scríobh teachtaireacht chuig do chara ag tabhairt cuireadh dó/di teacht leat chun páirt a ghlacadh sa champa spóirt. Luaigh na pointí seo a leanas:

- Eolas praiticiúil faoin gcampa
- Tabhair cuireadh do do chara
- Cúpla tuairim atá agat faoin gcampa.

Tá an póstaer agus nathanna úsáideacha ar leathanach 231 de do théacsleabhar.

✓ Seicliosta

Léigh mé an póstaer.

Luaigh mé eolas praiticiúil sa teachtaireacht.

Thug mé cuireadh do mo chara.

Luaigh mé cúpla tuairim atá agam faoin gcampa.

Bain úsáid as na nótaí ar leathanach 231 de do théacsleabhar.

Príomhscileanna

Bhain mé an-úsáid as an bpríomhscil seo: _____

Punann 8.2 - Próifíl de Phearsa Spóirt a Dhearadh

> Cén phearsa spóirt is fearr leat?

> Is í Laura Muir an phearsa spóirt is fearr liom mar tá sí tapa agus crua.

Smaoinigh ar phearsa spóirt a thaitníonn leat. Dear próifíl de/di.

Ainm	
Spórt	
Áit bhreithe	
Dáta breithe	
Airde	
Teaghlach	
Club spóirt	
Buaicphointe (*high point*) a shaoil/a saoil	
Tréithe	(i) (ii) (iii)

✓ Seicliosta

- Chuaigh mé ar líne agus rinne mé taighde ar phearsa spóirt a thaitin liom. ☐
- Liostaigh mé go leor eolais faoin bpearsa spóirt. ☐
- D'fhoghlaim mé go leor rudaí faoi/fúithi. ☐
- D'fhoghlaim mé go leor focail nua. ☐

Bain úsáid as na nótaí ar leathanaigh 228 agus 233 de do théacsleabhar.

Príomhscileanna

Bhain mé an-úsáid as an bpríomhscil seo: _____

Punann 8.3 – Postáil Bhlag faoi Ócáid Mhór Spóirt

D'fhreastail tú ar ócáid mhór spóirt. Scríobh postáil bhlag faoin ócáid. Luaigh na pointí seo a leanas:

- Eolas faoin ócáid mhór spóirt
- An áit a bhfuair tú na ticéid
- Roimh an ócáid mhór spóirt
- An ócáid féin
- Tar éis na hócáide.

https://www.ocaidi-spoirt.ie

https://www.ocaidi-spoirt.ie

> Malartaigh do chuid oibre leis an duine atá in aice leat. Tabhair aiseolas. Luaigh éacht amháin ✓ agus moladh amháin 💡.
>
> Swap your work with the person beside you. Give feedback. Mention one achievement and one recommendation.

✓ Seicliosta

Luaigh mé eolas faoin ócáid mhór spóirt agus an áit a bhfuair mé na ticéid. ☐

Luaigh mé cad a rinne mé roimh an ócáid mhór spóirt. ☐

Scríobh mé faoin ócáid féin. ☐

Luaigh mé cad a rinne mé tar éis na hócáide seo. ☐

➡ Bain úsáid as na nótaí ar leathanaigh 234 agus 235 de do théacsleabhar.

🗝 Príomhscileanna

Bhain mé an-úsáid as an bpríomhscil seo: _____

Punann 8.4 – Cur Síos ar Fhíseán Ceoil

Tá an chéad dréacht den chur síos ar fhíseán scríofa agat. Scríobh an leagan deiridh den chur síos anseo. Ar léigh tú an seicliosta ar leathanach 65?

✓ Seicliosta

Rinne mé plean. ☐
Rinne mé nasc idir (*a link between*) scéal an amhráin agus an físeán. ☐
Rinne mé cur síos ar scéal an fhíseáin. ☐
Rinne mé cur síos ar an suíomh (*setting*) agus ar na carachtair. ☐
Bhí mé cruthaitheach (*creative*). ☐

➡ Bain úsáid as na nótaí ar leathanach 239 de do théacsleabhar.

🔑 Príomhscileanna

Bhain mé an-úsáid as an bpríomhscil seo: _____

Turas 2: Mo Phunann

Focail agus Nathanna Tábhachtacha ó Chaibidil 8

Céard iad na focail agus na nathanna is tábhachtaí a d'fhoghlaim tú i gCaibidil 8? Déan liosta anseo. Déan comparáid le daoine eile sa rang.

Gaeilge	Béarla

Gaeilge	Béarla
Gaeilge	Béarla

Caibidil 9: Laethanta Saoire

Punann 9.1 – An tSaoire is Measa Riamh

Samhlaigh go raibh saoire uafásach agat. Scríobh deich n-abairt faoin tsaoire. Luaigh na pointí seo a leanas:

- An t-aerfort nó an eitilt
- An lóistín agus an bia
- An aimsir
- An ceantar agus na daoine.

Caibidil 9

_____
_____
_____
_____
_____
_____
_____
_____
_____
_____

> Malartaigh do chuid oibre leis an duine atá in aice leat. Tabhair aiseolas. Luaigh éacht amháin ✓ agus moladh amháin 💡.
>
> Swap your work with the person beside you. Give feedback. Mention one achievement and one recommendation.

✓ Seicliosta

- Scríobh mé faoin aerfort **nó** faoin eitilt. ☐
- Scríobh mé faoin lóistín agus faoin mbia. ☐
- Scríobh mé faoin aimsir. ☐
- Scríobh mé faoin gceantar agus faoi na daoine. ☐

➡ Bain úsáid as na nótaí ar leathanaigh 254 agus 255 de do théacsleabhar.

🔑 Príomhscileanna

Bhain mé an-úsáid as an bpríomhscil seo: _____

Laethanta Saoire

Turas 2: Mo Phunann

Punann 9.2 – Cárta Poist ó Pháras

Tá tú ar thuras scoile i bPáras. Scríobh cárta poist chuig cara leat. Luaigh na pointí seo a leanas:

- An t-óstán ina bhfuil tú ag fanacht
- Na háiseanna agus na siopaí
- Na rudaí a dhéanann tú
- An bia
- An aimsir.

✓ Seicliosta

Scríobh mé seoladh mo charad ar dheis. ☐

Bheannaigh mé do mo chara. ☐

Scríobh mé cúpla abairt faoi gach pointe urchair (*bullet point*). ☐

D'fhág mé slán ag mo chara. ☐

Rinne mé seiceáil litrithe. ☐

> Bain úsáid as na nótaí ar leathanaigh 262 agus 263 de do théacsleabhar.

🔑 Príomhscileanna

Bhain mé an-úsáid as an bpríomhscil seo: _____

Greamaigh stampa anseo

Seoladh:
_____
_____
_____
_____
_____

Faraor nach bhfuil tú anseo!

Laethanta Saoire

Punann 9.3 – Comhrá le Bainisteoir Bainc

Tá an chéad dréacht den chomhrá scríofa agat. Scríobh an leagan deiridh den chomhrá anseo. Ar léigh tú an seicliosta ar leathanach 73?

✓ Seicliosta

Bheannaigh mé don bhainisteoir. ☐
D'úsáid mé go leor focail agus nathanna nua. ☐
Ghabh mé buíochas leis an mbainisteoir. ☐
Sheiceáil mé litriú na bhfocal. ☐

Bain úsáid as na nótaí ar leathanach 281 de do théacsleabhar.

Príomhscileanna

Bhain mé an-úsáid as an bpríomhscil seo: _____

Focail agus Nathanna Tábhachtacha ó Chaibidil 9

Céard iad na focail agus na nathanna is tábhachtaí a d'fhoghlaim tú i gCaibidil 9? Déan liosta anseo. Déan comparáid le daoine eile sa rang.

Gaeilge	Béarla

Gaeilge	Béarla
Gaeilge	Béarla

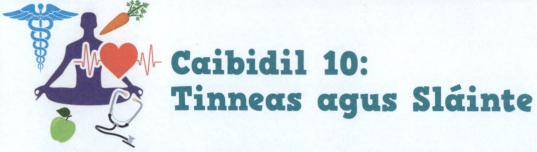

Caibidil 10: Tinneas agus Sláinte

Punann 10.1 – Scéalchlár faoi Dhuine a Bhí Tinn

Cruthaigh scéalchlár faoi am nuair a bhí tú féin (nó duine eile) tinn.
Bain úsáid as www.storyboardthat.com.
Cuir na pictiúir sna boscaí 1–4 thíos.

Scríobh abairt amháin faoi gach pictiúr. Bain úsáid as na noda seo, más mian leat:

1. Cathain a thosaigh an tinneas agus céard iad na siomptóim (*symptoms*) a bhí agat?
2. Cad a rinne tú nuair a bhí tú tinn?
3. Cad a rinne tú chun an tinneas a leigheas (*to cure the illness*)?
4. Cathain a tháinig biseach ort (*get better*)?

1.	2.

3.	4.

_____   _____
_____   _____
_____   _____
_____   _____
_____   _____
_____   _____
_____   _____
_____   _____

Caibidil 10

Tinneas agus Sláinte

✓ Seicliosta

Chuaigh mé go www.storyboardthat.com. ☐
Chruthaigh mé ceithre phictiúr. ☐
Scríobh mé abairt amháin faoi gach pictiúr. ☐
Bhain mé úsáid as na noda (roghnach (*optional*)) ☐

Bain úsáid as na nótaí ar leathanaigh 294–297 de do théacsleabhar.

Príomhscileanna

Bhain mé an-úsáid as an bpríomhscil seo: _____

Punann 10.2 – Biachlár a Dhearadh

Samhlaigh go bhfuil tú ag obair i mbialann. Dear biachlár blasta.

Ainm na Bialainne:

Bricfeasta	€	Lón	€
Deochanna	€	Sneaiceanna	€

Bain sult as do bhéile!

> Malartaigh do chuid oibre leis an duine atá in aice leat. Tabhair aiseolas. Luaigh éacht amháin ✓ agus moladh amháin .
>
> Swap your work with the person beside you. Give feedback. Mention one achievement and one recommendation.

✓ Seicliosta

- Dhear mé biachlár cruthaitheach. ☐
- Luaigh mé an bricfeasta, lón, deochanna agus sneaiceanna. ☐
- Luaigh mé an praghas a bhí ar gach rud. ☐
- D'úsáid mé go leor focail nua. ☐

➡ Bain úsáid as na nótaí ar leathanaigh 300 agus 301 de do théacsleabhar.

Príomhscileanna

Bhain mé an-úsáid as an bpríomhscil seo: _____

Tinneas agus Sláinte

Punann 10.3 – Dráma Gearr i mBialann a Scríobh

I ngrúpa, scríobh dráma gearr idir freastalaí i mbialann agus beirt chustaiméirí. Léirigh os comhair an ranga é. Bain úsáid as na nathanna úsáideacha ar leathanach 81.

Nathanna úsáideacha

Fáilte romhaibh chuig _____.	Welcome to _____.
Bord/Tábla do bheirt, le do thoil.	A table for two, please.
An bhfuil áirithint agaibh?	Do you have a reservation?
Leanaigí mise, le bhur dtoil.	Follow me, please.
Tagaigí an bealach seo.	Come this way.
Seo bhur mbord/dtábla.	Here is your table.
An dtógfaidh mé bhur gcótaí?	Shall I take your coats?
An féidir leat an biachlár a thabhairt dúinn, le do thoil?	Can you bring us the menu, please?
Ar ndóigh. Seo daoibh é.	Of course. Here it is.
Ba mhaith liom an _____ mar chéad chúrsa agus an _____ mar phríomhchúrsa, le do thoil.	I would like the _____ for starters and the _____ for mains, please.
Cinnte. Tá an _____ an-bhlasta.	Sure. The _____ is very tasty.
Gabh mo leithscéal, tá an _____ fuar.	Excuse me, the _____ is cold.
Tá an-bhrón orm faoi sin. Gheobhaidh mé ceann úr duit.	I'm very sorry about that. I'll get you a fresh one.
Bainigí sult as bhur mbéile.	Enjoy your meal.
An féidir linn an bille a fháil, le do thoil?	Can we get the bill, please?
Go deimhin. Nóiméad amháin, le bhur dtoil.	Of course. One minute, please.
Gabh mo leithscéal, tá fadhb leis an mbille.	Excuse me, there is a problem with the bill.
Ó, tá an-bhrón orm faoi sin.	Oh, I am very sorry about that.
Go dtí an chéad uair eile.	Until next time.

✓ Seicliosta

- Scríobh mé ról an fhreastalaí agus d'úsáid mé na frásaí cuí (*appropriate*). ☐
- Scríobh mé ról na gcustaiméirí agus d'úsáid mé na frásaí cuí. ☐
- D'úsáid mé go leor focail nua agus frásaí nua. ☐
- D'oibrigh mé i ngrúpa. ☐
- Léirigh mé an comhrá os comhair an ranga. ☐

Bain úsáid as na nótaí ar leathanaigh 302 agus 303 de do théacsleabhar.

Príomhscileanna

Bhain mé an-úsáid as an bpríomhscil seo: _____

Turas 2: Mo Phunann

Punann 10.4 – Scéal Bunaithe ar Shraith Pictiúr a Scríobh

Scríobh scéal bunaithe ar an tsraith pictiúr seo. Bain úsáid as na nathanna úsáideacha ar leathanach 83.

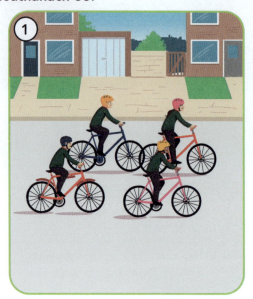

Nathanna úsáideacha

Lá breá brothallach a bhí ann.	It was a fine hot day.
Bhíomar ar an mbealach abhaile.	We were on the way home.
Go tobann, bhuail mo rothar cloch.	Suddenly, my bike hit a stone.
Thit mé den rothar.	I fell off the bike.
Thit mé ar mo bhéal is mo shrón.	I fell flat on my face.
Bhuail mé mo cheann ar an gcosán.	I hit my head on the pavement.
Thosaigh mo lámh ag cur fola.	My hand started bleeding.
Bhí mé i bponc.	I was in a fix.
Bhí mé in ísle brí.	I was down in the dumps.
Chonaic comharsa chineálta an timpiste.	A kind neighbour saw the accident.
Chabhraigh sí liom.	She helped me.
Thug sí síob dom.	She gave me a lift.
Ní raibh an dara rogha agam.	I didn't have any other choice.
Ghlaoigh mo chara ar mo thuistí.	My friend called my parents.
Chuaigh mé go dtí an dochtúir.	I went to the doctor.
Thit an lug ar an lag agam.	I became disheartened.
Baineadh siar asam.	I was taken aback.
Bhí an t-ádh dearg orm.	I was dead lucky.
Ba mhór an faoiseamh é.	It was a great relief.
Bhí mé an-bhuíoch den bhean chineálta.	I was very thankful to the kind woman.

Scríobh do scéal anseo.

Caibidil 10

Tinneas agus Sláinte

✓ Seicliosta

Scríobh mé cúpla abairt faoi gach pictiúr. ☐
D'úsáid mé go leor nathanna úsáideacha. ☐
Scríobh mé scéal suimiúil. ☐
Rinne mé seiceáil litrithe. ☐

Bain úsáid as na nótaí ar leathanaigh 304 agus 305 de do théacsleabhar.

🗝 Príomhscileanna

Bhain mé an-úsáid as an bpríomhscil seo: _____

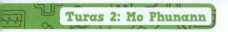

Focail agus Nathanna Tábhachtacha ó Chaibidil 10

Céard iad na focail agus na nathanna is tábhachtaí a d'fhoghlaim tú i gCaibidil 10? Déan liosta anseo. Déan comparáid le daoine eile sa rang.

Gaeilge	Béarla

Gaeilge	Béarla
Gaeilge	Béarla

FOOD CULTURES OF INDIA

FOOD CULTURES OF INDIA

Edited by

SARIT K. CHAUDHURI
DEBARSHI PRASAD NATH
DHURJJATI SARMA

MANOHAR
2025

First published 2024

© Individual contributors, 2024

Reprinted 2025

All rights reserved. No part of this publication may be reproduced or transmitted, in any form or by any means, without prior permission of the editors and the publisher.

ISBN 978-93-6080-855-6 (hardbound)
ISBN 978-93-6080-943-0 (ebook)

Published by
Ajay Kumar Jain *for*
Manohar Publishers & Distributors
4753/23 Ansari Road, Daryaganj
New Delhi 110 002

Typeset by Kohli Print, Delhi 110 051

Printed and bound in India

Contents

List of Figure and Tables 7

Acknowledgements 9

Introduction
DEBARSHI PRASAD NATH AND DHURJJATI SARMA 11

SECTION I: THEORIZING FOOD CULTURES

1. The History and Historiography of Indian Food: The State of the Field
   JAYANTA SENGUPTA 21

2. Food and Fellowship
   MIHIR BHATTACHARYA 39

3. Theorizing Food Studies: Gender and Ideologies
   SUKALPA BHATTACHARJEE 53

4. Anthropological Perspectives of Pregnancy Dietary Patterns among Indian Women
   CAITLYN D. PLACEK 65

SECTION II: FOOD IN FOLKLORE—BELIEFS, PRACTICES, AND SOCIAL REALITY

5. Food, Folklore and the Construction of Social Reality: Perspectives from Arunachal Pradesh
   SARIT K. CHAUDHURI 93

6. Sociality and Anxiety in the Foodways of Malabar
   HASHIK N.K. 111

7. Gastronomic Terrain of the Sikkim Himalaya
   UTTAM LAL AND CHARISMA K. LEPCHA 129

8. Garo Food Habits and Ethnicity: A Folkloric Perspective
   CHANDAMITA GOSWAMI 145

SECTION III: FOOD IN/AS FICTION—ONTOLOGY, IMAGINATION, AND IDENTITY

9. Edible Memories: Rasogolla and Food Fiction
   BIJAY K. DANTA — 163

10. Food and Narration: Encoding Pain and Fracture in Bangla Partition Literature
    SRAVANI BISWAS — 187

11. Food Mnemonics and Identity Construction
    SURANJANA BARUA — 197

12. Tea as Food: Tracing the History of Tea through Folktales and Fairy Tales
    YASHOMANA CHOUDHURY — 209

SECTION IV: FOOD AND FAMINE—MEMORIES OF LOSS AND SURVIVAL

13. Cultural Construction of Famine Food
    SUCHETA SEN CHAUDHURI — 223

14. Scarcity, Survival, and Memories
    KANCHAN MUKHOPADHYAY — 241

SECTION V: FASHIONING FOOD—REPRESENTATIONS THROUGH FILM AND NEW MEDIA

15. The Gustatory Metaphor: Decoding Food Images in Indian Films
    SWIKRITA DOWERAH — 257

16. Reconstructing Youth Through Popular Culinary Culture
    ANASUYA SREEDHAR — 271

17. The Nostalgic Foodie: Food Photography and the Representation of Assamese Cuisine on Social Media
    GAURAV RAJKHOWA — 287

List of Contributors — 315

Index — 323

List of Figure and Tables

FIGURE

7.1. 'Sikkimese' Food Served with Millet Beer   130

TABLES

7.1. Categorization of Food in Sikkim   133
7.2. Alcoholic and Non-alcoholic Brew in Sikkim   137
11.1. Linguistic Features Characterizing Salient Food Voice of Respondent R17   204
11.2. Linguistic Features Characterizing Salient Food Voice of R16   206

Acknowledgements

First, we would like to thank the administration and staff of Indira Gandhi Rashtriya Manav Sangrahalaya, Bhopal (IGRMS), for their support and collaboration in organizing the seminar on 'Food Cultures of India' in 2016 at Tezpur University, where the idea of this book first took shape. We also thank the concerned authorities of Tezpur University for their support in organizing the seminar. Special thanks are due to all the colleagues in the Department of Cultural Studies, Tezpur University. Special mention must be made of Dr. Jayanta Vishnu Das, who was one of the conveners of the seminar at Tezpur University. We would like thank all the contributors to this volume. The book also reflects the collective academic engagement within the North East towards exploring the varied food cultures of India, as epitomized by the convergence of three editors belonging to Rajiv Gandhi University, Tezpur University, and Gauhati University for this project. Last, but not the least, Manohar Publishers deserve special mention for having accepted the offer of publishing this volume.

Introduction

DEBARSHI PRASAD NATH AND DHURJJATI SARMA

Food is indisputably one of the most important constituents of our everyday lives. Since the advent of the 'cultural turn' in the sixties of the last century, many taken-for-granted-aspects of culture have come to be questioned in academic discourses. Food is a splendid example of this. When consumed daily, it is often considered as mere sustenance. The consumption of food is a common act, which, despite its importance for our survival, deceives us by its everydayness. This everydayness helps to underplay the way food pervades all aspects of our lives from the most intimate to the most professional practices. It is also a key factor as to how we view ourselves and others; today it is often at the centre of social and political issues and is also one of the mainstays of popular media.

As a topic of academic interest, food provides multiple points of entry. Food has been studied in history to look at its cultural, economic, and environmental impact. The more traditional field of culinary history focuses on the origin and recreation of specific recipes. Historians look at food as one of the most crucial elements of cultures, reflecting the social and economic structures of a community. Archaeologists/prehistorians tried to explore this dimension by linking food with evolutionary perspectives and issues of migration/diffusion of human populations.

Anthropology and history offer the opportunity to explore food historically and culturally. Marvin Harris explored the relationship between food and ecology, trying to understand how food practices are, in the final analysis, related to material conditions of life. Food habits, in terms of what is considered as edible or inedible by a community, is as powerful a marker of social identity as the incest taboo. Margaret Mead cited the relationship between the two taboos in the following proverb from New Guinea:

Your own mother, your own sister, your own pigs, your own yams which you have piled up, you may not eat (quoted in Rosman, Rubel, and Weisgrau, 2009: 86).

The proverb also highlights the symbolic aspect of food and women's relationship with it. Many literary writers have explored the symbolically cannibalistic nature of the relationship between the sexes in terms of food; in a society marked by unequal power relationship between the sexes who 'eats' whom (and what) is a political question. Everyone is aware of the surprisingly lesser number of representations of scenes of women consuming food in the literary and visual arts. The powerless can only be equated with food; she cannot 'eat'.

Sociology of food enables one to understand the connection between food and social identity. Food is also a marker of class and caste identification; for the sake of being included in a group, people will eat things that they hate and avoid perfectly tasty food that is on their forbidden list. The process of upward social mobility entails the learning and unlearning of food related practices. On the other hand, folklore enables one to look more closely at how traditional food is prepared and to draw the boundary between authentic culinary heritage and invented traditions. Practices of social change and continuity can thus be meaningfully interpreted through an exploration of the connection between food and folklore.

Though philosophers have generally stayed away from undertaking sustained analyses of food and food-related practices, in recent times there have been attempts made to address this issue academically. Two edited collections—Fritz Allhoff and Dave Monroe's *Food and Philosophy* and David M. Kaplan's *The Philosophy of Food*—bring together leading philosophers of our times to consider the most basic questions about food: the questions of ethics, choices and scarcity.

Food paintings constitute a separate line of development. Food images echo and revise the character of different schools of painting, but these are also never quite divorced from their own histories of places.

Management of food involves looking at the economics and business operation of food processing. It is possible to analyse food policies and their relationship with food industries. The scarcity of food and the political question of food aid (for example, which country will qualify for it in the event of a natural calamity) are vitally important questions.

Food science is an interdisciplinary field that thrives on the convergence of disciplines like biology, chemical engineering, and biochemistry. The objective of food scientists is to improve both the quality of consumable food and increase the quantity of production that can lead to food safety. Food scientists study the physical, microbiological, and chemical makeup of food. Today, the food one consumes every day is the result of research. Along with research on the improvement of food, food technology is concerned with the mass production of food products.

As discussed earlier, consumption of food is both a material practice as well as a symbolic act. What people eat, how and with whom, apart from what they feel about food and why they are crucial markers of the relationship between the members of a society. Theoretical frameworks for understanding consumption practices, commodification and food imagery are aplenty—one is of course immediately reminded of 'fetishism' as conceived by Marx and Freud, and the anthropological theories of Claude Lévi-Strauss.

More recently, Cultural Studies has provided several theoretical frameworks for understanding food cultures. In *Food and Cultural Studies*, Bob Ashley, Joanne Hollows, Steve Jones, and Ben Taylor have associated food with the idea of the circuit of culture, developed first by Richard Johnson (1986). They argue that 'the meaning or "life story" of any food cultural phenomenon—a foodstuff, a diet, and table manners—needs to be understood in relation to five major cultural processes: production, regulation, representation, identity and consumption' (Ashley, Hollows, Jones & Taylor 2004, vii).

In more recent times, Food Studies has emerged as an important interdisciplinary field of enquiry, situated at the convergence point of many disciplines. Several leading institutions around the world are offering courses on Food Studies. Food Studies is not only just about the study of food itself. One could argue that the trajectory of development of Food Studies has been along the same lines as Cultural Studies (which also, is not only about the study of culture per se). Food Studies deals with more than the mere production, consumption, aesthetic appreciation, and cataloguing of food related practices. It provides the vantage point to look at the relationship between food and people from the variety of perspectives offered by art, science, management, technology, sociology, cultural studies, economics, health, social justice, literature, anthropology and history.

In the context of the above discussion, the present volume brings together a collection of articles written by academics and scholars belonging to a wide range of disciplines and who have brought in their subject expertise towards analysing various dimensions of Food Studies. The volume has been divided into five sections. The first section titled 'Theorizing Food Cultures', containing four articles, provides certain crucial theoretical and historical perspectives on food as a cultural trope. Jayanta Sengupta, in his article on 'The History and Historiography of Indian Food: The State of the Field', delves into the annals of Indian history in order to explore the range of influences exerted on Indian food habits through cultural encounters with the Islamicate and the European world in the early modern period to the diasporic situation in the present-day globalized world. The second article, 'Food and Fellowship', by Mihir Bhattacharya deals with the twin aspects of preparation and consumption of food as a collective/community activity that is representative of the wider social milieu and its material and mental states of being. In the third article, 'Theorizing Food Studies: Gender and Ideologies', Sukalpa Bhattacharjee takes up for analysis the complex interplay between food and social–ideological forces determined by the prevalent dynamics of class, caste, and gender. The fourth article in the section, by Caitlyn D. Placek, entitled 'Anthropological Perspectives of Pregnancy Dietary Patterns among Indian Women', makes an interesting foray into the dietary behaviours of Indian women during pregnancy, which involves aversion towards certain kinds of food and, at the same time, craving for some items generally considered 'non-food' (like clay or soil), and thus the associated notions of appreciation and revulsion evoked within others as a result of such actions. The second section on 'Food in Folklore: Beliefs, Practices, and Social Reality' comprises four articles, the first of which by Sarit K. Chaudhuri and entitled 'Food, Folklore and the Construction of Social Reality: Perspectives from Arunachal Pradesh' has attempted to look into the food practices of the tribal communities inhabiting the frontier state. With folklore as the guiding principle, the article has shown how food production and consumption patterns are reflective of the ingrained belief systems of the tribal communities and how such processes have become, over a period of time strong markers of their respective social-cultural identities. The second article of the section, 'Sociality and Anxiety in the Foodways of Malabar', by Hashik N.K., explores the diverse food practices of Kerala, and explains the significance of food as a 'performative' commodity throughout history in fostering social relationships leading to communal harmony among the people of the region, particularly those living along for centuries along the coast of Malabar. The third article carries on with the spirit of 'gastronomical solidarity'—the authors Uttam Lal and Charisma K. Lepcha, in their article 'Gastronomic Terrain of the Sikkim Himalaya', undertake a brief survey of the eating habits of the people of the region and argue that the food culture in Sikkim has evolved over time to assume a heterogeneous character representing the mixing of various food styles, namely, those of Tibetan, Nepali, Bihari, Marwari and the indigenous Lepchas and Bhutias. This has also led to the problematization of the accepted notions of 'non-vegetarianism', particularly with reference to those visiting the state from outside. In the fourth article of the section, 'Garo Food Habits and Ethnicity: A Folkloric Perspective', Chandamita Goswami examines the twin processes of diffusion and acculturation in the food culture of the people of the community living in Assam. The study focuses on the cooking styles of the Garos, the ingredients used in the process, the recipes and the food habits prevalent within the community, and the transformations effected within them in the context of modernity.

The third section entitled 'Food in/as Fiction: Ontology, Imagination, and Identity' has four articles, and it begins with the article on 'Edible Memories: Rasogolla and Food Fiction' by Bijay K. Danta, where the author undertakes an in-depth critical-historical analysis of the rasogolla debate that ensued between Odisha and West Bengal. Referring to the said event as the 'rasogolla war', the author applies the notion of 'food fiction' in order to explore how the warring communities have fashioned fascinating narratives of ownership and invention *vis-à-vis* the cheese-ball sweet by invoking devotional texts, cultures, and precolonial/colonial events of their respective histories in order to legitimize their claims on the food item. The second article of the section, 'Food and Narration: Encoding Pain and Fracture in Bangla Partition Literature' by Sravani Biswas opens up a new possibility of decoding the painful narratives of Partition through the medium of food-memories, as represented by her brief analysis of Atin Bandyopadhyay's *Nilkontho Pakhir Khonje*. Food-memories, in her reading, are often juxtaposed with the deep physical and emotional recognition/recollection of the characters of their troubled states of being—just like the taste of specific food-items lingering on the tongue long after they are ingested, memories too tend to stay behind, as both physical and psychological sensations. In the third article of the section, entitled 'Food Mnemonics and Identity Construction', Suranjana Barua examines the deep association between food and memory by taking up case studies on language whereby she shows how specific references to or conversations on/about food can actually reveal various facets of one's own as well as the larger collective identity. The author contends that in a world of fluid identities, food (and the associated preferences) provides a stable perspective for identity construction. The fourth article in the section, entitled 'Tea as Food: Tracing the History of Tea through Folktales and Fairy Tales' by Yashomana Choudhury, situates the historical significance of tea as a common cultural marker across communities in Asia and Europe and also its presence as a popular trope in many folktales of the regions brought under discussion.

The fourth section on 'Food and Famine: Memories of Loss and Survival', comprising two articles, begins with Sucheta Sen

Introduction 17

Chaudhuri's submission on 'Cultural Construction of Famine Food', where she discusses the impact of famine upon the lives of various communities of Arunachal Pradesh and how these communities withstand the onslaught of the frequent famines through alternative food-production strategies based on their indigenous knowledge system. The other article in the section, 'Scarcity, Survival and Memories' by Kanchan Mukhopadhyay, attempts to critically examine the existent memories of past famines and of the resultant food scarcity among the Santals and thereby sheds light on the coping mechanisms developed within the community against such ordeals. The author emphasizes the role of memory in enabling the Santals towards building a repository of knowledge consolidated over a period of time through confrontations with famines, both natural and man-made.

The fifth and final section, entitled 'Fashioning Food: Representations through Film and New Media', contains three articles. In her article on 'The Gustatory Metaphor: Decoding Food Images in Indian Films', Swikrita Dowerah discusses the use of food imagery in films, and for that purpose, takes up three films, namely, *Adajya* by Santwana Bordoloi (1996), *Water* by Deepa Mehta (2005), and *Goynar Baksho* (2013) by Aparna Sen, to show how food becomes a regulating mechanism to exercise control over the women's body, particularly those of the widows, and how on the other hand, consumption of food signifies the very attempt by these women characters to fight against the patriarchal repression of their innate desires and predilections. In the second article of the section, entitled 'Reconstructing Youth Through Popular Culinary Culture,' Anasuya Sreedhar undertakes the study of culinary cultures, with reference to two food shows, set against the new culture of consumerism that builds on the prevalent ideas regarding health, fitness, and beauty. In his article on 'The Nostalgic Foodie: Food Photography and the Representation of Assamese Cuisine on Social Media', Gaurav Rajkhowa has shown how representations of Assamese culinary culture over and across social media platforms have presented new and interesting visions of a multi-ethnic food-consumption culture in Assam.

These articles on food cultures of India have presented a panoramic view of the theoretical as well as individual and collective patterns of food behaviour located and mapped across a wide cross-section of the Indian society. Food is seen not merely as are item for physical gratification, but as a potent signifier exercising its outreach over matters of identity and assertion (social, cultural and sexual). The legacy of food and the associated memories have been immortalized through their preservation and dissemination within the literary genres of orality and performance. Even the very lack or absence of food works towards heightening its regulating impact upon the collective thought processes and actions of the people affected by its scarcity. Furthermore, food also serves as a metaphor, constantly accruing new meanings onto itself through its representation in films and portals of new media. Food signifies both power and its subversion—what one ought to/is allowed to eat defines the identity of the subject within the ideological and gender based set up of the society. These articles have attempted to problematize a number of ideas enumerated above, and it is hoped that readers as well as future researchers on food studies will build upon the arguments posited here and also work towards formulating their own scholarly visions on the ever-expanding area of food cultures or food studies in India and the world.

REFERENCES

Allhoff, Fritz and Dave Monroe (ed.), 2007, *Food and Philosophy: Eat, Think, and Be Merry*. New Jersey: Wiley-Blackwell.

Ashley, Bob, Joanne Hollows, Steve Jones and Ben Taylor, 2004, *Food and Cultural Studies*, London and New York: Routledge.

Harris, M., 2001, *The Rise of Anthropological Theory: A History of Theories of Culture*. London: AltaMira Press.

Kaplan, David M., 2012, *The Philosophy of Food*, University of California Press.

Rosman, Abraham, Paula G. Rubel, and Maxine Weisgrau, 2009, *The Tapestry of Culture: An Introduction to Cultural Anthropology*, Lanham, Boulder, New York, Toronto, Oxford: Alta Mira Press.

SECTION I
THEORIZING FOOD CULTURES

CHAPTER 1

The History and Historiography of Indian Food: The State of the Field

JAYANTA SENGUPTA

THE STATE OF THE FIELD

If Indian history were a room, food history would not be a big elephant in it. Nurtured for several decades by the magisterial work of the lonesome pioneer figure K.T. Achaya, the alimentary aspects of modern Indian history and their connection with the complexities of colonial modernity and anticolonial nationalism have only recently started stoking serious scholarly interest. The path charted by scholars like Lizzie Collingham and Cecilia Leong-Salobir, in their studies of the relationship between food and regimes of power, has also welcomed those who have explored the culture and politics of food and cuisine as important constituents of the self-making of the educated middle class, including Srirupa Prasad, Utsa Ray, Rohan Deb Roy, and myself, among others.[1]

In India, as in other societies, food is one of the central elements of the culture of the subcontinent and reflects the social and economic structure of its society. Naturally therefore, any discussion of its food traditions needs to be mapped onto its cultural, economic, environmental and sociological features. The great size and immense diversity of the subcontinent belies broad generalizations. Its geographical features include long stretches of coastal land, thickly forested inland regions, mountainous territories, arid deserts and great stretches of plain land crisscrossed by rivers—a diversity that has shaped food availability and agricultural techniques. Social and cultural diversity has contributed greatly to this mix. While the vast majority of the Indian population are Hindus, India has also the world's third largest Muslim population (after Indonesia and Pakistan). Vegetarianism is a religious practice among nearly 30 per cent of Indians, while many among the Indian poor can little afford to consume non-vegetarian food for economic reasons. The contrast between India's poor—according to a 2005 World Bank estimate, 42 per cent of Indians live below the international poverty line[2]—and its fast-growing middle class, one of the largest in the world, also contributes to the divergence of food practices. And, despite the popularity of Indian restaurants in the west—where there prevails a widely shared perception of Indian food as spicy and primarily curry based—the enormous variety of regional cuisine in India too, cautions one against trying to generalize to any significant extent on a subject like food in the Indian subcontinent.

The basic division in scholarly discussion of Indian food lies in the examination of food as an aspect of material culture, on the one hand and that of food as an entity endowed with cultural and moral characteristics, on the other. Intriguingly, these two approaches are informed by two virtually opposite ideas of India. In as much as one seeks to write the history of Indian food as a temporal narrative of various dishes, their ingredients and their evolution through the rise and fall of political regimes, social and cultural systems and structures of economic production—best exemplified by the work of the Indian food historian K.T. Achaya—India invariably emerges as one of the most diverse societies in the world. For, it has borrowed food ingredients and cooking styles heavily and openly from all corners of the world.[3] Indeed, 'the story of Indian food,' as Ashis Nandy reminds one, 'is often the story of the blatantly exogenous becoming prototypically authentic.'[4] On the other hand however, a significant body of work—led by the researches of the Indian anthropologist Ravindra S. Khare—has examined what has been described as 'gastro-semantics', namely, how the symbolism and communication involved in the cultural language of food link the worldly aspects of Hindu society with

The History and Historiography of Indian Food

its other-worldly ones. Although it sheds important light on the ethnography of food as articulated in ideas of the cooked and the raw, the pure and the polluted, the sanctified and the profane, community, commensality, etc., such work has tended to exaggerate the pervasive cosmic presence of food in the Hindu moral universe and reinforce the Indological emphasis on India's exceptionalism and essential difference from the west.[5]

EVIDENCE FROM EARLY INDIA AND THE ORIGINS OF VEGETARIANISM

Historians speculate that the first humans came to the Indian subcontinent by sea from East Africa and by land from East Asia at different times, and that their pointed stone tools indicated a mainly meat based diet, possibly complemented with natural foods like honey, berries, fruits, roots, herbs and nuts. The development of Neolithic tools from about 5000 BC made possible the transition from hunting and gathering to agriculture, accompanied by new processes like the grinding of grain and spices. This soon led to the emergence of rice as a dietary staple, coupled with *ragi* (a kind of millet), lentils, pumpkin, eggplant, banana, coconut, pomegranate, jackfruit, orange, limes, watermelon, gourds and squashes of various kinds, and the edible parts of the lotus plant. By this time, the domestication of animals like sheep, goats and buffalos—for the purposes of farming, eating, and dairying—was a well marked feature of the culture of the subcontinent.

The Harappan civilization, which flourished from 2500 BC to 1600 BC, contributed richly to this developing mosaic of Indian food culture. Wheat and barley were the main crops grown by the Harappans, who prepared bread in round ovens similar to those used in the Middle East and Central Asia, and used animal fats for cooking. Among other foods consumed were rice, oats, peas, chickpeas, lentils and fruits such as dates, pomegranates and perhaps bananas. Bone remnants excavated from the Harappan sites indicate both excessive meat eating and the consumption of fish from the river and the Indian Ocean. During the ensuing thousand years or so, when groups of Indo-Aryan speakers from central Asia gradually migrated into the subcontinent, cleared the thick forests of northern India, and settled down along the valley of the River Ganges, the consumption patterns did not witness any dramatic changes, though an important innovation of this period growing out of the rising importance of the cow, was a significant consumption of milk and dairy products like butter, cream, yogurt or clarified butter (*ghee*), which itself quickly became an important cooking medium.

The really intriguing question with regard to food habits in ancient India is the emergence of the concepts of vegetarianism and abstinence as critically important ethical doctrines among significant sections of the Indian population who came to avoid the consumption of food that necessitated the taking of life. This is a curious development, given that meat-eating was widely prevalent in ancient India, both in the north and in the south. The researches of Om Prakash on food and drink in ancient India and of Jeannine Auboyer on daily life, document a large variety of animals—including cows, sheep, goats, horses, swine, deer and tortoise—whose flesh were consumed by Indo-Aryans in the Vedic period, often after ceremonial sacrifice, but also as part of more 'regular' meals and as offerings made to guests.[6] The use of sacrificial meat continued in the period after 800 BC, and even the Buddhist *Jataka* tales mention the practice of consuming the meat of the pigeon, partridge, monkey and elephant. Indeed, Buddha did allow the consumption of meat, especially if it was offered as alms to monks. The most famous medical treatises of ancient India—the *Charaka-samhita* (*c*. first century AD) and the *Sushruta-samhita* (probably originated in the last centuries of BC and had become fixed in its present form by the seventh century AD)—present formidable lists of edible meats which were deemed suitable for people of varying body types and health conditions. Francis Zimmerman's work on the concepts of ecology and traditional medicine (*ayurveda*) among Hindus in ancient India contends that the Indian equivalent of what the Europeans called 'the great chain of being' was a sequence of foods at the end of which were various cooked meats whose savours permeated the natural domain.[7]

However, early notions of vegetarianism were also developed in the midst of this widespread culture of meat-eating, perhaps as early as the Vedic period itself, when the taking of life for food began to be questioned. A textual critique of meat-eating began to develop in the later Vedic period, evident in the *Shatapatha Brahmana* and later in the *Dharma Sutras* and then in the *Dharmashastras* like *Manu Smriti*. The celebrated Indian food historian, K.T. Achaya, has shown that utilitarian economic needs—and not humanitarian impulses—led to the early prohibitions on the slaughter of milch cows or draught oxen, and a larger concern for the taking of animal life developed much later and as a gradual process.[8] Eventually, the Buddhists and the Jains prevailed in this campaign to put an end to Vedic animal sacrifices. The emergent concept of *ahimsa* or non-killing gradually began to resonate with a significant number of people and was made into a moral compass of the state by Ashoka, the Buddhist Emperor of the Maurya dynasty. This received strong endorsement from influential reformist and devotionalist schools of Hindu philosophy in early medieval India between around 800 AD and 1200 AD, and consequently—with the exception of those living in Kashmir, Bengal, and a part of Karnataka—Brahmans were gradually obliged to become vegetarians. The lower castes, however, were much less affected by the social taboo against meat-eating.

ISLAMIC AND EARLY EUROPEAN INFLUENCES

The Muslim influence on the style and substance of Indian food was profound. K.T. Achaya writes that the Muslims imported a new refinement and a courtly etiquette of both group and individual dining into the austere dining ambience of Hindu society.[9] Coming originally from modern-day Uzbekistan, Tajikistan, Kyrgyzstan, and Kazakhstan, the Mughals initially had a culinary style influenced by the nomadic lifestyle of the steppes, revolving around simple grilling and boiling. The later refinement came mainly from Persian sources, especially after Babur's son, Humayun, came back to India after spending a long period of exile in Kabul and the imperial court in Iran. He brought with him an entourage of Persian cooks who introduced the rich and elaborate rice cookery of the Safavid courts to India, combining Indian spices and Persian arts into a rich fusion that became the iconic dish of Islamic South Asian cuisine, the biryani.[10] In general, during the centuries of Muslim rule food items native to India were enriched with nuts, raisins and other dried fruits, saffron, musk, asafoetida and other aromatic spices and liberal doses of clarified butter (*ghee*). These materials went into the making of meat and rice dishes (*pulao*), marinated meat (*kabab*) grilled usually in a clay oven traditionally sunk into the ground (*tandoor*), oven baked or fried flatbreads (*naan* or *paratha*), spicy stews of rice and lentils (*khichri*), pastries with savory fillings (*samosa*), desserts (*halwa*), and sweetened drinks (*falooda, sherbet*).[11] It has been rightly said that by the time the Mughal Empire reached the peak of its power around the turn of the seventeenth century, royal cuisine 'had been elevated to the level of a state concern', as indicated by the significant space that the Mughal emperor Akbar's famous court historian, Abul Fazl, devotes to it in the imperial gazetteer, the *Ain-i-Akbari*.[12] In reality, it was the Mughals who first gave shape to the concept of an Indian cuisine, though it never acquired truly pan-Indian proportions. And, although its close association with a feudal lifestyle and expensive ingredients made it primarily an *haute cuisine*, pared-down versions gradually came to be adopted by the common people, especially in northern India.[13]

The other decisive influence on Indian food habits in this period came, of course, from the contact with Europe and through it with the New World. In 1498, six years after Christopher Columbus set foot on the West Indies, the Portuguese seaman Vasco da Gama found the sea route to India and landed on the subcontinent's southwestern Malabar coast. The Portuguese were followed soon by the Dutch, French, and British trading companies, the last of which eventually established their political hegemony in the subcontinent in the second half of the eighteenth century. The Portuguese presence by then became confined to their main outpost in Goa on India's western coast, but not before they had used their series of forts and factories stretching from Brazil to Japan to create an extensive trading empire that ushered India into the Columbian Exchange—a global exchange of food crops, populations, ideas, and diseases between the New World and the Old World following Columbus's voyage to the Americas. The other factor contributing to a global exchange was the Spanish conquest of the Philippines in the 1560s, which made it possible for the goods of the New World to make their way into India also from the opposite direction across the Pacific and the eastern Indian Ocean.

In India, the Portuguese introduced a wide range of new foods, including potatoes, tomatoes, chili peppers, kidney beans, maize, tapioca, papayas, pineapples, guavas, sugar-apples, cashews, peanuts, and sunflower seeds (the two latter products pressed for oil used in cooking), tobacco and turkey from the New World, okra and coffee from Africa, and tea, soybeans and litchis from China. The extent to which these products were assimilated in the regional cuisines was truly remarkable. In Goa itself, the interaction between the Portuguese influence and the local food of the Saraswath caste of western India gave rise to a distinctive cuisine. In Bengal in eastern India, the Portuguese generated a significant demand for cottage cheese, which was adapted by Bengali cooks into the chief ingredient of a wide range of sweetmeats. The potato quickly found general acceptance, and Indian cuisine gradually became one of the very few in the world to convert the potato from a side dish to the centrepiece of many recipes. Kidney beans, cooked like lentils, too became one of the staple dishes of northern India.[14] And chillies, of course, became the iconic marker of the spiciness of Indian cuisine, as well as an easily affordable ingredient for the common people to add some flavour and taste to their diet.

BRITISH COLONIALISM AND THE EVOLUTION OF FOOD HABITS IN INDIA

Although the Portuguese were the first to arrive in India, it was the British East India Company, which in the second half of the eighteenth century, went on to launch a subcontinental colonial empire. The transformation of the company into an imperial power was, however a long drawn out process, that started in Bengal and gradually came to engulf virtually the whole subcontinent by the

1850s. Until the early nineteenth century, the British sought to rule India through an Indian idiom and consequently, the Company's men in India often pursued a 'native' lifestyle, learning Indian languages, taking Indian wives and mistresses, and eating spicy Indian food made by local cooks as well as hybrid dishes conjured up by the English lady of the house, including rice *pulao*s, *biryani*s, Indian style pickles and relishes and *kedgeree*—an anglicized version of the Indian *khichri*.

European attitudes towards India and its inhabitants were varied and often ambivalent, yet there was one basic assumption underlying all British colonial medical texts from the 1770s to the 1850s—a belief in the uniqueness of the Indian tropical disease environment and the need for a fundamental reappraisal of European medical knowledge in the light of this. Most medical men believed that there was nothing inevitable about sickness in the tropics, and that it could be prevented by avoiding the inappropriate diet of Europeans, which revolved around an overconsumption of every sort of meat, including pork and beef, both roast and curried. Letters from Bengal written by the English traveller Eliza Fay reveal that, notwithstanding the oppressive heat of the tropics, their regular 'bill of fare' in the afternoons consisted of 'a soup, a roast fowl, curry and rice, a mutton pie, a fore-quarter of lamb, a rice pudding, tarts, very good cheese, fresh churned butter, fine bread, [and] excellent Madeira'.[15] Indeed, as Elizabeth Collingham's work has shown, during the early decades of the British East India Company's rule in India, such ostentatious and unhealthy dining habits 'served well to underline the status of the Company grandee in India'. With the increasing racialization of colonial rule after 1858—when, following the suppression of the first war of Indian independence of 1857, the Indian empire passed under the direct rule of the British Crown—the body of the colonial official in India became an even more powerful signifier of 'Britishness', and diet and dress became accordingly, cultural sites on which a sense of bodily difference between the British and their Indian subjects was maintained.[16] Though this entailed a refinement of the eating etiquette compared to the meat-eating excesses of the earlier period, elaborate meals continued to be the norm, until at least the advent of the twentieth century, when lighter meals acquired increasing favour.[17]

Similarly, Dipesh Chakrabarty's work on the culture of managerial power in Bengal's jute mills around the turn of the nineteenth century shows that the lifestyle—and especially the food habits—of the British jute mill managers contained an element of spectacle as an important aspect of their physical superiority vis-à-vis the millhands. In such circumstances, as Chakrabarty suggests, 'eating was a ritualised expression of a colonial ruling-class culture... signifying... excess and plenitude'. Thus, an early-morning 'small breakfast' (*chota haziri*) of a handful of toasts, a few eggs and a large pot of tea was duly followed by a regular breakfast consisting of 'fish, stewed steak and onions, eggs, curried fowl and rice, with the usual addenda of tea or coffee, with bread, butter and jam'. Some went further and gleefully downed a few pegs of whiskey and soda before going back to work.[18]

Just as these ostentatious eating habits were deployed as the cultural markers of a masculine, physically superior British Raj, the native kitchen or 'cookhouse' was very bleakly portrayed as symbolic of all that was filthy, dirty and uncouth about oriental cultures. The author of a cookbook described a typical kitchen in an Anglo-Indian compound as 'a wretchedly mean, carelessly constructed, godown [outbuilding]... inconveniently far from the house, and consequently open to every passer-by'.[19] Further, because of inadequate equipment, the cook had to use 'his cloth for a sieve, and his fingers for a spoon or fork'.[20] Given this description, it is perhaps not surprising that yet another cookbook cautioned, 'The native ways are not as our ways and the less you see of them over their cooking operations the more appetite you will have for the food set before you.'[21]

Generally speaking, the gastronomic habits of the British in Bengal—including conspicuous consumption bordering on gluttony in the early days of Company rule, and more refined but elaborate meals in the second half of the nineteenth century—served as a metaphor for the racial and physical superiority of the Raj. Although such dietary habits were firmly castigated from the 'scientific' viewpoint—most frequently by climatologists and medical men—the table manners of the Raj obviously valued symbolism over science. The Indian kitchen as an object of revulsion was the other part of the same worldview. The dark mysteries of the orient manifested themselves within the cookhouse in many ways—through the heat, smoke and filth, as well as through the cunning of foxy cooks or *bawarchis*, who pinched provisions, padded their accounts, and—worst of all—used their curry powder to enliven what a 1906 cookbook described as 'superannuated fish or meat'.[22]

Indeed, it was in such a hybrid world of cooking ingredients and styles that the concept of the 'curry' was born and gained acceptance in Anglo-Indian cuisine in the late eighteenth and through much of the nineteenth century. Towards the later part of that century its popularity went into a decline, though eventually—for most non-Indians—curry became a blanket catchphrase for every Indian dish. It has rightly been said that it was a British invention, both the word (adapted from the Tamil word *kari*, which means black pepper) and the ingredients that went into its making. As a generic term, curry designated a spicy stew of meat, fish or vegetables, cooked in clarified butter or oil, with a large array of dry roasted whole or ground spices, frequently involving onions, ginger and garlic, sometimes including tamarind and/or coconut milk or flesh, and typically eaten with rice. Colonial officials returning to Britain, no longer able to depend on Indian cooks, acquired commercial curry powder mixtures to try at home in the middle decades of the nineteenth century. Curry gradually became, as has been argued recently, 'not just a term that the British used to describe an unfamiliar set of Indian stews and ragouts, but a dish in its own right, created for the British in India'.[23]

COOKING, FOOD, AND THE MIDDLE CLASSES IN INDIA AND ABROAD

A recent important development in the field of Indian food history has been a growing interest in an examination of how themes related to cooking, food, nutrition and the relationship between dietary practice and health came to preoccupy the intellectual worlds of the educated middle classes in many parts of colonial India. With the growth of English education among the primarily Hindu upper caste, urban sections of the British Indian population, the articulation of a new set of values, prejudices and tastes for these middle classes often came to be deeply implicated in thinking and discussion about modernity and nationalism. Though this emerging literature is less about food *per se* than about cooking and eating as cultural practices, it touches on several themes intimately connected with food—for instance, the relationship between food habits and the rise of the health sciences, ideas of an 'appropriate diet' for different categories of Indians, debates about the place of cooking in the world of the educated, refined 'New Indian Woman' and the emergence of a well organized kitchen as the centrepiece of a new, reformed, efficient ideology of domesticity. This is a welcome development in the field, because it brings the history of Indian food squarely within the ambit of scholarship on the cultural politics of Indian modernity.[24] One of the most interesting instances of this literature is an examination of modern Indian cookbooks as cultural texts, leading to the argument that the making of a truly national Indian cuisine is a postcolonial process in which cookbooks have openly paraded the regional roots of their recipes, and so aided the 'culinary cosmopolitanism' of a multiethnic, polyglot, consumerist Indian middle class whose very cultural identity is defined by an 'interplay of regional inflection and national standardization'.[25]

Within the very broad north-south division in Indian political and cultural geography, there is an enormous regional diversity in Indian cuisine that belies most broad generalizations and the popular identification of 'Indian food' with the inauthentic, spiced-up Mughal-Punjabi fare dished out in the majority of Indian restaurants in the west. Outside of the southern half of the subcontinent, there are well defined regional food traditions in Kashmir, Punjab, Rajasthan, Gujarat and Bengal, among others.

The connection between the growth of a global Indian diaspora and the export of Indian food abroad is close, but often belies simple generalizations. Colleen Taylor Sen has shown that the first Indian restaurants—or 'curry houses' as they were called in the early nineteenth century—in Britain came up as early as 1809, much before the formation of any significant Indian immigrant population. It was, however, from the 1920s onwards, that Indian restaurants started increasing in popularity, eventually exploding in a remarkable boom from the 1980s onwards, as hordes of people from the South Asian nations—mainly India, Pakistan, and Bangladesh—began taking advantage of liberal immigration laws to make their way into Britain and hike up the demand for 'ethnic' food. Currently, Indian food is a $5 billion industry in Britain, and approximately 8,000 Indian restaurants in that country account for two-thirds of eating out, prompting the former British Foreign Secretary Robin Cook in 2001 to proclaim 'chicken *tikka masala*'—marinated pieces of chicken grilled and then simmered in a spicy sauce—a 'true British national dish'.[26] By contrast, in the United States, the relative affluence of Indian immigrants—and the difference in tastes compared to those of the poorer working-class immigrants to Britain—has stopped short of spawning a 'tandoori' or 'tikka' revolution of the kind witnessed in contemporary Britain through ubiquitous budget restaurants. Despite the relative growth of Indian restaurants in the last three decades, Indian food continues to lag far behind the most popular ethnic-restaurant options like Italian or Chinese. With a few notable exceptions, restaurants in both Britain and the United States have been largely unable or even unwilling, to serve food that genuinely represents the huge regional diversity of Indian cuisine, relying on a kind of hybrid Mughal-Punjabi fare (in Britain, often accompanied by a Bangladeshi style) as their staple. This is only inadequately compensated for by the increasing availability of a wide array of regional speciality dishes in the form of precooked and packaged ready-to-eat single-serving meals manufactured by processed food companies like House of Spices, Deep Foods, and MTR, and—increasingly in Britain—Patak's, and the ethnic foods section of the supermarket giant, Sainsbury's.

Other than its obvious contribution to the growth of an Indian food business overseas, the Indian diaspora has also in recent times featured some interesting new trends in the burgeoning field of Indian food history. The most significant of these has been an examination of how Indian immigrants seek to preserve their ties to a homeland—real or imagined—through their preservation of and participation in traditional customs and rituals of consumption. A number of studies attest to the strong connection between Indian ethnic food in the markets of the west and the national self-identification of diasporic Indians.[27] This connection has many facets—from the cooking of authentic Indian meals at home to the increasing number and popularity of Indian restaurants, and the growing availability of the specialized ingredients of authentic Indian cooking in specialty ethnic grocery stores. An interesting recent addition to this literature is a genre that can be best described as 'culinary nostalgia'—articulated through memoirs, written mostly by diasporic Indian authors, centred on the theme of food as a crucial catalyst of socialization, interspersed with recipes savoured and learned in childhood.[28] Though framed as personal narratives, these memories are important documents for food historians, precisely because they help to explore the interstices of history and memory through the trope of food.

TEACHING FOOD HISTORY IN INDIA: A CONCLUDING HOPE

That brings us to a concluding hope with which this piece is going to end. One has seen how the history of food and of cooking and eating as cultural practices has burgeoned in recent times and shows all signs of developing into a major strand of the history of South Asia. But is there a way of conveying the excitement of this new subfield to students in the classroom? In other words, can one teach courses on food history to our students in colleges and universities, to try and give them a sense of the interdisciplinary flavour that it brings, and the useful and interesting window it offers into the broader trends and patterns of Indian and world history. Needless to say, the most organic connection that such Indian food history courses must maintain is with larger themes of global and transnational history, such as human migrations and settlements, trade, travel, imperialism, colonialism, modernity and globalization. On the one hand, the study of Indian food has to be grounded in a history of India's evolving material culture, shaped invariably by its climate, social formations, patterns of state formation and economic production, historical contacts with the outside world, and the experiences of Muslim rule and British colonialism. However, food has also traditionally held many complex symbolic meanings in Indian society, and—in this particular sense—not only has its preparation, handling and sharing shaped rules of inclusion and exclusion in social interaction, but it has also been fetishized into national cuisines and driven nostalgic recollections of lost pasts or imaginary homelands. A course on Indian food history must design itself to take both of these aspects into account. Significant efforts have already been made in quite a few South Asia teaching programmes in universities in the west, so why should we be left behind? Let one strongly hope, therefore, that one will—sooner than later—have the teaching of culinary and alimentary history to chart out some preliminary pathways to some of the most fascinating insights into our civilization.

NOTES

1. See, for instance, Srirupa Prasad, 'Crisis, Identity, and Social Distinction: Cultural Politics of Food, Taste, and Consumption in Late Colonial Bengal', *Journal of Historical Sociology*, *19*(3) (2006), pp. 246-65; *Cultural Politics of Hygiene in India, 1890-1940: Contagions of Feelings* (New York: Palgrave Macmillan, 2015); Utsa Ray, *Culinary Culture in Colonial India: A Cosmopolitan Platter and the Middle-Class* (New Delhi: Cambridge University Press, 2015); Rohan Deb Roy, 'Debility, Diet, Desire: Food in Nineteenth Century Bengali Manuals', in Supriya Chaudhuri and Rimi B. Chatterjee (eds.), *The Writer's Feast: Food and the Cultures of Representation* (New Delhi: Orient BlackSwan, 2011), pp. 179-205; and Jayanta Sengupta, 'Nation on a Platter: the Culture and Politics of Food and Cuisine in Colonial Bengal', *Modern Asian Studies*, *44*(1) (2010), pp. 81-98.
2. World Bank Report, 'New Global Poverty Estimates: What it Means for India', http://go.worldbank.org/51QB3OCFU0, accessed on 20 April 2012.
3. K.T. Achaya, *Indian Food: A Historical Companion* (Delhi: Oxford University Press, 1994).

4. Ashis Nandy, 'The Changing Popular Culture of Indian Food: Preliminary Notes', *South Asia Research* 24(9) (May 2004), p. 11.
5. R.S. Khare, *Culture and Reality: Essays on the Hindu System of Managing Foods* (Simla: Indian Institute of Advanced Study, 1976); Ibid., *The Hindu Hearth and Home* (Durham: Carolina Academic Press, 1976); Ibid., ed., *The Eternal Food: Gastronomic Ideas and Experiences of Hindus and Buddhists* (Albany: State University of New York Press, 1992); Ibid., and M.S.A. Rao, eds., *Food, Society, and Culture: Aspects in South Asian Food Systems* (Durham: Carolina Academic Press, 1986). For a similar study of food symbolisms—which compares Khare's work on northern Indian Brahmans with fieldwork conducted among Brahmans of Tamil Nadu in south India—see, Arjun Appadurai, 'Gastro-Politics in Hindu South Asia', *American Ethnologist*, 8(3) (August 1981), pp. 494-511.
6. Om Prakash, *Food and Drinks in Ancient India: From Earliest Times to c.1200 AD* (Delhi: Munshiram Manoharlal, 1961); Jeannine Auboyer, *Daily Life in Ancient India, from approximately 200 BC to AD 700*, trans. Simon Watson Taylor (London: Weidenfeld and Nicolson, 1965).
7. Francis Zimmermann, *The Jungle and the Aroma of Meats: An Ecological Theme in Hindu Medicine* (Delhi: Motilal Banarsidass, 1999).
8. Achaya, *Indian Food*, p. 55.
9. Ibid., p. 154.
10. Sami Zubaida, 'The Idea of "Indian Food", between the Colonial and the Global', *Food and History* 7(1) (2009), pp. 191-209.
11. Achaya, *Indian Food*, p. 154.
12. Hashi Raychaudhuri and Tapan Raychaudhuri, 'Not by Curry Alone: An Introductory Essay on Indian Cuisines for a Western Audience', in *Food in Motion: The Migration of Foodstuffs and Cookery Techniques*, ed. Alan Davidson, Proceedings of the Oxford Symposium on Food 1981 (London: Prospect Books, 1981), pp. 45-56.
13. For detailed descriptions of the food habits of Mughal India, see Lizzie Collingham, *Curry: A Tale of Cooks and Conquerors* (New York; Oxford: Oxford University Press, 2006), pp. 13-45; Joyce Westrip, *Moghul Cooking: India's Courtly Cuisine* (London: Serif, 2005).
14. For the Portuguese contribution to Indian food, see Lizzie Collingham, *Curry: A Tale of Cooks and Conquerors*, pp. 47-80. For their impact on an important Indian regional cuisine, see Colleen Taylor Sen, 'The Portuguese Influence on Bengali Cuisine', in *Food on the Move*, ed. Harlan Walker, Proceedings of the Oxford Symposium on Food and Cookery 1996 (Blackawton, Devon, UK: Prospect Books, 1996), pp. 288-98.
15. Eliza Fay, *The Original Letters from India of Mrs. Eliza Fay* (Calcutta: Thacker, Spink & Co., 1908), p. 140.

16. E.M. Collingham, *Imperial Bodies: The Physical Experience of the Raj, c.1800-1947* (Cambridge: Polity Press, 2001), pp. 13-116.
17. For the food habits of the British colonial ruling class, see Cecilia Leong-Salobir, *Food Culture in Colonial Asia: A Taste of Empire* (London; New York: Routledge, 2011), pp. 12-38; David Burton, *The Raj at Table: A Culinary History of the British in India* (London: Faber and Faber, 1993); Lizzie Collingham, *Curry: A Tale of Cooks and Conquerors*; Achaya, 'The Coming of the Europeans', in *Indian Food*, pp. 163-78.
18. Dipesh Chakrabarty, *Rethinking Working-Class History: Bengal, 1890-1940* (Delhi: Oxford University Press, 1989), p. 167.
19. Wyvern [Arthur Kenney-Herbert], *Culinary Jottings: A Treatise in Thirty Chapters on Reformed Cookery for Anglo-Indian Exiles* (Madras: Higginbotham and Co., 1885), p. 499.
20. Ibid.
21. An Anglo-Indian [pseud.], *Indian Outfits and Establishments: A Practical Guide for Persons About to Reside in India* (London: L. Upcott Gill, 1882), p. 68.
22. Shalot [pseud.], *Things for the Cook: In English and Hindustani* (Calcutta: Thacker and Spink, 1906), p. 89. For a study of the deep-seated Anglo-Indian misgivings about the native 'bazar' and the Indian cook, see Mary Procida, 'Feeding the Imperial Appetite: Imperial Knowledge and Anglo-Indian Domesticity', *Journal of Women's History*, 15(2) (Summer 2003), pp. 123-49.
23. For the evolution of the curry as a culinary concept, see Lizzie Collingham, *Curry: A Tale of Cooks and Conquerors*; Colleen Taylor Sen, *Curry: A Global History* (London: Reaktion Books, 2009); Leong-Salobir, 'The Colonial Appropriation of Curry', in *Food Culture in Colonial Asia*, pp. 39-58; and Shrabani Basu, *Curry: The Story of the Nation's Favourite Dish* (Stroud: Sutton, 2003).
24. David Arnold, 'The "Discovery" of Malnutrition and Diet in Colonial India', *Indian Economic and Social History Review*, 31(1) (October 1994), pp. 1-26, Mary Hancock, 'Home Science and the Nationalization of Domesticity in Colonial India', *Modern Asian Studies*, 35(4) (October 2001), pp. 871-903; Chakrabarty, 'The Difference-Deferral of (A) Colonial Modernity: Public Debates on Domesticity in British Bengal', in *Subaltern Studies VIII: Writings on South Asian History and Society*, ed. David Arnold and David Hardiman (Delhi: Oxford University Press, 1994), pp. 50-88; Srirupa Prasad, 'Crisis, Identity, and Social Distinction: Cultural Politics of Food, Taste, and Consumption in Late Colonial Bengal', *Journal of Historical Sociology*, 19(3) (September 2006), pp. 245-65; Jayanta

Sengupta, 'Nation on a Platter: the Culture and Politics of Food and Cuisine in Colonial Bengal', *Modern Asian Studies*, 44(1) (January 2010), pp. 81-98; Utsa Ray, 'Eating "Modernity": Changing Dietary Practices in Colonial Bengal', *Modern Asian Studies*, 46(3) (May 2012), pp. 703-29.
25. Arjun Appadurai, 'How to Make a National Cuisine: Cookbooks in Contemporary India,' *Comparative Studies in Society and History*, 30(1), (January 1988), pp. 3-24.
26. Colleen Taylor Sen, *Curry: A Global History*, pp. 36-51; Lizzie Collingham, *Curry: A Tale of Cooks and Conquerors*, pp. 215-43; Jo Monroe, *Star of India: The Spicy Adventures of Curry* (Chichester; Hoboken: Wiley, 2005).
27. Krishnendu Ray, *The Migrant's Table: Meals and Memories in Bengali-American Households* (Philadelphia: Temple University Press, 2004); Ketu Katrak, for instance, has written about how—on coming to the United States as a graduate student—her childhood uninterest in food 'was transformed into a new kind of need for that food as an essential connection with home'. See Ketu Katrak, 'Food and Belonging: At "Home" and in "Alien-Kitchens", in *Through the Kitchen Window: Women Explore the Intimate Meanings of Food and Cooking*, ed. Arlene Voski Avakian (New York; Oxford: Berg, 2005), pp. 263-75; Uma Narayan, 'Eating Cultures: Incorporation, Identity, and Indian Food', in *Dislocating Cultures: Identities, Traditions, and Third-World Feminism* (London: Routledge, 1997), pp. 159-88; Purnima Mankekar, 'India Shopping: Indian Grocery Stores and Transnational Configurations of Belonging', in *Cultural Politics of Food and Eating: A Reader*, ed. James L. Watson and Melissa Caldwell (Oxford: Blackwell, 2005), pp. 197-214; and Sharmila Sen, 'Indian Spices across the Black Waters', in *From Betty Crocker to Feminist Food Studies: Critical Perspectives on Women and Food*, ed. Arlene Voski Avakian and Barbara Haber (Amherst; Boston: University of Massachusetts Press, 2005), pp. 185-99.
28. For typical representative samples, see Chitrita Banerji, *Life and Food in Bengal* (Delhi: Rupa, 1993); Ibid., The *Hour of the Goddess: Memories of Women, Food, and Ritual in Bengal* (Calcutta: Seagull Books, 2006); Ibid., *Feeding the Gods: Memories of Food and Culture in Bengal* (New York; Oxford: Seagull, 2006); Shoba Narayan, *Monsoon Diary: A Memoir with Recipes* (New York: Villard, 2003); Raghavan Iyer, *The Turmeric Trail: Recipes and Memories from an Indian Childhood* (New York: St. Martin's Press, 2002). For a recent study on how food shapes the cultural imagination of diasporic populations, see Anita Mannur, *Culinary Fictions: Food in South Asian Diasporic Culture* (Philadelphia: Temple University Press, 2010).

CHAPTER 2

Food and Fellowship

MIHIR BHATTACHARYA

THE REPUBLIC OF HUNGER

The most important fact about food and eating in India is that a third of its people go hungry to bed at night and that another third are chronically undernourished; consequently more than half of the Indian population are prone to disease and despair, their mind occupied less with the palate than with the tummy. This is why this writer has chosen the title of Utsa Patnaik's pathbreaking book as the first subheading (Utsa Patnaik, *The Republic of Hunger*, 2007). It's true that India has been a hungry subcontinent throughout history, just like most of the inhabited world before imperialism tweaked the wealth of nations into a system of plenty for the few and very little for most. The wealth of the few increased at a breakneck speed from the rapacious extraction of natural resources and ruthless exploitation of human labour, often enslaved and indentured and always oppressed today one has arrived at a juncture when the planet is becoming rapidly unsuitable for human beings as well as other living creatures and mankind is facing a permanent condition of war, anarchy and inequity. Talking of food and cooking in this context is all the more necessary because it shows up at one end the human resources of labour, invention and fellowship and on the other, the proliferating pornography of excess and indulgence and waste. What is often called 'popular' food belongs somewhere in-between and in India, the large world of snacks and what goes by the name of 'tiffin', shows a capacity for change—marked by ingenuity and regional variations—worthy of a special study. Street food is always a dynamic area, but the people's basic food, cooked mostly at home in both town and country has remained largely constant, and that is one of the things one wishes to discuss.

The contrast between the top and the bottom rungs of social structure turns starker from the last decade of the last century, when the neoliberal Structural Adjustment Programme sweeps all the nations into its ambit of globalization and the Soviet Union collapses and governments everywhere start squeezing the people in order to make the rich richer. The last three decades have seen an increasing immiseration of the working people in the global south (the advanced capitalist economies having set up safety nets for their own workers) and an income inflation for the creamy layer everywhere. A new wave of consumerism has therefore kicked in and the affluent in the poorer countries have started feeling smug and secure in their cozy gated communities. This we-have-never-had-it-so-good syndrome manifests itself in, among other things, an indulgence in comestibles, the two polarities of which are a globalized homogenization of taste and, on the other side, an appetite for the exotic and the different in food and drink. Coca Colization and McDonaldization co-exist happily with the cultivation of taste for Single Malts and *Cordon Bleu* cookery, describing two moments of the same group sanction. The proliferation of consumables has been mediated by a powerful media industry which makes you play the game of keeping-up-with-the-Joneses as a faithful lackey of corporate transnationals. Thus, the current phase of globalization has brought in a spontaneous process of absorption and incorporation of the articulate citizens into worship of idols of the marketplace, in spite of the daily spectacle of murder and mayhem and misery. The crisis of 2008-11 has not taught anybody anything. Neo-imperialism, meanwhile aligns happily with all regressive forces in the interest of primitive accumulation and expansion of markets. The times are the best for some and the worst for many. Talking of food at this juncture is very much a matter of the moment, for it is at the centre of things which mark the lineaments of the crisis mankind faces.

THE UNIFIED FIELD OF FOOD-MAKING: PRAJNASUNDARI'S RECIPES

Since one would be talking of Bengali food for the most part, including food for the rich and food for the poor, one can go back in time and pick out an important historical document from the late years of the nineteenth century to illustrate some of the points one will be making. This is a largish tome in Bangla called *amish o niramish aahar*, 'Non-vegetarian and Vegetarian Food', Part 1, by Prajnasundari Devi, second daughter of Hemendranath Tagore (one of the many elder brothers of Rabindranath) and Neepamoyee Devi. She had married Lakshminath Bezbaroa in 1891. This volume came out in the year 1900, and two subsequent volumes appeared later, with a separate volume on Assamese cooking, but the work for the book and the preparatory notes were largely gathered in the 1880s and 1890s, both before and after the author's marriage.

As was the custom those days, Prajnasundari continued to be an apprentice at first and then moved towards being something of a 'master chef', in two large affluent enlightened kitchens. The Tagore family was itself a considerable consumer of food and their kitchens had been sites of experiment and innovation throughout the nineteenth century, especially its second half, when educated and forward-looking scions of the family began to take an interest in matters of the domestic interior. This was part of the civilizational project which involved the search for modernity and enlightenment in both home and the world. Prajna's father, Hemendranath Tagore (1844-84), was a keen student of the natural sciences and had written a small treatise on the subject which was published posthumously. He was himself interested in cooking and encouraged the younger members of the family to try this 'fine art'; he had filled a notebook with recipes which he had found interesting (Chitra Deb, *thakurbarir andarmahal*, 'The Inner Household of the Tagores'). One doesn't know the date of Prajnasundari's move from the Tagore to the Bezbaroa establishment, but it is likely to have been soon after their marriage, when Lakshminath (b. October 1864) would be in his late twenties and Prajnasundari (b. 1870?) just past twenty.

It seems that she married late. Girls would be married off in pre-teenage and early teenage those days, irrespective of class, caste and community and stories of lost childhood and lost adolescence were nearly universal. But the Tagore family was an exception, and some of their girls—not all, including Rabindranath's daughters—married late and their period of upbringing in the huge joint family in Kolkata was full of activities. Very few went to school though, let alone college—formal education for women was just about starting—but most of the Tagore girls were well read, active and exceptionally accomplished. Prajna had attended the Loreto School run by Christian missionaries. The girls were moreover brought up to value cultural and social work and were therefore involved in enterprises which linked them to the world outside home. The family brought out journals, wrote poetry, fiction and essays, wrote and produced plays, drew and painted, learnt, composed and practised music, gave lessons to dependents and children, designed revolutionary dresses, formed societies and organized charities, preached reformed religion and spread the messages of social reform and political nationalism. The daughters and wives of the Tagores had a pioneering role in these enlightening enterprises. This added a discreet charm to the quantum of elegance they had acquired at home. Lakshminath, who was a near contemporary of Prajnasundari's uncle Rabindranath and was engaged in the modernizing project of Assamese culture, is reputed to have had one look at a photograph of young Prajnasundari and decided to marry her. The marriage took place in spite of his family's objections; Prajna was a sweet tempered accomplished and accommodating bride, and theirs was a very happy life together. One would like to think that Prajnasundari's cooking had something to do with this familial bliss.

She was an accomplished and innovative cook, as the recipes reveal. She states that each and every item has been cooked in her kitchen and tested by her family and guests. The food she offers has enormous variety. But much more remarkable is the idea of an integration of the food culture with an overarching elegance of living which was emerging at the time. Cleanliness, order, grace, and a certain exteriority of orientation in the organization of family life became a norm in certain circles. Women would come out of the interior and meet others—even strangers—and offer hospitality. The kitchen got a make-over; the dining-space was marked off and spruced up; furniture and utensils and tableware went through a process of aestheticization; cooking was not any longer a hole-and-corner activity away from the daily round of civilized living. Therefore, when one broaches this matter of 'new' cooking, one is talking about the dawn of a new era in the life of the educated middle and upper middle classes in colonial India. The basic and distinctive mode of Bengali cooking—the ingredients and the processing, that is—did not change much, but the whole ambience and culture of preparation and consumption of food changed drastically. One is of course talking of the tiny minority of affluent families which would invest in the new political economy of the household. Whereas the larger majority of the labouring poor carried on as usual with both the raw and the cooked, the cold and the hot parts of their daily diet; many affluent people remained strictly traditional in the kitchen and the inner household, observing the purity codes and the taboos, keeping their women confined to the interior parts. The kitchen continued to be a prison for womenfolk in many households. One has to remember Rasa Sundari Devi's (1809-99) desperate endeavour to educate herself in the secrecy of the traditional kitchen of a large Hindu household (as narrated in her autobiography, *amar jiban*, 'My Life'). But for a tiny minority, it became a site of freedom and creativity and fellowship. It is still the women's preserve; but a change is visible in the dynamic equation of food and gender.

THE ENLIGHTENED KITCHEN

There are nearly two and a half thousand separate entries in Prajnasundari's cookbook, collected in the three volume edition which came out in 1995, meticulously edited by her granddaughter, Ira Ghosh, who has painstakingly added a number of entries collected from old notebooks and journals. The work is voluminous but carefully organized. The first volume of the new edition, devoted to vegetarian food, follows the traditional order of eating: rice, boiled vegetable, fries, kinds of mixed stir-fried vegetable, bitter vegetable, *daal* (lentil soup and pea soup), curried vegetable of various kinds, chutney, and sweets. The array is mind boggling. The entries under plain rice, for instance, number 14, under vegetarian pulao 27, under *khichuri* or rice lentil mix 19, under *daal* 76; the other groups provide a similarly encyclopaedic range of ingredients and cooking processes. The total number of entries in the vegetarian volume happens to be 884, which includes a brief section on the diet for the sick and the convalescent. The second volume, on non-vegetarian cooking, has 1,019 entries, divided into sections on soup, fish, sauce and gravy, kebab, stew, chops and cutlets, game and poultry, curries, Bengali dishes, eggs, pudding and so on. The third volume of the new edition lists preserves and chutneys from various parts of the country. The slim volume on Assamese cooking, published as (*randhabara*), merges item by item into the main text.

The recipes come mainly from Bengal, Assam, and Orissa; the rich food of the Mughlai provenance and of Punjab and the frontiers has an honourable place. South India is rather neglected. European recipes get a great deal of attention. The range takes care of breakfast, lunch, tea, dinner and snacks; it covers everyday meals at home, small parties and lavish banquets; it takes equal care of what the poor eat and what the rich feed on, of what is suitable for the child and for the elderly and the sick. She envisages a unified field of food, where people of all classes and all kinds may participate to express themselves in one of the fundamental practices of civilized living. The average moneyed Indian of today, used to enterprising home makers or cooks at home and a variety of restaurants in India and abroad, would not manage to sample such a wide variety of dishes. The Bezbaroa family and their friends were lucky indeed to have enjoyed such a lavish spread over time. Though Lakshminath's home was in Assam, his business took him to different parts of Bengal and Orissa and other places in eastern India and the family lived away from Assam a great deal. Prajna picked up recipes wherever she went and tried these out.

The work would be remarkable indeed if it were just a collection of recipes; it would have immense historical value as such. But the book is a great deal more than that and explicitly documents the process of enlightenment which the educated Indian was struggling to achieve in the nineteenth century. Prajnasundari was into cooking and feeding, as were a great many women before and after her. But she is unique in making the claim that this mundane everyday labour of the woman is a theoretical practice as well and that it contributes to the social good. To quote from her 'Advertisement' to the First Edition:

> In our Bengal we do not see any sign of discipline in some things; there is little order or harmony. This Bengali trait is particularly evident in our eating habits. There is in our feasts a hotchpotch of fish and sweets, which is against ancient manuals and detrimental to health. One of my principal aims has been to rescue Bengali food from this disorder and to restore discipline and harmony to our eating. We shall never be able to put a backbone to Bengali cuisine unless we manage to do this. There is not much point in putting together a few recipes and publishing the thing in the form of a book. . . . The few books on food which have appeared in Bengali lack method and order. That is why I have started with the basic item of vegetarian cooking, which is rice, and have then moved step by step into other classes of dishes to be cooked. The reader will notice that vegetarian cooking by itself has so much variety that you do not need non-vegetarian food at all to satisfy your palate. But only a fraction of existing vegetarian dishes find place in the present 500-page volume; there are many more to write up, after which alone we can enter the class of fish, flesh and fowl. (*All translations mine*)

The order Prajnasundari is demanding comes from the reforming zeal which was sweeping across the mental landscape of modernizing Bengal. This movement was the work of the elite, a section of landowning gentry and higher professionals, and the Indian component of the colonial bureaucracy, mostly *orthograde* (my term for the so-called upper caste, as contrasted to *contragrade*, commonly called lower caste) Hindus, inspired by the noble ideals of freedom of thought and justification by reason. Some equality was sought, especially for women, though gender roles were to be kept intact carefully; liberty and fraternity were distant goals for a few, mostly manifest in sporadic attempts to move on from charity to philanthropy. But everyday life was seeing changes. The stranglehold of existing dispensations of class, caste, gender, religion and race, however, made sure that transgressions were confined to the margins. Prajnasundari accepts that existing traditions, particularly rules of purity, will continue to matter in the overall structure of Hindu eating habits. Widows will be vegetarian and shun even garlic and onions and certain kinds of *daal*; beef will not be allowed in the kitchen. But she has included lots of chicken dishes, unobtrusively countering the existing Hindu prejudice, which nearly amounted to taboo. She brings in game and goes into great detail about suitability and preparation and cooking of wild birds; she has elaborate recipes for venison and boar and hare, combining both Mughlai and European modes. Chefs from outside Hindu caste society were welcome into the rich men's kitchens for this kind of cooking, and enterprising housewives benefitted from their tuition. Prajnasundari writes:

Hindu widows are famous in society for the purity of their practices. I have seen that they bathe and change into a separate set of white clothes before cooking food. To cook and serve food in soiled clothes is not only disgusting but also unhealthy. . . . We generally engage Brahman cooks for preparing indigenous foodstuff like rice, daal, etc. But for outlandish meat dishes like roast, chop, curry and so on, we engage low-caste Hindu or Burmese or native Christian cooks (Prajnasundari Devi, op. cit., vol. 1, p. 58).

There are records of frequent engagements of Muslim *bawarchis* (chefs) in affluent Hindu households. Renuka Devi Chaudhurani (1909-85), who married into a landlord family somewhat later, fondly recalls her mentor, a Muslim *bawarchi* who taught her a great many things to do in the kitchen (*rakamari niramish ranna* 'Kinds of Vegetarian Cooking'; *rakamari amish ranna* 'Kinds of Non-Vegetarian Cooking'). One has already seen a certain kind of gustatory revolt on the part of some Hindu younger men throughout the nineteenth century; eating forbidden meat and drinking alcohol became a kind of fashion statement as well as a gesture of defiance against orthodoxy. Gradually, some of the *outré* dietary innovations—derived from Muslim and European cuisine—found a place on the tables of the rich. Prajnasundari was one of the few enlightened women one knows of who fell in with the ways of the menfolk in this respect and struck a culinary blow for the social rejection of tradition and prejudice.

Food and Fellowship 47

A great deal of important work has been done on the position of women in the nineteenth century, documenting the inner world of women in their particular interior space in the household. The Bengali Hindu *bhadralok*'s investment in the idea of the sanctity of women and their inviolable inner space at home has been ascribed to the reaction against the ignominy of colonial rule. Prajna's life and that of her sisters and cousins and aunts demonstrate a contrary movement, in which even cooking—along with other clever and creative things some women were up to—demands a site for experiments in well being and hospitality and social bonding. It's ludicrous to assume that British rule made it possible to open up this hitherto closed universe of women. The colonial control over India was an unmitigated evil for its people and if a tiny fraction of the relatively privileged Indians thought and acted for some improvement of their lives in some areas, it was not because of British rule, but in spite of it. The colonial government did everything possible to stall social reform. It was pressure from a section of the elite which made it move in some directions. Food was not on the agenda of social reform, not seriously, though some young men made a fetish of their taste for the exotic; it was a tiny fraction of women in enlightened households who undertook a mission of expanding the horizon of taste and hospitality. This did not do much for the enormous majority of labouring people, just as the other platforms of the enlightenment project—education, culture, religion, social reform, politics and so on—did not in general touch their lives, but it puts in place a kind of model which would be meaningful in future.

COLONIAL RULE AND HUNGER

But the reality of poverty and hunger is the necessary point of reference to the innovations in food making in nineteenth-century Bengal. Prajnasundari is aware that ordinary people live very different lives and she includes a great many recipes from the repertoire of what may be called 'poor food'. But she addresses the women of upper income households who may want to break out of the stranglehold of unenlightened cooking and unreformed hospitality. She seeks to integrate the area of food making by an inclusive approach to geographical, economic and social divisions in the field.

Let one move from the upper end of society to the lower. India has always been a very hungry country throughout history, as Sukumari Bhattacharjee's well documented work (2012) shows. Medieval records confirm the extreme poverty of those who labour, especially the indigenous people who had been driven to the social and geographical margins of settled peasant society (for instance, the episode of Fullara and Kalaketu in *chandimangal*). Invasion and conquest exacerbate the situation, increasing the gap between the rich and the poor and subjecting the latter to periodic famines and epidemics. The beginning of the reign of the East India Company in Bengal, for instance, saw a horrendous famine, described in a terrifyingly vivid passage in Bankimchandra Chattopadhyay's *Anandamath* (1882). The year, in contrast, saw an increase in the Company's revenue. The fag end of the British Raj was marked by another terrible famine in 1943, entirely man-made, caused by the colonial government's massive transfer, without compensatory supply, of foodgrains to the eastern theatre of war. This cost the Exchequer nothing, but it cost Bengal three million lives. Famines are often extreme manifestations of a perpetual state of deprivation and misery. One has elsewhere written on the representation of the Bengal famine in the fiction of Bibhuti Bhushan Bandyopadhyay and Manik Bandyopadhyay (see Bhattacharya 2000). Let's have a look at one instance where a middle class reformer encounters chronic hunger.

Haraprasad Shastri tells this story about Ishwarchandra Vidyasagar. In September 1878, young Haraprasad had travelled to Karmatnar, a small town on the borders of Bengal and present-day Jharkhand, to see Vidyasagar, who had been going away regularly from Kolkata to live among the tribal Santals for most of the year in the last phase of his life. Haraprasad had arrived in the afternoon and had a prolonged chat with Vidyasagar on scholarly matters till dinner time, after which the careful old man locked up all the shutters in his bedroom and instructed him to lock his door before going to bed, for fear of burglars. Haraprasad was curious about one empty room with shelves on the four walls; when asked, Vidyasagar replied enigmatically that he would find out tomorrow. Next morning, as soon as the sun was up, an adivasi man appeared with half a dozen cobs of maize in his hand and demanded five annas which he needed for the treatment of his son. Vidyasagar took the maize and put it on a shelf in a separate room and gave the man five annas. A little later, another Santal came and demanded eight annas for a basket containing a large quantity of maize. Vidyasagar kept the basket and gave him eight annas. Haraprasad was surprised at the procedure under which the rules of the market do not operate and the buyer accepts the variable price demanded by sellers. This went on all morning and by eight o'clock all the empty shelves of the room were filled with heaps of maize. But the maize buying spree still went on. Tribals came in ones and twos to sell their crop, and each was paid at the price determined by the need of the moment perceived by the person concerned. Vidyasagar disappeared for a while after the buying stopped to attend to a sick *adivasi* child a couple of miles away, but he walked back to find his yard full of other groups of Santals. All of them addressed Vidyasagar in the dialectal mode, avoiding the usual honorific vocative, all of them demanding food. The maize was brought out. Each group had brought faggots and dry leaves and they proceeded to build small fires to roast the corn on the cob and have a large feast of this simple fare. When they went away satisfied, the stock of maize was exhausted. The Santals blessed him, saying, 'You've fed us well, man' (Shastri 1989). The food was the fruit of their own labour, the cooking elementary and bereft of the elaborate paraphernalia of elite households, such as Prajnasundari's. Vidyasagar would not insist that everybody should eat such fare, but he was practising the primordial model of equity, 'from each according to his ability, to each according to his need'. Later on, this work of economic management would devolve on the welfare state, but so far, no formal democracy in the world has really accomplished it.

This article is not about the entire universe of mankind's relationship with food. Food is the result of gathering, hunting, tilling and rearing; is mediated by butchering, harvesting, sifting, sorting, grinding, processing, manufacturing and preserving; is stored, carried, combined, cooked, arranged, served, sold and of course eaten, commonly thought of as the final destiny of all vegetable, animal and synthetic matter called food. These processes are largely collective and often commercial, and things would collapse if mankind had not evolved ways of working together to produce food and prolong lives. But a great deal of food and foodstuff are never eaten by human beings; animal feed and fertilizers and industrial processes consume a good part of what would recognizably constitute human comestibles; a great deal of food, both raw and cooked, is wasted and left to rot. Recent reports state that the waste food in the advanced nations would feed the entire population of the world's poor. This is too large a matter to sum up in one paper.

This writer merely touched upon the matter of the distribution of food which, just like its production, is a complex story by itself. Food is often eaten by a single person, particularly in cities and towns where there are a great many single people, but it is produced communally, and the story of civilization tells us that food has been largely a collective affair, intimately linked to family, community, region, and nation. Hence, food has to be seen as something integrally and intimately connected with the material and mental life of peoples. You can't hope to write about food and avoid all references to any part of this ongoing and interconnected story. But I have stuck largely to food-making, which is a bigger matter than cooking, and the cooking part comes from a particular region of the Indian subcontinent, namely Bengal, meaning both Bangladesh and the Indian state of West Bengal, with certain neighbouring areas and the Bengali diaspora thrown in. The idea is to approach a food culture—rightly identified as a proper subject of study in academic writings—rather than a geographical area. And since this is not entirely about recipes and cuisine and good food and ethnic dishes and restaurants and chefs and so on, one has used 'food-making' rather than 'cuisine' or 'cookery' or good old simple 'food' to stay away from the world of professional foodies and TV chefs and eating out guides. Food pornography is best left to mass purveyors of entertainment.

REFERENCES

Bhattacharjee, Sukumari, 2012, *Prabandhasangraha*, 'Collected Essays', vol. 2, 2012.

Bhattacharya, Mihir, 2000, 'Realism and the Syntax of Difference', in *The Making of History: Essays Presented to Irfan Habib*, eds. K.N. Panikkar, Terence J. Byers and Utsa Patnaik, pp. 478-99.

Chattopadhyay, Bankimchandra, 2010, *Anandamath* (1882). Translated by Basanta Koomar Roy, Orient Paperbacks.

Chaudhurani, Renuka Devi, 2013, *Rakamari Amish Ranna*, India: Penguin Books.

——, 2013, *Rakamari Niramish Ranna*, India: Penguin Books.

Deb, Chitra, 2016, *Thakur Barir Andarmahal*, Ananda Publication.

Devi, Prajnasundari, 1995, *Amish o Niramish Ahar*, vol. 1, Ananda Publication.

——, 2000, *Amish o Niramish Ahar*, vol. 2, Ananda Publication, 2000.

Devi, Rasa Sundari, 2015, *Amar Jiban*, Dey's Publication.

Patnaik, Utsa, 2007, *The Republic of Hunger*.

Shastri, Haraprasad, 1989, *Haraprasad Shastri Rachana Samgraha*, vol. 4, West Bengal State Book Board.

CHAPTER 3

Theorizing Food Studies: Gender and Ideologies

SUKALPA BHATTACHARJEE

Contemporary perspectives on food variety and cultures of consumption have turned Food Studies into a critical site for a better understanding of history, culture, economics and society. Scholars working in this field have analysed food as a powerful cultural signifier (Arvela 2013). While food and the act of eating can connote membership of a group, comradeship and belonging, it can also generate revulsion, animosity and social hierarchy, demarcating boundaries between us and the other. Food can produce mnemophilia as much as it can produce mnemophobia. Several scholars have analysed how food has not only nutritional value but is semiotically powerful (Appadurai 2009). Food also defines the body politic of a nation and like the modern nation, food is also a site of hegemony and exclusionary politics of the centre and the periphery. Ethnic and caste-based food is always considered to be the other of the national cuisine causing threat to the idea of a national mainstream food. Non-dominant food preferences and practices thus become a site of struggle where the idea of 'national' is challenged, destabilized and re-invented. Thus, Food Studies is an emerging interdisciplinary field of study that examines the complex relationship between food, culture and society and is today largely the study of food and its relationship to various multi-layered human experience (Almerico 2014). One can see how class, caste, race and gender hierarchies are maintained through control over food and how consumption patterns and cooking methods are classified as either civilized or barbaric. In other words, who decides what is palatable and what is unpalatable. In fact, the history of civilizations has been constructed on the basis of who eats 'raw' and who eats 'cooked' food and how the transition happened from one kind to the other. Thus this transition from raw to cooked is often used as a framework to understand who is more civilized.

In recent times, in India food preferences and eating habits have come to constitute a major issue of contestation and conflict. Dalit activists across India have questioned the dominant hierarchies of taste and have celebrated their liking for non-vegetarian cuisine and in particular beef. Vegetarianism is a dominant ideological position in contemporary India, followed very strictly in some states and legitimized by certain political positions. As mentioned by G. Arunima,

Vegetarianism in India is the result of enforced normative caste practice, continually reproduced over the past many hundreds of years through the rigidities of Brahminical Hinduism. While today, not just Brahmins but many other aspiring upper and other castes have become vegetarian, it is worth remembering that this is a combination of force (invoked in the instance of 'The Hindu' by 'legal' means) and ideology (Arunima 2014).

Food practices thus, are inherently political whether they are politicized or not. Again, food and food practices are intrinsically connected to one's identity. Food discourse and the power relations embedded within it and which it produces, along with early bodily experiences of eating, construct one's identity (Lupton 1996). Food not only nourishes but serves as a social marker of class status and social hierarchy. One's choice of shopping certain goods reifies class distinctions or differentiations and demonstrates to others what his/her class position is. Women also assert their gendered caste or class identities through their role as producer or consumers which places them in a certain position in the power structure. This is how food liberates its consumers and at the same time becomes the source of their oppression, demonstrating the various ways in which power operates in human lives. The politics of othering that operates through food is indirect and subtle, because it is not seen as a tool of oppression or exclusion and yet it excludes the other.

Theorizing Food Studies: Gender and Ideologies 55

Closely associated with the idea of othering that operates on the basis of food habits, food preferences, manner of eating food and cooking, a contemporary term 'food politics' has been introduced by scholars working in this field. As mentioned by Marak, Food politics can be understood as politicizing food at one level, or the politics involved in the control over food or the policies on production, distribution and consumption of food, which makes food 'ethnographic in nature', particularly in the context of the internal structures of communities, on the one hand and in the context of the tribal societies' interface with other communities (Marak 2014). If food is the text that invites decoding, issues of hierarchy, inclusion and exclusion, shame and honour, national and peripheral imaginings of culture and traditions become the subtexts. Descriptions of food, eating habits and the sociology of hunger become central to experiences of caste and race. In the racial context of slavery, for example, Frederick Douglass' first memoir, *Narrative of the Life of Frederick Douglass*, describes the way he ate:

Our food was coarse corn meal boiled. This was called mush. It was put into a large wooden tray or trough, and set down upon the ground. The children were then called, like so many pigs, and like so many pigs they would come and devour the mush; some with oyster-shells, others with pieces of shingle, some with naked hands, and none with spoons. He that ate fastest got most; he that was strongest secured the best place; and few left the trough satisfied (Douglass 1845).

The passionate narrative of someone like Frederick Douglass, who says that hunger was his childhood companion writes this in *My Bondage and My Freedom*,

I have often been so pinched with hunger, that I have fought with the dog – 'Old Nep'—for the smallest crumbs that fell from the kitchen table, and have been glad when I won a single crumb in the combat, ... Many times have I followed, with eager step, the waiting-girl when she went out to shake the table cloth, to get the crumbs and small bones flung out for the cats.

Through these heartbreaking narratives in his three autobiographies, Douglass explains how slave owners used food as a means of control over the slaves. The analogy drawn between hungry humans and dogs or pigs here is significant, as it robs a human of his humanness or makes him animal like as an inevitable consequence of his battle for survival or in fulfilling his basic elemental need. In the same vein, Marathi poet, writer and Dalit activist from Maharashtra, Namdeo Dhasal writes, 'Hunger stalks Dalit lives', like the slaves in America mentioned above. He used many vivid and hungered descriptions of food. A food component of the Dalit called *dhal* is used as a metaphor to understand dalit condition because dhal means split. The term Dalit comes from the same root—broken and crushed by society (Doctor 2014).

Although food had been a very important field of study for anthropologists for understanding cultures, there are many ideological issues which have made food the 'most visible' marker of identity and difference and a space for inscribing the politics of difference. As mentioned by Marak,

As early as the 1900s, anthropological writings briefly mentioned food within the context of a culture's diet, tending to favour lists rather than analysis. From 1950s to the early 1970s the anthropology of food moved toward a biological orientation with nutritive studies becoming popular. On the other hand, there were those anthropologists who were interested in tracing the origins of particular foods. In the 1970s and 1980s, anthropologists began to move toward conceptualizing food as a symbolic substance that was embedded and invested with meaning. Current studies on food emphasize the cultural and social aspects of food, rather than its nutritive qualities (Marak 2014).

Such a shift from the dietary perspective on food to the biological and subsequently to the symbolic realm in the 1970s and 1980s as mentioned above has been theorized further from an intersectionalist approach to food, highlighting the interlocking issues of gender, race, class and sexuality. Notions of food justice coupled with rights movements of women, subalterns and indigenous peoples across the world transformed Food Studies into an interdisciplinary field. Forson and Wilkerson, in their essay 'Intersectionality and Food Studies' (2011), have examined the intersection of Food Studies with Women's Studies and Gender Studies and how such intersections lead to the place of food in LGBT Studies or Disability Studies. Some scholars have also studied the relationship between gender and indigeneity and food in their study of food insecurity among the ultra-poor Garo women in Bangladesh (Munro, Parker & McIntyre 2014). Their position is that indigenous populations may experience food insecurity differently compared to non-indigenous people, indicating that right to food is linked with the right to produce, which leads to issues of land and property rights. Besides cultural dislocation, forced assimilation, or other aspects of political violence experienced by indigenous populations deprive them of their right to land and resources. Contemporary political movements of indigenous groups centre round political definitions of indigeneity and citizenship which include and exclude people from land and resources. For example, the displacement of peoples caused by the partition of the Indian subcontinent has resulted in food insecurity, impoverishment and malnutrition as an inescapable condition of existence of millions of people. It may be stated in this context that the position of indigenous woman of the global south at the intersection of gender and ethnicity in a postcolonial context is the most vulnerable one. Her exclusion from economic, political, social and cultural processes as well as being away from the developmental intervention of states or non-governmental bodies being the fall out.

Again, in postcolonial societies, food becomes a metaphor and reminder of one's own roots or belonging—a home, locating or dislocating them from one culture to another. In the context of globalization and with the floating of peoples and capital across transnational borders, food has also travelled as a part of culture. For example, eastern food chains in various metropolis of the west also become sites of coming together of people of similar cultures, who recreate their home away from home through food. Different foods have different appearance and smell which creates a social hierarchy of people who associate a certain smell with what they would consider pleasant or offensive. For example, the smell of bamboo shoots or fermented dry fish, which is a delicacy for one culture, is extremely unbearable for the other. Human attitude to different smells in different food is thus highly differentiated and socially stratified. Very closely connected to the issues discussed above is the issue of untouchability in the Indian society and the concept of leftover of food. Narratives of caste discrimination in India reveals the humiliation of lower caste people if they had touched an upper caste brahmin's food. Besides, it was an accepted practice that leftovers which would be dropped into the hands of the lower caste people from above. It is important to note here the parallel between the position of lower caste people and women in Hindu cultural practices whereby in Hindu rituals, wives are directed to eat the leftover of their husbands. Thus, it is clear that the understanding of food has to go beyond the framework of survival and locate it in the context of food as marker of patriarchal hierarchy.

Scholars of Food Studies have also analysed critically how the control of food production, distribution and consumption is based on gender relations that defines and legitimizes the social value of the male and female and the constructions of their identities. Power and Foodways have been linked in two ways: firstly, men and women do not have equal access to food, secondly, they do not have equal means to control its production, consumption or distribution. Power is constructed on the basis of this access or denial of food to men and women. Men and women's appetite, their priority to health also determines their attitude to their own bodies and self (Counihan 2013). In the Indian subcontinent, narration have eulogized virtuous women who can fast and can renounce hunger as a mark of their loyalties to patriarchal rituals and ceremonies. While hunger is seen to be an absence of power, as it denies the woman her basic elemental need which is food, counternarratives of virtue and chastity are internalized by women themselves who think that renouncing of hunger constitutes their spirituality. Again, food can be both a site and a sign to understand how bodies are constructed, ideals are maintained and monitored, and how control over food can be the basis of control over bodies and sexualities.

Scholars have called for a new field of feminist food studies which stresses on the connections between women's food work in the labour market (material), their responsibility for food related work at home (sociocultural), and their relationship with eating (corporeal) (Avakian & Haber 2005). Until recently, these areas have been both understudied and unconnected, with little integration of the material, sociocultural, and corporeal domains. Other gender issues, including the relative absence of a feminist agenda despite women's increasing involvement in leadership roles in the food system, remain neglected. For example, the role of women in the cultivation or production of rice in India's northeast is not proportionate to the position that she holds in the private or public spheres. Scholars have mentioned that rice cultivation has traditionally been in the women's domain of knowledge and that the variety of rice in the region reflects women's range of knowledge of seeds and of plant breeding (Krishna 2005). Women's identities are clearly tied to their often problematic relationship with food. Susan Bordo suggests that women seek emotional heights, intensity, love and thrills from food. She also explains how restriction of food and denial of hunger serve as central features of the construction of femininity in a patriarchal culture. A certain class of women, who are driven by the logic of the culture industry, consider thinness as a precondition to be included in the media and the fashion world. This constitutes groups of women who can afford to eat well but fear exclusion from the glamour world which prescribes specific measure of bodily structures for women. This results into problems and diseases such as anorexia nervosa, bulimia, and obesity (Forson & Counihan 2013). Women seem to actually have a very ambiguous relationship with food as also mentioned earlier. Williams and Counihan write,

> Women cannot help but be caught up in some form of schizophrenic positioning with regard to food—eat more, eat less; eat well, eat badly—due to the contradictory and simultaneous marketing of thin-ness and food indulgence (Williams & Counihan 2011).

Some Women's Studies scholars have discovered that food practices and their representations can be the sources for construction of social history of time and place and can offer insights into the specificities of women's lives. Therefore, feminist food studies establish that food practices are gendered.

Another important and interesting analysis of this field of study is that the kitchen is both a space of domesticating women and, at the same time, it is also a site for women's creativity and appropriation of patriarchal ideology. A woman's food work mostly happens in kitchens where through her gendered role as food-giver she is able to have some amount of control over food. As mentioned earlier, anthropology is one of the earliest disciplines to study the pivotal role that women perform in ethnic communities, particularly as food providers. One can turn to myths and folk tales to see how women have organized themselves as groups and individual rebels in and around the kitchen which was the sole uninterrupted space, away from patriarchal gaze. Avakian's anthology, *Through the Kitchen Window: Women Writers Explore the Intimate Meanings of Food and Cooking* (1997-8), highlights the agency of powerless or dispossessed women through their food work. Alice Walker's *In Search of Our Mothers' Gardens: Womanist Prose* (1983) discusses the gardens of poor southern African American women which served as an outlet for their creativity when no other existed and when cooking may have provided a vehicle for women's creative expression. Therefore, myriad narratives on the lives of women in their various contexts tell one about the meanings embedded in women's relationships to food. Again, eating vegetarian food or non-vegetarian food also signifies one's own ideology and construction of the self. For example, eating meat can symbolize strength, and therefore, the consumption of meat is often associated with men and masculinity (Fischler 1988).

Thus, human relationship to food is a complex one running through at least two dimensions: firstly, from the biological to the symbolic and secondly, from the individual to the collective. The logic stated in favour of vegetarian food to be consumed by Hindu caste widows in India is essentially based on restraint, celibacy or renouncing of her sexuality. The same logic does not apply to the male counterpart. While food is essential for nutrition, the need for nutrition in females is often underplayed in cultural terms. Food and masculinity go hand in hand, generally delegitimizing a woman's need for it even when she is pregnant or nursing children. Once the significance of materiality of food reaches a symbolic status through a patriarchal culture of exclusion of the female in the map of food consumption, the nutritional value of the food becomes secondary in importance and the political contestation over power takes precedence (Parraga 1990). Therefore, Roland Barthes says that a meal signifies much more than feeding the body, for it also encompasses 'a system of communication, a body of images, a protocol of usages, situations, and behavior' (Barthes 1979). Mary Douglass also writes about the symbolic function of food in society in her essay 'Deciphering a Meal' and states that 'the meanings in our food system should be elucidated by much closer observation' (Douglass 1972).

It is also important to examine the stereotyping of women's relationship to food. The projection of the feminine as food provider also imposes the responsibility of food provisioning on women. This is very loudly pronounced in food advertisements whereby hungry children straight from the playground come and ask their mothers to provide food in 'two minutes'. Research conducted along these lines suggests that women perform the majority of work associated with food and often feel that it is a part of their role as 'wife' or 'mother' to feed their family. Feeding others is always highlighted so as to subvert women's own need to be fed. Domestic work of women of the global south centres mostly around procuring, producing, cooking and serving of food to members of the family. Social etiquettes are constructed on the basis of gender ideologies which prescribe that women should eat after all male members and children of the household have eaten. In appropriation to the stereotypical relationship between food and women, one can see how women constitute themselves as rebels in defiance of food for a political cause. While hunger strike is a significant mode of democratic protest, the decade long hunger strike by Irom Sharmila was an example of defiance of the stereotypical relationship between food and human life particularly between food and women. Sharmila's act of fasting takes one beyond the binary between aggressor and victim by turning consequences of repression against itself. Body without food here plays a multidimensional role. She had transcended 'suffering' in the conventional sense by 'participating' in that subjected body, which was not only her own but which demonstrated the effect of bearing the suffering of others. Her imprisoned, incarcerated and monitored body in the hospital-prison was a social body that belonged to the domain of every other suffering self in which Sharmila could participate. Her refusal to eat was a political message of refusal to live a life with denial of human rights under Armed Forces Special Power Act.

As mentioned earlier, food advertisers also perpetuate gender ideologies that suggest that women should limit the amount of food that they eat, so that they can lose weight and become beautiful. Despite the fact that women are central to food practices, they have been relegated to the margins of Food Studies. However, it is significant that women from such marginalized positions have appropriated the gender ideologies that fix women to their stereotypical roles more as a provider of food and less of a consumer. Cookbooks and recipe books have been the space for creative expression of women whereby they have turned cooking into a liberatory activity and the kitchen has turned to a space of resistance. The kitchen which was supposed to be a space of forced confinement for women and the actual space of their domestication, has been turned into a creative space. Scholars have mentioned how Chicana and Native American women have reclaimed their ethnic and gender identities through writing about food and in the process creating a ground for resistance to the 'commodification of their culture'. These women often assume a communitarian identity when they speak of their culture, which is reflected in kitchen related activities. Food-writing thus becomes autobiographical, where food-related discourse centring around the kitchen becomes a source of identity and also empowerment (Avakian & Haber 2015). It may be mentioned here that housework had been hitherto addressed by Women's Studies scholars as domesticity, and the issues around cooking were ignored as a marker of patriarchal oppression. The emergent discourse of kitchen culture has unfolded what could be learned from and about women's relationship to food practices and how this culture influences the society at various levels (Inness 2015). For many women, a 'kitchen of their own' has come to symbolize what Virginia Woolf called 'A Room of One's Own'. In an age of globalization, women are exposed to greater varieties of cooking products in the global market which become the resources from which women learn how to cook differently and become a part of global culinary literacy. On the one hand, this becomes a site of creativity and, at the same time, allows women to attain expertise and economic empowerment.

REFERENCES

Arvela, Paula, 'Ethnic food: the other in ourselves', Faculty of Law, *Humanities and the Arts—Papers*. University of Wollongong, 2013.

Avakian, Arlene Voski and Barbara Haber, *From Betty Crocker to Feminist Food Studies: Critical Perspectives on Women and Food*, Liverpool: Liverpool University Press, 2005.

Appadurai, Arjun. 'Gastro-politics in Hindu South Asia', *American Ethnologist*. 8:3, Version of Record online: 28 October 2009.

Almerico, Gina M., 'Food and identity: Food studies, cultural, and personal identity', *Journal of International Business and Cultural Studies*, 8 June 2014.

Arunima, G., 'Being Vegetarian, the Hindu Way', *Economic and Political Weekly*, G. Arunima's blog, 2014.

Barthes, Roland, 'Toward a Psychosociology of Contemporary Food Consumption', in *Food and Drink in History*, edited by R. Forster and O. Ranum. Baltimore: Johns Hopkins University Press, 1979.

Counihan, Carole M., *Food and Gender*, Routledge, 2013.

Douglass, Frederick, *Narrative of the Life of Frederick Douglass, an American Slave*, Anti-Slavery Office, United States, 1845.

———, *My Bondage and My Freedom*, New York and Auburn: Miller Orton & Mulligan, 1855.

Douglas, Mary, 'Deciphering a Meal', *Daedalus, 101*(1), *Myth, Symbol, and Culture* (Winter 1972), pp. 61-81, Published by The MIT Press on behalf of American Academy of Arts & Sciences.

Doctor, Vikram, 'Garam Masala: The many meanings of Dalit food', in *On My Plate, The Economic Times Blogs*, 16 January 2014.

Fischler, Claude, 'Food, Self and Identity', *Social Science Information, 27*(2), Sage, 1988, pp. 275-92.

Forson, Williams and Carole Counihan, *Taking Food Public: Redefining Foodways in a Changing World Psyche*, Routledge, 2013.

Forson, Psyche William and Abby Wilherson, 'Intersectionality and Food Studies', in *Food, Culture and Society: An International Journal of Multidisciplinary Research, 14*(11), March 2011.

Gorringe, Hugo and D. Karthikeyan, 'The Hidden Politics of Vegetarianism Caste and The Hindu Canteen', *Economic & Political Weekly*, 49(20), 17 May 2014.

Inness, Sherrie A., ed., *Kitchen Culture in America: Popular Representations of Food, Gender, and Race*, University of Pennsylvania Press, 2015.

Krishna, Sumi, 'Gendered Price of Rice in North-Eastern India', *Economic & Political Weekly*, 40(25), 2005.

Marak, Queenbala, *Food Politics: Studying Food, Identity and Difference among the Garos*, Cambridge Scholars Publishing, 2014.

Munro, Jenny, Barbara Parker and Lynn McIntyre, 'An Intersectionality Analysis of Gender, Indigeneity, and Food Insecurity among Ultrapoor Garo Women in Bangladesh' *International Journal of Indigenous Health*, 10(1), 2014.

Parraga, I.M., 'Determinants of Food Consumption', *Journal of the American Dietetic Association*, 90(5), 1990.

CHAPTER 4

Anthropological Perspectives of Pregnancy Dietary Patterns among Indian Women

CAITLYN D. PLACEK

INTRODUCTION

What do fasting, soil cravings, and being disgusted by the smell of meat all have in common? For starters, these behaviours commonly occur during pregnancy. Second, each dietary behaviour carries cultural norms of permissibility, with some behaviours met with stigma and shame (e.g. soil consumption), whereas other behaviours (e.g. religious fasting) are often met with community praise and perceived religious reward (Placek et al. 2021a, Young 2010). Third, and perhaps most surprising, is that despite having such varied cultural undertones, these dietary behaviours share a hypothesized etiology for occurrence in pregnancy, which is to reduce ingestion of toxic and pathogenic agents (Fessler 2002, Placek et al. 2017, Profet 1995, Young 2010). The aim of this article is to introduce pregnancy dietary behaviours that are common among some populations of Indian women and the hypothesized biocultural explanations that explain their persistence.

OVERVIEW OF DIETARY PATTERNS IN PREGNANCY

Dietary changes along with nausea and vomiting are considered hallmarks of pregnancy and evidence for these sometimes-peculiar shifts are found across human societies. Pregnant women report increased aversions toward specific food and smells, increased cravings for foods and other substances they would not normally desire and adherence to culturally transmitted dietary rules geared toward improving maternal-infant health outcomes (Henrich & Henrich 2010, Patil et al. 2012, Orloff & Hormes 2014, Young 2010). Research indicates that Indian women follow similar dietary patterns that are found across other human societies (Nag 1994, Placek et al. 2017), yet nearly 30 years have passed since an anthropologist has written comprehensively about cultural influences of pregnancy dietary patterns in India. In 1994, Moni Nag compiled data about pregnancy dietary patterns across India, with an aim to highlight the importance of understanding the interconnections between social inequalities, cultural norms of prenatal diet and maternal malnutrition. While Nag's article offers insight into the cross-cultural similarities and differences regarding Indian women's dietary preferences, and how these might influence nutritional health, more data has since emerged with fresh insight into the biocultural factors that influence diverse dietary practices in pregnancy. Note that while this article presents data on Indian women's dietary preferences in pregnancy, this is by no means an exhaustive review of the literature nor an attempt to generalize these patterns across India, a heterogenous country with noteworthy variation in religion, caste, socio-economic status and other demographic markers.

BIOCULTURAL APPROACH

In this article, the following dietary patterns will be discussed: pica, cravings and aversions, food avoidances and fasting. A biocultural anthropological framework is used to present the current evidence and theories regarding why and how women alter their diets during pregnancy. Biocultural anthropology considers emic (or local views), evolutionary, political-economic, and social-ecological factors to understand and explain aspects of human behaviour. According to Wiley and Cullin (2016), the term 'biocultural anthropology' can take on different meanings and the levels of analysis can vary, depending on the research question. For example, Young (2011) describes how pica, the urge to eat culturally defined non-food items, is influenced by micro- and macro-level social and physical environmental factors along with ideational/cultural factors. Biocultural research can also account for the evolutionary underpinnings of a behaviour (e.g., Placek et al. 2017), or how culture might impact variation in a biological trait (e.g., Dressler et al. 2005). This approach is useful because it shifts explanation away from individual factors and provides evidence for the contextual factors that shape behaviour. This approach is particularly relevant in India, because some dietary patterns are stigmatized, or viewed as a form of psychopathology (e.g., Patil et al. 2010, Srinath et al. 2005), which can prevent women from openly reporting their cravings and other preferences.

PICA

Pica is the craving and subsequent consumption of culturally defined non-food items, and can consist of an array of substances, such as clay (geophagy), unprocessed starches (amylophagy), ash (stachtophagia), and charcoal. Geophagy has been studied in India for over 100 years and has been documented across the country among diverse castes and religions (Hooper & Mann 1906, Laufer 1930, Nag 1994, Rao 1985, Thurston 1906). According to Hooper and Mann (1906), 'In India itself there are earth-eaters belonging to every main ethnological division and to every type of climate.' Descriptions of earth-eating, specifically, date back to Kalidasa's poems of the fifth century AD. In one instance, Kalidasa provides the following description of the queen of Ayodhya, Sudaksina, while she was pregnant with Raghu, the future king: 'As if premeditating that her son will subsequently enjoy (i.e. rule over) the whole earth, just as Indra rules over heaven by driving his chariot to all the quarters thereof, the queen first felt a hankering for eating baked clay only to the exclusion of all other well-flavoured articles of food' (Hooper & Mann 1903).

Geophagy in pregnancy, therefore, has deep historical roots in India, yet the behaviour in modern times is often met with stigma and shame. In one's own research, one has attempted to study geophagy in four diverse cultural settings. During the first field trip to India, located in a small village near Tiruvannamalai, Tamil Nadu, one embarked on an ethnographic investigation of pregnancy health and diet, which it was hoped would serve as the initial steps of the dissertation. At the time one was not exactly certain about the specific topic of study, as one knew little about the local culture and wanted to choose something that people in the village studied also found worthwhile to investigate and discuss. Using Agar's (1980) ethnographic funnel approach, one led with the question, 'What do women crave during pregnancy?' One was surprised to hear cravings for clay were common and that women preferred specific soil mounds to collect their secret substance. It is recalled one older mother of four who talked at length about her cravings for red clay, how she began in pregnancy and how every time it rained, the sweet smell of the wet clay would trigger her desire to consume a small handful.

One was eager to learn more about why women engage in this behaviour and the potential health outcomes of eating clay, so one returned to India a year later with semi-structured and structured surveys, only to discover that very few women openly reported clay consumption. When asked about eating clay, women would shyly look away and answer with a quiet 'no'. Instead, women were quick to admit consumption of uncooked rice, or amylophagy (Placek & Hagen 2013). In this focal village, consuming uncooked rice was not considered taboo and was even viewed as a consumable item that fell somewhere in between the continuum of 'food' and 'non-food'.

Based on the field experience, the social stigma surrounding many pica substances in India prevents researchers from fully understanding why women crave these substances and the resultant impact they have on health. Community members and participants often talked about how nurses at their local clinics and family members would scold them for craving clay, which made them feel ashamed to admit their cravings. One woman purposely bought and consumed Ayurvedic tooth powder as a replacement for clay for fear of retribution from the members of her family. This is not out of the ordinary when considering the broader literature on pica; research has found that cravings for crumbly powder is a consistent quality of pica consumers across cultures (Young 2009).

Hiding substances from peers was another topic of conversation among pica consumers, with the main impetus to avoid being scolded by family members. One woman interviewed hid her charcoal in a small bag under her bed and snuck samples whenever she found a moment of privacy. Stigma towards clay consumption has roots in Indian psychology. Similar to western psychology, pica is sometimes viewed as a form of psychopathology, psychological distress, or mental illness in need of intervention (Srinath et al. 2005, Singhi & Singhi 1983). This is perhaps partly based on research showing that pica is associated with adverse psychological states, such as anxiety, as well as reports of people who have an uncontrollable urge for non-food substances like cravings for alcohol and tobacco. One study conducted in India, for example, found a high correlation between pica and tobacco cravings (Boatin et al. 2012). Importantly, adverse psychological traits that are often associated with pica might not be the cause of stigmatized cravings, but rather a product of the shame women feel for desiring a taboo substance.

If pica is not driven by mental illness, then why do pregnant women crave non-food items? One approach anthropologists take to understand human behaviour is by focusing on the *emic*, or insider's view. Jeffrey et al. (1989), for example, found that pregnant Indian women described their cravings for ash as a sign that a woman would give birth to a girl, whereas cravings for dust were indicative of a boy. The collaborative research in Tamil Nadu found that pregnancy cravings were largely associated with desire, or *acai*. In this community of study, *acai* in pregnancy could only be quelled by giving women a *cimantam* or *valaikappu* (pregnancy ceremony), if she was pregnant with her first born, which often included elaborate gifts of bangles, clothes, and delectable foods. Failure to satisfy her cravings could lead to unwanted cravings, including tabooed non-food items (Placek & Hagen 2013).

Anthropologists also consider *etic* explanations for human behaviour, such as environmental, biological, and cultural factors.

Geophagy, specifically, is frequently correlated with micronutrient deficiencies, such as iron deficiency anemia and low plasma zinc concentrations (Miao et al. 2015, Young 2011). This correlation, which is found cross-culturally, has led researchers to wonder whether geophagy causes micronutrient deficiencies, or if geophagy replenishes micronutrients. Research has found that some clays provide bioavailable iron to consumers, however, this is not a consistent finding. In some cases, geophagic substances bind to iron, rendering consumers iron deficient (Young 2011). Therefore, researchers consider the fact that, in some cases, geophagy and other forms of pica *could* offer nutritional benefit, particularly in resource-scarce environments.

But why would someone consume a substance that can leach nutrients, particularly in pregnancy when nutritional demands increase during the second and third trimesters? Another hypothesis of pica addresses this question and proposes that geophagy and other forms of pica could function as a pathogen and toxin avoidance strategy by coating the intestinal wall or binding directly to toxins and pathogens in the intestines, thereby rendering a protective benefit (Young 2011). The protective benefits of geophagy are relevant during immuno-compromised states, such as the first trimester of pregnancy when cell-mediated immunity is down-regulated to support placentation and organogenesis, leaving pregnant females at greater risk of certain extra-cellular pathogens and toxins (Kourtis et al. 2014, Kraus et al. 2012, Mor and Cardenas 2010; Pazos et al. 2012; Racicot et al. 2014). Given that India is a tropical region with high pathogen density, the pathogen and toxin protection hypothesis warrants further consideration— along with consideration of micronutrient deficiencies among consumers.

FOOD CRAVINGS

Pregnancy is also marked by an increase in cravings for foods that are deemed unusual or not typically preferred outside of pregnancy (Flaxman & Sherman 2000; Orloff & Hormes 2014). For example, 'pickles and ice cream'—two foods that are usually not paired—constitute stereotypical pregnancy craving in the United

States. In India and across other South Asian countries, women commonly report cravings for mangoes—of both the ripe and unripe varieties (Nag 1994, Placek 2017). In East Africa, on the other hand, Turkana and Datoga women report cravings for meat and dairy (Young & Pike 2012). What causes these cravings, and why does there appear to be cross-cultural differences, yet within-culture similarities?

One influential study of pregnancy cravings found similarities in the categories of craved foods and the timing in which they occurred in pregnancy (Flaxman & Sherman 2000). According to this cross-cultural study, cravings emphasized foods that were sweet and/or high in fat and calories. The authors concluded that pregnancy cravings could be an adaptive response to high caloric need during the second and third trimesters of pregnancy and could allow for the replenishment of nutrients that are lost from heightened nausea and vomiting in the first trimester (Flaxman & Sherman 2000, Hook 1978). This study was limited by the inclusion of primarily Western European and North American countries, thereby preventing generalization of the results. Food cravings in India, for example, do not appear to follow similar trends as found in the Flaxman and Sherman study (Nag 1994, Placek 2017).

While pregnant Indian women *are* known for craving sweet foods (Jeffrey et al. 1989), they also desire bitter-tasting and sour foods (Nag 1994, Placek 2017). Interestingly, although cravings for mangoes and tamarind are pervasive in India, these foods are often met with similar ambivalence as one found in this research on amylophagy (Placek & Hagen 2013). Why would these cravings elicit mixed feelings, especially if they are so widespread? A biocultural perspective can shed light on this question. From an emic perspective, unripe mango and unripe tamarind are considered heat-inducing foods. According to Ayurveda, consuming too many 'hot' foods can increase *pitta* (fire) in the body. Pregnancy is viewed by many as being a heat-generating state that must be balanced with cooling foods, such as buttermilk or cucumbers (Nichter & Nichter 1983, Van Hollen 2003, Placek et al. 2021a). Consuming too many hot foods in pregnancy can lead to undesirable effects, such as spontaneous miscarriage (Placek & Hagen

2015). Pregnant women, however, are not always responsible for their cravings, which might contribute to some of the ambivalence. In an ethnographic study conducted in Tamil Nadu, respondents thought that the type of cravings (*acai*) a woman has is dependent on how her family has treated her during pregnancy. If she is given the foods she desires, then she is unlikely to crave tabooed items (Van Hollen 2003).

From an etic, or outsider's perspective, unripe mango and unripe tamarind can provide ample amounts of Vitamin C. This critical micronutrient can reduce teratogenic effects of environmental toxins that can make their way across the placental barrier and disrupt fetal development (Simán & Erikkson 1997), thereby serving as a pathogen or toxin avoidance strategy. In addition, pregnant women require additional antioxidants because placentation disrupts the amount of antioxidants that are bioavailable for women (King 2000). Given that unripe mangoes and unripe tamarinds are both high in antioxidants and Vitamin C, are abundantly available in the Indian subcontinent yet are perceived to increase heat, the ambivalence surrounding these cravings is understandable when viewed through a biocultural lens.

Cravings can also be influenced by cultural and environmental factors. One study conducted in Tamil Nadu found that cravings for foods high in toxins and pathogens were predicted by resource scarcity and pressure to give birth to a son (Placek 2017). In other words, women who experienced both resource stress and cultural stress were more likely to desire taboo foods. These findings carry strong symbolism—in a region where women have less control over their reproductive health and abortion is stigmatized, do taboo cravings signal that a pregnant woman wants to terminate her pregnancy? Further research is needed to address this question properly.

AVERSIONS

Pregnancy-related food and drug aversions are also found cross-culturally. For the sake of clarity, food is any substance with actual or socially ascribed nutritive benefit, whereas drug is any 'chemical compound that, when brought into contact with the human body, produces a change in that body's functional condition, especially the mental and emotional states' (Page & Singer 2010). Drugs can include caffeine and nicotine, along with illicit drugs, such as heroin and non-prescription methamphetamine. The line between what constitutes a food or drug are blurry, especially when using an emic lens through which to understand these categories. For example, these definitions indicate that caffeine is a drug, however, many people consume items containing caffeine and categorize them under the umbrella of food. In this section, one will refer to the combination of food and drugs as 'substances' for simplicity, although using the term 'substance' is often criticized for being too vague (Page & Singer 2010).

Early research on aversions focused on western populations, with results indicating that aversions occurred most during the first trimester of pregnancy and often targeted bitter tasting substances and animal products (Hook 1978, Flaxman & Sherman 2000, Tierson et al. 1985). The most frequently mentioned averted substances were those that could have teratogenic effects. Nicotine is an example of a teratogenic substance. Nicotine exposure *in utero* can lead to adverse neurobehavioural effects in foetuses, impacting attention, temperament and cortical functioning (Liao et al. 2012). Along with nicotine, women have reported aversions to other plant foods containing toxins, such as heightened aversions toward spicy foods (Hook 1978). Spices can provide many health benefits, such as antioxidant and antimicrobial effects, but in high amounts can be deleterious to health, particularly in pregnancy (Flaxman & Sherman 2000, Profet 1995). However, aversions to spicy foods seem to be less common than aversions to animal products in non-vegetarian populations (Flaxman & Sherman 2000, McKerracher et al. 2016).

The consistent finding that meat is a cross-cultural aversion is not surprising given that raw and undercooked meat are particularly harmful. These foods run a high risk of transmitting pathogens such as *Listeriosis* and *E. coli* (Fessler 2002). Infections with these illnesses in pregnancy can have extreme deleterious effects, such as pre-term labour, miscarriage, and other birth complications (Dautt-

Leyva et al. 2018, Pazos et al. 2012). Aversions to both meat and plant based toxins are both therefore hypothesized to limit ingestion of toxins and pathogens, thereby functioning as a maternal-foetal protection strategy. However, whether these aversive patterns carry in an Indian context was unknown at the time early studies were being conducted and is worthy of consideration given the higher rates of vegetarianism, frequent use of diverse spices for cooking, and higher rates of tropical diseases compared to western populations.

One sought to explore pregnancy aversions in India through the lens of maternal-fetal protection. The populations one worked with had low levels of meat consumption due to religious reasons and lack of financial resources, so one wondered what types of aversions women would report given this important cultural and environmental distinction. Food aversions between the *Jenu Kurubas*, a resettled Scheduled Tribe community and neighbouring mixed-caste farmers (Placek et al. 2017) were compared. The findings revealed that grain aversions were the primary aversion among women in each location, a finding that does not align with the pathogen and toxin avoidance hypothesis. However, women also reported aversions to spicy foods, which can potentially contain teratogenic chemicals (Placek et al. 2017). In a quantitative model, spicy food aversions were inversely related to months pregnant and heightened nausea, two associations in line with the pathogen and toxin avoidance hypothesis. What, however, could explain aversions to grains?

The finding that grains were the most common aversion among both the *Jenu Kurubas* and the mixed caste farmers was indicative of another hypothesis, namely the dietary diversity model of food aversions (Demissie et al. 1998). This model hypothesizes that pregnancy aversions will target staple foods that are consumed daily as a strategy to 'encourage' consumption of nutritionally diverse foods. In contrast to the maternal-foetal protection hypothesis, where aversions are typically concentrated during early pregnancy, the dietary diversity hypothesis can encompass other phases of pregnancy since women's nutritional demands increase as pregnancy progresses. A study conducted in East Africa with the Datoga and

Turkana found support for this hypothesis: pregnant women reported cravings for meat and aversions toward staple grains (Young & Pike 2012).

From an emic perspective, food aversions are viewed as a natural part of pregnancy and are linked to iron deficiency anemia. Among pregnant women in Mumbai, appetite loss, food aversions, and nausea were viewed as the underlying cause for anemia (Chatterjee et al. 2014). Dietary changes in pregnancy—both in reference to cravings, aversions, and avoidances—are also perceived to be driven by what the foetus desires, and not solely the wants of the pregnant woman (Kant 2014, Vallianatos 2016). Women explained that the preferences must be influenced by the foetus because their preferences changed across pregnancies. Apart from the studies detailed here, little research has been conducted documenting Indian women's food aversions.

FOOD AVOIDANCES

Pregnancy in India is heavily marked by an adherence to proscriptions, or foods and drugs women are told to avoid. Food proscriptions, or avoidances, differ from aversions in that the former are culturally determined and socially transmitted, whereas the latter are driven by physiological sensations (Placek et al. 2017). These dietary patterns do not necessarily overlap and can often be at odds—for example, a pregnant woman might be told to avoid a food but experience intense cravings for the item, or experience strong aversions toward certain foods while also following proscriptions for a different set of substances. Among the *Jenu Kurubas* of Mysore district, many women report chewing tobacco in pregnancy (Placek et al. 2021b) yet are also told to avoid this substance because of the harm it can bring to the developing foetus (Placek et al. 2017).

Pregnancy food avoidances among Indian women consist of numerous foods, such as papaya, pineapple, unripe mangoes, unripe tamarind, jackfruit, black foods such as dark purple grapes, eggplant and jamun, egg, sesame, and drumsticks (Chanchani 2019, Khanum & Umpathy 1976, Nag 1994, Nichter & Nichter

1983, Patil et al. 2010, Placek & Hagen 2015, Placek et al. 2017). Several of these foods, such as papaya, mango (typically unripe mango), and jackfruit, are classified as 'hot' foods, which are perceived to be dangerous to pregnant women, whereas 'cold' foods are often proscribed during the third trimester as a method to prevent the soon-to-be born foetus from catching a cold (Chanchani 2019). Unfortunately, certain food proscriptions—like cravings for pica substances—are often the target of stigma among Indian scholars. A study conducted in Pondicherry by Patil and colleagues (2010) reports 'misconceptions' and 'old scientific tales' about pregnancy diet; their findings indicate that the majority of respondents believe that pregnant women should consume saffron to have a fair-skinned child and avoid specific fruits and vegetables for fear that they could cause abortion. The authors claim that illiteracy is the cause of these misconceptions, yet these claims lack proper scientific investigation and cast judgement on community belief systems and cultural practices. When considering the prevalence of dietary avoidances found cross-culturally, illiteracy cannot be the primary explanation for pregnancy food avoidances.

Accumulating evidence suggests that environmental cues and perceptions of pathogenicity influence ingestion of potentially harmful substances (Henrich & Henrich 2010, Placek & Hagen 2013, Placek & Hagen 2015). For example, socially transmitted pregnancy food taboos in Fiji targeted the most toxic marine species on the island (Henrich & Henrich 2010). This author's collaborative research in Tamil Nadu and Karnataka supports the notion that avoidances seem to be an additional strategy to protect the foetus, similar to other dietary shifts in pregnancy. Pregnant women frequently learned about avoidances from their maternal relatives and indicated that the avoided foods could be abortifacients or cause some other harm to the developing foetus (Placek & Hagen 2015, Placek et al. 2017). Fruits, which are reported avoidances across Indian studies, are generally not a category deemed harmful in pregnancy. Certain fruits including papaya and unripe mango, however, contain latexes, which can lead to anaphylaxis in pregnancy (Cipollini & Levey 1997, Wagner & Breiteneder 2002). Natural latexes provide defence against herbivores (Konno 2011); therefore, pregnancy avoidances that target them is consistent with the evolutionary model of foetal protection from plant teratogens (Hook 1978, Profet 1988).

FASTING

In India, fasting (*vratas*) is widespread across religions, and has deep roots in Hinduism, with early mentions of the practice found in the ancient *Puranas*, dating back to 250 CE (Collins 1988, Sastri 1988). Fasting is believed to liberate Hindus from the cycle of rebirth (Laidlaw 2005, Pearson 1996) and lead to health benefits, such as the elimination of toxins and increased longevity (Verma 2013). Fasting also occurs among pregnant Indian women (Placek et al. 2021a). Despite the deep history and widespread occurrence of fasting in India, little biocultural research has been conducted on the various fasting protocols and subsequent health outcomes among pregnant women representing diverse religions and cultural settings.

From an evolutionary perspective, pregnancy fasting is a paradox. Why would a woman restrict her food intake during a period of increased nutritional need? Compared to non-pregnant healthy individuals, the physiological costs of fasting in pregnancy are amplified: pregnancy is characterized by insulin resistance due to increased nutrient transfer to the foetus, where women require an average of 300 additional calories per day to maintain individual health and promote foetal growth and development (Sonagra et al. 2014). Under 'normal' pregnancy circumstances, fasting induced hypoglycemia leads to higher levels of fat metabolism, causing both decreased nutrient transfer from mother to the foetus, as well as an increase in ketone production. In some cases, these sudden shifts can generate a cascade effect where a woman's blood pH drops, leading to organ failure, and finally, intrauterine death (van Ewijk 2011). Pregnant women who skip meals can therefore experience the effects of starvation more rapidly than non-pregnant individuals, increasing the risk of adverse pregnancy outcomes. Within the context of evolutionary theory, pregnancy fasting is therefore an enigma because abstaining from food opposes adaptive predictions that centre on increasing caloric intake during the second and third trimesters of pregnancy when fasting sometimes occurs (Alwasel et al. 2010, Ziaee et al. 2010). Several hypotheses have been proposed to explain pregnancy fasting, but more empirical data is needed. Current hypotheses include gender inequality, pathogen and toxin avoidance and emic explanations.

The gender inequality model posits that fasting is a response to situations where women occupy a subordinate social, political and economic position (e.g., Counihan 1989). Scholars have noted that gender inequality in India is deeply rooted in patriarchal structures that are expressed and reinforced through the dowry system and patrilineal inheritance, which leads to the devaluation of females and perceptions of them as costly (Brulé & Gaikwad 2021, Malhotra et al. 1995). The devaluation of women is widely studied across numerous domains; for example, Indian women frequently lack power in household decision-making (Stroope 2015), have less control over their fertility and health (Palitto & O'Campo 2005) and are responsible for domestic work, which is valued less than paid work (Singh & Pattanaik 2020). Gender discrimination in Indian households is often expressed through unbalanced distribution of food between males and females. For example, adolescent and adult females in Indian households often eat less and eat last, contributing to adverse health outcomes (Neogy 2010). During pregnancy, in-laws sometimes restrict food to pregnant women as a form of neglect and abuse (Raj et al. 2011). Research indicates that dietary patterns and nutritional status are correlated with markers of economic empowerment for Indian women, with iron deficiency anemia being more common among women with less control over household financial decision-making (Krupp et al. 2018).

Fasting is hypothesized to be a way that women who lack power across social, economic and political domains rebel against patriarchal structures and gain moral authority (Counihan 1989, Menon & Shweder 1998). This is relevant in India, where food is a central component of women's lives and is one domain that they often control (Mathu & Jain 2008). Supporting evidence suggests that Hindu women sometimes fast to elicit emotional support from others (Egnor 1980), experience appetite loss when fighting with their husbands (Snell-Rood 2015), or fast to build 'moral capital' (Menon & Shweder 1998, Placek et al. 2021a). Specifically, Menon and Shweder (1998, 184) state that for Oriya Hindu women, 'fasting, eating less, and eating leftovers are seen as ways to garner moral authority'. South Asian ethnographic research therefore supports the perspective that fasting is used to exert power and control within certain contexts (Counihan 1989); however, the extent to which fasting is driven by specific indicators of gender inequality have not been directly measured.

Pregnant women might fast in response to pathogenic infection. Fasting, or pathogen-induced anorexia, appears to be a response to pathogen exposure in non-human organisms (Hart 1988). Research has found that organisms stop eating in response to fever and become otherwise selective about their dietary intake when immunologically challenged (Hart 2010, Konsman et al. 2002). Evidence for this hypothesis in pregnant women, however, is unavailable. The pathogen response hypothesis is relevant in India for the primary reason that reproductive-aged Indian women suffer from high rates of iron deficiency anemia. Iron deficiency anemia can be caused by a multitude of factors, such as dietary norms that discourage consumption of iron-rich foods, as well as helminth infections (Breymann 2015, Rammohan et al. 2012). Intestinal helminths, such as hookworms (*Necator americanus* and *Ancylostoma duodenale*) can cause nausea, vomiting, pathogen-induced anorexia, and high levels of blood loss. India is endemic for soil-transmitted helminths (Salam & Azam 2017), including roundworm (*Ascaris Lumbricoides*), hookworms, and whipworm (*Trichuris trichura*). This scenario presents an opportunity to test if fasting (or perhaps appetite loss, more accurately) is a response to helminth infections co-occurring with iron deficiency anemia in pregnant women.

The third hypothesis for pregnancy fasting centres on ethnophysiological perceptions of pregnancy. The *ease delivery* model, proposed as an emic explanation, suggests that fasting reduces pregnancy complications and can ease pain associated with a difficult delivery (Nichter & Nichter 1983). An earlier study found that pregnant women in Karnataka viewed the foetus as occupying the same physiological space as wind, food and urine (Nichter & Nichter 1983). Food consumption therefore influences the size of the baby and subsequent pregnancy outcomes. Other research indicates that cultural norms to 'eat down' to reduce the size of the baby is a cultural adaptation to reduce maternal and infant mortality (Christian et al. 2006, Rush 2000). Having a large baby can increase the risk of having an obstructed labour, particularly among women who have a short stature. In this author's ethnographic research with Hindu women in Mysore, pregnancy fasting is perceived to ease delivery by reducing infant size (Placek et al., unpublished data). Are 'eating down' and other forms of fasting associated with having a smaller baby? Lebanese Muslim women who fasted in Ramadan had significantly lower cesarean delivery rates than women who did not fast (Awwad et al. 2012); however, other biomedical research indicates that pregnancy fasting had no effect on intrauterine growth or anthropometric measurements of infants after birth (Moradi 2011, Ziaee et al. 2010). Although this research indicates that fasting is perceived to ease delivery for Hindu women, more research is needed to elucidate the how and why of this process.

CONCLUSION

Across cultures, human pregnancy is characterized by several dietary changes, such as intense cravings for soil and other culturally 'odd' foods, a heightened sense of disgust and food aversions, as well as the abstention of certain foods and drugs. The aim of this article was to describe these behaviours in an Indian context and provide current biocultural explanations and available evidence of these behaviours. As demonstrated throughout, evidence suggests that pathogen and toxin avoidance is a significant underlying factor that can explain the patterning of dietary preferences but does not negate the importance of other models that describe the persistence and impact of these dietary shifts.

This research is relevant in India because reproductive-aged women suffer from high rates of iron deficiency anemia. While iron deficiency can be caused by a multitude of factors, such as dietary norms that discourage consumption of iron-rich foods (Breymann 2015, Rammohan et al. 2012), existing research has not considered co-occurring dietary shifts; for example, vegetarianism might be included, but avoidances, aversions, and other behaviours described herein are omitted. One hereby offers a few suggestions for researchers interested in pregnancy diet specifically and reproductive health more generally. First, research protocols should consist of both food intake measures as well as questions that elicit cultural meanings of intake and abstention. Second, include study questions that measure external factors that contribute to dietary patterns, such as food and water insecurity (e.g., Placek & Hagen 2015). Third, engage in community education regarding possible etiologies of dietary shifts and the importance of avoiding stigmatizing language when discussing dietary changes and nutrition with pregnant women. Fourth, investigate statistical associations between dietary patterns and biological markers, especially hemoglobin levels, to determine if dietary shifts impact nutritional health. Fifth, collect data across regions of India and among women who vary according to caste, religion, socio-economic status and other key demographic markers, as India is heterogeneous and findings presented in this article may not be generalized and applied to other populations.

Summing up, dietary shifts in pregnancy occur cross-culturally. While there are several robust biocultural theories to explain several behaviours among Indian women, further evidence is needed to understand why women engage in these shifts and the subsequent maternal-infant health outcomes.

REFERENCES

Agar, M., 1996, *The Professional Stranger: An Informal Introduction to Ethnography*, Academic Press.

Alwasel, S.H., Z. Abotalib, J.S. Aljarallah, C. Osmond, S.M. Alkharaz, I.M. Alhazza, G. Badr and D.J.P. Barker, 2010, Changes in Placental Size during Ramadan. *Placenta*, *31*(7), pp. 607-10. https://doi.org/10.1016/j.placenta.2010.04.010

Awwad, J., I.M. Usta, J. Succar, K.M. Musallam, G. Ghazeeri and A.H. Nassar, 2012, The effect of maternal fasting during Ramadan on preterm delivery: A prospective cohort study, *BJOG: An International Journal of Obstetrics & Gynaecology*, *119*(11), pp. 1379-86. https://doi.org/10.1111/j.1471-0528.2012.03438.x

Boatin, A., B. Wylie, M.P. Singh, N. Singh, K. Yeboah-Antwi and D. Hamer, 2012, 671: Prevalence of and risk factors for pica among pregnant women in Chhattisgarh, India, *American Journal of Obstetrics & Gynecology*, *206*(1), S299. https://doi.org/10.1016/j.ajog.2011.10.689.

Breymann, C., 2015, Iron Deficiency Anemia in Pregnancy. *Seminars in Hematology*, *52*(4), pp. 339-47. https://doi.org/10.1053/j.seminhematol.2015.07.003.

Brulé, R., and N. Gaikwad, 2020, Culture, Capital, and the Political Economy Gender Gap: Evidence from Meghalaya's Matrilineal Tribes, *The Journal of Politics*, *83*(3). https://doi.org/10.1086/711176.

Chanchani, D., 2019, Maternal and child nutrition in rural Chhattisgarh: The role of health beliefs and practices, *Anthropology & Medicine*, *26*(2), pp. 142-58. https://doi.org/10.1080/13648470.2017.1361654.

Chatterjee, N. and G. Fernandes, 2014, 'This is normal during pregnancy': A qualitative study of anaemia-related perceptions and practices among pregnant women in Mumbai, India, *Midwifery*, *30*(3), pp. e56-e63. https://doi.org/10.1016/j.midw.2013.10.012.

Christian, P., S.B. Srihari, A. Thorne-Lyman, S.K. Khatry, S.C. LeClerq and S.R. Shrestha, 2006, Eating Down in Pregnancy: Exploring Food-Related Beliefs and Practices of Pregnancy in Rural Nepal, *Ecology of Food and Nutrition*, *45*(4), pp. 253-78. https://doi.org/10.1080/03670240600846336.

Cipollini, M.L., and D.J. Levey, 1997, Secondary Metabolites of Fleshy Vertebrate Dispersed Fruits: Adaptive Hypotheses and Implications for Seed Dispersal. *The American Naturalist*, *150*(3), pp. 346-72. https://doi.org/10.1086/286069.

Collins, C.D., 1988, *The Iconography and Ritual of Siva at Elephanta: On Life, Illumination, and Being*, SUNY Press.

Counihan, C.M., 1989, An anthropological view of western women's prodigious fasting: A review essay. *Food and Foodways*, *3*(4), pp. 357-75. https://doi.org/10.1080/07409710.1989.9961961

Dautt-Leyva, J.G., A. Canizalez-Román, L.F.A. Alfaro, F. Gonzalez-Ibarra and J. Murillo-Llanes, 2018, Maternal and perinatal complications in pregnant women with urinary tract infection caused by Escherichia coli, *Journal of Obstetrics and Gynaecology Research*, *44*(8), pp. 1384-90. https://doi.org/10.1111/jog.13687.

Demissie, T., N.M. Muroki and W. Kogi-Makau, 1998, Food Aversions and Cravings during Pregnancy: Prevalence and Significance for Maternal Nutrition in Ethiopia, *Food and Nutrition Bulletin,* 19(1), pp. 20-6. https://doi.org/10.1177/156482659801900104.

Dressler, W.W., M.C. Balieiro, R.P. Ribeiro and J. Ernesto Dos Santos, 2005, Cultural consonance and arterial blood pressure in urban Brazil. *Social Science & Medicine,* 61(3), pp. 527-40. https://doi.org/10.1016/j.socscimed.2004.12.013.

Egnor, M., 1980, On the meaning of sakti to women in Tamil Nadu, In *The Powers of Tamil Women.* Syracuse: Maxwell School of Citizenship and Public Affairs.

Fessler, D.M.T., 2002, Reproductive Immunosuppression and Diet: An Evolutionary Perspective on Pregnancy Sickness and Meat Consumption. *Current Anthropology,* 43(1), pp. 19-61. https://doi.org/10.1086/324128.

Flaxman, S. M. and P.W. Sherman, 2000, Morning Sickness: A Mechanism for Protecting Mother and Embryo, *The Quarterly Review of Biology,* 75(2), pp. 113-48.

Hart, B., 2010, Beyond Fever: Comparative Perspectives on Sickness Behavior, in *Encyclopedia of Animal Behavior,* 1, pp. 205-10. https://doi.org/10.1016/B978-0-08-045337-8.00133-9.

Hart, B.L., 1988, Biological basis of the behavior of sick animals, *Neuroscience & Biobehavioral Reviews,* 12(2), pp. 123-37. https://doi.org/10.1016/S0149-7634(88)80004-6.

Henrich, J. and N. Henrich, 2010. The evolution of cultural adaptations: Fijian food taboos protect against dangerous marine toxins, *Proceedings of the Royal Society of London B: Biological Sciences,* 277(1701), pp. 3715-24. https://doi.org/10.1098/rspb.2010.1191.

Hook, E.B., 1978, Dietary cravings and aversions during pregnancy, *The American Journal of Clinical Nutrition,* 31(8), pp. 1355-62. https://doi.org/10.1093/ajcn/31.8.1355.

Hooper, D., and H.H. Mann, 1906, *Earth-eating and the Earth-eating Habit in India.* Asiatic Society.

Jeffery, P., J. Patricia, R. Jeffery, A. Lyon and P. Jeffery of S. of S. A.R., 1989, *Labour Pains and Labour Power: Women and Childbearing in India.* Zed Books.

Kant, A., 2014, Experiencing Pregnancy: Negotiating Cultural and Biomedical Knowledge, *Sociological Bulletin,* 63(2), pp. 247-62. https://doi.org/10.1177/0038022920140204.

Khanum, M.P., and K.P. Umapathy, 1976, Survey of food habits and beliefs of pregnant and lactating mothers in Mysore city, *Indian Journal of*

Nutrition and Dietetics. http://agris.fao.org/agris-search/search.do?record ID= US201303066476.

King, J.C., 2000, Physiology of pregnancy and nutrient metabolism, *The American Journal of Clinical Nutrition*, 71(5), pp. 1218S-25S. https://doi.org/10.1093/ajcn/71.5.1218s.

Konno, K., 2011, Plant latex and other exudates as plant defense systems: Roles of various defense chemicals and proteins contained therein, *Phytochemistry*, 72(13), pp. 1510-30. https://doi.org/10.1016/j.phytochem.2011.02.016.

Konsman, J.P., P. Parnet and R. Dantzer, 2002, Cytokine-induced sickness behaviour: Mechanisms and implications, *Trends in Neurosciences*, 25(3), pp. 154-9. https://doi.org/10.1016/S0166-2236(00)02088-9.

Kourtis, A.P., J.S. Read and D.J. Jamieson, 2014, Pregnancy and Infection, *New England Journal of Medicine*, 370(23), pp. 2211-18. https://doi.org/10.1056/NEJMra1213566.

Kraus, T. A., S.M. Engel, R.S. Sperling, L. Kellerman, Y. Lo, S. Wallenstein, M.M. Escribese, J.L. Garrido, T. Singh, M. Loubeau and T.M. Moran, 2012, Characterizing the Pregnancy Immune Phenotype: Results of the Viral Immunity and Pregnancy (VIP) Study, *Journal of Clinical Immunology*, 32(2), pp. 300-11. https://doi.org/10.1007/s10875-011-9627-2.

Krupp, K., C.D. Placek, M. Wilcox, K. Ravi, V. Srinivas, A. Arun and P. Madhivanan, 2018, Financial decision making power is associated with moderate to severe anemia: A prospective cohort study among pregnant women in rural South India, *Midwifery*, 61, pp, 15-21. https://doi.org/10.1016/j.midw.2018.02.014.

Laidlaw, J., 2005, 'A life worth leaving: Fasting to death as telos of a Jain religious life', *Economy and Society*, 34(2), pp. 178-99. https://doi.org/10.1080/03085140500054545.

Laufer, B., 1930, *Geophagy: vol. Field Museum of Natural History, Publication 280, Anthropological Series XVIII, No. 2*. Chicago. http://indianmedicine.eldoc.ub.rug.nl/root/L/60346/.

Liao, C.-Y., Y.-J. Chen, J.-F. Lee, C.-L. Lu and C.H. Chen, 2012, Cigarettes and the developing brain: Picturing nicotine as a neuroteratogen using clinical and preclinical studies, *Tzu Chi Medical Journal*, 24(4), pp. 157-61. https://doi.org/10.1016/j.tcmj.2012.08.003.

Malhotra, A., R. Vanneman and S. Kishor, 1995, 'Fertility, Dimensions of Patriarchy, and Development in India', *Population and Development Review*, 21(2), pp. 281-305. https://doi.org/10.2307/2137495.

Mathu, A. and A. Jain, 2008, Gender Equality in India in *Gender and Development in India: The Indian Scenario*, pp. 13-38. Gyan Publishing House.

McKerracher, L., M. Collard and J. Henrich, 2016, Food Aversions and Cravings during Pregnancy on Yasawa Island, Fiji. *Human Nature*, 27(3), pp. 296-315. https://doi.org/10.1007/s12110-016-9262-y.

Menon, U., and R. Shweder, 1998, 'The Return of the "White Man's Burden": The Moral Discourse of Anthropology and the Domestic Life of Hindu Women', in *Welcome to Middle Age!: (And Other Cultural Fictions)*. University of Chicago Press.

Miao, D., S.L. Young and C.D. Golden, 2015, A meta-analysis of pica and micronutrient status. *American Journal of Human Biology*, 27(1), pp. 84-93. https://doi.org/10.1002/ajhb.22598.

Mor, G. and I. Cardenas, 2010 'The Immune System in Pregnancy: A Unique Complexity', *American Journal of Reproductive Immunology (New York, N.Y.: 1989)*, 63(6), pp. 425-33. https://doi.org/10.1111/j.1600-0897.2010.00836.x.

Moradi, M., 2011, The effect of Ramadan fasting on fetal growth and Doppler indices of pregnancy. *Journal of Research in Medical Sciences: The Official Journal of Isfahan University of Medical Sciences*, 16(2), pp. 165-9.

Nag, M., 1994, Beliefs and Practices about Food during Pregnancy: Implications for Maternal Nutrition, *Economic and Political Weekly*, 29(37), pp. 2427-38.

Neogy, S., 2010, 'Gender inequality, mothers' health, and unequal distribution of food: Experience from a CARE project in India', *Gender & Development*, 18(3), pp. 479-89. https://doi.org/10.1080/13552074.2010.522027.

Nichter, M. and M. Nichter, 1983, 'The Ethnophysiology and Folk Dietetics of Pregnancy: A Case Study from South India', *Human Organization*, 42(3), pp. 235-46. https://doi.org/10.17730/humo.42.3.430814452 35366lk.

Orloff, N.C., and J.M. Hormes, 2014, 'Pickles and ice cream! Food cravings in pregnancy: Hypotheses, preliminary evidence, and directions for future research', *Frontiers in Psychology*, 5. https://doi.org/10.3389/fpsyg.2014.01076.

Page, J.B., and M. Singer, 2010, 'Comprehending Drug Use', in *Comprehending Drug Use*. Rutgers University Press. https://www.degruyter.com/document/doi/10.36019/9780813549934/html.

Pallitto, C.C., and P.O'Campo, 2005, 'Community level effects of gender inequality on intimate partner violence and unintended pregnancy in Colombia: Testing the feminist perspective', *Social Science & Medicine*, 60(10), pp. 2205-16. https://doi.org/10.1016/j.socscimed.2004.10.017.

Patil, C.L., E.T. Abrams, A.R. Steinmetz and S.L. Young, 2012, 'Appetite Sensations and Nausea and Vomiting in Pregnancy: An Overview of the

Explanations', *Ecology of Food and Nutrition*, *51*(5), pp. 394-417. https://doi.org/10.1080/03670244.2012.696010.

Patil, R., A. Mittal, D.R. Vedapriya, M.I. Khan and M. Raghavia, 2010, 'Taboos and misconceptions about food during pregnancy among rural population of Pondicherry', *Calicut Medical Journal*, *8*(2). https://www.cabdirect.org/cabdirect/abstract/20103306697.

Pazos, M., R.S. Sperling, T.M. Moran and T.A. Kraus, 2012, 'The influence of pregnancy on systemic immunity', *Immunologic Research*, *54*(1-3), pp. 254-61. https://doi.org/10.1007/s12026-012-8303-9.

Pearson, A.M.,1997, *Because It Gives Me Peace of Mind: Ritual Fasts in the Religious Lives of Hindu Women*. SUNY Press.

Placek, C., 2017, 'A test of four evolutionary hypotheses of pregnancy food cravings: Evidence for the social bargaining model', *Royal Society Open Science*, *4*(10), 170243. https://doi.org/10.1098/rsos.170243.

Placek, C.D. and E.H. Hagen, 2013, 'A test of three hypotheses of pica and amylophagy among pregnant women in Tamil Nadu, India', *American Journal of Human Biology*, *25*(6), pp. 803-13. https://doi.org/10.1002/ajhb.22456.

——, 2015, 'Fetal Protection', *Human Nature*, *26*(3), pp. 255-76. https://doi.org/10.1007/s12110-015-9239-2.

Placek, C.D., P. Jaykrishna, V. Srinivas and P. Madhivanan, 2021, Pregnancy Fasting in Ramadan: Toward a Biocultural Framework. *Ecology of Food and Nutrition*, *60*(6), pp. 785-809. https://doi.org/10.1080/03670244.2021.1913584.

Placek, C.D., and P. Madhivanan, 2017, 'Exploring the perceptions of pregnancy loss between two populations of South Indian women: A pilot study', *Public Health*, *148*, pp. 9-12. https://doi.org/10.1016/j.puhe.2017.02.019.

Placek, C.D., P. Madhivanan and E.H. Hagen, 2017. 'Innate food aversions and culturally transmitted food taboos in pregnant women in rural southwest India: Separate systems to protect the fetus?' *Evolution and Human Behavior*, *38*(6), pp. 714-28. https://doi.org/10.1016/j.evolhumbehav.2017.08.001.

Placek, C.D., R.E. Magnan, V. Srinivas, P. Jaykrishna, K. Ravi, A. Khan, P. Madhivanan and E.H. Hagen, 2021, 'The impact of information about tobacco-related reproductive vs. General health risks on South Indian women's tobacco use decisions', *Evolutionary Human Sciences*, *3*. https://doi.org/10.1017/ehs.2020.61.

Profet, M., 1988, 'The evolution of pregnancy sickness as protection to the embryo against Pleistocene teratogens', *Evolutionary Theory*, *8*(3), pp. 177-90.

———, 1995, 'Pregnancy Sickness as Adaptation: A Deterrent to Maternal Ingestion of Teratogens', in *The Adapted Mind: Evolutionary Psychology and the Generation of Culture: Evolutionary Psychology and the Generation of Culture*, USA, Oxford University Press.

Racicot, K., J.-Y. Kwon, P. Aldo, M. Silasi and G. Mor, 2014, 'Understanding the Complexity of the Immune System during Pregnancy', *American Journal of Reproductive Immunology*, 72(2), pp. 107-16. https://doi.org/10.1111/aji.12289.

Raj, A., S. Sabarwal, M.R. Decker, S. Nair, M. Jethva, S. Krishnan, B. Donta, N. Saggurti and J.G. Silverman, 2011, 'Abuse from In-Laws during Pregnancy and Post-Partum: Qualitative and Quantitative Findings from Low-income Mothers of Infants in Mumbai', India. *Maternal and Child Health Journal*, 15(6), pp. 700-12. https://doi.org/10.1007/s10995-010-0651-2.

Rammohan, A., N. Awofeso and M.-C. Robitaille, 2012, 'Addressing Female Iron-Deficiency Anaemia in India', Is Vegetarianism the Major Obstacle? *ISRN Public Health*, *2012*, pp. 1-8. https://doi.org/10.5402/2012/765476.

Rao, M., 1985, 'Food beliefs of rural women during the reproductive years in Dharwad, India', *Ecology of Food and Nutrition*, 16(2), pp. 93-103. https://doi.org/10.1080/03670244.1985.9990852.

Rush, D., 2000, 'Nutrition and maternal mortality in the developing world', *The American Journal of Clinical Nutrition*, 72(1), pp. 212S-40S. https://doi.org/10.1093/ajcn/72.1.212S.

Salam, N., and S. Azam, 2017. 'Prevalence and distribution of soil-transmitted helminth infections in India', *BMC Public Health*, 17(1), p. 201. https://doi.org/10.1186/s12889-017-4113-2.

Sastri, S. M.N., 1903, *Hindu Feasts, Fasts and Ceremonies*. Printed at the M.E. Publishing House.

Simán, C.M., and U.J. Eriksson, 1997, 'Vitamin C supplementation of the maternal diet reduces the rate of malformation in the offspring of diabetic rats', *Diabetologia*, 40(12), pp. 1416-24. https://doi.org/10.1007/s001250050844.

Singh, P. and F. Pattanaik, 2020, 'Unfolding unpaid domestic work in India: Women's constraints, choices, and career', *Palgrave Communications*, 6(1), pp. 1-13. https://doi.org/10.1057/s41599-020-0488-2.

Singhi, P. and S. Singhi, 1983, 'Nutritional status and psycho-social stress in children with pica', *Indian Pediatrics*, 20(5), pp. 345-9.

Snell Rood, C., 2015, 'Marital Distress and the Failure to Eat: The Expressive Dimensions of Feeding, Eating, and Self-care in Urban South Asia', *Medical*

Anthropology Quarterly, 29(3), pp. 316-33. https://doi.org/10.1111/maq.12184.

Sonagra, A.D., S.M.D. Biradar and D.S.J. Murthy, 2014, 'Normal Pregnancy- A State of Insulin Resistance', *Journal of Clinical and Diagnostic Research: JCDR*, 8(11), pp. CC01-CC03. https://doi.org/10.7860/JCDR/2014/10068.5081.

Srinath, S., S.C. Girimaji, G. Gururaj, S. Seshadri, D.K. Subbakrishna, P. Bhola and N. Kumar, 2005, 'Epidemiological study of child & adolescent psychiatric disorders in urban & rural areas of Bangalore', India. *Indian Journal of Medical Research*, 122(1), p. 67.

Stroope, S., 2015, 'Seclusion, decision-making power, and gender disparities in adult health: Examining hypertension in India', *Social Science Research*, 53, pp. 288-99. https://doi.org/10.1016/j.ssresearch.2015.05.013.

Thurston, E., 1906, *Ethnographic Notes in Southern India*, Superintendent, Government Press.

Tierson, F.D., C.L. Olsen and E.B. Hook, 1985, 'Influence of cravings and aversions on diet in pregnancy', *Ecology of Food and Nutrition*, 17(2), pp. 117-29. https://doi.org/10.1080/03670244.1985.9990886.

Vallianatos, H., 2016, *Poor and Pregnant in New Delhi, India*. Routledge. https://doi.org/10.4324/9781315422374.

van Ewijk, R., 2011, 'Long-term health effects on the next generation of Ramadan fasting during pregnancy', *Journal of Health Economics*, 30(6), pp. 1246-60. https://doi.org/10.1016/j.jhealeco.2011.07.014.

Van Hollen, C.C., 2003. *Birth on the Threshold: Childbirth and Modernity in South India*. University of California Press.

Verma, M., 2013. *Fasts and Festivals of India*, Diamond Pocket Books (P) Ltd.

Wagner, S., and H. Breiteneder, 2002. 'The latex-fruit syndrome', *Biochemical Society Transactions*, 30(6), pp. 935-40. https://doi.org/10.1042/bst0300935.

Wiley, A. S. and J.M. Cullin, 2016, 'What Do Anthropologists Mean When They Use the Term *Biocultural*?: What Does *Biocultural* Mean?' *American Anthropologist*, 118(3), pp. 554-69. https://doi.org/10.1111/aman.12608.

Young, A.G., and I.L. Pike, 2012, 'A Biocultural Framework for Examining Maternal Cravings and Aversions among Pastoral Women in East Africa', *Ecology of Food and Nutrition*, 51(5), pp. 444-62. https://doi.org/10.1080/03670244.2012.696013.

Young, S., 2009, 'Evidence for the consumption of the inedible', in *Consuming the Inedible: Neglected Dimensions of Food Choice*. Berghahn Books.

Young, S.L., 2010, 'Pica in Pregnancy: New Ideas About an Old Condition', *Annual Review of Nutrition*, 30(1), pp. 403-22. https://doi.org/10.1146/annurev.nutr.012809.104713.

——, 2011, *Craving Earth: Understanding Pica—the Urge to Eat Clay, Starch, Ice, and Chalk*. Columbia University Press.

Ziaee, V., Z. Kihanidoost, M. Younesian, M.-B. Akhavirad, F. Bateni, Z. Kazemianfar and S. Hantoushzadeh, 2010, 'The Effect of Ramadan Fasting on Outcome of Pregnancy', *Iranian Journal of Pediatrics*, 20(2), pp. 181-6.

SECTION II

FOOD IN FOLKLORE: BELIEFS, PRACTICES, AND SOCIAL REALITY

CHAPTER 5

Food, Folklore and the Construction of Social Reality: Perspectives from Arunachal Pradesh

SARIT K. CHAUDHURI

> Food derives its 'power' from the web of interrelations it evokes.
>
> POTTIER 2003, 240

Food remained one of most essential elements in the struggle for existence as well as in the evolutionary history of mankind. Its pervasive role in everyday life is manifested irrespective of cultural and geographical boundaries. According to Mintz and Bois (2002, 102), 'Next to breathing, eating is perhaps the most essential of all human activities, and one with which much of social life is entwined.' Pottier says, 'As the most powerful instrument for expressing and shaping interactions between humans, food is the primary gift and a repository of condensed social meaning' (2003, 238). Food, as a concept, has multiple implications for a community or communities, region, or even a nation as such, and these have led to the academicians as well as policymakers to come forward and look into various issues associated with this concept. Food plays many and also complex roles in human society (Dawar 2019, 7). According to Mukhopadhyaya (2020, xi), 'Ideas and practices related to food are integral components of varied forms of lifeways that are influenced by dominant ideologies of social and economic inequalities. . . .'

Undoubtedly, this has provided a real ground of interdisciplinary works. The discipline of anthropology has a long association with food habit, and it can be traced back to Garrick Mallery's article, 'Manners and Meals' which was published in *American Anthropologist* in 1888 (vol. 1, no. 3). Since then, there have been many valuable studies, such as Hamilton 1920, Franz Boas 1921, Andrew Richard 1939, Levi Strauss 1965, Mary Douglas 1966 and Appadurai 1981 though Jack Goody's (1982) classic ethnography on *Cooking, Cuisine, and Class: A Study of Comparative Sociology* remained a landmark as it reoriented the trajectory of anthropological study on food and eating.[1] In fact, for a long time, field based anthropologists have harped on human diets, specifically in the socio-cultural determinants of diet; changing pattern of food production; markets; and food security at community and household levels, etc. (Pottier 2003, 240). Linkages of food with ecology, rituals, and symbolism are well reflected and even anthropologists tried to underscore how food functions in social allocation, in terms of identity, nationality, class, individuality, and gender (Mintz & Bois 2002, 108). Within this backdrop, the present study is an attempt to look in the context of Arunachal to locate how pervasive food stuff is in the life of the tribes of this frontier state.

Arunachal Pradesh, the erstwhile NEFA, is located in the extreme northeastern corner of India. It is bordered by Bhutan in the west, China (Tibet) on the north and northeast and the states of Assam and Nagaland to its south. It is here the Himalayan range changes its eastwest orientation to a northsouth one (HDR 2005, 3). Being the largest state in northeast of India, this state is blessed by nature with extraordinary resources in terms of diversity, though the population density is quite low—13 people per square kilometre (according to the 2001 Census). The remoteness and the insularity of the area till very recently, was a contributing factor to the legacy of persisting bountiful natural resources (Das 2005, 169). This state is the homeland of 26 major tribes with more than 100 subtribes located in 14 districts.[2] Each tribe has its own distinct identity though some threads of commonality can also be traced looking at their latent and manifested aspects of culture. Some scholars tried to divide the tribes in two broad cultural zones based on the distribution of tribes in to hills and plains which is problematic.[3] Depending on the concentration of the tribes, some have preferred five cultural zones. Depending on the religious beliefs and practices, the tribes however cannot be divided into Buddhist and non-Buddhist tribes as Christianity is a dominant phenomena today, and even the Hinduized ideological frame has gradually accentuated among some of the tribes.[4] However, foodstuff or the food habits of the tribal population helps us not only to understand the question of cultural specificity, but also a lot of commonality which is directly linked up with their ecology, belief system as well as the ongoing process of acculturation and emerging social realities. This also helps one to understand how this has given an added dimension to their existing plethora of folklore tradition.

FOOD AND FOLKLORE

Traditionally, a majority of the tribes are dependent on shifting hill cultivation leaving a few who practise wet rice cultivation, such as the Apatanis, Khamptis, etc. And most of such tribes also practise both hunting and gathering along with fishing. Such productive strategies ultimately decide the nature of foodstuff and also the consumption pattern. Undoubtedly, rice is the staple food for a majority of the tribes though a few are dependent of maize and millet.[5] Besides numerous roots, shoots, wild vegetables, there is a unique concept of famine tree which is associated with some tribes, such as Nyishi, Adi, Miji, Mishmis, etc., but it has special association with the Sulungs, for whom this sago plant still constitutes their major food item whereas others use it for feeding their domestic animals. This plant (tree fern of genus *Alsophilia*) has different nomenclatures. Almost 60 years back, Stonor had mentioned that, 'Among the Daflas (now known as Nyishi), *tacheh* is entirely a reserve food, for the times of famine, but among the Sulungs, who are still partly food gatherers, it is said to be fairly frequently used under normal circumstances, although sago made of wild palms is preferred' (1958, 137).[6]

Some of the high altitude tribes, such as Miji, Monpa, Sherdukpen as well as subtribes of the Adis (Tangam, Bori, Pailibos, etc.) use maize as their staple food. All tribes are non-vegetarians and generally, meat of all domestic, semi-domestic, and wild animals and birds are consumed depending on their availability within the habitat of the people. Next to meat, fishes of different local varieties are part of non-vegetarian food item followed by eggs which have a great ritual value for many tribes. Milk is hardly consumed except by a few high altitude Buddhist tribes, like, Monpa and Sherdukpen. Each and every tribe has a strong tradition of drinking which is brewed in almost all households by using different locally grown cereals, and this can be a fascinating subject to study.[7] Similarly, smoking is a very common habit though addiction to opium is restricted to a few tribes having a long history as reflected in official colonial reports[8] and today opium is a real problem in the Lohit district and to some extent in Tirap district also.[9]

RICE

Rice is one of the most important staple crops, and Arunachal tribes are growing enormous varieties of the same in both hills and plains. Already 1866 rice germplasms are collected by Assam Rice Collection series, ICAR Complex for NEH region, and National Bureau of Plant Genetic Resources (Hegde 2003, 35). The Khamptis of Lohit district are producing 21 varieties of rice as reported by Singh et al. (2000),[10] and the Monpas are producing rice at an elevation of 3,000 m msl.

Interestingly, rice or paddy is one important source of folklore materials in Arunachal Pradesh. Dai (2005, 15) narrates a tale explaining how rice reached man:

> In Arunachal mythology rice is of divine origin. It is a gift of gods that came to a race of sky dwellers in the land of fish stars. The story goes that during the great hunt the faithful dog of a legendary hunter lost his way and stayed in to the kingdom of the great earth mother, the goddess of grain. The dog told her how he had lost her way. The goddess heard him out and gave him a few seeds of rice, which the faithful dog carried back to the land of the sky dwellers in the crease of his ear.

Mopin, one of the most popular festivals of Arunachal, which can be perceived as one of the most important identity markers of the Galo tribe is centred around the myth of rice or paddy. The rice powder and rice paste are considered as sacred objects by this tribe and they believe that rice originated from a corn that was a gift of goddess Mopin (Anyi-Pinku-Pinte) and she also favours its use. There are different versions explaining how rice or paddy reached or in a larger sense cultivation was initiated by man. These are basically linked with the myth of Abo Tani—the mythical ancestor of Tani group of tribes (which includes the Galo) and even mankind as a whole.

The first man Abo Tani and his brother Taki were born out of Earth (Sisi). Taki was extremely jealous of Tani which soon grew into hatred, and he planned to kill his brother. Once, he managed to persuade Tani to go rowing with him, took him towards a waterfall and shoved him down in it. He had already fixed a fish trap (Takom) further downstream and the body of Tani as it floated down got caught in it. Taki had thought that none had seen but a bird (Jiku Miku) saw it. As man would be born of Tani, he decided to bring Tani back in life. And finally, after a lot of effort he succeeded in the revival of Tani who became a man. Many gods and goddesses who were anxiously waiting to see Tani's revival, then blessed Tani before their departure with several things for his survival, such as bravery, bow and arrow, mustard seed, gourd and paddy (Daji Dane), etc. And all these were left with the Mopin—the deity of wealth, who would hand these over to Tani when he grew up and performed a ritual sacrifice for his prosperous life.

There are other versions explaining how the Mopin goddess gave paddy or taught the art of cultivation to Tani.[11] It may be mentioned here that Galos believe that rice has a divine power; so, during Mopin rice powder (*Iti*) is sprayed over the Mopin images and altars. It is also smeared on the baskets of women, on the sacrificed animals, sacrificial weapons and on the face of each and every participant which they believe purify the minds and bring happiness as well as prosperity to individuals.[12]

Rice or, in other sense, cultivation of paddy crop can also be taken as identity marker of another two tribes of Arunachal Pradesh, namely, Apatani and Khampti. Apatanis are famous for their advanced irrigated rice fields—a unique display of traditional mode of resource management. In the 1960s, the introduction of paddy-cum-fish cultivation had added another success story to the Apatani farmers which has now become part of their tradition or identity marker.[13]

Among the Adis, a good number of festivities are linked with the production of foodgrains, such as rice or millet and even harvesting or storing of grains. *Unying* or *Aran*, which is celebrated for the better production of paddy crop, is linked with a myth which says that the most beautiful woman *Nyanyi Mete* decided to glide down to the world of human being. When she arrived to the surface of the earth with beautiful dress and attires, the world of creatures, humanity, wild animals woke up and raised their voice to welcome her. The flowers of different colours and leaves appeared on the trees and creepers, birds started singing and dancing. The human world woke up to welcome the beauty in a befitting manner. *Kine Nane*, the mother of plenty, raised a basketful of food items with which the humanity should arrange a feast. Then all started singing and dancing in admiration of the beauty (Dupak 2004, 3-4).

Similarly, the *Kombi* festival is also celebrated for the prosperity of thee crops,[14] and *Rikti* is linked to the storage of crops in the granaries as a purifying act.[15] Similarly, *Pinneng* or *Dorung* festivals are linked with the harvesting of millet (*Mirung*).[16] The biggest celebration of the Adis is Solung festival where Miri (expert singer) recites Abang[17] which narrates the myth of the origin of different crops, like paddy, maize, millet, etc. during *Ponung*.[18]

Use of rice powder as sacred object is also found among some other tribes. Among the Apatanis *Murung* is one of most important family based festivals where people seek blessing from their ancestors as well as *Murung* gods for multiple reasons.[19]

However, the most popular and important festival of the Apatani is Dree, which can be perceived today as one of the identity markers of the tribe, and is generally celebrated in the month of July in the Apatani valley. Interestingly, myth related to the origin of the festival is associated with the origin of paddy which Dai (2005, 27) textualized in her book.

MITHUN

Another important food item is the meat of mithun which is considered as a delicacy for the majority of the tribes under the Subansiri, Siang, and Lohit areas leaving a few (Monpa, Memba, etc.) who reside in high altitude areas or where mithun are not found (Wangcho). This is not only a popular and a huge food store, but it has a huge sacred value. Mithun is sacrificed in almost all major festivals or even for worshipping various gods and goddesses for the well being of family or clan or even to ward off evil spirits causing sickness or misfortune to individuals or families or even villagers, etc. Naturally, possession of this food recourse is linked with social as well as economic status of individuals in most of the tribes.[20] Here also, one can trace various myths related to the mithun which symbolizes the pride of Arunachal even today. In fact, each tribe has its own tale to tell.

The Khowas (Bugun) and the Akas of Kameng district, the Adis of Siang and the Mishmis of Lohit district—all have their own legends about the origin of the mithun. Each one differs from the other. However, one common belief among all the tribes is that the mithun as well as buffalo and the pig were created to be sacrificed in the honour of the gods and goddesses. Most of the stories contain imaginary episodes relating to the most miraculous way the mithun had come into being. The Adis, during their Solung festival, as well as the Miri narrate the origin of life on the earth which is popularly called 'Abang'. In the first part of Abang (Limir Libom), the Miri narrate the tales related to the origin of mithun which is given in brief:

Long ago there appeared a gigantic object with huge legs, beautiful horns and cars and ears. For the people it was a terrifying object. The huge body had blocked the route through which 'Donying Bote', the god who does well to mankind, used to maintain communication with Kine Nane, the goddess responsible for the welfare of humanity. It had blocked the passage through which came the sunlight. Ultimately, one 'Dadi Karki Bote' coming from the 'Dadi Somi' land could identify the object as the great 'Mapong Bon Sedi' who symbolized greatness. The object was named 'Limir Sobo'. Hundreds of people representing various lands decided together to drive away the ominous looking beast. All their attempts to get rid off it ended in failure. Heroes and valiant fighters like 'Dadi Miko Pokbo', 'Dadi Miru Lejung', and 'Dadi Mire Legeng' fought gallantly but the great thing remained where it was. Finally, a great hero named 'Dadi Karki Bote' succeeded in inflicting fatal injury on it. Limir-Sobo was slain. The 'Engo Takar' people cut the animal into pieces and distributed the flesh to the tribal world. After some time, it was found that the varieties of grasses, trees and plants had grown at place where the animal had been thrown. One part of the animal was sent to the land of 'Donying Ang' and sown there. After some time, a creeper of 'Epun' or gourd sprouted from it. With the passage of time, the creeper spread out in all directions, one of its branches spread out in all directions, one of its branches reaching as far as the land of 'Dadi Somi'. In course of time, it bore a fruit which turned out to be a huge gourd. When the gourd attained maturity, a strange sound could be heard inside it to the great awe of all who decided to break the gourd and see what it was all about. A large 'Tapum' or worm came out of the torn gourd. Nobody could recognize it and therefore, an expert called 'Dadi Komi Yomko' collected the grasses, plants and leaves grown out of the flesh of the great 'Limir-Sobo' and affixed them on the body of the worm. The face of the worm was immediately transformed into an 'Eso' or mithun. The first-ever mithun on earth was thus born to the great jubilation of mankind.[21]

Versions of such myth can be traced among many other tribes, such as Bugun, Miji, etc.[22] Origin myths are also available with some other important animals which constitute major meat items for the Arunachal tribes, such as pig, rat or squirrel, chicken, monkey, etc.[23]

BAMBOO

Bamboo, which is considered as wonder plant, is valuable in multiple ways, such as ecological, economical, and cultural and even the survival of some of the endangered animals and species depends on this wonder grass (Furniss 2004, 58-65). In the context of the majority of tribes of the northeast, it is also a pleasure plant as its products, especially bamboo shoots, are considered as a delicacy as food stuff or even as spices. Naturally, Arunachal is not an exception to this aspect. Bamboo shoot (Eeku) is the most favourite item of the Galo tribe though preparation of bamboo shoot from raw bamboo is really a laborious job usually done during the month of September or October by the group of families or individuals having kinship relations. Two different varieties of bamboos are used which are locally called Aenee and Aejoo though the first one is more delicious. Preparation of fermented bamboo shoots involves a lot of procedures[24] and generally four varieties of the stuff are produced, such as, Kuupee, Eekuu, Eenee and Kuutee. Earlier, these were made for domestic consumption but now these are sold in the market and have become a source of earning for the villagers. For instance, one bamboo tube full of Eekuu will cost fifty rupees and other varieties are less costly ranging from 10 to 20 rupees (Lollen 2007, 95-6). Such a bamboo shoot is used in various ways, not only in everyday life but also during community feast, festivities or ceremonies. In most of their food preparations, whether vegetables, meat, pork, or fish, they prefer to add this fermented bamboo shoots to make them more delicious. Among the Lisus or Yobin, a little-known tribe of Arunachal, residing in Tirap district, one of their delicacies is young bamboo shoots which are pounded, boiled with meat, and served (Dutta 1979, 64).

Among the Adis, one can trace at least three varieties of food items prepared from bamboo, such as *Ikun* (fermented bamboo shoot which is sour in taste), *Ip* (dried bamboo shoot) and *Iting* (green bamboo shoot used as vegetables). For preparing such items, first bamboo roots are collected during the new shoots season, then after cleaning off its sheath, it is cut into pieces and consumed after boiling. But, in order to make the fermented veriety, pieces of bamboo shoots are filled in the bamboo tubes which are then kept in the muddy area for initiating fermentation process which takes almost one week. Then those are taken out as per the requirement and these can be preserved for two years. Another way of preserving shoots is to put the shoots in the baskets made of cane by using some wild leaves and kept in shady areas, such fermented shoots can be kept for one year. Usually, various bamboo shoots are consumed with meat, fish and meat of rodents. Padams believe that bamboo shoot locally known as eyom is the tastiest among all varieties (Megu 2007, 37). At least 12 varieties of wild and eight varieties cultivated bamboos are intricately associated with the lives of the Padams, and this has also given rise to number of folklores explaining how bamboo is originated on the earth. Long oral narratives are textualized by Megu (ibid., 21-4). However, a brief translation is given below (ibid., 24):

Originators of the beads and ornaments known as '*Sedi Linggen Sobo*' was shot dead by *Kari*, an expert hunter, with bow and arrow made of iron which was made by the mythical priest known as *Ninur Lomang*. At that time bamboo was not found on the earth. When Linggen Sobo was shot, out of pain he also injured Kari *Babing* below the armpit. Because of this injury, *Siking Kingkang e Kari* also died in the outskirt of the *Nomgu-nomnang* land, the land of the spirits of hunting. The funeral rite of the Siking Kari was done by the *Sipit* (a kind of bird) and the people of *Karpung Karduk* visited to offer food to his buried soul locally known as '*Goram Ginam*'—a ritual where family or relatives of the diseased person offer food to the departed soul at the grave. There they observed a tiny plant germinated from the bow and arrows by which *Linggen Sobo* was shot dead. That plant had grown into a bamboo. That's why bamboo became so strong and durable especially when harvested during dark phase of the moon or '*polo ruruk*', as it grows out of that iron bow and arrows.

It may be mentioned here that, out of 115 species reported in India, 60 species are traceable in Arunachal. Dai (2005, 60) writes, 'Sooner or later the visitors to be assailed by the distinct aroma of bamboo shoot that is used almost daily in a variety of local preparations. Pickled, cooked or fresh, bamboo shoot is served as an appetizer, and is believed to possess healing and curative properties with protease activity that helps the digestion of proteins.' She also mentions that, in Upper Siang district, bamboo also has mythical tales narrating its origin. One type of bamboo grew out of the body of a spirit who died when he was trying to climb a high tree to lay his trap for catching birds. This bamboo, known as Dibang is very strong and flexible and is used for making bows and arrows. Another kind of bamboo, the *eppo*, is believed to be sprouted from the naval of a spirit called *Tonang-botte*. This is bigger but weak bamboo which is used for making tubes for storage purposes, Dai added (ibid.).

It can be added here that the Apatani tribe is associated with a unique variety of bamboo which never flowers (*Phyllostachys sp.*)

and now popular as Apatani bamboo. Apatanis not only linked it with migration routs but also their folklore explains why Apatani bamboo doesn't flower, where scientists have seen some real sense.[25] Another interesting fact is that Adis are aware about the predicament of bamboo flowering which they call *'Talam-lamnam'* but they simultaneously believe that only lucky persons can witness bamboo flowering during their lifetime as it is a rare phenomenon (Megu 2007, 62).

WILD VEGETABLES

As a majority of the tribal population depends on shifting hill cultivation, they produce a huge variety of vegetables as well as spices, such as ginger, chilly, etc. The Wanchos of Tirap district harvest about 28 varieties of products and about 20 varieties of wild vegetables and 59 varieties of wild fruits they collect from surrounding forests (Wangpan 2001). Adis grow about 15 varieties of vegetables in the jhum field and collect 8 different types of tubers, 15 types of vegetables and 11 varieties of edible fruits from forests (Dupak 2004). Mibang reported about more than 40 wild leafy vegetables and 50 wild fruits used by the Adis of Jomo village (Mibang 2004, 18). He also mentioned an Adi saying, *neyi pulunge punamko, neyang belo e garnam ko* which means, 'Children being fed and brought up with wild leafy vegetables, become healthy and robust' (ibid.). The Galos collect at least 16 varieties of edible wild fruits,12 varieties of wild tubers, wide varieties of leafy vegetables from the forests (Lollen 2007). Akas of West Kameng district collect 16 varieties of vegetables,13 types of fruits (Nimachow 2002). Nyishis are also habituated in taking large number of wild roots (at least 14 types), leafy vegetables, fruits besides growing huge variety of foodgrains and cereals in the jhum fields. According to Tara (2005, 60), Nyishis do not maintain any special diet in their life time, rather they are capable of living on wild food items months together in the absence of rice. Food stuff cultivated in jhum field or collected from forests constitute about 65 varieties for the Hill Miris of Upper Subansiri district (Laa 2000).

FOOD PREPARATION

Among the Arunachal tribes, five basic consumption patterns are found, such as boiling, roasting, smoking, porridge and consuming mainly raw fruits and a few vegetables, depending on the food items. In general, boiling rice or other cereals, meat, fish or vegetables is an every day affair for the preparation of food adding a little bit of salt, chilley, ginger and preferably fermented bamboo shoots. However, in most of the tribal villages, if one enters a traditional house and carefully observes the hearth place, one can locate at least a piece of meat or may be many other food stuff that are kept hanging on the hearth allowing for becoming smoke dry. This is precisely because meat, fish or varieties of forest animals or birds, rats or even insects are found every day. Naturally whenever they get these in large number, they try to preserve them so that they can use as per their need. Sometimes such well smoked items are preserved inside the bamboo tube or even inside baskets for a long time, especially they store such items for days of scarcity or even to entertain special guests. Duarah (1990, 85) mentioned that the Apatanis preserved pork, locally called as 'Ya-acho' for a period up to 10-15 years. In fact, in urban areas such smoked fish, squirrels, and meat items are very common and have good commercial value. Similarly, roasting fresh fish, meat, wild roots, tubers, animal skin in fire is very common which are generally preferred along with locally brewed wide varieties of drinks adding a few spices like, chilly, salt or sometimes black pepper (ibid., 86). In Lohit district, such roasted fish is considered as a delicacy, specially the *Paa-Ping*—fish roasted using bamboo skewer (Dai 2005, 24) and roasted pork (*Waak ngam*) of Changlang district or roasted beef (*Sihi yo sangkho*) of Lower Subansiri district (ibid., 40-2). Another form of food consumption is porridge or paste which is again common to tribes who are producing rice or other cereals. Tribes like Sulung (Puroik) who depend largely on *Tache* prepare such porridge out of the stem of this fern tree and consume the same by adding a little bit of salt. Bur many other agriculturally advanced tribes prepare paste or sometimes bake by steaming such paste made of rice, fish or various other food stuff and some of these are considered as delicacy, such as, bamboo rice (*Khau-Laam*), *Khaupuk* (steamed sticky rice), *Tongtep* (steamed pancake wrapped in leaf), *Khautek* (roasted sticky rice mixed with molasses and made into balls), *Khaumouning* (steamed rice cookie) of the Khamptis of Lohit district (ibid., 23).

FOOD TABOO OR FOOD AND INEQUALITY

For each and every tribe of Arunachal, there are certain food items which are taboo depending on the various social realities or contextual belief systems. But structurally these are linked to a great extent with life cycle rituals. For instance, among the Minyongs, in case of any death, members of the family maintain taboo for certain food items, such as, Ikung, Iyup, animal meat. Even the person who is carrying the corpse to graveyard doesn't take small fish, rice cake, banana, rat meat for one to two months. Every ritual which is linked with healing mechanism in order to drive away evil spirits follows some food taboo (Dupak 2004, 60-5). Drinking milk is taboo for the Bokar of West Siang district but they are habituated in preparing milk products which they barter in order to strengthen their economy (Banerjee 1999, 126). The Pailibo girls do not eat heart, lung and stomach of hunted animals and the Bori girls or women do not consume dog meat and similarly Idu Mishmi girls of Dibang valley district are almost vegetarian though they take some fish and bird meat. Taboo is comparatively lesser in lower and upper Subansiri districts. The Tagins and Nyishis never take intestine of their domesticated animals, such as pig, mithun, etc. whereas taking some portions of sacrificed meat is tabooed to the younger generation of the Apatanis and a few clan members. Among the Khampti and Singhpho, in two Mahayana Buddhist tribe of Lohit district, an expectant mother is tabooed from taking honey and egg (Duarah 1990, 89). Digaru and Miju Mishmi girls are not allowed to consume meat of any variety from their menarche to menopause. According to Nyishi tradition, during menstruation period, a woman is not allowed to take roasted meat of wild animals. She is not even allowed to dine with other members of the family and also debarred from taking part in rituals like *Amper Wiyu* and *Yullo* or to take meat of such rituals (Tara 2005, 19). Another common belief is that a person while going for fishing should not eat any variety of meat (Bagang 2006). For the Wancho women as such there is no rigid food taboo though pregnant women never take crab or prawn as they believe that the newborn baby's hair may become grey and yellow. Some of the Wancho clans, like *Joham*, never eat *Nya-me* fish as they believe that they emerged out of that fish only. In general the community avoids taking meat of tiger, fox, wolf, wild cat and snake. Among the many tribes of Arunachal Pradesh, the killing of tiger is regarded as a bad sign and in order to get rid of that, lot of rituals and taboos need to be observed. Among the Galo, a tiger-hunter has to observe a lot of food taboo and he has to prepare his own food for months and he has to avoid consumption of ginger (Takee) and one variety of local onion (Diplap) throughout his life. Such a hunter cannot take part in various festivals and rituals for a few years (Lollen 2007, 103).

CONCLUSION

From the whole discourse, it is evident that the tribes of Arunachal Pradesh are accustomed to a huge variety of food stuff which they produce as well as acquire from their surrounding ecosystem. Undoubtedly, a majority of the population, irrespective of their tribal background, are still largely rooted to their age old tradition so far, as their food stuff is concerned, or for that matter, nature of food preparations they are habituated to. But understanding such food habits becomes comprehensive when one tries to understand not only the food items but the consumption pattern or consumption norms and their belief system which is so pervasive in their family as well as social life that it has given rise to a rich folklore tradition. Food studies also help one to understand existing inequalities as well as growing disparities in contemporary Arunachal. It also reveals how various food stuff or food linked ceremonies or festivities become the identity markers of the tribes. Finally, food as an essentially cultural phenomenon is subjected to the process of negotiation in the market and the media-driven globalized world. However, sometimes, food habit may also lead to the construction of ethnic stereotype bringing the so-called 'mainstream' and 'periphery' syndromes to the centrestage which calls for sensitization. Lastly this study, perhaps, helps one to understand why Arunachal, the largest frontier state, can be looked at as the state of possibility and paradox.

NOTES

1. For a detailed historical understanding of anthropologists' study on food, one can look at S.W. Mintz and C.M.D. Bois's review article on *The Anthropology of Food and Eating*, first published online as a review in *Advance* on 10 May 2002.
2. Different literatures reflect the total number of tribes as well as subtribes differently. So, some confusion remained regarding the actual number of major tribes as some reported 26 and some 25. This relates to the existing dynamics of identification of tribes evident in this state.
3. In some parts of Arunachal, one can locate that a single tribe is scattered in both the hills and plains, such as, Nyishi, Mishmi, Adi, etc.
4. Christianity is a reality among some of the dominant tribes of Arunachal, such as, Nyishi, Adi, Galo, Apatani, etc. which has wider implications in terms of bringing socio-cultural change as well as food intake of the tribes, specially, ritual or sacrificial food stuff.
5. Varieties of rice, meze and millets are locally grown.
6. Stonor has given very useful information about the use of this fern tree by the Adi, Nyishi and the Sulung which came out of his visit to so-called Abor (Adi) Hills and Dafla (Nyishi) Hills between 1947 and 1948. He says that the use of tree ferns for sago is known along the whole length of Assam Himalayas but it seems quite unknown to any hill areas lying beyond south of Brahmaputra. He added that the same species was available in the Naga, Lusai, Khasi and Garo Hills but without any traditional utility value for the people of those areas (1948, 137).
7. Preparation of beverages are essentially women's job in most of the tribes and there are varieties of such drinks available where one can trace tribe specific delicacies. This can be a separate theme of discussion in the context of Arunachal tribes.
8. One can find long notes by the colonial officers regarding the use of opium and ganja by the then tribes of NEFA.

9. The tribes like Khampti and Singpho of Lohit and Wangchos of Tirap are addicted to opium which is usually produced by the Mishmis. Many NGOs, both national and international, as well as government departments are involved in tackling this addiction problem but the success stories are very marginal. During field work in 2004-5 among some of the Khampti villages this author has seen how this addiction is leading to disruption in Khampti society as this has severely affected their male population who are identified as *Kanias* (*Kani* is the popular term for opium).
10. Arunachal Pradesh State Biodiversity Strategy and Action Plan (Hedge 2003, 35) contains detailed information regarding rice diversity in Arunachal which represents 24 per cent of the total rice germplasm.
11. For different versions please see Mibi's (2006, 9-16) dissertation (unpublished) or Dutta's (1976) book on Mopin festival.
12. Traditionally, smearing of rice paste was restricted to the Galos only but today anyone participating or observing Mopin will have the same. Of course, this is linked with the changing face of Mopin or for that matter other festivities in Arunachal which are becoming identity markers of the tribes in the contemporary context.
13. N.A.
14. This is done one week after Aran festival by the elderly male persons of the village who erect a bamboo altar at the corner of a dwelling place on which they put white rice powder and ginger paste. Every household prepares rice cakes and apong—the local drink (Dupak 2005, 8).
15. This is done by individual households by sacrificing chickens. However, rice cake is an important component of this ritual (ibid.).
16. Dorung is also known as hunting and trapping festival and similarly during Pinneng villagers generally organize community hunting called Kiruk (ibid.).
17. Abang is long oral epic narrative found among the Adi tribe of Arunachal Pradesh.
18. Ponung is an important and popular festival of the Adis.
19. Murung is celebrated if a family suffers from illness for a long time or domestic animals are afflicted with unusual disease or a rich man can celebrate this to enhance his status or even for begetting a son (Yabyang 2006, 22). During Murung celebration, Apatanis try to propitiate Tiigo Uiis, a benevolent deity, so that members of the family are blessed with wealth and prosperity. Depending on the number of mithun or cow sacrificed, this Murung is divided into two types—Rontii and Ronser. In order to have an understanding about the priest/shaman's involvement and oral tradition associated with Murung one can see Takhe Kani's work (1996).

20. Each adult mithun will cost at least 15,000 rupees. In most of the villages, those who are economically well off or influential have a huge number of mithuns—the number can even cross 100. Even leaders, may be urban based, but having root in rural areas, possess a huge number of mithuns in their respective village areas. It is interesting to observe that during various elections, competing candidates display a sort of competition on the number of mithun they sacrifice to feed the village people during election campaign.
21. Details about the tales related to mithun is given in NEFA information published in 1968, pp. 23-7, by the NEFA administration.
22. The myth among the Khowas (Bugun) can be found in Elwin's book (1993).
23. See V. Elwin's *Myths of North East Frontier India* (1993), Directorate of Research, Government of Arunachal Pradesh, Itanagar.
24. It involves a distinct division of labour, selection of proper site and specific techniques which can be perceived as IKS of the Galos.
25. Folklore says, 'Our ancestors told us that once long time ago, there was a huge seed-bearing flowering. They were so beautiful and aromatic that birds devoured them all. Bamboo was unhappy; they realized that if they produced seeds like these, they would not be able to multiply because of the birds. So, they decided to raise their families hidden from the birds, through the roots. Since that time there is no flowering (Chakraborty 2003, 5).

REFERENCES

Banerjee, B., 1999, *The Bokars: An Anthropological Research on their Ecological Settings and Social Systems*, Itanagar: Directorate of Research.

Bagang, K., 2006, *The Nyishi belief and Ritual Practices related to Economy: A Case Study*, M.Phil. dissertation, AITS, RG University, Itanagar.

Chakraborty, S., 2003, 'Bamboo Flowering in the North-East: Crisis Beckons Opportunities', *Indian Folk Life*, 2(3), January-March.

Dawar, J.L., 2019, *Food in the Life of the Mizos: From Precolonial Time to Present*, Shimla: IIAS.

Dupak, N., 2005, *The Festival of the Adis (With Special Reference to the Minyong)*, Unpublished Seminar Paper, Department of Tribal Studies, Arunachal University, Itanagar.

Dutta, D.K., 1979, 'A Little-Known Tribe of Tirap', *Resarun*, *1*, Spring & Summer.

Dutta, P., 1976, *Mopin: A Festival of the Adis of Arunachal Pradsesh*, Itanagar: Directorate of Research.
Furniss, C., 2004, 'The Wonder Plant with an Uncertain Future', in *Geographical*, 76(8) August.
Hedge, S.N., 2003, *Arunachal Pradesh State Biodiversity Strategy and Action Plan*, Itanagar: SFRI.
Johan, P., 2003, 'Food', in *Encyclopedia of Social and Cultural Anthropology*, eds. Alan Barnard & Jonathan Spencer, London: Routledge.
Kani, T.,1996, *Socio-religious Ceremonies of Arunachal Pradesh*, Guwahati: Purbadesh Mudran.
Laa, R., 2000, *Forest and Tribe: Study of the Hill Miris of Upper Subansiri District of Arunachal Pradesh*, M.Phil. dissertation, AITS, RG University, Itanagar.
Lollen, K.E., 2007, *Food Habit of Galo*, unpublished M.A. dissertation, AITS, RG University, Itanagar.
Megu, O., 2007, *Cane and Bamboo in the Life of the Adis of Arunachal Pradseh: An Anthropological Study on the Indigenous Knowledge System*, unpublished M.Phil. dissertation, AITS, RG University, Itanagar.
Mibang, T. and M.C. Behera, 2004, 'Jomo: Reminiscences of a Villager', in *Tribal Villages in Arunachal Pradesh: Changing Human Interface*, New Delhi: Mittal Publications.
Mibi, R., 2006, *Mopin Festival of the Galos of Arunachal Pradesh: A Study of Continuity and Change*, unpublished M.Phil. dissertation, AITS, RG University, Rono Hills.
Mukhopadhyaya, K., 2020, *Food and Power: Expression of Food-Politics in South Asia*, New Delhi: Sage Publications India Pvt Ltd.
Nimachow, N., 2002, *Forest and Tribe: A Study on the Akas of Arunachal Pradesh*, M.Phil. Dissertation, Department of Tribal Studies, Arunachal University, Itanagar.
Richard, A.I., 1939, *Land, Labour and Diet in Northern Rhodesia*, Oxford: Oxford Universy Press.
Singh, K.A., 2000-1, *Study of Traditional Rice Varieties grown by Khampti Tribe of Arunachal Pradesh*, Basar, Arunachal Pradesh, ICAR.
Stonor, C.R., 1948, 'On the Use of Tree-Fern Pith for Sago in the Assam Himalayas', *Man*, 48, p. 137.
Tara, T.T., 2005, *Nyishi World*, Itanagar: Eastern Horizon.
Wangpan, S., 2001, Food Habits of the Wangchos, unpublished M.Phil. seminar paper, Department of Tribal Studies, Arunachal University, Itanagar.
Yabyang, K., 2006, *A Study on the Murung Festival of the Apatanis*, unpublished M.Phil. dissertation, AITS, RG University, Itanagar.

CHAPTER 6

Sociality and Anxiety in the Foodways of Malabar

HASHIK N.K.

The foodways in Kerala vary widely across region and community. The present study tries to examine Malabar food practices in general and the cuisine, serving style and the nature of social interaction between different communities in particular. The performative act of food helps to foster social interactions and communal harmony among the people of the Malabar region ever since the arrival of Arab traders to the coast of this region. This social interaction through food is changing among the communities due to the anxiety about the influx of outside/foreign food in the everyday life of Malabar region.

MALABAR AND ITS PEOPLE

Being the provenance of Islam in India, Malabar (the six northern districts of the Kerala state—Palakkad, Malappuram, Kozhikode, Wayanad, Kannur, and Kasargod) is considered an important place in the history of Islam in India. The pre-Islamic trade relationship of Arabians with Kerala and the support of the local rulers, especially of the Zamorins of Calicut, helped the peaceful propagation of Islam in Kerala (Miller 1992). They did not use any kind of force while propagating Islam and hence the conversion that happened in the Kerala society was peaceful in nature. Muslims of North Kerala are generally called Mappillas or Moplahs. Many of them are descendants of Arab traders who married women from Kerala. The social structure of Kerala in this period had influenced much in the process of conversion. The main reason behind this conversion was the social and economic condition of the lower caste class natives of Kerala. Before the advent of the Arabs and Islam, these natives had lived like slaves under the rigid laws of the upper caste class Hindus. When the Arab Muslim traders began their missionary activities, it was not the upper caste/class people, but the backward caste class people such as Thiyyas, Parayas and Cherumans who came forward to embrace Islam (Panikkar 1989, Samad 1998). This brought about a huge change in the social domain of Kerala. As in other parts of Kerala, Hindus constitute the majority in Malabar region. But, 67 per cent of the Muslim population in Kerala is in the Malabar region (Miller 1992).

MALABAR FOOD PRACTICES

The discussions on food beliefs, customs and its association with religion are necessitated by the fact that people overtly and readily make these differentiations. Evidently, food becomes a language of meaningful discourse and practice as well as one of contention and of religious and ethnic identity, which goes much beyond into the social interactions of everyday life. The culture based meaning of food signifies this body of verbal and non-verbal tradition as an instrument of cultural continuity, a sign of folk identity and a crucial aspect of community culture. Studies on the culinary aspect of food has provided the early anthropologist scope to observe culinary habits and enabled him/her to differentiate between people along regional lines. Later, foodways was more likely to focus upon particular foods as significant choices, implicitly rejecting physical determinism of food in favour of a cultural model—one in which the food that people eat are believed to say more about who they are. While Bourdieu insists that different social groups express their distinctive 'social habitus' through material practices such as food (Bourdieu 1984), Sutton explores food as a product of the phenomenon of food memory (2001). The insistence upon the 'authenticity' and 'centrality' of certain items which must have been, at one point, 'new' or 'foreign', is common across India—as has been opined by Achaya and lately debated by Nandy (Achaya 1994, A. Nandy 2004, 9-19). In matters of food, this constructed 'traditional' seems, over the twentieth century, to have congealed into a series of food cultures which have been increasingly communalized and disciplined by food values, leading up to recent attempts to extend the fundamentalist intervention to the food habits of South Asia in general and Kerala in particular.

Islam instructs that no food should be wasted. It stresses on charity, the necessity to share food with others. Fasting is a compulsory ritual, which is related to eating. All these factors indicate that food is also of prime importance to believers in Islam. In view of this attributed importance, food culture of Malabar Muslims cannot be separated from its religious connotations. Malabar Muslim food itself is well known outside the community and is highly specific and known especially in Tellichery, Kannur and Kozhikode as a distinct entity. The cultural difference, of Malabar Muslims from other Muslims in Kerala, is reflected in their food habits as well. After the arrival of Islam along with the Arab traders to the Malabar coast (much before the advent of Islam to other parts of India), local people were converted in large scale. The Muslims blended their food habits with those of newly converted people and a new food culture emerged with its richness and variety. Muslim influence refined the hitherto Kerala cooking style and dietary habits by adding many food varieties such as *ghee-rice, nan, roti, kurma, kulcha, thandoor, paratha, biriyani,* etc. (Osella 2008, 170-8), to name a few.

Malabar Muslims follow their dietary habits based on the *Quran* and the *Sunnah*. Swine flesh and grasshoppers are prohibited, but sea food is permitted. It is mandatory to provide water to the animal and utter the name of God when one cuts the jugular vein of any animal before using it for consumption, differentiating Halal (permissible) from Haram (forbidden). Interestingly, Mappilas never differentiate between the two while eating. The onus lies on the butcher who performs and prepares the halal meat. If he has not followed the prescribed religious norm, he would be solely responsible and will incur the sin from the Almighty. The dishes of the Mappillas are mostly meat based. Biryani is a dish in which meat and rice are cooked together within the Kozhikode version, with very light spicing, a prodigious quantity of ghee fried onions and a good amount of rose water. Biryani is an inevitable part during special occasions, especially at weddings. Mappillas also prepare sweet delicacies. *Muttamala* (egg garland), the chain like strings of egg yolk cooked in sugar syrup, is a distinctive sweet. Many of their dishes are made from rice and wheat with added coconut, coconut milk, spices, sugar, egg and dry fruits. There are special dishes to mark certain festive and life cycle ceremonies and Muslim kitchens prepare special dishes during the month of Ramzan. The rich culinary tradition of the Mappillas has influenced the other cuisines of Kerala. The traditional Muslim flavour has entered into kitchens of other religious communities also.

HOSPITALITY AND FEASTING

In many communities, food regulations separate insiders and outsiders and indeed the two are often connected. Concern about sharing meals with and eating even non-meat food prepared by Christians or Hindus became a subject of contention from the mid-nineteenth to the mid-twentieth century in India. Refraining from consumption of problematic food not only differentiate between Muslims and non-Muslims but also, as for the medieval Muslims, between good Muslims and bad Muslims (Masud 2000).

For much of the relatively brief history of Malabar foodways, cookery has held the high ground, subjugating all else to context. Most apt for performance studies, the centrality of cooking as transformation, focuses attention on skills as well as secrets. Unfairly reduced to the brief notation of recipes, cooking is, by definition, individuated and non-reproducible. The traditions associated with cooking range from gender specified roles and settings to elaborate 'scripts' that contain, enact and signify the relationship between host and guest, sacred and profane. What people do with food when it is ready to be eaten is simply to express with it and through it, the substance of identity, sentiment and community.

One of the most striking differences of Malabar, compared to other parts of Kerala, is the centrality of food in everyday Muslim sociality. Although food customs and habits vary significantly, spatially and temporally, feasting often occurs at key points in the social life of a community. The *thakkaram* (hearty welcome) is a ceremonial meal that reaffirms social solidarity while providing culinary gratification to an assembly of individuals. It is the symbolic display of food and represents surfeit of consumption. As eating beyond the point of satiation, *thakkaram* is forever shadowed by its obverse. In addition, offering of food has sacrificial connotations which can be equated with socially mediated hunger, food asceticism or fasting. In all the life cycle ceremonies of Muslims *thakkaram* and offering of food has a pivotal role. There are two very powerful sources of contemporary practice. First, it is the practice of inviting non-Muslim neighbours and friends for feasting organized by the family at the time of annual Eid and other festive occasions and second, the family invites the newly married couples of their family/relatives to their home in the form of *thakkaram*. The invitation to non-family members and neighbours comes from a self-consciously sociable ethos. Malabar Muslims pride themselves on knowing how to participate gracefully—as host or guest—in occasions of hospitality. The hospitality becomes performative and indicates the degree to which Muslims themselves participate to showcase their unique food customs which is clearly apart from other communities. The male guests may be friends or acquaintances outside the home; their womenfolk will often meet for the first time and forge friendship with the women of the guests. This event is specifically to bring together friends and family, and is a way in which strong social networks are maintained, expanded and intensified. This is also applicable when after the wedding in a family, the groom's family visit the home of the bride and vice versa. The *thakkaram* guests are urged to taste the prepared dishes, but are permitted to help themselves and choose what to eat. Food is considered to be a pleasure and no prestige is lost by expressing appreciation of one dish over the other. While interrogating food practices cooking your way to another heart becomes the centre of the narratives in both cases.

Food is often controlled by women and used accordingly, to not only control and transform the self, but also effect change within a community. Solidarity between social groups may be invoked through exchanges that include food sharing, as in the case of funerary feasts of the Mappilas. The acts of cooking and eating are an inseparable part of the narratives, demanding our attention to the need to interrogate these practices with relation to our daily life. The *thakkaram* to other community acts at forming interpersonal relationships, whereas *thakkaram* among the relatives affirms and strengthens familial bonds. Food, as a vibrant and popular medium which engages with reality from many vantage points, also signifies the myriad implications on how one uses food. All of this is strongly expressive of several aspects of specifically-Muslim sociality. The eating styles, dishes eaten and serving practices are all highly particular and different in many striking aspects from the food habits of other communities.

In the everyday situation, food is an essential ingredient, as it plays a crucial role in deciding ones existence and sense of body and self. Evidently, the love for cooking constructs alternative narratives where the act of cooking and related food practices opens up larger socio-cultural debates. The men are professionalized for cooking in the outdoor function of the family, whereas the women are assigned to cook in the indoor function of the family. The Malabar women are crafted with the unique food preparation of the family. The women in the house resist the entry of men into the kitchen and thereby the interference of the latter in the cooking practices. By appropriating the decision of what to cook in the kitchen, women resist patriarchal practices by using food as an accessible point in the processes of identity formation.

There was a 'proper' way of eating food among the Muslims during rituals. It is served on a 'san' (a large plate holding food for more than one person) and is placed in the middle of a circle of people, who help themselves to the food served on it. This eating habit has been borrowed from the Arab traders (which is the part of traditional eating style of the tribal community in the Arabian Peninsula) who visited the homes of Malabar Muslims as guests in the first CE. It shows the equality between the host and the guests. This reminds that everybody should actually eat directly with the hand from the 'san', sharing one plate. As much as the food items, styles of eating are also quite distinctive between different communities. This style of eating, replicated in the Muslim domestic sphere, where men folk of the family sit together around a table and are served by the women in the traditional joint family, where age hierarchies are strictly observed to separate people into different 'sittings' and where family women will generally hover around the table to serve food. This is rather different from nuclear family styles, where all members of family sit and serve each other. In the former way of eating, a particular bodily habitus is inculcated and is made all the more potent by being associated with the synesthetic experience of eating (Osella & Osella 2008). Thus, food production and consumption are deeply interwoven with family structures within the ladder of hierarchy.

The menfolk meet in the evening or weekends and invite friends for meals in the restaurants. On most evenings men get together in groups to enjoy each other's company in a tea shop by ordering *sulaimani* (a brew of black tea with cardamom). The *sulaimani* that is found across North Kerala carries with it a regional specific legacy of being a Malabari drink. Further, they select the person as a sponsor of tea on that evening based on lot. These regular gatherings of friends and their presence in the form of '*iftar*'[1] where social relations are tied up strongly through the consumption of food becomes particularly strong when they are fasting in the month of Ramadan.

Food rules and practices manifest formative ethical ideals about meaningful human social activity—it is part of '*din*' (religion). Moosa argues that it signifies practices with salvific ends in mind, but that does not mean it eliminates worldly or secular concerns (Ebrahim Moosa 2009, 139). Moreover, Muslim food practices are inextricable from food norms and practices in the places where Muslims dwell. Muslims can draw on religious resources to encourage self-scrutiny and moderate consumption, to avoid extreme self-denial, to evince concerns about refusing hospitality, and to guard against setting oneself up as morally superior to others.

EXCLUSIVE PRIVATIZED IDENTITY AND FOODWAYS

Transgression to the food habits of other community is a remarkable element in the foodways of Malabar. During the feast of Onam and Vishu festival, the people of South Kerala abstain from non-vegetarian food as they believe the 'inclusion' of non-vegetarian food make the festival food polluted. Whereas for the people of Malabar, non-vegetarian food is inevitable in the cuisine. Here, the people of Malabar try to break the notion of pollution through the inclusion of non-vegetarian food in the Onam/Vishu festivals. While the non-vegetarian Muslim family could cook a vegetarian meal at home, a crossing over from vegetarian to non-vegetarian in the home is also regarded as an equivalent act and is generally welcomed by other communities. This highlights the point that the notions about the polluting qualities of meat, or the ritualized purity of the kitchen in the other parts of Kerala, were severely negated by the Hindu communities of Malabar, and this strengthened the possibilities for cosmopolitan experimentation with food. The Hindus make special food items during Onam (a state festival among the Malayalis, connected with the king Mahabali legend) and serve them to Muslims. The Muslims in turn reciprocate with *pathiri* (a particular type of round-shaped food made out of rice) at the time of Ramadan (fasting among the Muslims in the holy month of Ramadan). The Muslims also give *mundu* (a kind of plain cloth commonly used under the waist among the people) to Hindus during Onam. Such practices are hardly continued today. At present, participating in the festival of the other community, distributing food to other community during ritual occasions, donating for the construction of religious institution/rituals of another community, has become a bone of contention among the followers of religious communities. Most of the priests dictate that it is forbidden.

All other divisions in society pale before religion because it defines the other indicators of a 'group', such as food habits, dressing modes, ways of courtesy, etc. This is evident if one looks at the sociality of food in the Marad region of Kozhikode district in the pre- and post-riot situation. Before the riot, all the Hindus of Marad attended the *Milad-i-Sherif* (the commemoration of Prophet's Birthday) in the mosque and they had the food there, or the Muslims would take the food to the Hindu temple. Many Hindu children tied the amulets sanctified by the *usthad* (the Muslim priest), and the Muslim child normally visited *Avathan Muthappan Kavu* (sacred grove) dedicated to God Muthappan to cure fever. The Araya community bore the expense of conducting the ritual to be blessed for more catch from the sea. The *Milad-i-Sherif* and the *Mandala vratam* (observance of spiritual rules for 41 days in connection with the pilgrimage to Sabarimala temple) were celebrated by Muslims and Hindus alike. The Araya Samajam sent items for the preparation of ghee-rice to the Muslims and they gave their due to celebrate the Mandala Period. The Muslim fishermen crowded at the precincts of the Vettakkorumakan Kavu to celebrate the Utsavam (temple festival) and collect the pieces of coconut after the ritualistic ceremony of coconut throwing. These practices are losing their significance in the present society. This could be read in association with the exclusivism practised in the new food practices which were created by the growing anxiety among the communities. The lack of 'intercommunity' relationship widens the conflict among the communities in the present situation. Offers and exchanges of food helped people to internalize social relations and allegiances and hence made them intimate and also obligatory. Sutton also accounts for the extraordinary power of food memory as partly due to synesthesia—the crossing or synthesis of different sense registers (Green 2008, F. Osella & C. Osella 2003, 109-39).

Evidently, this is one among the many events that calls attention to the changing and evolving meanings of food and food practices in the twenty-first century; particularly in a place like Malabar. Here one is not concerned with what Malabar food is but how food becomes Malabar. This process of indigenization that brings in, adapts, and then subsumes external culinary influences, especially the influence for the Arabs and the regional Kerala cuisine makes the cuisine of Malabar dynamic, emergent, fluid, evolving and improvised. This helps one to locate food as structure that imposes order for sociality in the everyday life of Malabar Muslims. The debates about this notion may create the opinion that foodways either offer a path for preservation or that food serves purposes. Hence, food works as an encompassing agency, power and subjectivity in the life of Malabar Muslims. It also helps to reconnect the mind and body, thereby bringing the mental, discursive worlds of cultural history with a material, embodied understanding of the past.

At present, under the regime of purification of religious and caste identities, Hindus and Muslim communities of Malabar have increasingly normalized and excluded each other as well as other communities in their everyday life. The cultivation and focus on Hindu-Muslim differences which one observes in contemporary Kerala foodways are closely linked to gulf migration, socio-economic development, socio-political changes post-Babari Masjid effect, the invasion of foreign military on the soil of Iraq, post-9/11 incidents and communal riots in different parts of India, etc., evoked multiple responses from Muslim organization in Kerala and the Persian Gulf. The mass media under the ownership of different organizations manipulated the paranoia of Kerala Muslims and Hindu community. One of the consequences of this was an increased ambivalence towards and among the community. This in turn created a new tendency that many people tend to orient themselves to the *nadan* (traditional food from the region), whereas Muslim food cultures were clearly and explicitly termed as *videsham* (foreign) and linked to gulf countries. Such differences are recognized, carefully cultivated, and celebrated as part of modern projects of forging essentialized and differentiated *Qaum/sammudaym* (community) within the cultural landscape of Malabar.

Ironically, hotels and restaurants with a permanent infrastructure also began to call themselves *thattukadas* (covered carts on the roadsides which sell the traditional food of Kerala) in order to take advantage of its popularity as the destination of traditional food. Many people are prone to be the regular visitors of this *thattukadas*. Hotels in Malabar have started adopting distinctive and innovative Malayalam names to win attention of the customers and attract people. Christianizing eateries in vernacular names are the new trend across Malabar. Most of the towns of Malabar are dotted with *thattukada* with vernacular names in English. Such names evoke curiosity and comfort of familiarity among the people. People relate to it and are aware about the specific cuisine that in served in these shops. The *Maapilakkada* (shop of Mappila), specialize in the cuisine from North Kerala, especially the cuisine of Mappila community. The red fish curry, kappa, meat and traditional meals are the special items in the *Shaapukari thattukada* (toddy shop). There are some places exclusive for *puttu* (cylinders of ground rice layered with coconut) and fish curry; *nadan sadhya* (traditional meal), and so on. The names range from functional to nostalgic such as *Eruvum Puliyum* (spicy and sour), *Chaayakkada* (teashop), *Usthad Hotel, Adaminte Chayakada* (teashop of Adam), *Uppum Mulakum* (salt and chili), *pathayoram* (highway), *puthuma* (novelty) and so on.

Here, the idea of food and its authenticity has to be seen in relation to a certain ambience provided by space and this further imposes the idea of the *nadan* food (native food), which is facing possible threats of extinction. The anxiety about the decline of regional food culture generates more divide among communities. The wide shared food practices of Malabar which stand iconically for the specificity of the state within the boundary and which mark out its difference from the neighbouring states are in turn questioned in the present cultural imaginings. It is interesting to note that the new food culture of Muslims of Malabar never turned the taste and food systems of Malabar upside down, never changed the old taste or changed the indigenous kitchen, but incorporated the local food culture into the kitchens of Malabar. The food menu that the people of Malabar consume daily is the combination of both local and middle eastern Muslim cuisine, thereby also moving away completely from the food logics observed in the *nadan* food, where what is local, imagined as 'traditional' and whose provenance is known is valorized and other culinary forms being subject to distrust. It points us instead towards different set of values: experiments for new cuisine, an interest in imported items; a taste for innovation, including modern manufactured products (Osella & Osella 2008). Not only do Malabar Muslims accept new food influences, they seem actively to seek them out as part of their generalized interest in food, feasting and eating out.

The role of food in the sociality of Malabar has been in use by the conservative groups in urban areas of Malabar (Arafath 2014). This dietary conflict will turn even more deep as Muslim-owned eateries have started offering Arabian cuisines like, *malhooth, hamoous, shawai, manti, majboos, kabsa,* and also provide space for Arabian dining experience (eating together from one plate). Muslim migration to Gulf countries from Malabar elevated their socio-economic status and gained prominence in Kerala society. This new wave into the transnational circulation of labour and money has produced a cultural politics of globalization within Kerala (Ritty Lukose 2005, 924). The continuous flow of huge amount of money ensues the family to change the consumption and spending pattern of the household (Leela Gulati 1998, 195). The studies on the impact of Gulf migration on Malabar attest to the fact that the new economic mobility had helped to change the food consumption as well (R. Surya Murthy 1994, 15).

It is interesting to note the increasing number of *kudumbasangamam* (family get-together) venture and its influence in the social sphere of Malabar. Family meets are conducted in each village based on their religion and caste affiliations. The religious institutions are the ones who call the meeting in the locality and give sermons to the families. This has been continuing on a large scale, and the invitation to families is done by distributing invitation letters which mention the programme schedule. This new development has created a gap between interreligious/caste dialogues across Malabar. Each social group shrinks into religious/caste unit, and the interdining chances are getting weaker in contemporary society. These programmes are conducted in the hotels, and the committee runs by individual donation from each family. The families are connected through their telephone directory. They introduce newly-wedded couples in the community along with distributions of scholarship to the students who have scored good marks in the school and college examinations along with other entertainment programmes in the *kudumbasangamam* (family get-together) functions such as praying for their ancestors, creating awareness among the young about social issues, distributions of pension for the elders, free medical camp, feast and so on. This is normally conducted either under religious institutions such as temples, churches or mosques or the clubs based on kinship/lineage, religious/caste affiliations. Therefore, what one finds in the new context is the creation of different exclusive dietary spaces, which inadvertently generate different sociabilities when the politics of food is intrinsic to the entrenched process of 'othering' in this age. These ways of creating distance through food is a new strategy of right wing communal organization as well. This is one of the ways to create paranoia among the public. In Malabar, the identities of religious communities are essentialized in terms of public belief and that essential interests are primarily negotiated in the context of the other community.

During eighteenth and nineteenth centuries, eating food prepared by a lower caste person/family was a taboo in the caste-based Kerala society (Wiertsema 1984, 82; Menon 1978). The social reformers in Kerala launched *Panthibhojanam* (interdining) or community feasts where people belonging to various castes and communities used to participate. The message of this attempt was to create a casteless and creedless society. Though one vehemently denies harbouring any such discrimination, it is interesting to note that this segregation continues to exist in present-day Kerala society in general and Malabar in particular. The 'caste-centred' segregation has deviated into a 'religion-centric' difference in present-day Malabar. One cannot ask caste/religion, speak about caste but it endures in the everyday life of Malabar.

The new fringe elements, especially under the banner of Muslim and Hindu religious organizations, insist that a Muslim and a Hindu should not adopt the customs of other community and should not befriend them either. This advocates a closed system of belief that has no intention of intermingling with the other, except from a position of dominance. This insularism clearly manifests in the rejection of cumulative weight of historical baggage. As perceived, these elements are uninterested in history. By emphasizing a future golden age in Islam/Hinduism, it ignores or demonizes the balance of community history. This new fringe element carried a contemporary orientation that is anchored in profound feelings of anguish, alienation, and resentment. The product of this alienation is from the institutions of power of the modern world and also from the memory of victimhood in communal violence. This constructs extreme polarization and denigrates the value of other community and the non-believers too. It reacts to the apprehension of marginalization and discrimination with the symbolic display of belief and practice. These groups' symbolic acts of power become uncompromisingly fanatic and violent.

Observing the course of events over the last decades, the manipulation of rhetoric can be considered an indication of the religious polarization that is intense and can be experienced in the public spaces of everyday life of Malabar. Unfortunately, this hostile rhetoric creates indirect feelings of hate and anxiety which is favourable to the making of aggressive religious bodies and exclusive cultural zones in the present-day Malabar. Consequently, the communal ideologues nourish their ferocity with the making of the 'good believer' and this in turn is used to mobilize against the other community. Such attempts negate the existence of public and familial spaces in the form of community oriented rituals and festivals in contemporary Malabar. The destruction of public and familial spaces has also engineered in a cultural motif through the penetration into new media, films, etc. to create a notion of being a pure community. As the religious purists find new leaders in the regions, festivals, social relationships and intercommunity engagements are deteriorating into the trap of community based identity assertions that are both parochial and hostile. Moreover, the new rich who have been experiencing socio-economic mobility due to gulf migration, whose intercommunity relations are limited, became influential on religious preachers in the formation and promotion of community-based cultural identity formation.

CONCLUSION

Practices of interfaith relations in the form of *thakkaram* and other intercommunity events challenge the exclusive interpretation of religious demands because they challenge the language of privacy by recasting the demands of religion in terms of interfaith engagement and deliberation about the common good. These interfaith food practices are political in nature because they do not assume that religious food ethics are a matter of individualized/privatized identity. Instead, these practices are the results of the attempts to translate religious food ethics into shared objectives. The framing of foodways in terms of an exclusive privatized identity creates a moral disjunction that can be potentially addressed by embracing greater inclusivity and a moral economy through the cultivation of communal virtues.

The foodways of Malabar were framed primarily within the language of inclusivity. The discourse on the changing foodways of Malabar is characterized by the language of exclusive privatized religious identity (made possible by intolerance) and by individual consumerism (made possible by market economy). The focus is more specifically on the way liberal subjects, Muslims or otherwise, are shaped by tolerance in various historical periods. In this regard, foodways presses a point about which much is assumed but little is said: is tradition cause or consequence? People are involved in foodways when food enables them to connect with members of the family or friends, practise their faith, or assist someone less fortunate. Special occasions in which food plays a prominent role, such as *thakkaram* or feast, are of particular interest because they are invested by those who participate with a high degree of significance and importance. The need to know how people express themselves through food demands attention to circumstance and process, intention and outcome.

Islam has spread and grown in different parts of the world through incorporating local practices of the place. The concept of *taqwa* (consciousness and fear of God) is important in understanding how the virtues cultivated at the individual level may translate into the communal level. The political approach to food ethics in the social sphere of Malabar challenges the limits of exclusive individualistic conception of both ethics and religious belief by challenging the language of privacy. The value of interfaith activism lies in its potential to challenge not only market commodification of religion, but also the multicultural appropriation of religion as identity politics. That is to say, interfaith relation through foodways may provide the language that allows people to think of food-related issues beyond the language of exclusive privatized ethics, religious belief and identity and the language of individual consumerism.

NOTE

1. The term '*iftar*' has a specialized use to describe major gathering after the *magrib* prayer (evening prayer) at the time of Ramadan.

REFERENCES

Achaya, K.T., 1994, *Indian Food: A Historical Companion*, Delhi: Oxford University Press.
——, 1994, *The Food Industries of British India*. Delhi: Oxford University Press.
Ali, Kecia, 2015, 'Muslims and Meat-Eating, Vegetarianism, Gender, and Identity', *Journal of Religious Ethics*, 43(2), pp. 268-88.
Arnott, Margaret L., 1975, *Gastronomy: The Anthropology of Food and Food Habits*, Paris: Mouton.
Bakhtin, Mikhail, 1984, *Rabelais and His World*. Bloomington: Indiana University (originally published as *Tvorchestvo Fransua Rable*, Moscow, 1965).
Bourdieu, P., 1984, *Distinction: A Social Critique of the Judgment of Taste* (trans. R. Nice), London: Routledge.
Bynum, Caroline, 1987, *Holy Feast and Holy Fast: The Religious Significance of Food to Medieval Women*, Berkeley: University of California Press.
Camp, Charles, 1989, *American Foodways*. Little Rock, AR: August House.
Cussler, Margaret and Mary L. de Give, 1952, *Twixt the Cup and the Lip: Psychological and Socio-Cultural Factors Affecting Food Habits*, New York: Twayne.
Derrida, Jacques, 2001, *Cosmopolitanism and Forgiveness* (translated by Mark Dooley and Michael Hughes), London: Routledge.
Green, N., 2008, 'Breathing in India, c.1890', *Modern Asian Studies*, 42(2), pp. 283-315.
Gulati, Leela, 1995, 'Migration and Social Change in Kerala: Progress and Paradox', *India International Centre Quarterly*, 22(2), pp. 191-202.

Gutierrez, C. Paige, 1992, *Cajun Foodways*. Jackson: University Press of Mississippi.

Isaac, T.M. Thomas and S. Mohana Kumar, 1991, 'Kerala Elections, 1991: Lessons and Nonlessons', *Economic and Political Weekly, 26*(47), pp. 2691-704.

Jones, Michael Owen, Bruce Giuliano and Robert Krell, eds., 1983, *Foodways & Eating Habits: Directions for Research*, Los Angeles: California Folklore Society.

Kan, Sergei, 1989, *Symbolic Immortality: The Tlingit Potlatch of the Nineteenth Century*, Washington, DC: Smithsonian Institution Press.

Kristeva, Julia, 1991, *Strangers to Ourselves* (translated by Leon S. Roudiez), New York: Columbia University Press.

——, 1993, *Nations without Nationalism* (translated by Leon S. Roudiez), New York: Columbia University Press.

Lukose, Ritty, 2005, 'Consuming Globalisation: Youth and Gender in Kerala', *Journal of Social History, 38*(4), pp. 924-5.

MacCulloch, J.A., 1912, 'Feasting', in James Hastings (ed.), *Encyclopedia of Religion and Ethics*. New York: Charles Scribner's Sons, pp. 801-5.

Masud, Muhammad Khalid, 2000, 'Ideology and Legitimacy', in Muhammad Khalid Masud (ed.), *Travellers in Faith: Studies of the Tablýghý Jamaat as a Transnational Islamic Movement for Faith Renewal*, Leiden: Brill, pp. 79-118.

Menon, A. Sreedhara, 1978, *Cultural Heritage of Kerala—An Introduction*, Cochin: East-West Publications Pvt. Ltd.

Miller, Roland E., 1992, *Mappila Muslims of Kerala: A Study in Islamic Trends*, Madras: Orient Longman.

Mintz, Sidney W., 1986, *Sweetness and Power*, New York: Penguin Books.

Moosa, Ebrahim, 2009, 'Genetically Modified Foods and Muslim Ethics', in Congrad G. Brunk & Harold Coward (eds.), *Acceptable Genes? Religious Traditions and Genetically Modified Foods*, New York: State University of New York Press, pp. 135-57.

Murthy, R. Surya, 1994, 'Emergence of Consumerism in Kerala', Seminar Paper, International Congress on Kerala Studies (AKG Centre, Thiruvananthapuram, 27-9 August).

Nandy, A., 2004, 'The Changing Popular Culture of Indian Food: Preliminary Notes', *South Asia Research, 24*(1), pp. 9-19.

Neustadt, Kathy, 1992, *Clambake: A History & Celebration of an American Tradition*, Amherst: University of Massachusetts Press.

Osella, Caroline and F. Osella, 2008, 'Food, Memory and Community: Kerala as Both "Indian Ocean" Zone and as Agricultural Homeland in South Asia', *Journal of South Asian Studies, 31*(1), pp. 170-98.

Osella, F. and C. Osella, 2003, 'Migration and the Commoditization of Ritual: Sacrifice, Spectacle and Contestations in Kerala', *Contribution to Indian Sociology,* *37*(1), pp. 109-39.

Panikkar, K.N., 1989, *Against Lord and State: Religious and Peasant Uprising in Malabar 1836-1921,* Delhi: Oxford University Press.

Samad, Abdul M., 1998, *Islam in Kerala, Groups and Movements in the 20th Century,* Kollam: Laurel Publications.

Sutton, David E., 2001, *Remembrance of Repasts: An Anthropology of Food and Memory,* Oxford: Berg.

Weiser, Francis X., 1958, *Handbook of Christian Feasts and Customs: The Year of the Lord in Liturgy and Folklore,* New York: Harcourt Brace.

Wierstema, Wiert, 1984, 'The Caste System and the Hindus and Muslims of Kerala', *Journal of Kerala Studies,* *11*(1), pp. 82-5.

Yaseer, Arafat P.K., 2014, 'Should Muslims Fear the Kiss? Body as Resistance in the Times of Hindutva', *Economic and Political Weekly,* *49*(49), pp. 35-9.

——, 2015, 'Kerala: Cultural Sanitation and the Making of a Hatesphere', *Mainstream Weekly,* *53*(50).

CHAPTER 7

Gastronomic Terrain of the Sikkim Himalaya

UTTAM LAL
CHARISMA K. LEPCHA

Food is more than nutrition. In recent years, the nutritional value of a food item has become an important factor in determining what one eats. But much of what one consumes is a product of what is available and how the same is processed as 'culture defines how possible nutrition is coded into acceptable food' (Lévi-Strauss 1966). What one eats and drinks on a daily basis or on special occasions is largely determined by cultural specifics connected to the history and geography of it as well. Food is therefore rooted in time and space, as the ecological and economic conditions should not be ignored either, as there are various factors that aid the food we consume. However, culinary preferences remain one of the powerful mediums for mobile population to remain connected to one's cultural core across geographies. Sikkim has not only been a melting pot of mountain societies, but also a site of social intercourse between the mountain, hills and the plains. As people moved to and from Sikkim at different points in its history, they picked up as well as transmitted various traits of cultural institutions, including gastronomic preferences. Hence, despite being a predominant Buddhist landscape, material culture of Sikkim has been an impressive motley rather than a homogeneous terrain. Hence, food consumed in Sikkim is obviously one of the prominent reflections of its historical space relations.

IS THERE A SIKKIMESE FOOD?

Whenever a friend or a colleague visits Sikkim, they want to eat 'Sikkimese' food, and the hosts have to think twice about what to serve, as it becomes important to understand who/what is a Sikkimese. Historically, 'Sikkimese' has been an exclusive term to identify the ruling aristocrats of Sikkim society. The word Sikkim is of Limbu origin *Su him* which means 'new home' or 'new place'. It is said that marriage between Limbus and Lepchas (the oldest settlers of the land) were common and when a Limbu girl married a Lepcha and reached his place, she would call it *su him* or 'new home'. Lepchas are believed to be the earliest inhabitants along with Limbus who made Sikkim their home by the thirteenth century before the advent of Bhutias from Tibet who would go on to establish their kingdom. Under the influence of the British, workers from Nepal were encouraged to settle in Sikkim so as to carve out new agriculture fields and till the land. In due course, the Nepalis became the largest ethnic group of Sikkim followed by the Bhutias and the Lepchas. Colonial India also registered some footfall of

Figure 7.1: 'Sikkimese' Food Served with Millet Beer

Marwaris and Biharis as different ethnic groups made home in this small Himalayan state of Sikkim. As the different ethnic communities came from different regions and climate types, they brought their culinary and taste preferences with them. Thus, 'Sikkimese' food is not any specific indigenous culinary tradition or taste, rather it is a composite mixture of the gastronomic traits of different ethnic groups residing in Sikkim.

SIKKIM AS THE MELTING POT OF CULTURAL GEOGRAPHIES

Sikkim is the second smallest state of the country with dramatic climatic variations over short distances. People's adaptability from subtropical climate type to cold-arid conditions in its high altitudinal regions are also reflected in their dietary adaptations and acceptance of culinary preferences. Despite hosting a population of diverse ethnic stock, Sikkim society's classification of 'what is food and what is not' is however not rigid across different ethnic and religious groups. If there are those who observe purity and pollution in terms of food, there is appreciable tolerability of non-vegetarian food, including beef. The culinary experience of Sikkim has therefore been appreciated by visitors while keeping the different communities connected as food has been a way to present oneself and a means for cultural exchange (Monatanari 2007).

Sikkim, like its immediate neighbourhood, is known for its *momo, sha-phale,* and *thukpa* as well as its numerous variations like *thenthuk,*[1] *gyathuk, bhakthuk* which came from Tibet. Likewise, *gundruk,*[2] *sinki*[3] and *dhindo* are part of the traditional Nepali culinary. *Bhat-dal* and *roti* which have been a staple diet of the multitude in India and Nepal have also been regulars in Sikkim kitchens of all ethnic composition along with the culinary traditions of their own kinds.

CATEGORIZATION OF FOOD IN SIKKIM

In *The Raw and the Cooked* (1964), Lévi-Strauss' explores the binary categories at culinary level as it is the socio-cultural aspect which determines what is food and what is not food. The distinction between what is 'edible/inedible is founded in cultural rather than a physical basis', writes Elyada. Cooking transforms the food from raw to cooked and this transformation is an acquired cultural phenomenon. Food is therefore 'structured by the culinary triangle: raw/cooked/rotten'. It is a triad of binary oppositions as food in Sikkim can also be roughly categorized into three subgroups:

1. Processed Food: Pickled, Brewed, Smoked, and Sun-dried.
2. Direct from Forest.
3. Direct from Farm/Market.

Processed food would be the rotten kind which is usually fermented, pickled, brewed, smoked, and sun dried. Direct from forest would be raw, and direct from market are the cooked kind. Table 7.1 will give a gist of food in Sikkim organized in three categories and further organized according to its source, name, type, significance, and prevalence among the community. It is a nascent attempt to categorize the different kinds of food with suitable examples consumed by the population of Sikkim. The list is not all-inclusive as only those the authors felt popular have been included.

TRADITIONAL FOOD PROCESSING

While the produce from forest and the ones easily available in the market are a given, traditional food processing is important to understand as it has been societies' ingenious response to minimize waste, increase shelf life of food produce, and work towards food security. It has been required more so in remote mountainous societies of harsh ecological settings like Sikkim. The following paragraphs will discuss the different processed food that is consumed among people of Sikkim.

(a) *Dairy Processing*: Geography and genetics have set the contours of gastronomic trait in Tibet. Even though there has been a high intake of dairy products among Tibetans and have traditionally met almost one-third of their calorie intake from dairy products,

TABLE 7.1: CATEGORIZATION OF FOOD IN SIKKIM

S. No.	Base Material/ Source	Food Name	Type	Significance	Prevalence Among the Community
1.	Processed	Dried *sha*,[4] dried & regular *churpi*[5]	Animal protein	Increasing shelf life, minimizing waste and ease in transporting the stored item	Dried *sha*-Bhutias, Tibetans, Sherpas, *churpis* - all ethnic group
		Gundruk	Dried fermented leafy greens	-do-	Of Nepali origin; prevalent among all ethnic groups
		Sinki	Fermented & dried radish tap root	-do-	-do-
		Chi/Tongba	Plant: Millet-drink	Fermented-brew	Lepchas and Limbus
		Raksi	Drink	traditional distilled alcoholic beverage	Among the Nepalis
		Chhaang	Drink	Barley or rice beer	Bhutias and Nepalis
		Kinema	Plant Protein	fermented soybean	Nepali origin
		*Nakima**	Plant (edible Orchid's Florescence)	Non-timber Minor Forest produce; Consumed as vegetable and pickle	Among all community; traditionally used by Lepchas and Nepalis
2.	From Forest	*Ningro**	Plant	Fern from wilderness; cooked as vegetable	Among all communities in Sikkim
		Tama	Plant	Tender Bamboo shoot Consumed as vegetable and pickle	by all communities but mostly among Lepchas and Nepalis

(*Contd.*)

TABLE 7.1 (Contd.)

S. No.	Base Material/ Source	Food Name	Type	Significance	Prevalence Among the Community
		Sisnu	Plant	Stinging nettle soup taken along regular meals	Among all community; traditionally used by Lepchas and Nepalis
		Sikkim Sundari (Rhubarb)	Plant	Mostly Eaten as pickle	Mostly among the Bhutias and Nepalis
3.	From Farm/ Market	Sel roti	Bread	Ring-shaped slightly sweetened deep fried rice bread	Nepali origin
		Thukpa	Noodle	Among the staple food	Tibetan origin
		Momo	Meat/dumpling	Eaten as snacks and regular diet	Tibetan origin
		Shaphale	Meat/vegetable stuffed deep fried bread	Eaten mostly as snacks	Tibetan in origin
		Khabje	Deep fried cookies	Eaten as snacks, mostly prepared during festivals	Tibetan in origin
		Jiro	Deep fried cookies	Eaten as snacks, mostly prepared during festivals	Tibetan in origin
		Khuri	Buckwheat pan-cake roll	Eaten with veggies and meat flour inside the roll Mostly the food of occasions	Lepcha origin, consumed by other communities of Sikkim as well

Note: * = Minor forest produce which is sold in market of and on.

they have been Lactose intolerant. Lactose is milk sugar which cannot be digested in the absence of Lactase enzyme in them. Hence, Tibetans and other related highlanders have traditionally been non-milk drinkers despite having nomadic to pastoral economy. Rather they have been traditionally processing milk into hard and soft cheese (*Chhupi*) as well as into butter. The hardened *chhurpis* are both sun-dried and as well partially smoked.

Processing of milk is suited logistically as well. As the society traditionally depended on their large herds of domesticated yaks, goats and sheep and largely lived a nomadic life, storing milk or carrying it around was a challenge. Solidified milk products were not only easier to store for longer and lug around distances, it was also suitable for consumption of a largely lactose intolerant population.

The harsh climate and limited growing season of the cold-arid trans-Himalayan landscape required protein rich and energy efficient culinary tradition. Cold-arid conditions of the high altitude meant not only limited supply of fuelwood but also more fuel supply for cooking. Thus, the Tibetan culinary system appears to be placed well in the prevailing harsh climatic setting. Most traditional cuisines like *thukpa, momo, ti-momo* are either boiled or steamed and loaded with animal protein and fat. Sikkim being a mountainous state with about 200 square kilometres of Tibetan plateau as part of Sikkim and as a sizeable proportion of Sikkim's citizens are of Tibetan ancestry; so traditional Tibetan culinary tradtion is very much ubiquitous across Sikkim kitchens and so does the *chhurpis*.

(b) *Dried meat* has been traditionally consumed by the Tibetans. In the cold-arid climatic conditions, meat used to be sun-dried, smoked and snow-frozen to increase its shelf life. Air in the trans-Himalaya is normally so desiccating that most food products are sun-dried. However, in the green verdant valleys of Sikkim where humidity normally remains high, sun-drying is usually not feasible and if attempted, the meat gets infested with moulds and maggots sooner. The community which has been routinely storing extra meat for later usage, almost entirely smoke it to increase its storage in Sikkim. As per the 2011 Census of India, about 57.7 per cent of Sikkim population is Hindu and a sizeable proportion of it does not eat Yak or cattle meat. Besides this, these animals are bigger in size, so the storage of the leftover meat has been a rather tenable practice among Bhutias and other highlanders of Sikkim. Unfortu-nately, what was suited in Tibet's geography was not ideal in Sikkim's setting. The dried meat in Sikkim is almost entirely smoked meat which has been found to be highly carcinogenic (WHO 2015). There have been sizeable cancer incidences in places like Lachen, Lachung, Yuksom, etc. in Sikkim where smoked meat has been a usual gastronomic element.

(c) *Pickling*: It is simply a process to preserve or extend the lifespan of food by either sopping it in vinegar which is a strong acid where few bacteria can survive or by soaking it in salt brine to encourage fermentation. In the humid ecological setting of Sikkim food items are often spoilt by microbial growth. Thus, people in Sikkim have been traditionally pickling both meats such as beef to vegetation edible products like *nakima* (flower of an edible orchid), radish, carrots, cauliflower, ginger, wild fruits like *lopse* (Nepali Hog Plum), chilies, etc. Even tomato and soft *chhurpi* are pickled in chutney form.

(d) *Brewing*: It is the process of preparing a drink by steeping, boiling, fermentation or by infusion of hot water and fermentation. Traditional brew of a place is often aligned with the ecological realities and food storage aspects. Seasonal surplus of crops and minor forest produces have often been brewed by communities. Such processes, apart from merely producing intoxicating drinks, practically take care of the seasonal surpluses which may be spoilt by storing the food calories in the form of brew. *Chhang* and *chi/Tongba/Roksi* are the common traditional alcoholic brew in the Sikkim Himalaya.

Brewing can further be divided into alcoholic and non-alcoholic brew (Table 7.2).

Tea has been a significant non-alcoholic brew of Sikkim. There are diverse teas in the state. Apart from consuming the conventional Tea (dried, fermented leaves of *Thea Sinensis*) which is consumed as tea with sugar or salt and the quintessential Tibetan butter-tea

TABLE 7.2: ALCOHOLIC AND NON-ALCOHOLIC BREW IN SIKKIM

S.No.	Non-Alcoholic	Alcoholic
1.	Tea-Salt & Sugar; Butter (*Pocha*) & non-butter tea	*Chi, Chhang, Tongba, Roksi*-made out of Rice, Ginger, Rhododendron, etc.

(*Pocha*) have been commonly used among the highlanders of Sikkim. Communities in Sikkim can be broadly categorized on the basis of how they drink their tea. Most Sikkimese Buddhists trace their ancestral roots in Tibet where sugar has been a luxury and salt a metabolic necessity. Various brackish water-lakes of Tibet have been salt-producing areas, hence, making salt readily available for consumption; whereas Tibet did not produce sugar. Sugar had to be imported as an item of luxury. So, Tibetans become accustomed to sipping mostly salt tea and adding butter to it as environmental compulsion for intake of more protein, a taste they carried even in Sikkim. In many Bhutia households, the regular tea is salt tea; sugar tea is prepared mostly for guests or the younger generation who have come to share a bit of taste with their Nepali counterparts.

HOW ORGANIC IS THE FOOD IN SIKKIM?

In recent years, Sikkim has received worldwide attention for its organic mission. It is easily assumed that all food in Sikkim is organic as we question the same. Food basket of a usual Sikkim kitchen has been considerably dependent on conventional agriculture, animal husbandry as well as minor forest produce till about 1980s. Hence, sizeable amount of food items of the kitchen of a household used to be produced within the state which included both organic and inorganic food items. Till 2002, Sikkim practised regular agriculture as prevalent in other parts of the country; thus employing usage of chemical pest killers, fertilizers, etc. However, having a mountainous and forested landscape with limited carrying capacity, Sikkim still imported majority of its food requirement through the North Bengal town of Siliguri.

Hence, the majority of food stuff in a regular Sikkim kitchen would be inorganic in nature. The proportion of inorganic items to Sikkim's produce have only increased in a regular Sikkim kitchen over a period of time.

Subsequently, two noteworthy developments in Sikkim's gastronomic terrain unfolded during the last many decades. First, prohibiting grazing in 1993; second, banning import of chemical fertilizers, pest-controlling chemicals, etc. in 2003. These two events further increased the dependence of Sikkim on the import of food items from the rest of the country through Siliguri. The fact that Sikkim was declared world's first 100 per cent organic state in the year 2019 by the UN Food and Agriculture Organization (FAO), after beating 51 nominations from around the world, did not bring any change in its consumption pattern. Rather, it drove Sikkim further away from being self-reliant in terms of agricultural produce. As the octogenarian Pokhrel from Pakyong in the east district says,

> even though organic Sikkim sounds a prudent policy, I am not sure if it is sustainable. I used to be self-reliant in so many food items, including oils. But now we have to buy these items. I don't remember ever buying mustard oil from market earlier. I grew some mustard every year which will yield me oil to last the entire year consumption for my household. However, ever since the government banned import and banned usage of fertilizers and other chemicals in agriculture, flowering in the mustard crop has been affected. It bears too little seeds to be used for extracting oils. So I had to abandon cultivating it altogether. This ban has similarly affected the horticultural produce such as oranges. So, I have largely abandoned agriculture.

While the state promotes organic farming, it is to be remembered that organic produce is slightly more expensive for regular people as affordability of organic products is a question at hand for local people.

SIKKIM AS PERCEIVED GASTRONOMIC LANDSCAPE

On a holiday trip, Beniwal and his friends along with their respective families reached Sikkim. The very first afternoon of their arrival, they were eagerly looking for a 'good restaurant' to have their lunch at Gangtok's M.G. Marg. They randomly stopped me to ask for restaurant recommendations. When I referred a few decent eating joints nearby which serves traditional cuisines as well, one among the two friends said they don't want to go to any restaurant where non-vegetarian food is served because they may be serving beef and other meats while they eat only mutton, fish, and poultry products. So, despite being non-vegetarians themselves, they were looking for a vegetarian restaurant. In fact, there has been a stereotyped image of Sikkim as a predominantly non-vegetarian society with majority being beef- and pork-eaters. The fact that a sizeable part of its citizens are vegetarians as well as non-beef eating non-vegetarians normally remain masked under its carefully crafted Buddhist image of Sikkim, meaning thereby that it is an ethnic community dominated landscape with a population of primarily meat-eaters. Contrary to the perception of many as Buddhism being the main religion in Sikkim, above 57 per cent population of Sikkim follows Hinduism. Among them, many follow the purity and pollution notions associated with food like societies in the larger part of rest of India. As Sikkim draws a lot of domestic tourists, many among them travel to Sikkim with purity and pollution dogma associated with food. Several such travellers try to stick to pure vegetarian restaurants as they find such eating joints safer to eat in, irrespective of whether or not they are non-vegetarians themselves. In fact, the main shopping alley of Gangtok city has at least two very conspicuously placed 'pure vegetarian' eating joints catering mostly to travellers and its patrons in the typecast gastronomic landscape of urban Sikkim.

STREET FOOD Vs. EATING OUT IN SIKKIM

According to a study conducted by the UN Food and Agriculture Organization (FAO) in 2007, about 2.8 billion people eat street food every day. Thus, being a subset of general cuisine of a place, street food in one way or another is a reflection of the culture as well. However, street food is deeply tied with the economic set up, influenced by the cultural milieu and, at the same time, governed by the political structure of the place. Consequently, street food culture quite often varies from one city to another even within a region of short distances. Most cities have their share of street foods but the place it occupies in the urban gastronomic landscape varies a great deal. While some cities have much famed street food diversity, it reinforces tourism with its gastronomic street offerings. Obviously, these categories of street food do have appeal across different classes of people, while in certain other urban centres, street food remains largely confined to low-income group. Now an obvious question one encounters is, where does Gangtok in particular and Sikkim in general stand with respect to street food. A careful scanning for food in the urban centres in Sikkim, suggest that the state belongs to none of the two blocks with respect to street food. The place has at best nascent street food culture. In fact, if one does not know the state well, one might not even notice street food set ups. In Sikkim, it is largely conspicuous by its absence. It is not that the state does not have it, rather street food in Sikkim is in quite an early stage. Thus, it barely exists as compared to other states which have a comparatively larger population, hence, more supply and demand regarding street food.

Whether or not there is a thriving food culture in Sikkim can easily be understood from its market place visuals. Street food is certainly not noticeable in and around Sikkim's urban spaces. There are extremely limited number of street food options in Sikkim and the place wherever it is found remain somewhat obscure because of lesser number of buyers; one really has to know those stalls in the city to reach them. Such eateries do not gather much attention and patron because Sikkim still prefers to eat at 'decent' eating joints, which often, people refer to as hotels and restaurants, rather than at roadside open places and from mobile vendors. Perhaps Sikkim is a little more class conscious than neighbouring Darjeeling or Siliguri towns. Upon missing the street food culture, a student from outside state said, 'When I first came to Sikkim, I asked my friend to treat me with some famous street food item of Sikkim and my friend took me to one corner of Lal Bazar[6] where fresh *aloo dum* and *chana* was sold. It tasted nice.' But if it isn't for a local guide/contact a person would have a tough time

Gastronomic Terrain of the Sikkim Himalaya 141

finding this place that mainly serves local students, porters and vendors.

How the city eats is also about how the city earns and what they value. The available street food in Sikkim draws not only from Tibet and Nepal but also beyond. *Momo* (dumplings), *shafale, roti sabji*, tea, *jhaal-muri* (puffed rice mixture with lentil) and others stuffs, beaten rice *aloo-dum* (spicy potatoes), pastries are items which fill up the void of an absent street food scenario in Sikkim. The nascent street food is by and largely remain the food preferred by students and those working firms in the market area. They are served mainly by a handful of mobile street vendors and a few carts here and there. But why are these vendors so less in number?

One reason is that the market is regulated in better fashion by municipal corporation and related civil bodies than many other places in the country. The mobile vendors are regulated by issuing permits; such permits are issued only to those who have domicile in the state. Interaction with such vendors suggest that most of them are from outside state and operate on the basis of kind of permit-tenancy to some locals. Even though people in the state like to eat out, street food has not come up in prominence in the state. In order to understand how Gangtok eats, 42 students from university and 12 professionals were interviewed. Out of the 42 university students, everyone except three among them said they like to eat outside. Among them at least 81 per cent eat out at least once a week and 59 per cent responded that they eat more than twice a week. Among the 12 professionals, 9 responded that they cannot recollect how many times in a week they eat out. They all opined that they eat out regularly. Among all the respondents 38 per cent said that they have kind of become familiar faces for the eateries. Among these 38 per cent people, none said that like to eat the street food of Sikkim rather they look forward to their visits to Siliguri and other cities to enjoy street food. On being asked why they don't eat the same in Sikkim, a somewhat average response was lack of variety, hygiene, and the fact that they can barely be located in the state.

CONCLUSION

Sikkim has neither been geographically secluded nor ethnically excluded at any point in history to have developed a distinct gastronomic culture of its own. The history of Sikkim has been intertwined with that of Tibet, Nepal, Bhutan and the neighbouring district of Darjeeling and so has its gastronomic character too. It always had a space relation with its neighbourhood. Their connection with the neighbourhood resulted in the shared culture as well as taste. Hence, the gastronomic personality of the state has overlapped its national and international boundaries. Cuisines in general have transitional boundaries and space relation as well. How a place eats suggests how they have travelled and with whom they communicated.

Thus, Sikkim through its traditional food suggests that it looked and frequently communicated to its North, South and East; and thus picked up its cultural traits, which permeate Sikkim's kitchens as well. Despite being the second smallest state of India and nestled in the Himalaya, contrary to the commonplace belief of many, Sikkim has been a geographical corridor as well where mixing of blood between communities did take place. So did their taste and preference. Hence, Sikkim rather than having a culinary tradition unique from that of her neighbours, can boast of a shared gastronomic personality. No walks of Sikkim's life have remained untouched by the motley mix of culture and cuisines. It can be witnessed, not merely in the households kitchens and pantries of eating joints', but also in community messes such as the famed monasteries of Sikkim, where a monk can be seen being served not only Tibetan dishes, but also a simple rice-dal meal. On the other hand, elders can be seen sipping sugar tea as well even though their favourite is often the butter-tea. This preference of tea is of course the opposite for younger generation. Similarly, in a Nepali kitchen, Tibetan delicacies are not for-the-occasion food rather it is something of a regularity. Even the kitchens of Bihari and Marwari families have imbibed this shared taste heritage of the place. So, there is nothing called Sikkimese food because taste does not confine to narrow geographical limits and neither does a particular cuisine. Instead, it teaches one that food is a part of shared heritage.

NOTES

1. *Thukpa*—noodle soup of Tibet.
2. *Gundruk*—fermented leafy vegetable usually prepared using leaves of mustard leaves or spinach.
3. *Sinki*—wrapped in plastic bag Radish buried in the soil for ½ weeks wrapped to ferment. And thus it acquires a distinct taste and odour.
4. *Sha*—Tibetan word for meat.
5. *Churpee*—Himalayan Cheese (exists both as dried-hardened and as moist soft chunks).

REFERENCES

Derek, M., 2020, 'Ethnic Cuisines in Urban Spaces', in A. Kowalczyk and M. Derrek (eds.), *Gastronomy and Urban Space: Changes and Challenges in Geographical Perspective*. Springer, pp. 225-37.

Lévi-Strauss, Claude, 1964, *The Raw and the Cooked.*

Montanari, Massimo, 2007, *Il cibo come cultura* (Italian). Loteraza, Rome.

Thomas, C.A., 2015, International Agency for Research on Cancer (WHO), Paris.

CHAPTER 8

Garo Food Habits and Ethnicity: A Folkloric Perspective

CHANDAMITA GOSWAMI

Since the prehistoric past to the modern age, consumption of different foods and drinks has been considered a basic human need. Every culture or every community living in a particular geographical and climatic setting has a food habit different from another group of people living in another geographical setting. It is the culture and religion also which allows a particular group of people to have a particular kind of food. There are some allowances and restrictions in every culture to have or not to have specific food items. Vegetarianism or non-vegetarianism is also determined according to the culture. The traditional domestic cooking process and preparation with regional variations is folk cookery. The cooking process and food habits in domestic life are determined by the regional tradition. Folk cookery includes the food, its morphology, preparations, preservation technique, the social and psychological functions of the food habits and consequences in other aspects of folk culture. The main or staple food of the Garos of the North East is rice. They consume rice with various seasonal vegetables and different kinds of meat and fish. Apart from the traditional food habits new food habits and food items have entered the Garo culture. The distinctiveness of an ethnicity is reflected through the food habits of a community among other traits of culture. This article documents and analyses the process of diffusion and acculturation as reflected in the food culture of the Garos in the selected locales.

The article is based on the collection of both primary and secondary data on the Garos living in Assam. Field work is done extensively on the Garos living in Guwahati and in South Kamrup tribal belt. The common food items and recipes along with their methods of preparation have been considered in this study. A number of changes and variations mark their food items. However, they still value their traditional food items. Garos living in hilly areas do jhum cultivation, and the Garos living in Assam and plain areas do plough cultivation. The jhum cultivators, after migrating to the plains, assimilated with the neighbouring communities thereby adopting their plough cultivation. Horticultural products are also available within their residential plots. The main crop of their cultivation is paddy. In their transition from Songsarek to Christianity, rice has held an important role in Garo culture. The Garos are fond of different types of meat. They eat different kinds of pulses, maize and vegetables. Fish is another delicacy for them. Dried fish is one of the most common food items taken by almost every Garo household. The Garos living in Assam have converted to Christianity, so there are some changes related to religious aspects of food preparation.

OBJECTIVES OF THE STUDY

(i) The main objective of the study is to look at the food habits of the Garos from a folkloric perspective.
(ii) Ingredients, cooking method and significance of the food items, recipe, food habits are focused here.
(iii) To find out the variation and causes of variation in food habits is another objective of this study.
(iv) A major objective of this study is to analyse how traditional food habits represent ethnicity

METHODOLOGY

Various studies have been done on the Garos living in Meghalaya. But studies on the plain Garos are limited. So this writer has decided to study the Garos living in Guwahati specially in the area of Panikhaity, Narengi and the Garos living in Rani, Chaygaon and Boko subdivisions of South Kamrup tribal belt. The Garos of South Kamrup area share common language and culture whereas the Garos living in Panikhaity area of Guwahati have undergone a drastic change in their culture. The process of acculturation is so high that influence of modern lifestyle and other people have wiped out many cultural practices from them. Regarding food habits, some are common food items which are present in both areas, only the names are different. To collect data on food culture and folk cookery observation, method of interviews have been adopted. Before going to the field, secondary data has been collected from journals, articles and books available on Garo culture. To record and store data, digital cameras as well as mobile phone have been used.

THE GAROS: A SHORT PROFILE

Linguistically and ethnically, the Garos belong to the great Bodo family. As per their oral history, the Garos originally migrated from Tibet and settled in the Brahmaputra valley. There is a place called Garu Pradesh and people living there are known as Garo or Garu. So, it is believed that Garos living in India migrated from Tibet. According to Milton S. Sangma, the term Garo is derived from the Bodo language. It is also believed that Garos are descendent groups of the Bodo. In Bodo language Garo means 'separate', so it could be because the Garo is a separated branch of the great Bodo family. The Garos are sturdy people. Their skin colour is yellowish with a flat nose. The women are short in stature compared to the men folk. The young men and women are physically fit and healthy. Many of them are educated in formal institutions nowadays. The split Garo groups of people moved to different areas. Some moved to the hills and some settled down in the plain areas. Due to these regional variations, there are differences in their languages and cultural variations. Garos are divided into eleven groups: A'kawes or A'wes, the Chisaks, the Duals, the Matchis, the Matabengs or Matjangchis, Chiboks, the Rugas, the Garas or Ganchings, the Atongs and the Me'gams. These groups have gradually disappeared due to a number of reasons, conversion to Christianity being one of them. Now the entire Garo people call themselves as 'A-chik'.

Originally there were eleven groups each inhabiting different parts of the Garo hills and Assam with distinct dialects and culture. The Garos now follow nuclear family system. A Garo family consists of husband, wife and their unmarried children. Their children leave their house after marriage and build their own house. But they live near their parents' house. They follow matrilocal form of residence. According to traditional custom, the youngest daughter inherits the property and becomes the heiress of the house. The elder daughters leave their parents' house after marriage. They leave their parents' house after one or two years right after their marriage and live with their husband separately. Within this period, they manage to build their house. Till then the husband also lives with his wife in his in-laws' house. They get a share in their Jhum field. Their houses are built by the money of their parents in the common village and the villagers offer help in building the house.

The traditional domestic cooking process and preparation with regional variation is folk cookery. The cooking process and food habits in domestic life are determined by the regional tradition. But the commercial, institutional and scientific-nutritional versions of cooking are not connected with folk cookery. The food habits of some communities have nutritional and medicinal values. Folk cookery includes the food, their morphology, preparations, preservation technique, the social and psychological functions of the food habits and consequences to other aspects of folk culture. Since the prehistoric period when men learned to fulfil their hunger by killing animals with crude weapons and used their teeth and nails to eat them to the invention of fire and preparation of roasted meat and fish in fire, all the processes came through different stages of evolution. People, through their experiences and knowledge discovered different techniques of preparation as well as production of food. In the study of folk cookery and food habits the utensils, preparation method, recipes, ingredients, socio-economic value of food habits and changes as well as diffusion are studied. There are a number of variations of the same food item in its preparation and cooking method. Eating habits depend on the geographical settings and climatic conditions. As a result, food habits and cooking methods are different in various regions. The ethnic background, taboos, religious beliefs also determine the food habit of the people living in a particular area. Rice is the main or staple food for the majority of population in India whereas wheat and wheat made products are staple for other parts of the world. Red meat is taken as the main food in the cold countries. Red meat in India is prepared and eaten as a delicacy as well as occasional food. Different tribal groups relish the meat of some wild animals too.

The ingredients and preparation method are different according to the taste, occasions, weather and seasons. The dominant crop and its product became the staple food of a particular region. There are some traditional food habits which are of interest in the study of culture. It is important to know how they cook and how they offer such food to their deities and community people. There are some herbs which are consumed to cure some diseases or illness. Such foods and drinks have medicinal value.

The drinks are also an important item of study. There are some habitual, some occasional drinks in every group of people. Some are herbal beverages, some are fruit based and some rice beer. There are some occasional drinks which are mandatory on some special occasions like ritual offerings, marriage ceremonies, death rituals and community feasts.

REVIEW OF LITERATURE

Ethnographic studies were carried out by the British Indian Officers for administrative purpose which were like ethnographic notes on the different tribes living in the North East. Eliot (1788-9), Mills (1854), Dalton (1872) and Mackenzie (1884) made important ethnographic reports on the Garo tribes about their socio-economic conditions and in order to know them for a smooth administration. In different journals, Allen (1909), Ayrest (1863) and Buchanan (1820) had also written reports on the Garo people, their physical appearances, their way of living and so on. Since then, there is a trend of studying the tribes that started among the Indian anthropologists like N.K. Bose (1935, 1938), Mukherjee (1955) and Sinha (1966) who had studied the different aspects of the social institutions of Garos.

An in-depth study on the patterns of family and kinship system was made by Chie Nakane in 1954 and reprinted in 2021. *Some Cultural and Linguistic Aspects of the Garos* (1958) by B.N. Choudhury is about the origin and history of the Garos, their physical characteristics, geographical distribution, social institutions, marriage, clan organization, family structure and law of inheritance. He also mentioned that Garos originated from great Bodo stock. *The Garos and the English* (1978) by Bhattacharjee is a comprehensive and critical analysis of the relation between the Garos and the British East India Company when they took over the charge of governing the Garos. Along with the social and cultural life of the Garos he also discussed the social changes among the Garos.

D.N. Majumdar, in his book *A Study of Culture Change in Two Garo Villages of Meghalaya* (1980), had studied two Garo villages Matchakolgiri and Wajadagiri in Meghalaya. He made extensive study of the two villages and the rapid cultural change taking place in the Garo society along with the studies on history and origin of the people, geographical settings, social and cultural institutions, economy, subsistence economy. He studied how with Christianity the changes in their cultural and social life are happening and how their social and cultural institutions are responding to these changes.

Rengsanggri, Family and Kinship in a Garo Village (1963) by Burling had studied and described the tribe, marriage, family structure, and kinship system of the Garos. *Social Institution of the Garos of Meghalaya: An Analytical Study* (1972) by M.C. Goswami had discussed the family, marriage, lineage, clan, women's role in society, inheritance of property. The author used diagrams and charts to explain certain topics of the Garos. *Tribes of Assam* in three volumes by B.N. Bordoloi, G.C. Sharma Thakur and M.C. Saikia contains a broad outline of different tribes of Assam, with different aspects briefly.

Parimal Chandra Kar's *The Garos In Transition* analyses the socio-economic changes in the life of Garos, Indrani Medhi in her thesis,

Society and Economy of the South Kamrup Tribal Belt discussed about the society and economic conditions of the tribal communities found in the south Kamrup area. Major A. Playfair in his book, *The Garos* described the Garos, explaining all aspects of their life specially the Garos living in Garo Hills, Meghalaya. Milton S. Sangma has written about the society, culture and the historical background of the Garos in his book *History and Culture of the Garos* with every minute detail.

MATERIAL CULTURE

There is a link between the material culture, ritual and everyday used material. The materials used for everyday purposes, ritualistic purposes and others are different. So, it is very important to know and study the purpose of manufacturing artifacts, their uses and purposes.

Ritualistic purposes are served in special places, sometimes in natural settings by making altars, specifically structured buildings or houses having a particular construction model. The shape and size of materials used in ritualistic purposes have special shape and size. There are certain symbols, idols and books in every religion. The connection or belief in a specific deity or power is reflected through the use of cult image. Religious performances are followed by offering prayers and special arrangements of special settings and decorations. Foods and beverages are prepared and served according to the religion. Specific dress and ornaments are also associated with the performance of religious activities. There is interring linkage of material culture or physical folk life of a particular group of people. The pattern of living places is different from religious places. There is a difference between the equipment used everyday and religious or occasionally used materials.

Due to modernization and communicational advancements different food items have permeated in different cultures. Among the tribal population, who prefered eating boiled food have now started consuming oil, ghee and different types of other spices available in the market.

The function of folk cookery in a community plays positive as well as negative roles in religion. If one studies the food habits of a community, one can see that the food which are cooked in religious festivals are different from the daily food they have. If one sees the hinduized group of people during festivals, the preparation of food items are different from food taken daily. Similarly, the Christians during Christmas and Easter celebration bake cakes, breads and arrange feasts for the community. The Garo living in South Kamrup prepare different kinds of food during Christmas.

When one studies folk cookery, the process of food preparation, production, ingredients, methods, preservation techniques, utensils, kitchen types, etc. are studied together. So, while one studies the food habits and main food, one has to study the sources of food, techniques of cultivation and implements of cultivation. The utensils and kitchen tools used for cooking are also considered for study. The infrastructure of the kitchen, the hearth, etc. are important part of study. Among the tribes of the North East, preservation of meat, fish and vegetables are seen which are kept over the hearth on a hanging bamboo platform known as *Dhowa Chang*. Similarly, fish is dried in the sun. Pickling the fruits and vegetables is another way of preservation. Among the Garos and Mising people of Assam a popular preserved food item is dried fish mixed with ginger garlic paste, salt and tapioca leaf and kept in a bamboo container. The item is used with other veggies or used as chutney.

The techniques used in the preparation of the traditional food items are relatively easier. Notably, the ethnic food is given utmost priority in the current scenario. In restaurants and commercial eateries, ethnic food is a priority. The beverages of different ethnic communities and their delicacies are now available in different fairs and festivals. Ethnic food festivals and annual festivals of different communities are examples where the ethnic food items have high value. Thus, the commercialization of ethnic foods has now become commonplace. The rising awareness and consciousness of ethnic identity are the driving force behind such fairs and festivals.

FOOD HABITS AND RECIPES OF THE GAROS

Panikhaity Area: The staple food of the Garos is Rice. Dry fish is one of their favourite foods. Pork and chicken are consumed too. Rice powder is added with meat. Soda (*Karchi*) is added in almost every dish with fish or meat. Some items of day-to-day food menu include *Kharchi Phura*, i.e. Pork with rice, *Nakham Bitchi* (dry fish with soda). Some of the favourite foods are:

Kaldah Nakham Bitchi—*Kaldah* is a kind of sour plant. Its leaf is added with chillies while cooking dried fish. The green leaf of *Kaldah* is boiled in a pot with salt and chillies, when the leaves are bolied, dried fish are added and cooked for another four-five minute and served with rice.

Nakham Jagua—*Nakham Jagua* is the dried fish, i.e. *Heedol* fish. It is processed by adding some ingredients like *khar*, salt and stored in an earthen pot and buried under the ground for some days. Afterwards it is collected and cooked.

Occasional food includes rice cake, cake, etc., especially during Christmas and Good Friday. The rice cake which is an essential food on occasions is called *Sakham Kata*. *Sakham Kata* is prepared with rice powder, sugar, sesame and salt according to taste. The process of preparing this special cake is that rice powder, sugar, sesame and salt is mixed with water and the whole thing is cooked in vapour in a pan or cooker. It is offered to every guest.

The daily food habit of the Garos includes rice. They take meals in the morning and evening. At noontime, they take tea or some light food.

South Kamrup Tribal Belt: Rice (*Mi*) is the staple food for them. With rice (*Mi*) they eat curry (*Sam*), vegetables (*Bi.jak*), meat (*Be.en*), rice powder (*Phura*) mixed with curry of meat, banana stem (*Keda* or *Resu*) cooked with meat, bamboo shoot (*Me.a*) as curry with pork or pickle, soda (*Kachi*), sour curry (*Me.seng*) with fish or meat is also taken by them. Fried silk worm (*Jong*) is another delicacy for them. Dried fish (*Nakam Jagua*) is one of the frequently used and loved food items of the Garos. Maize is a jhum product cultivated by the Garos. They eat corn by roasting and boiling. During my field study, I have had the opportunity to taste and know about some of their recipes as below:

(i) *Wanthi* (Rice cake)
Wanthi is a kind of sweet snack prepared on the eve of Christmas. It is made with rice powder and sesame powder, sugar, salt or sometimes coconut powder. It is like the rice cakes prepared by the Assamese people during Bihu festival. *Wanthi* is served with tea and taken as breakfast. They offer it to their guests during their Christmas and New Year festivities.

(ii) *Bona Bhat*
In agricultural societies rice and rice powder play a very important role. *Bona bhat* is an essential part of their Christmas and New Year celebration. *Bora rice* is soaked in water and after that packed in bamboo leaf. The layers of sesame powder sugar and salt are added with it. Then the prepared packed rice is kept in a steamer. At the bottom, water is kept and on the strainer the packets of rice are kept to steam. After half-an-hour or forty minutes, the item is ready to eat. It is eaten as breakfast or snacks with tea. It is an important dish made in every household during Christmas.

(iii) Coconut sweets are also prepared on the eve of Christmas and New Year.

(iv) *Do.o Modipol* (Chicken with Raw Papaya)
The desired amount of chicken pieces is taken, and it is cooked with ginger (*Aching*), green chilli, soda and raw papaya. The chicken along with salt, ginger and chilli is thrown into the pan and then soda is also added. The chicken is then let to cook in its own juice for some minutes. After the chicken is dried the chopped pieces of papaya are added. Then the chicken is left to cook on a low flame for 10 minutes. After that the item is served with steamed rice.

(v) *Do.O.Eching*
When a baby is born, a special kind of soup is given to the mother for one week. This is called *Do.O.Eching*. It is

prepared by boiling chicken with ginger (*Aching*), garlic (*Rasin*) and black pepper (*Jalik*). It is served to the mother for a couple of days and the ladies who are with the lady during pregnancy, delivery and after delivery.

(vi) *Do.o. with Gal'da* leaf (Roselle or red sorrel leaves)
The desired amount of chicken meat is taken. After washing, they cook it with little bit of oil adding onion, green chilli, garlic and ginger paste. Salt is added. After that the chicken is left to cook in its own juice. After water is absorbed, finely chopped fresh tangy green leafs (*Gal'da*) are added with it and sautéed. After that enough water is added for it to bcome a curry. Thus, sour and tangy chicken curry is prepared. The curry can be cooked without oil also. If rice flour is added the curry is sautéed continuously.

(vii) *Keda* or *Resu* (Banana stem) with *Wak* (Pork) or *MatchuBe'n* (Beef)
Beef or pork is cooked with banana stem. The meat is boiled with salt (*Kari*) and after the water is absorbed the grated banana stem is added to it followed by edible soda (*Ka.chi*). Pork and beef are also cooked with dried roselle leaf powder. Potato is occasionally used. Seasonal vegetables are sometimes used with it. *Thekera Tenga* is also used to cook tangy meat or fish curry. Rice powder is added at the end.

(viii) *Janko* (Wild cat) curry
During field study at Santipur, this writer found a recipe which was cooked by four to five Garo boys. They trapped a wild cat at the hill and they brought it home. They killed the animal, cut it into pieces and cooked it with onion, ginger, garlic and curry leaves. They made dry fry of this item.

(ix) On the occasion of Christmas, beef or pork is the main food served to everyone gathered for the feast. Pork is sometimes boiled with *thekera tenga* or sometimes fried with oil. Beef is cooked with banana stem or roselle. The intestine and other parts except the meat are cooked with *Kachi* or soda.

(x) Fish is also cooked with bamboo shoot (*Me.a*) or small tapioca. When the fish is cooked with tapioca *Thekera Tenga* or elephant apple is added with it followed by ginger, garlic and green chilli. Oil (*To*) or soda is not added. The recipe is prepared by boiling.

Fish is also boiled with ginger, garlic, onion, chilly with water and after boiling it they add sour leaves to it and make a sour curry. Now, their children love to eat fried fish and fish curry with other spices and ingredients, etc.

(xi) *Nakam Jagua* (Dried Fish)

The Garos are fond of dried fish. They dry it on their *Onggal* over the fireplace or in sunlight. They store it in bamboo container. They prefer to enjoy dry fish with soda or *Kachi*. Dried fish is also added sometimes with the vegetables they cook.

(xii) *Galdah Nakam*

Dry fish is mixed with salt, green chilli and fresh roselle leaves left to cook over medium flame. As salt is added, the green leaves release water and the fish becomes soft and tender with it. It is then ready to serve.

(xiii) *An chi Kapa* (Blood Fry)

One of their delicacies is baked animal blood. But now they prefer to fry the animal blood in oil with salt, ginger, garlic, onion and chilli.

(xiv) Tapioca with dry fish

Tapioca is washed and peeled off. It is boiled with dry fish and smashed. It is taken as *Chatni* with pulses.

(xv) *Rongchu* or Chira is also taken by them after harvesting the paddy.

(xvi) Bamboo shoot pickle.

After cutting the bamboo shoot, it is soaked in water for one day or it is covered with banana leaf for one day. After that, the pieces of bamboo shoot are mixed in turmeric and dried for two days by spreading it on a *dala* or winnowing fan. It is then stored in a jar by adding oil and chillis. Mostly the wild variety of bamboo shoot is used. The sour water is not thrown; it is served to the fowls with cooked rice. Sometimes pork is also cooked with this leftover water. Fish is also cooked with this sour water. Rice powder is added with it.

There is a lot of variety nowadays in their food items. Other food and products from markets have now permeated into their day-to-day menu. *Puri-sabji, maggi, buns, biscuits, snacks* and similar items have now replaced some of these items. Easy processing and less time consuming items are now used by them.

During field study in Chaygaon and Boko area, this writer had found small food stalls in the market place where Garo women sell tea, snacks (*Puri-Bhaji*), noodles to the visitors. During the Ukium festival held in the month of December on the bank of the river Ukium in Chaygaon, ethnic food stalls are set up serving traditional Garo food items. Even the non-tribal people set up food stalls and sell Garo traditional food items. A process of commercialization of the ethnic food can be seen at work here.

Betel nut holds a special place in Garo society. Betel nut and leaf (*Gui* and *Pan*) is also offered to the guest as a representation of hospitality. It is a symbol of great honour to guests who visit a Garo family. They drink milk or black tea (*Cha*) and also offer it to their guests. Before Christianity traditional rice beer *Chu* was offered to the guests but after converting to Christianity drinking and brewing rice beer is completely prohibited in the Garo society. Now they offer tea to the guests with rice cake, readymade snacks available in the nearby market. During Christmas festivities a feast is arranged for all the villagers where traditional food items including meat, fish, rice are offered to the villagers and guests who visit them during celebration. Along with feast rice cake, coconut sweets are made and served to everyone during Christmas time. Due to assimilation with Assamese people, they prepare rice cake similar to *pitha* during *bihu* celebration. As the Garos are a matrilineal society most of the time it is seen that cooking is associated with the women. Only during festivals, male members are seen to engage in cooking during the feast for the villagers. The women prepare other sweets and rice cakes during festivals. Some food items are associated with some special context and limited to a specific gender. *Do.O.Eching,* a special kind of chicken soup, is given to the mother who gives birth to a baby for a couple of days every evening or noon.

The cooking vessels previously used were earthen pots. Now these are replaced by iron pots and aluminium cooking pans and *kadhai*. Pressure cooker and LPG gas are now used by every household. Alongside the amenities of a modern kitchen, the fireplace, earthen hearth and the hanging bamboo platform to keep and preserve food can still be seen in every kitchen.

Diffusion is a universal process responsible for cultural growth in almost every culture in the world. It is a process through which new ideas and novel concepts from another society or culture are adopted by the local culture or society. The hotels and tea stall in the villages one has studied sell food items which previously did not belong to them. Buns, cakes, Chinese cuisine, *puri* and *sabji* or *ghugni* (green peas gravy) are some such food items now available in their shops and students and teachers from nearby schools enjoy these food items in their lunch break.

While studying the Garos in Assam, especially in South Kamrup region, one notices that there is not complete acculturation but the process of modernization and the influences brought by the British rule that have led to changes in their material culture and religion. Conversion to Christianity had completely demolished the *Sonserek* activities among them in Kamrup. So, the materials related to performance of *Sonserek* customs and festivals have become nearly obsolete now.

CONCLUSION

In this study of the Garo folk cookery, the changes and variation in their food habits have been found. The process of diffusion and acculturation brought many outside varieties of food items into the Garo food habit. Due to the fast-moving market economy, the propensity to integrate the food habit other than their own have also increased. But during their festivals or ceremonial occasions traditional food items are still cooked and savoured by the community members.

Continuous contacts, communication with urban centres are the reasons of accumulation of different lifestyles and behaviour of the Garos. Market economy, business, and technological aids, modern equipments are now part of each and every society.

However, despite the challenges of market economy and the influence of dominant cultures, the Garos have retained their recognizable cuisine including a specific set of cooking traditions, preferences and practices. The presentation of various food items in different fairs and festivals of the Garos is an effort to showcase and represent their ethnic identity. Like every ethnic community in the North East, the Garos also practise their political consciousness by showcasing food as a marker of their ethnic distinctiveness.

REFERENCES

Bhattacharjee, J.B., 1978, *The Garos and the English, 1765-1874*, New Delhi: Radiant Publisher.

Datta, Birendranath et al. (eds.), 2015, *A Handbook of Folklore Material of North-East India*, Assam: ABILAC.

Dorson, Richard M., 1972, *Folklore and Folklife: An Introduction*. Chicago: University of Chicago Press.

Dundes, Alan, 1965, *The Study of Folklore*, New Jersey.

Sangma, Milton S., 1981, *History and Culture of the Garo*, Today and Tomorrow Printers and Publishers.

Sarma, N.C., 2011, *Introduction to The Folklore Material of North-East India*, Guwahati: Kamakhya Gate.

Playfair, Major A., 1975, *The Garos*, Guwahati: United Publisher, Panbazar.

SECTION III

FOOD IN/AS FICTION: ONTOLOGY, IMAGINATION, AND IDENTITY

CHAPTER 9

Edible Memories: Rasogolla and Food Fiction

BIJAY K. DANTA

> *Ahare bhala manda nahin*
> *Je sthane jemanta milai*
> [No food is good or bad
> You eat as you get it][1]

The lines cited above are from Jagannath Dasa's Odia *Bhagavata*. Here *Abadhuta*, the archetypal wandering minstrel, tells King Parikshit about his twenty-four gurus. His gurus include the sun, the moon, the sky, the sea, the mountain, the dog, the tree, the honeybee, the fly, the courtesan, the serpent, the wind and the widow. Each of these teachers has taught him, in different contexts, the meaning of steadiness, change, flexibility, wealth, endurance, perseverance, freedom, sharing, tolerance and non-attachment, among other things. One guru particularly—the python, as a matter of fact—tells him that one should eat what is available and that it is pointless to talk about the class or quality of food. The fly consumes excreta and converts it into manure, a vital ingredient for food production. The honeybee drinks the sap of flowers and converts the vegetal sap into honey. It is pertinent that honey produced by the honeybee is consumed by other species, opening up what is perhaps one of the earliest natural foodways. However, the fact that the honeybee does not get to consume its own produce also implies that in the foodway one's loss is another's gain. This is where food narratives enter the scene.

This article began as a talk at a seminar on food cultures organized by the Department of Cultural Studies, Tezpur University, in December 2016. This writer could not have spoken on food without referring to the 'rasogolla war'[2] raging at that stage between Odisha and Bengal.[3] The media threw up all kinds of stories on whether Odisha or West Bengal should have the bragging rights over the iconic cheese ball sweet, favoured in both communities, in the wake of a book published in 2015.[4] Let it be confessed that one has more information on the origin and literary-cultural journey of rasogolla than one had when the seminar was held.[5] However, let me also say that one was not interested then, and one is not interested now, in settling what is, at best, a neighbours' quarrel. Several arguments made then, albeit with references to literary and historical texts, are no longer useful. This is said in retrospect, not because this author's contentions were wild or speculative but because several of his claims have been substantiated since with verifiable evidence.[6] Again, while one referred to some humorous conversations involving members of both communities, primarily to direct public attention away from the media, one finds those comments too dated and remote to merit inclusion in a printed volume now.[7] That said, the focus on rasogolla in the seminar somewhat obscured ones thoughts on food legitimacy, food pride, and food rights that come through narratives on food, which one would like to call food fiction.

This author's aim is to show how food is among the greatest and darkest human inventions, both in the sense of narrative and bio-political interventions. This is not to say that food is unreal—in the sense that stories are unreal—but that the truth of food is too painful to bear, and too complex to explain. Still people eat and tell stories about food. The story of rasogolla or rosogulla is one such story, with variations provided or legitimized by contexts that may not always be accurate. As no story is ever fully told, the story of food is told in seven instalments. You may call them seven versions of a food story. Rasogolla features in some of them.

A STORY OF TWO SONS

In *Serve It Forth* (1937), later collected in the iconic *Art of Eating* (1954), Mary Frances Fisher retells the biblical story of Esau and Jacob, twin sons of Rebecca and Isaac. Esau, unwilling to stay home, follows his father's footsteps, hunts all day and comes back home with his catch in the evening. He makes savoury roasts and stews of the day's killing and shares his cooking with his father, much to the latter's delight. Jacob, on the other hand, stays home and diligently learns from his mother the art of cooking a fine lentil pottage. In the course of time, Jacob perfects the art of selling cooked food to the workers. Esau, contrary to his mother's expectations, enjoys lying by the fire talking about food, again to his father's great appreciation, comparing and contrasting a particular day's delight to several others.

One sees in Fisher's retelling of the biblical story a food historian's perspective. For, Fisher describes Rebecca as 'a good cook and a good teacher of cookery for one purpose or another, but never for pleasure' (*Art* 170). She also adds—humorously, one may add—that Rebecca's sons can be seen as the pioneers of two kinds of food cultures emanating from the same family history. Fisher sees Jacob as the father of all *restaurateurs* and Esau of *gastronomers* (*Art* 170). While biblical exegetes may not agree with Fisher's retelling of the story and indeed the concomitant displacement of the moral content of the original story, one sees in this interpretation her attempt to show how our most familiar stories simultaneously delineate and 'defamiliarize' the form and content of food cultures.

Fisher's retelling anticipates what Fredric Jameson says in *The Political Unconscious: Narrative as a Socially Symbolically Act* (1981). Each narrative, says Jameson, whether of heroism or trade or beauty or books, is a socially symbolic act. Narratives are arguably performative acts of encoding and decoding—simultaneously erasing and recording the specificity of particular contexts—that include economic secrets, cultural anxieties, as well as social and historical contradictions (*Political* 110). Works such as Crosby's *The Columbian Exchange: Biological and Cultural Consequences of 1492* (1973), Bordieu's *Distinction: A Social Critique of the Judgment of Taste* (1979), Mintz's *Sweetness and Power: The Place of Sugar in Modern History* (1985), and Lizzie Collingham's *The Taste of Empire: How Britain's Quest for Food Shaped the Modern Word* (2017) present persuasive histories of food that draw on social history, environmental ethics and postcolonial geography. Each of these books highlights why it is necessary to see, qua Lévi-Strauss, 'cooking as a symbolic language, showing how the cook transforms raw materials into socially sanctioned edibles, and suggesting that food in its raw, cooked, and rotten forms constantly traverses the boundaries of nature and culture' (Coghlan 2). The moment one looks at cooking as a symbolic language, not to forget Jameson's symbolic act, one begins to see that food—the staple food that is consumed out of habit, often without reflection, and the special treats one consumes with matching performance and rhetoric—has a political grammar and that the cook is a producer and consumer of political narratives.

One has to consider how over millennia, Esau's and Jacob's cooking stories drew on and circulated across time and space. These stories would invariably be stories where efficient and intelligent—to those who lose out, these people are nothing but barbaric, crafty, cruel, inhuman, treacherous, wily, etc.—human beings learn to produce food to meet expected and unexpected needs and desires. Thus, one sees humans inheriting and passing on through these stories, complex and coded messages of survival, control, domination, and pleasure.

STORIES OF FOODS AND FOODWAYS

Like the history of empires, the history of food is never told in full. The fact is that all stories of cooking—found in, say, ancient rock paintings, folk songs, oral narratives, religious and literary-critical texts, including *The Mahabharata*, Homer's *Odyssey*, *The Bible*, Shakespeare's plays, Defoe's *Robinson Crusoe*, James Joyce's *Ulysses*, J.M. Coetzee's *The Life and Times of Michael K*, popular cookbooks, or commercial shows and customized recipes—are accompanied by tall tales, bragging rights and descriptions, divinations or fantasies of increasingly efficient ways of killing and cooking.

As these stories circulate in and out of communities, they are invariably seasoned with methods not only of catching, killing and cooking animals—drying, roasting, grilling, barbecuing, broiling, steaming and pickling—but growing and enhancing food resources through animal husbandry, pisciculture and agriculture, among others—with shared, purchased, or 'stolen' expertise. Restaurants have historically converted cultural markers into assets and marketed them. As one sees with greater clarity now, there are 'invisible bullets' (to use Stephen Greenblatt's timeless phrase used in his reading of Shakespeare's histories), that carry forward stories of eating, which should be read as stories of eating rights. In other words, what one calls food has played a major role in the circulation of social energy that codified the military, economic and environmental interests of communities.

Human search for more food has also translated into predatory economic practices seen in colonialism and plantation slavery. The history of slavery, legitimately examined as a history of greed, exploitation and darkness, throws up an aspect of food history that was known to experts but not examined scientifically until recently. This section will be concluded with a brief mention of two books: Carney and Rosomoff's *In the Shadow of Slavery: Africa's Botanical Legacy in the Atlantic World* (2009) and Covey and Eisnach's *What the Slaves Ate: Recollections of African American Foods and Foodways from the Slave Narratives* (2009).

These two books, between them, draw extensively on research tools, archival records and resources not accessed by earlier scholars—this includes the work of an international cast of scholars of different disciplines from across Africa, Europe and the US—to suggest, one, that African slaves carried and grew African food crops and, two, that a considerable amount of such efforts were either financed or supported by slave traders and plantation owners. It is interesting to note that African men and women—slaves who were forced to lead the lives of beasts—wrote books and created old and new recipes with African-origin materials and that these writings and recipes would circulate anonymously without credit or acknowledgement.

Dilsey's kitchen offers a fragmented narrative of African cooking in Faulkner's *The Sound and the Fury* (1929). One sees Jane Pittman's extensive culinary memories in Ernest Gaines' *The Autobiography of Miss Jane Pittman* (1971). One gets to know of Sethe's job as a cook, first in the Garner home and then in a restaurant, in Toni

Morrison's *Beloved* (1987), but the story of her cooking is only partially told. Southern slaves hunted and cooked wild game and depending on how their owners arranged or viewed their diet, organized little feasts and picnics (Covey & Eisnach 2009, 113-14). These required improvisations and experiments and often produced culinary delights that reproduced African recipes with the meat of animals indigenous to America (117).

These foods, cooked by slaves for their own consumption, would eventually move to the masters' table. Clearly, American slave trade and the antebellum plantation economy depended on African foodways and saw the continuance and creation of a culinary tradition that remained unacknowledged until the late 1990s and early 2000s. What is presented as ethnic food in restaurants across the world is the product of a combinatorial food logic born in diasporic and colonial foodways constituted at different periods by Africans, Asians, Americans, Arabs and Europeans, seen in isolation from one another. In fact, humans have followed and are followed by other species into other countries and continents. In retrospect, several basic ingredients of food as well as techniques of cooking have crossed and re-crossed borders, and have been claimed and reclaimed as indigenous.

THE GASTRONOMIC UNCONSCIOUS

Food stories are part of complex needs and conflicting desires that push national, regional, linguistic and religious affiliations and identities in unexpected ways. It is necessary therefore to examine the formal and constitutive attributes of foods—access, cost, presentation, taste, style, safety—and their seemingly natural protocols of circulation. Cultural historians point to ideological apparatuses that determine the form and function of food. Whenever one talks about robust culinary traditions, one tends to ignore the fact that such traditions owe as much to narrative masterworks as to complex networks of production, circulation and consumption of food. In culinary productions, one also tends to oscillate between exaggerated accounts of form and content. To this extent, food narratives show how both fasting and feasting help create structures—as well as classes and constituents—that would make up the culinary equivalents of Jameson's 'political unconscious'. To further one's point, an African quest narrative retold by Jonathan Bishop Highfield in his *Food and Foodways in African Narratives: Community, Culture and Heritage* (2017) is cited:

Anansi, the original spider-man of West Africa, is starving. He tells his wife he will find food for the village and sets off. After a long journey, he finds a village of anthropomorphic plantains who beg him to roast them, but he deserts them when they tell him of a village of yams, which he loves far better than plantains. After another long journey, he finds the village of yam people who beg him to bake them, to pound them into fufu, to fry them in palm oil. Anansi is just about to feast upon them when the yams mention a village of rice. Now, Anansi likes rice even more than yams, and again he leaves the village hungry for a taste of something else, traveling to the village of rice. He enters the rice village and the rice people beg him to cook them up in a variety of tasty sounding ways, but when they mention a village of meat, Anansi leaps up and heads out of the village, his mind and taste buds set for the tastiest destination of all—a village full of meat begging to be eaten. After another long and arduous journey he spies the village and enters triumphantly, only to find he has returned to his own village of starving humans.

As Highfield rightly suggests, the story shows how Anansi's greed pushes his community to further starvation. The fact that there are references to food crops that talk indicates 'the spectre of cannibalism'. More importantly, however, the story points to the lure of distant foods. The story of the African spiderman, retold across Africa, allegorizes the territorial and cultural penetration of Europe into West Africa in the sixteenth century. In effect, the story of the trickster, carried by slaves from West Africa to America and the West Indies, is a symbolic act of resignation and resistance to ecological imperialism.

In what Crosby calls the Columbian Exchange, the European decides what indigenous crops and animals must perish in order for him to grow what brings profit, not sustenance. Here Crosby shows what makes food an ideological apparatus. That said, it is not difficult to see why people valorize the uniqueness of their food cultures. Such valorizations, whether at national, regional, or continental levels, invariably block out the mixed histories of food,

food crops and animals as well as their journeys to specific locations. Alternately, people highlight the universal nature of essential food items, foregrounding the science that determines the contents, in the process ruling out natural and cultural factors that separate food from waste. In other words, it is not food value alone that determines what is eaten, and how, or what is considered taboo. It is pertinent to note that while analysing dietary legitimacy in Africa and America, Highfield and Crosby show how such legitimacy is more dependent on race, gender, colonial rule, slavery, and public policies than on availability, access, and individual choices (Highfield 2017, 50-86; Crosby 2003, 76-125).

RASOGOLLA-KOKAKOLA FIGHTS IN WESTERN ODISHA

Much before Coca Cola pulled out of India in 1977, small time carnival artists in rural markets of western Odisha used to sing a satirical song about rasogolla and Coca Cola. They sang and generally performed to the accompaniment of a *ghudka*, a hollow drum-and-string instrument, and a hornpipe. The song was about the lure of the western beverage. In the song, the village boy upbraids his girlfriend, presumably for her disaffection with rasogolla and her new-found love for Coca Cola. As the song moves to its close, the singers substituted food items with whatever struck them as appropriate, repeating words of their choice for maximum effect. The audience was free to join after the first round was completed by the performers.

Here is the anxious village boy, worried about his girlfriend's fascination with Coca Cola:

kali rasuthilu para rasogolla
aji rasiluni dekhi kokakola
kali kahaku rasibu kihe jana
rasu paritrana hari paritrana.
aji pita lagilani chhenapoda
tora kataka kataki chhenaguda.

[Until yesterday you ran after rasogolla
And today you are mad about coca cola

Edible Memories: Rasogolla and Food Fiction 171

Who knows what you'll like tomorrow
Save me oh lord from this syrup of a girl.
Today you are bored with chhena poda
Damn your town and town-dwellers.][8]

The village boy's anxiety underscores the younger generation's lack of respect towards tradition, symbolized here by the iconic sweetball. Coca Cola, *chhena-poda*, and Cuttack represent a deeper anxiety in western Odisha over the lure of attractive—and alien—foods and beverages coming from the more developed coastal areas. Much like the story of the African Anansi told by dispossessed Africans, one sees in this song on rasogolla and Coca Cola a subtle critique of the commercial exploitation of the western region by the dominant coastal districts. The battle between rasogolla and the American beverage is not a battle for rasogolla as such. It is a battle for the rural artisan and the rural market.

The end of the show, however, in these village market performances provided a carnivalesque free-for-all where sweets and sweetened drinks—substitutes for rasogolla and Coca Cola—were offered to the participants.

RASA ASWADATE: A RASOGOLLA-EATER'S ESSAY ON COGNITIVE LOGIC

Years ago, this author found in our school library a newspaper cutting from the Odia newspaper *The Prajatantra*. The cutting, a short excerpt from a longer piece, went like this:

Eha rasogolla brutanta. Rasogolla khaiba purbaru mana asthira heba. Rasogolla khaila pare mana adhira heba. Rasogolla khaila belaku mana kintu mdhura heba.
[Here goes the story of rasogolla. Now, you can be uncertain before eating a rasogolla. Also, you can be unhappy after eating a rasogolla. But you can only be happy while eating a rasogulla.]

The cutting did not carry the author's name or the date of publication of the item. On the left margin of the cutting, somebody, presumably the collector of the item, had entered the following four digits vertically: 1975 (1 on top, 5 at the bottom). This author had no way to find out whether 1975 referred to the year of publication or to the day of publication, that is, 1 September 1975. For years, one tried to figure out who wrote it but had no success. Then one saw this statement by Ina Garten: 'You can be miserable before you have a cookie and you can be miserable after you eat a cookie but you can't be miserable while you are eating a cookie.' One came across this quote accidentally on the net while trying to find a suitable opening sentence for one's talk. This quote gave this author a kind of closure and one stopped looking for the source of the Odia newspaper-cutting.

The piece before me is a text that can be analysed as any other text. In cognitive terms, the prospective rasogolla-eater's unhappiness *before* eating it can be attributed to the following five reasons: One, he (assuming that the rasogolla-eater is a man) has to pay for it. Two, he is apprehensive that the rasogolla may not be as good as it was the other day. Three, he knows for sure that the iconic cheeseball sweet is more expensive now than it was during one's childhood. Four, he is worried about the link between rasogolla and diabetes. Five, he is worried that there may be spies who will report his indiscretion at home. And so it goes.

Similarly, there are five different reasons to justify the rasogolla-eater's unhappiness *after* eating it. One, he realizes, having tasted the sweet ball, that it was a bit stale this time and not as tasty as it was last time. Two, he is worried that it won't be as tasty the next time. Three, he is worried that his blood sugar levels are already up. Four, he is worried that somehow or the other the story of his blood sugar levels will circulate. Five, and the most important worry: the same heavenly sweet ball will be bought by his neighbour who will someday write about *his* prized sweet balls. And so it goes.

In the ancient poetic text, there's a saying *rasa asvadate iti rasa*. That which can be tasted or savoured is sweet, that whose sweetness can be tested or verified is sweet. However, there is no guarantee that that which is full of *rasa* (juice) will give *madhura rasa*.

Conclusion: The production, consumption, and circulation of rasogolla is backed by a discursive tradition that is older than anything else known to any other culture, and justifies further

Edible Memories: Rasogolla and Food Fiction

affective, cultural critical, dietary, medical, psychological, political, sociological, stylistic, new critical, new historicist and new materialist scrutiny.

RASOGOLLA, NATIONALISM, AND *VAKROKTI*

This story is based on facts that do not need any more verification than the cartographic existence of Odisha before 1 April 1936 needs verification. Each and every Odia will tell you *this* story with suitable additions and alterations.

Listen: Our readers may recall that Odisha—Udra, Utkala, Orissa—was created in 1936 combining areas from adjoining states. But that is not for today. Once an Odia gentleman (call him Bholanath babu), who worked in Cuttack *bada kacheri* (High Court, in English, for those who need a translation) sent his servant (call him Bhola) to receive his friend (this bhadralok's name is not important here) from the bus stand.

He gave him one *tanka* (a rupee) and said: 'Four annas for the rickshaw to the bus stand, four annas for the ride back, but as you go buy rasogollas worth eight annas from Gopi Sahu's shop. That makes it sixteen annas, mind you. My friend is very fond of rasogollas.' Bhola of course knew that friend or not, his master is very fond of rasogollas. Ever his master's true follower, Bhola went up to Madhu Sahu's shop as directed.

That said, this Bhola is not as stupid as our readers may imagine. As he went to buy rasogollas, as directed, he thought it is meaningless to waste four annas on a rickshaw ride when God has given human beings two legs to walk. He *thought* why not use the money to check if Gopi Sahu's rasogolla is as good as *bada babu* thinks.

Now he sat down at a corner table and asked the waiter to give him as many rasogollas as he would get for his four annas. The waiter said you get one for four annas but three for eight annas. Bhola cut him short, saying 'I know I know don't you teach me. Do you think I am a chuda or lump of *chhena guda*?'

Bhola put on his thinking cap (so to say), and thought: 'After a day's bus ride our master's friend will certainly enjoy a relaxing walk, so why waste four annas on a rickshaw ride that is nothing but ill-health? For, once master's friend falls ill, I have to do the nursing and who knows how long he'll be unwell, so why not remove the very foundation of the threat? In sum, why not utilize the remaining four annas for testing the efficacy of Gopi Sahu's claim to fame?

Bhola bought three round sweet syrupy balls for the master, as directed, and decided to use the remaining four annas, meant for paying the rickshaw fare, in order to conduct a test on Gopi Sahu's rasogolla. This test was indeed a national requirement, for then only could he confirm if Gopi Sahu's rasogolla was indeed Odisha's pride. He quipped: '*Sugale bhugale khyati, rasagola, bhunja jati.*' In other words, considered in terms of the most discriminating throats (*su gala* or fine throats) and geography (*bhugala*), what gives fame to this *jati* is rasogolla eating.

The rest of the account is equally fascinating; one may even call it hilarious. Bhola uses his relentless logic to eat up all the rasogollas. When he goes to the bus stand, the guest had already walked home after waiting for a long time. He is of course thoroughly plastered by his master for the indiscretion triggered by his Odia nationalism.

Now he hates it each time *bada babu* talks about the history and heritage of Odisha. He hates it more when his master lectures to him on the need to indigenize western axioms. *Bada babu* says that the taste of chhenapoda lies in the eating. Whether it is the English pudding or the Odia chhenapoda, why should the proof be left only to the master eating whatever it is that needs to be eaten? He thinks: *Chhenaguda jati priti. Chhenaguda sugola bhugola. Chhenaguda khiradahi rasgolla chhenapoda khia babu poda muhan.* Damn nationalism! Damn good throats and geography! Damn this accursed black-faced eater of cheese and jaggery and curds and rasagola! (Tripathy 2004, 45-7).

The story shows that it is class that determines one's relationship to national artefacts and assets and creates a language to legitimize that relationship. Bhola's curse is like Caliban's curse in *The Tempest*. If *bada babu* can subvert the language of imperialism, Bhola, too, can subvert the language of *bada babu*'s class. Here Bhola produces and partakes of the sly pleasure of *vakrokti* or *hasya* rasa. Bhola and Caliban are burdened with food secrets and that they are required to share with the master. They do not like it, so they learn to curse, as Greenblatt suggests, or make fun of the master when their situation permits them.

CHHENA GUDA Vs. BRANDED RASOGOLLA

In an essay titled *Chhena Guda* (Casein and Jaggery) published in the Odia magazine *Naba Bharata* (1939), the iconic Odia cultural historian and satirist Govinda Triapthy makes fun of the people of

Odisha for neglecting two food items produced at home—*chhena* (cottage cheese, casein, unripened cheese) and *guda* (jaggery or gur)—in the process favouring the mass-produced and market-driven rasogolla. He says:

> *Chhena* and *guda* are indigenous, both are undoubtedly of Odia origin, and both are genuine offerings of the Odia village farmer. They neither smack nor smell of the greed of Capitalism nor bear any relation to the gravity of Communism. In them there is no inkling of colonial trade, nor any sign of the dark mud of treason. These are authentic local goods. (46)

He is not sure that local customers will appreciate the beauty and food value of the indigenous produce. The tone of Tripathy's remarks is similar to that of the village boy's complaints against his Coca-Cola-loving girlfriend:

> Even in this land of great heroes, cheese-jaggery neither looks good nor tastes good until it is made over into the marketable Chittaranjan brand baboo-patronized *rasogolla, sandesh, leddikini, pantua, chhanabara* or *chhanakhoi*. Even though *chhena tadia, parijataka*, and *amrut rasavali* of the Jagannath Temple, and even though *chhenamunda, chhenapura* and *chhena curry* of our villages are made of *chhena* and *guda* (cheese and jaggery) their very sight draws massive frowns, creating a thousand wrinkles on our foreheads. The reason: they are made in our villages, from our sugarcanes, from the milk of our cows and buffaloes. (46)

Tripathy directs his ire at 'Chittaranjan brand baboo-patronized . . . *sandesh, leddikini, pantua, chhanabara* or *chhanakhoi*'. These sweet items are associated with recipes that appear to have come from elsewhere. It is remarkable, however, that he adds rasogolla to the list, suggesting that it should be treated as an alien food product along with other imports. This article was written in 1939, three years after Odisha became an independent province. Read in the context of the 'rasogolla war' between Odisha and West Bengal, this article would appear blasphemous.

Tripathy, however, is not interested in dividing people and foods along communal or parochial lines. His primary target is the colonial market, which he thinks will destroy indigenous foods and food crops associated with them. Tripathy is aware that the modern rasogolla makers favoured sugar, not jaggery, to make the syrup. Once jaggery is out of favour, its low demand would impact the village sugarcane farmer and his sustenance farming. One has seen how ecological imperialism resulted in the extinction of hundreds of indigenous flora and fauna in Africa. In other words, Tripathy's seeming hostility towards rasogolla is a critique of colonial modernity. Tripathy anticipates what modern food historians like Crosby and Highfield say about food narratives and ideological networks.

THE RIGHT TO RASOGOLLA

In the last few years, scholars have attempted to revisit the social ecology that drives the competitive rhetoric surrounding food and foodways. The case of *the* rasogolla is no different. It makes sense to look at three aspects of the 'bittersweet war': (a) the circulation of social energy to establish bragging rights before strengthening business rights and ownership; (b) the rhetoric of competitive antiquarianism that informs what is clearly a layered like-dislike relationship that only neighbours can have; and (c) the politics of partial memories in all food cultures.

In the wake of efforts made by the government of West Bengal to secure GI for rasogolla, three commissions have been set up by the government of Odisha to wrest the initiative in favour of rasogolla. Bhowmik has directed the attention of researchers to the Portuguese origin of sweets made of curdled milk to contest the claims of Odias.

Odisha has now adopted a day in its calendar as International Rasogolla Divas, coinciding with Niladri Bije, the last day of the Puri Rath Yatra. Odia scholars led by Asit Mohanty have turned to sixteenth-century texts such as Balarama Dasa's *Dandi Ramayana* to produce information and evidence on the Odia origin of the sweet. While the evidence is not as ambiguous as it is made out to be, the claims and counterclaims point to a layered relationship not only in a culinary neighbourhood but also intertwined histories of appropriation and counter-appropriation. Food cultures and food rights are informed as much by the materiality of neighbourhood historiography as by biopolitics and commercial interests.

Edible Memories: Rasogolla and Food Fiction 177

As biosocial markers, our food items carry narratives that tell us, as well as the world, who we are, and why we are what we think or claim to be. Mohanty's references to *chhena*-based foods and sweets in medieval and precolonial texts of Odisha illustrate how memories of food production and consumption circulate. However, such memories circulate partially. For, stories of food and war circulate by occluding and erasing stories that do not fit into specific food fictions or are ideologically incompatible to the stories told.

In the food culture of Odisha, *chhena* or cottage cheese is seen as indispensable part of ritual temple offerings including items such as milk, ghee, honey, camphor and *navata*. While offering *chhena* bhog to temple deities is discouraged in temples of North India, especially at Varanasi, *chhena* and *chhena*-based offerings are common to Odisha temples. In the Jagannath temple, no bhog offering is complete without a *chhena* recipe. To this author's mind, this practice has more to do with the social ecology of milk production and consumption in Odisha than with food rights and food pride.

It is important to note that most food items reserved for gods and kings in medieval Odisha—one may say that this practice is not exclusive to Odisha—are highly exoticized, enriched, or dressed up versions of indigenous items. The mention of the rasogolla in Odia scriptural texts and *puranas* dating back to the time of Sarala Dasa's *Mahabharata* and Balaram Dasa's *Jagamohana Ramayana* or *Dandi Ramayana* is to be seen in terms of medieval local colouring. The Odia writer, keen to indigenize pan-Indian cultural narratives and icons, brings in local words and references into free translations of Vyasa and Valmiki.

It should be noted further that the iconic rasogolla migrated to other parts of India, especially Bengal, when brahmin cooks and sweet makers, who traditionally depended on feudal households and temple establishments for a living, left home in the wake of the devastating famine of 1866. These cooks served as 'foodways' as they carried and experimented with Odia recipes to entertain their employers. In other words, in the same way that African foods became household items in the American South or the humble Indian curry became a British 'subject', the rasogolla of Odisha was 'invented' in nineteenth-century Bengal. This 'invention' of rasogolla, in this sense, is best seen as part of food invention narratives—models are available in colonial scientific invention stories that carried 'authentic' reports of 'experiments' with form and content—that grew out of 'new' market expectations.

The expectations included, among others, enhanced shelf life of food items and issues of body and health. As elsewhere in India, issues that we euphemistically called wellness now, were first mentioned in texts of Ayurveda but were diffused through *puranas* such as *Dandi Ramayana*. The line to mark out here is line 6: *kora rasogolla je amruta rasaabali* (sweet shredded coconut pulp and rasogolla with heavenly *rasavali*). The reference to rasogolla is clear.[9] How one interprets and situates this line and the accompanying text depends on one's willingness to look at the relationship between language diffusion and food diffusion (Mintz 2007, 202), at different points of time in specific locations.

SELLING FOOD/TELLING FOOD

This author would like to end the article with a few references to Odisha's putative links with rasogolla, both corroborative and contestable. When one first talked about this in the seminar on food cultures in 2016 and made some points on the evidence used to establish or deny the connection, one was not sure that one would be able to back up the views and readings with the right kind of evidence.

This author wishes to go back to the fact that the extract used by Asit Mohanty (quoted above) is from the Odia translation of Ramayana popularly known as *Jagamohana Ramayana* or *Dandi Ramayana*.[10] Mohanty argues that the use of the word rasogolla in Balarama Dasa's book predates the lexical evidence cited in Bhowmik's book (2017a, 24-5). In this manner, Odisha's claims on rasogolla would be clear.

There is a suggestion that the aforementioned evidence is not necessarily conclusive. For, it can be argued that rasogolla (the sweet and the word), may have come to Odisha from Bengal with

Edible Memories: Rasogolla and Food Fiction

Sri Chaitanya and that Balarama Dasa's use of the word can be traced to his association with Chaitanya. Now, it is agreed that Balarama Dasa completed *Jagamohana Ramayana* during the reign of Purushottam Deva. The poet was thirty-two at that time, which would mean that the book was composed before 1497, the year of the Gajapati King's death.[11] The point is that Balaram Dasa and Sri Chaitanya did not meet before the latter's visit to Odisha in 1509. In other words, any suggestion that the word rasogolla and the sweet travelled to Odisha from Bengal with Sri Chaitanya is not only misleading but also preposterous. Again, K.T. Achaya suggests that the sweet- and cheese-making tradition of Bengal owes substantially to the cheese-making art and science of the Portuguese (Achaya 1998, 22-3). Bhowmik and others use this argument to suggest that Bengal's rasogolla does not have anything to do with the tradition followed in Odisha. Here one needs to note that Vasco da Gama landed in Calicut on 20 May 1498. Achaya suggests that by 1650, there was a Portuguese colony of about 20,000 people in Hoogli, and it is logical to assume that the Bengali sweet-makers got the art of cheese-making from the former.

If the Portuguese tradition of cheese-making was indeed followed by Bengal's sweet-makers—that would make the Bengal cheese sweet-making tradition independent of other indigenous traditions such as the one prevalent in Odisha—the process would have started much after Sri Chaitanya's arrival in Odisha in 1509. The other point is that there was a strong Portuguese presence in Balasore from around the second decade of the sixteenth century. Asit Mohanty rightly suggests that any tradition of cheese-making that Bengal's sweet-makers picked up from the Portuguese would also have been picked up by the Odia sweet-makers, too. So, to think that the Portuguese passed their art to only one section of the Indian population excluding others who were similarly positioned does not make sense (Mohanty 2017a, 24-6, 48).

Even if one accepted the claim, for the sake of argument, that it is the Portuguese who taught Bengal and possibly Odisha, how to make cheese, there would still be inexplicable references to cheese and sweets in iconic texts of Odisha that need fuller explorations and explanations. One such text is Sarala Dasa's *Mahabharata*, completed during the reign of Kapilendra Deva (1435-67), the first Gajapati King of Odisha. This text predates Balarama Dasa'a *Jagamohana Ramayana* by at least thirty years. These two texts, between them, are remarkable for a new kind of vernacular energy that played, to one's mind, a huge role in linguistic and culinary diffusion.

Given the fact that the border territories of Odisha and Bengal remained vaguely defined for centuries, one would say that cultural and culinary diffusions explain the food links to a great extent. One would revisit Govind Tripathy and argue that the introduction of the railway and other new apparatuses in colonial trade gave the sweet-makers of Bengal the opportunity to expand their visibility in the Indian market. In an expanding trade world, appropriation provided a good and safe trading route. As elsewhere in colonial India, the indigenous producers of goods found themselves making way for traders and sellers who knew how to work the colonial facilities.

In the global food market, food is made famous by packaging companies, not by original producers. In the contemporary food market ecology, gastronomers seem to have cleared the stage for restaurateurs. The consumer is no longer, at least not necessarily, from the community that produces, or used to produce, a certain delicacy or a specific culinary wonder. Memories, in this sense, are as edible as the foods. One reason is that one's memories circulate more strongly than the things we call food.

NOTES

1. The translations from Odia texts, unless otherwise indicated, are this author's.
2. Rasogolla is also spelt rasagola, rasagulla, rosogulla, rosogullo, and rasgulla. One has used the spelling mostly used in Odisha.
3. Here one gives samples of widely read and cited social media entries here: Ishita Unblogged, 'Roshogolla or Rasgulla: Bengali's Own Sweet' (16 April 2012): [https://ishitaunblogged.com/2012/04/16/rasgulla-or-roshogolla]; Sanchari Pal, 'TBI Food Secrets: The Fascinating History of Rasgulla and the "Sweet" Battle Over its Origin'. (18 January 2017): [https://www.

Edible Memories: Rasogolla and Food Fiction 181

thebetterindia.com/82618/ history-rasgulla-origin-odisha-west-bengal]; also see P.K. Vasudeva, 'Tale of a Bittersweet Battle' (*The Statesman*, New Delhi, 17 November 2017) [https://www.thestatesman.com/opinion/tale-of-a-bittersweet-battle-1502529643.html]; also see Shreya Thapliyal, 'Rasgulla GI: A Year on, Looking Back at the Sweet Battle between Bengal and Odisha' (*The Statesman*, New Delhi, 13 November 2018) [https://www.thestatesman.com/bengal/rasgulla-gi-year-looking-back-sweet-battle-bengal-odisha-1502707638.html].

4. The book is Haripada Bhowmik's *Rasogolla: Banglar Jagatmatano Abishkar* (Kolkata: Gangchil, 2015).
5. Charmaine O'Brien's comment in *Penguin Food Guide to India* sets the tone for a sociology of food neighbourhoods: 'One food item that is the subject of particular dispute between the two states is the chhena-based sweet rasogolla. Oriyas claim it was invented in the kitchens of the Puri temple more than 300 years ago to appease Lord Jagannath's consort Mahalakshmi for being ignored on the last day of the Rath Yatra. (On this occasion, Jagannath is taken out of the temple and paraded through Puri on a massive chariot; the word 'juggernaut' derives from this event.) Bengalis place the rasogolla more recently decreeing that it was invented in the nineteenth century by a Calcutta sweet-maker for sale to mere mortals. The most likely story is that the rasogolla came into Bengal from Odisha but was commercially produced and popularized in Calcutta. As an interesting side note, the round shape of the rasogolla represents Lord Vishnu's rule of the globe (Penguin Books, 2013), p. 160.
6. Asit Mohanty and Anita Sabat use literary, historical, and archival information to contest Bhowmik's book, the former suggesting that more than heritage, it was the prospect of winning a GI tag that prompted Bengal's sweet-makers to endorse Bhowmik's book. As of now, the *rasgola* (Odisha) vs. *rasogolla* (Bengal) story seems to have ended, each side claiming its victory. *Banglar Rasogulla* and *Odisha Rasogolla* have been granted independent GI tags, respectively, in 2017 and 2019. See Mohanty, 'Rasagola: The Ritual Offering of Odisha' (2017b), and Sabat, 'Rasogolla and Rasagola Dibasa' (2019).
7. This extract from *The Times of India* sums up the spirit of a happy ending: 'They say, All's Well That Ends Well and indeed, it became true for the long-run battle over "Rasagola" between West Bengal and Odisha. The controversy over the scrumptious dessert resulted in a sweet ending for Odisha when it received the geographical indication (GI) tag for the famous eastern sweet. Odisha rasagola is made of cottage cheese and has a distinct colour and texture of its own. Chena is cooked in sugar syrup to get a soft

and juicy consistency. Its unique colour is due to the caramelized sugar and distinct method of cooking that makes for a mouth-watering delicacy' (see https://timesofindia.indiatimes.com/life-style/food-news/gi-tag-to-odishas-rasagulla-and-10-famous-sweets-of-odisha).

8. Benudhar Pradhan (also known as Benudhar Pradhan) of Surundi Village, Harbhanga, Boudh, Odisha, used to sing this song until his death in the late 1980s. A reference is available in an unpublished collection of popular stage songs of western Odisha, currently in the possession of his family. Pradhan seems to have toured all over western Odisha with a group of folk artists and performed in small and big events.

9. Balaram Dasa, *Dandi Ramayana*, Ayodhya Kanda, ed. Gobinda Rath (Gobind Rath Prakashan, 1912), no page; While the pagination of the book's first edition (1912) is not clear, the second edition (1921) carries clearly carries references to the food offerings made to Rama in Ayodhya Kanda (pp. 75-6; also see Mohanty, pp. 70-1). The author translated the following extract from the Odia original for his use:

ଏମନ୍ତେ ଅନେକ ଦ୍ରବ୍ୟ କେ ପାରେ ବଖାଣି ।
ନାଡ଼ୀ ସରପୁଲି ଯେ ଅରିଷା ଛେନାପୁରୀ ।
କାକର ଛେନା ଲଡୁ ଯେ ମାଲପୁଅ ପୁରୀ ।
ସଜମରା ଘିଅ ଆଣି ଦଣ୍ଡି କରା କରା ।
ଗଜା କଚୁରୀ ପଣସ ଖୋସା ବିରି ବରା ।
କୋର ରସଗୋଲା ଯେ ଅମୃତ ରସାବଳୀ ।
ମଣ୍ଡା ନାନମାନ ଅମୃତପାଣି କଦଳୀ ।
ଝୁମ୍ପା ଝଁରିରେ ଯେ ଭରି ନାନାତୀର୍ଥ-ଜଳ ।
ତହିଁରେ ଦେଇ ସୁବାସ ଦ୍ରବ୍ୟ ଯେ ସକଳ ।
ଯଣସିଧ ମଣ୍ଡା ଯେ ଲଡ଼ୁଣୀ ପାଣି ପଣା ।
କେ ପ୍ରକାରେ ଭଳା କେହୁ ପ୍ରକାରେ ଯେ ଛଣା ।
ଯେଣୀ ଅଥମୁଆଁ ସର ନାନାକର୍ଣ୍ଣୀ ପିଠା ।
ଖାଇ ଖାଇ ଦେଖନ୍ତୁ ଯେ ମାଣ୍ଡିଲାକ ଠଠା ।
ପରଷନ୍ତୁ ଲୋକେ ଯେ ଭୁଙ୍କୁ ଛେନା ମଣ୍ଡା ।
କେହୁ ମୁଗମଣ୍ଡା । କେହୁ ପେଢ଼ି ଖସାମଣ୍ଡା ।

> emante aneka drabya kepare bakhani
> nadi sarapuli je arisha chhena puri
> kakara chhena ladoo je malapua puri
> sajamaraa ghia ani dyanti badhaa badhaa
> gaja kachuri panasa khosha biri bara
> kora Rasogolla je amruta rasaabali
> manda naana maana amruta pani kadali
> jhumpa jharire je bhari nana tirtha jala
> tahinre dei suvasa drabya je sakala

*panasia manda je labani pani pana
ke ghrutare bhaja kehi ghrutare je chhana
phena khudumuan sara nana barne pitha
khai khai lokanku je madileka chita
parashanti loke je bhunjanti chhena manda
kehi muga manda kehi pesi khasa manda.*

[What a variety on offer, too many to tell here/sweet noodles, crusted top of milk, chhena puris and arisha pitha/chhena-stuffed kakara, ladoos, and malpuas/pitcherfulls of fresh ghee to top/gaja, kachuri, jackfruit arils, blackgram vadas/kora [shredded coconut pulp with sweet cheese], rasagola, and heavenly rasavali [amruta rasavali]/stuffed mandaas (doughnuts) of all kind, heavenly banana drinks that taste-like nectar/water brought from many holy places in jhumpa jhari [decorated pitchers]/flavoured with sweet-smelling condiments/jackfruit doughnuts, salted drinks/delicacies sauted in ghee and deep-fried in ghee/tender honey kernel, crispy mua ladus, sara [top of milk], varieties of pithas/People were full and fed up with these, there was so much/people still served and people still ate chhena mandas (cottage cheese doughnuts)/Some serve moong doughnuts, some sesame doughnuts.]

10. 'Dandi' is derived from the Odia word 'daanda' or village street which was the most notable common public sphere of the land. Hence street songs would be known as daandi songs. 'Dandi' also refers to a fourteen-syllable metre peculiar to the compositions of medieval devotional poets of Odisha called *daandi-britta* devised by Sarala Dasa, the composer of the Odia *Mahabharata.*
11. While Surendra Mohanty and Asit Mohanty suggest that the book was completed during 1467-97, Dipti Ray, in her *Prataparudradeva: The Last Suryavansi King of Odisha* (2007), argues that the book was composed in in 1503. It is still several years before Vasco da Gama's landing. So, a cheese-making tradition that borrowed from the Portuguese, and operated independently of the indigenous cheese-making tradition of Odisha, can be dated only post-1498.

REFERENCES

Achaya, K.T., 1998, *A Historical Dictionary of Indian Food.* Oxford University Press.

Bhowmik, Haripada, 2015, *Banglar Jagatmatano Abishkar* (Bangla). The Global Invention of Bengal. Gangchil.

Bordieu, Pierre, 2010, *Distinction: A Social Critique of the Judgment of Taste*, translated by Richard Nice, with a new Introduction by Tony Bennet, Routledge.

Coghlan, Michele J. (ed.), 2020, *The Cambridge Companion to Literature and Food*, Oxford University Press.

Collingham, Lizzie, 2017, *The Taste of Empire: How Britain's Quest for Food Shaped the Modern World*. Basic Books.

Covey, Herbert C. and Dwight Eisenach, 2009, *What the Slaves Ate: Recollections of African American Foods and Foodways from the Slave Narratives*. Greenwood Press.

Crosby, Alfred W., 2003, *The Columbian Exchange: Biological Consequences of 1492*. 30th Anniversary Edition. Praeger.

Dasa, Balarama, 1921, 'Ayodhya Kanda'. *Dandi Balmiki Ramayana*, 2nd edn. (Odia), edited by Gobinda Rath. Nityananda Pustakalaya.

Dasa, Jagannatha, *Bhagavata*. Book XI (Odia). https://odisha.gov.in/sites/default/files/202007/bh11.pdf.

Dash, G.N., *Hindus and Tribals*, 1998, *Quest for Co-Existence: Social Dynamics in Medieval Orissa*. Decent Books.

Fisher, Mary Frances, 1954, 'Serve It Forth' (1937). *The Art of Eating*. Houghton Mifflin Harcourt Publishing Company, pp. 55-224.

Highfield, Jonathan Bishop, 2017, *Food and Foodways in African Narratives: Community, Culture, and Heritage*. Routledge.

Mazumdar, B.C., (ed.), 1921, *Typical Selections from Oriya Literature*, Calcutta: Calcutta University Press.

Mintz, Sidney W., 2007, 'Asia's Contributions to World Cuisine: A Beginning Inquiry' in *Food and Foodways in Asia: Resource, Tradition and Cooking*, edited by C.H. Sidney, Cheung and Tan Chee-Beng, Routledge, pp. 202-10.

———, 1986, *Sweetness and Power: The Place of Sugar in Modern History*, Penguin Books.

Mohanty, Asit, 2017a, *Sri Jagannathanka Rasogolla* (Odia), The Rasogolla of Sri Jagannatha. Aama Odisha.

Mohanty, Asit, 2017b, 'Rasagola: The Ritual Offering of Odisha', translated by Supriya Kar, *Odisha Review*, pp. 76-94.

Mohanty, Surendra, 1995, *Odia Sahityara Madhya Parva O Uttara Madhya Parva* (Odia). A History of Medieval and Post-Medieval Odia Literature. Cuttack: Cuttack Students' Store.

O'Brien, Charmaine, 2013, *The Penguin Food Guide to India*. Penguin Books.

Sabat, Anita, 2019, 'Rasogolla and Rasogolla Dibasa', *Odisha Review*, pp. 127-37.

Tripathy, Govind, 2004, 'Chhenaguga: Cheese and Molasses', *The Indian Mind: Essays of the Inimitable Govind Tripathy*, edited by Biyotkesh Tripathy and Bijay K. Danta. Gyanjuga Publication, 2004, pp. 43-54.

CHAPTER 10

Food and Narration: Encoding Pain and Fracture in Bangla Partition Literature

SRAVANI BISWAS

Malati had come to look for the 'hargile' bird she heard crying out in despair. An uncanny feeling that a snake had caught the bird led her towards the wild undergrowth near her hut. While walking, she felt that Spring had come. She saw Shamu and asked him to help her in gathering soft tendrils of cane. She had been fasting as Hindu widows often do; boiled cane tendrils with flavourful rice and butter after fasting was her favourite meal. Shamu obeyed her as he had always done in the past. He followed her mesmerized. Without looking back, Malati could feel his gaze. Covering her naked shoulders with her sari, Malati realized with embarrassment the 'knora' bird that lurked within her calling out. She felt the thrill spreading all over her body. This is a situation this writer described from Atin Bandhyopadhyay's *Nilkontho Pakhir Khonje* (In Search of the Indian Roller). The purpose of putting it in the beginning is its dense encoding of hunger. Malati is a young and beautiful widow who lost her husband in the Dhaka riot. She lived with her brother's family in her village where she was born. On that spring afternoon, she was looking for the distressed 'hargile' bird which was perhaps caught by a snake. She was hungry too after her ritual fasting. She was already imagining the soft-boiled cane with rice and butter and had asked Shamu or Shamsuddin to collect some for her. Though Shamu was a Muslim youth, her natural right to order him was her childhood bond and her later growing awareness of love between them. They had never imagined marrying each other for they were habitual participants of the Hindu–Muslim dichotomy. But the body has a different language and leaves them hungry. Her naked shoulder and the feel of his hungry eyes encode the hunger of spring when creation asks for food to facilitate growth. Thus, the season of spring acquires a different dimension. It is not simply associated with joy and birth. It is also a time of yearning for food. It is only the sophisticated official world that compartmentalizes. Folk imagination thrives on paradoxes. If spring is the season of new birth, it has to survive on death. Its promise cannot escape the possibility of violence. The snake is hungry after its long hibernation through winter. Malati is hungry after her day-long fasting. The young man is hungry because his love will never be consummated. The apparently innocent passage can turn out as highly metaphoric.

But the passage spills out from the folk metaphor of nature into the structured world of human history. The partition of Bengal's has its own structured logistics—the structure of Hindu-Muslim cultural, religious and economic dichotomy, the structure of the politics of demography of the leaders. Partition was an oversimplified solution as it was based on such monolithic and structured political thought. But this affected the masses that live away from such structured ideology. They live an instinctive life. Their lives are tuned to the seasonal cycles and the spontaneity of everyday materiality. This yawning gap between the nationalist ideologies that mobilized partition and the ontological aspects of human life results in chaos. The passage with its paradoxes questions the monolithic discourse on partition. The snake's ingesting a huge bird looks brutal, a widow's craving for food is a violation of social stricture and a Muslim youth's love for a Hindu woman sounds almost profane. Yet in the passage the images of hunger, a natural instinct, are aesthetically humanized.

The aim of partition literature does not end with realistic description of the chaos—the bloodshed, the trains loaded with dead refugees, the rapes, honour killings, and betrayals. If it ends there, the error of generalizing human nature as intrinsically noble or cruel cannot be avoided. Partition did not just reveal these extreme qualities of man in crisis; it exposed the dynamics of the condition of mediocrity, that is, just to be, the inability to act on the face of a complexity that most of the victims faced—a complexity woven with social, political, geographical as well as personal questions. The tragedy of partition lies in underplaying these grey areas of human reality and the fact that this was ignored by the architects of partition; even the ideology of nationalism was monolithic. The role of literature does not end here. It has to execute a deeper exploration of human condition because it is equipped with the elasticity of form and language to do so.

The absence of gory descriptions in numerous Bangla partition novels actually facilitates attention to those grey areas of reality. One does not want to imply that novels that have a higher doze of violence ignore these grey or fluid areas. In fact, victims facing or witnessing such violence undergo this complex experience of emotional gallimaufry. But the shock of violence as experienced in words become so overwhelming in comparison to those more subtle questions that the reader is incapacitated to go beyond the surface.

It is interesting to note that many partition novels in Bangla focus on the mind of the affected rather than the violence itself. These novels are replete with descriptions of nature's bounty, memories of innocence of childhood and very prominently, food. The probable reason is the aim to focus on the mediocre actors who take form only within the dynamics of everyday life. There is no doubt that the crisis of partition gave birth to many tales of heroism and sacrifice. Even the ice-candy-man in Bapsi Sidwa's novel turns heroic when he leaves his home in search of his beloved. In *Train to Pakistan*, there were numerous others who remained glued to the habitual and instinctive life of everyday materiality and such heroic love was a far cry. To turn the spotlight on this mediocrity, the novel must use certain tools. The use of metaphors dramatizes the non-dramatic and helps to put to relief the tragic elements of their lives, especially during the time of crisis.

The passage that had been quoted in the beginning is one interesting example. From the metaphors of food and hunger, it took an overwhelming shape, dramatizing that which is a common story of the partition victims.

Malati's life remained connected to that of Shamu and turned into a map of Shamu's changing career along with his changing consciousness. When it changed from love to hatred, Malati's body bore the burden; she was raped by some strangers. When it turned destructive, it destroyed Malati. But it did not happen in a day because it took some time to move from the depths of Shamu's unconscious to his consciousness. In the meantime, unknown to Malati, Shamu observed her from oblivion. He admired the beauty of her blooming youth. He was pained to see her in her widow's pale attire. He watched her brooding, sitting by the pond while her pet ducks engaged in their amorous play. But his frustration did not remain personal and he joined the Muslim League. The use of metaphors thus joins the individual to the greater scene of history.

Shamu's joining the League is not unusual because one knows the crisis period gave many the excuses to mete out personal revenge. But Malati's life acquires a tragic dimension because it bears an uncanny quality of fate that was predicted even before her destruction. That very spring afternoon she and Shamu had found the 'hargile' bird devouring a snake. Thus, ingesting as a symbol outgrows its natural connotation to turn into a violent destiny.

Then she discovered the bird. The bird was tired and resigned. Its faint cry was of submission to fate. A huge black snake with red eyes was devouring the bird. Half of its body had already disappeared in the amazing wide and elastic mouth of the snake. How could a snake swallow such a huge bird!

She looked at Shamu who was watching the horrid scene with her. Shamu had grown a thin moustache like that of the Hindu deity Kartik. He pleaded with her to go back home because the snake could turn dangerous. But she hung on. Together they watched the snake ingest the bird. After that the snake's mouth and inflated neck returned back to the normal shape. It then looked lifeless and hung from the tree. It was its time of digestion.

The scene turned preternatural. It looked like a dark foreboding of a different future where Shamu and Malati would change their roles; they would play the roles of the snake and the bird.

The change came soon. Shamu's frustrated love for Malati turned convoluted. He transformed himself; he shaved his fine moustache, grew a beard like the 'mullaha' following the Islamic law. Malati had torn his posters again and again. He decided to be aggressive. One day he stuck a poster on the same tree and walked into her courtyard. He had now broken a taboo and had committed the sacrilege of violating the sanctity of private space. Malati was shocked to see the transformation in his appearance and behaviour.

Again, frequent descriptions of nature's bounty like fields full of crops and rivers alive with fish indicate human paradoxically limitation, anxiety and helplessness as against order, cosiness and plenty. Adhir Biswas, in his *Desh-bhager Smriti* (Memories of Partition) speaks of poverty in the child protagonist's prepartition life in East Bengal. Descriptions of plenty in nature do not signify enough food for all, thus underscoring the man-made economic discrepancy. In Adhir's book, it is a poor Hindu family whereas in Atin's novel *Nilkontho Pakhir Khonje* there is a stark contrast of rich Hindu festivities used as foil to the struggle of the Muslims for everyday existence. The question of food does not end in eating: the procuring of food is significant in understanding human condition. In the partition novel, memory of food further gains in significance and underscores the great change in the very fabric of the refugee's mental life.

When he grows up, he remembers the pangs of hunger and the hard work to earn a mouthful while in East Bengal. Yet, he admits that he was a happy child. During the monsoon, they sold grass, and the meagre amount they earned enabled them to buy a bag of vegetables and fresh fish wrapped in arum leaves. They forgot how their hands went raw from cutting grass and how boils erupted endemically during particular seasons. Here, in spite of poverty, the reader receives a positive vibe. Memory here indulges in a nostalgic view of poverty—a concession to hardship in one's own soil because it implies freedom and rootedness.

But the nature of procuring food as refugees in India changes in character and quality. Away from the vast rural scene, in the middle of the crowded city, it loses the possibility of grace that comes after physical hardship. It shows mental degeneration, servility even in a child.

'The refugees, for the government and their officials are not individual cases but a bunch of creatures, always hungry and dirty, a shame to the city. A little child dances for food-rice, khichri or even a biscuit. The onlookers are amused, 'Oh, take a biscuit and stop your pranks—you son of a "bangal",' (Biswas 2008, 34) they shout.

Food in partition narrative helps the writer encode violence and degeneration. It also poses a pertinent question—did partition lead to degeneration or was it social and moral degeneration that facilitated partition. Ritwik Ghatak, in his film *Subarnarekha*, has shown how the refugees who had come to India together, when settling in their ramshackle colonies recreated the same social boundaries and taboos that had divided them in prepartition times. Partition and the struggle for a new beginning had not resurrected them from the ashes. Old and dilapidated institutions of caste and class survived. This is effectively shown in Prafulla Roy's *Keya Patar Nouko* (The Keya Leaf Boat). Jugal, the household help of a prosperous family, after partition, had fled to India. Very soon, he realizes that coming to India is not the solution of all problems. Sealdah, the railway station where the refugees took shelter, is like hell. So, he leads a group of refugees to Mukundapur where he occupies land and soon builds a colony. He makes no discrimination and initially people live a community life, helping each other and eating together from a common kitchen. Initially it looks ideal but it is not so. This hurts Jugal. The Brahmins who had given up all their inhibitions in the crowded Sealdah Station, even eating from the 'langarkhana' meant for the masses, when settled in the colony resume their sectarianism. They no longer agree to join the rest when it comes to sharing food. Jugal feels angry and frustrated. During the partition, people had lost everything, but they still clung to the old useless social institutions.

Again, while dealing with the paradoxes—uncontrollable hunger in the midst of abundance of food, the writers not only hint at one of the causes of partition but further humanize the breaking of social and moral codes. When the body turns berserk, it creates its own codes of survival which is, for the victim a law in itself. Joton in the novel *Nilkontho Pakhir Khonje* (In Search of the Indian

Roller) is a Muslim widow. She survives on 'shaluk', a plant that grows in abundance in the endless water-bodies of East Bengal's. It keeps hunger at bay but does not provide nourishment. She is hungry for a handful of rice. After fasting for two days, she turns desperate. She goes to the paddy fields in search of turtle eggs. She would take them to the women of the Thakur family and barter them for a bowl of rice. But while looking for eggs among the ripe abundance of golden crop, she cannot restrain herself from stealing a few strands of paddy. She cuts the stalks with the help of a snail shell and hides them in the folds of her sari. She considers it Allah's mercy. When one is hungry, she tells herself, nothing is sinful.

Jalali, another Muslim woman, steals Malati's pet duck. Her husband, a boatswain, has gone to the sea, and she is left to survive on her own. After going without food for days, she turns into a desperate fox. After strangling the duck under the water, she runs home and immediately starts plucking at its feather. Then, kneeling on the floor naked with the water from her body making a dirty pool around her, she begins to roast the duck. She has no oil to grease it. She falls on her food and, like a greedy animal, polishes off every morsel of meat from the bones. In the darkness outside her hut, she hears Malati's voice crying out for her favourite duck. Jalali had always wanted to be as beautiful as Malati.

The same scene is witnessed by Shamu, and here the moral code is reiterated. Shamu, guessing the identity of the thief quietly walks to Jalali's hut.

He moved the cane bush with his hand and peeped through the bamboo netting. He saw a lamp burning. The half-naked Jalali was sitting on a low wooden stool. She was sucking at the bones from the platter. Not a single trace of meat was left on the bones. She gnawed at the bones, cracking them with her teeth. Then she drank water. Shamu noticed how the face of the cunning fox he had seen floating on the water, at the end of the day, after the feast of meat, had turned simple and beautiful. The face was remembering Allah. While drinking water, twice she uttered the name of Allah. Now Shamu, for these poor humans, wanted to walk in the deep wilderness. The thought of Malati's stolen duck or his resolution to punish Jalali disappeared from his mind. Because Jalali now spread a torn 'hogla' leaf mattress to read her 'namaz'. Her face looked like 'rasul', her hands were spread before her in prayer. Shamsuddin could not utter a word. He was as if rooted to the ground. (74).

Partition literature is mnemonic in the sense that history is fictionalized in order to bring out what partition denotes to the narrator or author. But memory is not a simple function of retrieving what was permanently etched within the mind. According to Fabio Parasecoli, memories are not pure images mirrored in the Cartesian subject. When one speaks of food as remembered by partition victims or even the use of food images by the narrators, it should be noted that food had always strong emotional undertones. So, images of food in whatever form are transitory and interact constantly with one's physical, emotional or motivational state. According to Sanchez Romera, a particular food item acquires its connotation of the environment when it was taken—the company, warmth, landscape and the specific time of life. One is immediately reminded of Marcel Proust's famous Madeleine. For Proust, the Madeleine acted as a stimulus which shows a connection between body and mind. Partition novels, when dealing with memory as nostalgia, uses the solidity and sensuality of food in order to revive what Proust spells out as the meaning of a time which was apparently dead. The moment of resuscitation is real without being actual, ideal without being abstract, and immediately the permanent and habitually concealed essence of things is liberated and one's true self, which seemed dead but was not altogether dead, is awakened and reanimated (Time Regained 264-5). What is this essence? Interestingly it is not the particular food but the very essence of the experience of time and space which the particular edible exorcizes like a ghost. Thus, food becomes an effective means of encoding the indefinable feelings of fracture and pain that the victims experienced. The difference between Proust's example and the writing of partition is that Proust's was pure nostalgia awakening the writer to the essence of a particular time that was lost; while, in case of partition literature, it entails a negative emotion—the putrid feeling of degeneration. In Sunil Gangopadhyay's *Arjun*, the memory of the boy's village is related to Amaladidi. She was childless and generously fed the little children with sweetmeats like the milky white coconut 'tokhti' that melted in one's mouth. She knew why the boys always came to their house on the pretext of asking for water, pretending to be thirsty. Amaladi was always ready with those heavenly 'toktis'. An aura of noble innocence surrounded her and no scandal could touch her young widowed life. She was, though young, an eternal mother figure. It is interesting to note that the group of boys who enjoyed her affection consisted of both Hindus and Muslims. Arjun's best friend was Altaf. Amaladi had a special attachment to a motherless Muslim boy called Abbas who spent most of his time with her. Whenever Arjun remembers his village, he remembers Amaladi and her sweets. It could have been Proust's Madeleine, but if one takes Sanchez's words, the sweets acquire a different meaning; the meaning of partition and all the fractures of body and mind of its victims. The boy connotes the image of Amaladi feeding the boys with sweets to his own fractured self. While playing hide and seek, the boys had discovered her naked body among the ripe corns and somehow sensed that she had become a victim to some different hunger. Later, when the boy leaves his village with his newly widowed mother, for the first time he realizes that his mother is a young woman and should be protected from strangers.

Memory is a complex process of the body and the emotions associated with it, like pleasure, pain and fear, influence the way memories are stored and eventually retrieved. The rational process cannot be isolated from the irrational and instinctive. They are beyond the mind–body split. Proust had tried to find the source of happy memory in the little cake itself but it was hidden in his soul. Partition had completely changed the fabric of the victims' mind. For the narrator of partition, food images unlock that secret chamber.

REFERENCES

Alhoff, Fritz and Dave Monroe (ed.), 2007, *Food & Philosophy: Eat, Think, and Be Merry.* Oxford: Blackwell Publishing.

Bandyopadhyay, Atin, 2012, *Nilkontho Pakhir Khonje*, Kolkata: Karuna Prakashani.

Biswas, Adhir, 2008, *Deshbhager Smriti (Part 2),* Kolkata: Gungcheel.
Bruschi, Isabella, 2010, *Partition in Fiction: Gendered Perspectives.* New Delhi: Atlantic Publishers.
Gangopadhyay, Sunil, 1971, *Arjun.* Kolkata: Ananda Publishers.
Holtzman, Jon D., 2016, 'Food and Memory.' *Annual Review of Anthropology* 35(2006), pp. 361-78. JSTOR. Web.
Lane, Robert E., 2016, 'Self-Reliance and Empathy: The Enemies of Poverty: And of the Poor', *Political Psychology* 22(3) (September 2001), pp. 473-92. JSTOR. Web.
Roy, Prafulla, 2012, *Keya Patar Nouko,* Kolkata: Karuna Prakashani.
Roy, Rituparna, 2010, *South Asian Partition Fiction in English,* Amsterdam: Amsterdam University Press.

CHAPTER 11

Food Mnemonics and Identity Construction

SURANJANA BARUA

INTRODUCTION

It is a given that food is an integral component of our sociocultural and religious identity. What one eats and does *not* eat is a reflection and extension, of who one is both as a community and as an individual (whether one looks at it from economic perspectives or sociocultural/ethnocentric ones). In today's food conscious world, how one eats is also tied to identity issues—hence the ways in which *experience* of ethnic cuisine is highlighted in today's consumerist society. This article will examine the role of *memory about* food in conversation—how eliciting information of one's favourite food together with evoking the memory of one's first (perceived) encounter with that food actually establishes and reiterates personal identity. An analysis of the language in use in such food mnemonics will help establish the intimate relation that food has with one's salient self-image and identity. As such, thought about food truly becomes food for thought.

As one of the key components to survival itself, food has always been at the centre of human existence. Recent academic discourses involving food have however spilled over from its sustenance status to involve other aspects of human culture and civilization. Food is now understood as a marker of identity and emerging disciplines such as Food Studies examines the deep psychological and socio-economic bonds existing between food, culture and societies from multiple disciplines within the humanities, social sciences and sciences. Almerico states that not only do food choices made by people reveal views, beliefs, passions, assumptions, background knowledge and personalities of people, 'they also tell stories of families, migrations, assimilation, resistance, changes over times and personal as well as group identity' (2014, 1). Thus, the quotidian experience of food consumption for survival and nourishment may also imply greater issues of personal choices, group preferences and human identity as a whole and by delving into the common occurrence of eating, one can draw greater inferences, have a greater acceptance and more understanding of oneself and others.

As noted above, the human experience of food has over centuries metamorphosed into an integral part of culture: food is no longer just for survival and nourishment but in a manner quite distinguishing of modern *homo sapiens* as a species. Humans have learnt not just to gather, cultivate plants, raise livestock but through the discovery of fire and its taming, they have also learnt to cook, use utensils to eat. In course of time, there evolved in every culture, complex sets of rules with a corollary code of etiquette to govern how to eat appropriately. Thus, not only do 'Humans do not feed, but eat' (Almerico 2014, 3), but they have evolved *food habits* (Kittler et el. 2012) uniquely. Food habits—variously known as *foodways* or *food cultures*—are thus inextricably linked to the manner in which humans have come to use food: this includes everything from how it is chosen, how it is acquired, distributed, by whom it is prepared to how it is served and who eats it. The significance is so much in today's world now that food has left behind its mere sustenance origins and also surpassed its epicurean associations to become an integral component of our very sociocultural and religious identity. What one eats and does *not* eat is a reflection, and extension, of who we are both as a community and as an individual today, whether one looks at it from economic perspectives or sociocultural and ethnocentric ones. Moreover, in today's food conscious world, how one eats is also tied to identity issues—hence the ways in which the *experience* of ethnic cuisine is highlighted in today's consumerist society. This method of recreating the ethnic experience of food may be seen as attempts to provide distinctive identity associated with food culture.

This article will examine the role of *memory about* food in conversation and attempt to show how eliciting information of one's favourite food together with evoking the memory of one's first (perceived) encounter with that food actually establishes and reiterates group and personal identity. An analysis of the language in use in such food mnemonics will help establish the intimate relation that food has with one's salient self-image and identity.

SOCIAL AND PERSONAL IDENTITY VIS-À-VIS FOOD MNEMONICS

In this section one will put forward a few theoretical positions that would be tenable for an analysis of food in language. The chief amongst these is the concept of *food voice* introduced by Hauck-Lawson (2004) who had suggested that what one eats or chooses not to eat communicates aspects of a person's identity or emotion in a manner that words alone cannot. Food choices enable one to understand and situate oneself in the greater context of social order and, it is hypothesized here, that speaking about choices would result in a greater realization given the positioning of oneself with respect to the social groups that one belongs to and functions in. There are studies that have delved deep into the socio-psychological factors which influence people's food choices and habits. For example, Larson and Story (2009) examined influences on the choices people make in food consumption and showed that children tend to have food admired by adults like their teachers but not their parents. More recently, Brown (2011) showed that social conscience and peer pressure impact food choices and group approval or disapproval of a given food has an impact on the choice of food. This article will examine data from peer group conversation with the hope of throwing further light on the choice of food and the role of language in positing/asserting/ justifying or negating such choices while linking it in the greater context of social identity. Since peer group is a strong social group with emotional ties and social hierarchies inherent in it, peer conversations regarding food may throw up interesting socio-psychological and cultural dimensions pertaining to food. One may be expected to choose to eat food that is mnemonic of the peer group identity. In the following section, one will examine such data to see what aspects of identity come to light in terms of food when it is represented in one's language.

THE LANGUAGE IN FOOD: CONSTRUCTING THE SALIENT IDENTITY

The speech extracts pertaining to food habits that will be analysed here is from data collected for a project by the current author at Tezpur University, Assam.[1] A total of 17 respondents (13 female and 4 male) who were students of an interdisciplinary course, that the current author was offering, as part of a postgraduate programme had volunteered to take part in the study. The students were from different departments of the University and were staying in hostels. The respondents were all in their early twenties and the study required them to take or give interviews. In the initial questionnaire that the respondents were asked to fill up, apart from supplying personal information, they had to indicate whether they preferred the role of an 'interviewer' or 'interviewee'. Respondents who preferred the role of interviewer were interviewed individually by the author and were then asked to interview any two of their peers who preferred to be interviewees. Thus, while the interviewee pair interacted with a peer group interviewer, the latter himself or herself was interviewed by the current author who was their teacher. The social position of the interviewer (whether teacher or peer) inevitably played a role in the context of interlocution. It is to be noted that in the case of the those who preferred to be interviewers, the author was the only person present during the recording whereas any respondent who took the interviewee preference typically had two peers present during the recording—the peer who interviewed her/him and the peer who was a fellow interviewee.

The speech extracts that shall be analysed here are, as mentioned above, from data collected for a project by the current author and the analysis broadly follows a Conversation Analysis framework.[2] The interviews were semi-structured, in the sense that interviewers were given a set of pre-selected questions which they were free to ask in any order that they liked. This was done to ensure that the interviewer (in case it was a student) was comfortable and familiar with the questions and could present them in a manner which s/he found most suitable. One of the 'ice-breaker' questions that the interviewers had to ask in the semi-structured interviews was the following:

- What is your favourite food and when did you first have it?

This question was given as a filler question in case the interview got too 'heavy' for the interviewers and to lighten up the situation of interlocution. Since food always elicits animated discussions, the response to this question was also no different than anticipated and respondents pitched in with reminiscences or narratives of their encounters with their favourite food. However, as will be clear from the analysis below, it also threw up remarkable linguistic evidence of the manner in which food is tied to one's essential identity. The manner in which encounters with one's favourite food were narrated also became yardsticks of the salience that these encounters had for their identity.

In the extract below which is a speech situation between three male peers R14, R16 and R17,[3] R14 is interviewing the latter two who happen to be in the same department and also the same hostel. The three of them had been together for a few semesters and shared a good rapport amongst them. The interviewer R14 asked his peers the favourite food question more than twenty minutes into the interview. His question turn is the first line in the first extract below:[4]

EXTRACT 1

[DAHZ000016: 23:08]

1. R14: *tuma::luke ki khai bhaal pua* ↑ *??*
   You (pl) what eat good get

   What do you (plural) like eating?

2. R17: *a::: ↑ a:mi oxo ↑↓ miya manuh ↑ (.) bhotuwa ↑ (.)*
   we Assamese people rice-eaters

   'We are Assamese people. Rice eaters'

3. *bha::t* khai bhaal pao ↑ (.) *prodha::n koi* (.)
   Rice eat good get1. mainly

'We/I like eating rice...means...mainly.'

4. >*ma:r hator bha::t ma:ne bira::t priyo* ↑<
   Mother hand-gen rice means very favourite

'Rice[5] cooked in Mother's hand is very favourite'

5. *a:ru ta::r logote moi::: fas fud kha:u* ↑ (.)
   And it-gen with I fast food eat

'And with that I eat fast food.'

6. *a::ru bira::t mane moi siken fraid rais kha::i bha::l pao*
   (marked structure)
   And very means i-nom chicken fried rice eat good get 1

'And...very...means...I like chicken fried rice a lot'

7. *guwa* ↑↓ *hatit thakute ekhon asile* ↑ *resturant* (.) *for sizens buli* ↑.
   Guwahati-loc stay-hab one pst restaurant Four Seasons quot

'When I was in Guwahati, there was a restaurant. Four Seasons.'

8. @*ta::t ami pra::i logor emutha goi addaa:: mari mari*
   there we often peer handful go adda[6] beat beat

9. *siken fraid rais khaisilu*@   (pitch variations)
   chicken fried rice eat 1

'There a handful of us used to go and eat chicken fried rice while gossiping'

10. *a::ru bele::g ki a::ru* ↑ (.)
    and other what and

'And other than that, what?'

11. *oxomiya:: jitu tha::li* ↓ (.)   (marked word order)
    Assamese rel-pro platter

'The Assamese thaali.'

12. >*bixexke kobole gole guwahatit* (.) *paradaizor oxomiya tha:litu*<
    specially say go Guwahati-loc paradise-gen Assamese platter-cl

'Specially if one has to say the Assamese thaali at Paradise in Guwahati'

13. *a:ru khorika:r oxomiya tha::litu (.) mur bira::t priyo* ↑
    and khorika-gen Assamese platter-cl i-gen very favourite

'And the Assamese thaali of Khorika is my favourite'

14. >*aru: ghoror ma::r hator*<
    and home-gen mother hand-gen

'And (anything) cooked by mother at home'

In the above extract, following the first turn of R14 in line 1 in which he posits the question 'What do you like eating?', R17 responds by asserting a community identity first—'We are Assamese people. Rice eaters.' He extends the assertion of the Assamese identity when he reiterates that given that he is an Assamese, he is also a rice eater. In line 4, he introduces the family identity when he says that he likes meals cooked by his mother and in line 5 he adds new information by stating that he eats 'fast food'. This latter becomes characterized when in line 6, he says that he likes 'chicken fried rice' a lot. In a very marked syntactic structure, he fronts the intensifier *biraa:t* (very) along with a filler *maa:ne* (means) and then starts the sentential clause with the nominative subject *moi* (I). The salience of this food choice can be gleaned from the fact that it is this food item that merits a narrative: his turns in lines 7-9 to recreate his encounters with chicken fried rice in restaurants in Guwahati where he used to hang out with his friends. Following this underscoring of the peer identity which gets coagulated through the conjuring of food image, he goes back to the community identity of Assamese food: his lines 11-13 are about the Assamese platter which he has had in popular restaurants of Guwahati. He ends his turns in line 14 by once again going back to home food cooked by his mother.

R17's food voice (Hauck-Lawson 2004) and food habits (Kittler et al. 2012) along with their accompanying linguistic features can be summarized as follows in Table 11.1.

TABLE 11.1: LINGUISTIC FEATURES CHARACTERIZING SALIENT FOOD VOICE OF RESPONDENT R17

Salient Identity	Accompanying Linguistic Features (Line numbers)
Community (Assamese)	Pitch variations (2/3)
	Marked syntactic structure (11)
Familial identity (Mother's food)	Fast speech (4)
Individual identity (fast food)	Pitch variations (5/)
	Marked syntactic structure fronting of intensifier/filler (6)
	Fronting of verb (7)
	Elaboration (7-9)
Peer identity	Pitch variations (7/9)
	Animated speech (7-9)

The same question was also asked to the second peer R16 who responds with his first line as cited below.

EXTRACT II

[DAHZ000016: 23:30]

1. R16: *moi tu bha:t khai bha::l pao* (.)
   (R17 laughs) (discourse marker)
   i-nom dm rice eat good get 1
   '(As for me) I like eating rice'

2. R14: *bha:t khai bha::l pua* (.)?(.hehe) *bhatot ke a:ru beleg nai neki?*
   rice eat good get2 hehe rice-loc com and different neg q mkr
   'You like eating rice? Isn't there anything other than rice?'

3. R16: *jolpa* ↑↓ *::n*   (no elaboration)
   jolpaan[1]

4. R14 @*arre kua tumi bule ga::khir khai bohut bha::l pua*@
   dm say2 you quot milk eat very good get2
   'Say—you reportedly like to have milk a lot.'

5. R16: *o ga::khir kha:l bha::l pao* ↑.
   yes milk eat good get
   'Yes, I like to have milk.'

6. >*moi khawei moi etiyao khao, a:gor pora khau*<
   'I have it (habitually); I have it now also and used to have it from earlier'

7. R14: *jolpa::n ma::ne kenekua dhoronor jolpa:n* ↑?
   'Jolpa::n means what kind of jolpan?'

8. R16: *sira* ↑.
   Flattened rice

9. R14: *sira* ↑:?
   Flattened rice?

10. R16: *si* ↑↓ *ra*: (.) *doi* (.) *gur* (.)
    Flattened rice curd molasses.

In extract II above, food choices become not only a matter of individual preference but also potential peer ridicule. Like R17, R16 too starts his response in line 1 by stating that he likes eating rice. R17 laughs in the background and it prompts R14 in his interviewer role to elicit a different response from R16. In response to the prodding by the interviewer, R16 says in line 3 that he likes *jolpaan* (see footnote 7). To this laconic reply, there is an unexpected challenge from R14 who in animated voice asks R16 to say on record that he likes milk. The specific choice of food item seems to be intentional and directed towards eliciting a certain kind of response because R16's next turn in lines 5-6 seems highly defensive: it is characterized by pitch variations, is spoken very fast and is highly guarded. R's 16 spirited defence of food choice in that line makes his peer interviewer redirect to the original question as to what kind of *jolpaan* he likes to which R16 says *sira*: (flattened rice). And he qualifies it further by saying he likes it with curd and molasses. A linguistic analysis of R17's food voice may be as follows:

TABLE 11.2: LINGUISTIC FEATURES CHARACTERIZING
SALIENT FOOD VOICE OF R16

Salient Identity	Accompanying Linguistic Features (Line numbers)
Community	Discourse marker (1) suggesting continuity with R17
(Assamese)	Lexical item choice with no elaboration (3)
Familial identity (Mother's food)	Fast speech (4)
Individual identity	Pitch variations (5)
(fast choice defence: *milk*)	Fast speech (7-9)

ANALYSIS

Sadella and Burroughs (1981) had proved that different food choices may come to imply personality types. The research had listed foods distinct to five different diets, viz., (i) fast food, (ii) synthetic food, (iii) health food, (iv) vegetarian food and (v) gourmet food and it was learned in the study that participants associated different personality types with the food choices made. Thus, people who had fast food and synthetic food were classified as religious conservative; health food personalities were characterized as antinuclear activists and Democrats; vegetarians were perceived as pacifists and gourmet eaters were seen as individuals who were liberal and sophisticated. The stereotypes were established through self-description and personality tests. In the current context, the food associations had very strong identity affiliations in both cases: while *in the case of R16, his food voice had encompassed community, family, individual and peer identity as salient* and through different linguistic features as noted in Table 11.1, in the case of R17, it became a question of strong defence of his individual food choice so as to negate any negative associations of his choice of favourite food with peer characterizations ('being a little boy who liked milk' or other possible and implied psycho-sexual associations). In this manner, food habits and voice become a strong marker of identity and assertion and specially in the peer group setting, it became imperative to not just say what food ones likes but also enumerate or defend on why one likes a particular food.

As such, rice, home cooked food/chicken fried rice, milk—all become assertions of community/family/peer or individual identity.

CONCLUSION

In a postmodern world where identities are so fluid, food becomes a relatively stable marker of identity. It not only justifies an experience of salient personal identity but also it plays an iterative role in reminding one *Who I am and what is important to me?*[2]

As such, *contextual and linguistic negotiations of food become mnemonics by which personal identity is retrieved, posited and reconstructed in conversation in a peer group context.* It is predicted that the same would also be true of any other situation of interlocution which brings together the self and the other in the context of food. Thought about food then is really food for thought.

NOTES

1. At the Centre for Assamese Studies, Tezpur University where the author was working previously.
2. Conversation Analysis in the study of talk-in-interaction and typically uses minutest details of everyday talk to analyse macro phenomenon. While the transcription symbols to be used in the data are explained in the table at the end of the paper, readers may kindly refer to any basic text such as Hutchby and Woofitt (1998), etc. for further elucidation and references on CA.
3. The notations for respondents are as per Conversation Analysis perspective where symbols and or number indicate the speaker and real names are not used in order to protect identity.
4. Each Assamese word is followed by a gloss in the next line and a translation in the one thereafter.
5. The term 'rice' is used metonymically here to mean 'meal'.
6. *Adda* is a very typical term in languages like Assamese, Bengali, and Hindi to signify a meeting point of peers to while away time, hold discussions and exchange gossip. It is used both as a noun to signify the place of meeting and as a verb to mean the action.
7. Assam, jolpaan is a breakfast meal which could comprise puffed rice and other savouries usually taken with milk or curd.

8. I am thankful to members of the audience at the 'National Seminar on Food Cultures of India' held at Tezpur University (1-2 December 2016) for their observations and comments on the data presented here. It has made the analysis more comprehensive.

REFERENCES

Almerico, Gina M., 2014, Food and Identity: Food Studies, Cultural and Personal Identity, *Journal of International Business and Cultural Studies 8*, pp. 1-7.

Brown, A., 2011, *Understanding Food: Principles and Preparation* (4th Edition), Belmont, CA: Wadsworth.

Hauck-Lawson, A., 2004, Introduction to Special Issue on the Food Voice. *Food, Culture and Society, 7*, pp. 24-5.

Hutchby, I. and R. Wooffitt, 1998, *Conversation Analysis: Principles, Practices and Applications,* Cambridge: Polity Press.

Kittler, P.G., K.P. Sucher and M.N. Nelms, 2012, Food and Culture (6th Edition). Belmont, CA: Wadsworth.

Larson, N. and M. Story, 2009, A Review of Environmental Influences on Food Choices, *Annual Behavioural Medicine, 38.* Supplement 1, pp. 56-73.

Sadella, E. and J. Burroughs, 1981, Profiles in Eating: Sexy Vegetarians and other Diet-based Stereotypes, *Psychology Today* (October), pp. 51-7.

CHAPTER 12

Tea as Food: Tracing the History of Tea through Folktales and Fairy Tales

YASHOMANA CHOUDHURY

Tea is an important part of food culture as it is one of the world's most popular and desired beverages. For the Chinese, tea culture is intricately linked with the culture of the country and plays a crucial part in shaping the economic and gastronomic development. For the Japanese, tea was part of the religious tradition which slowly developed as a daily practice. The relationship between the British and tea culture goes back to the sixteenth century and represents the transition of British history, which went from being an 'oriental beverage' to being their national drink. Today, tea is an important food item of Indian households, and Indian tea culture again has a rich, exotic, and grisly history.

Tea is called a beverage. But can tea be merely dismissed as being just a beverage? Food is mainly considered to be something we 'chew' and 'swallow'. Yet there are liquid foods like soup which we cannot chew but drink and swallow. How would one clearly demarcate between food and beverage? Beverage is the liquid food which completes a meal. Do beverages complete a meal or does one need solid food with beverage to complete a meal? Tea is seldom served or taken alone. A tea break or an afternoon tea is not just plain tea but served with other food items so that it becomes a small or a whole meal. The idea of tea being served with other food items or the need of tea at a certain time along with evening snacks or breakfast makes tea such a vital 'food' in our life. Hence, tea is assigned a privileged status as a beverage which has a rich, long and complex history of colonial power and legacy. It is considered as the world's most popular drink and known to have both commercial and cultural trade value. The tea trade was a huge empire which is intricately related with British colonization.

Food is a cultural product and food habits are one of the legitimate means of expressing and recognizing diverse social and cultural identities. In a world of differences, it is interesting to recognize the remarkable role food plays in differentiating social cultural entities and also acting as a unifying factor, a universal ground for people to identify with. In constructing an identity through the food habits, tea can be studied as an important marker in history which has shaped our history and still continues to shape our culture. Tea is a major food habit of countries like China, India, Japan and England. The historical significance and its impact on the human population have established tea as a major gastronomic necessity.

The article will focus on the historical significance of tea in different folktales and fairy tales and how it helped shape culture; especially the folktales, myths, legends and fairytales of China, Japan, and the British Isles. This article will study tea as a conventional food, its evolution through the ages in various forms to form different cultural identities; discovering tea as a common, universal identity, a cultural marker and the impact of tea in India and its evolution as a significant part in the present world.

When one uses the word conventional or traditional, one is already marking the subject with societal and historical significance. Conventional is synonymous with traditional. The word conventional for tea indicates tea has a rich cultural history and has helped in shaping traditions through different ages.

The concept of food is associated with social hierarchy, power relations, social stereotyping and cultural identity. Culture is the elemental base of traditions and philosophy which governs a society, a community, or a tribe. It provides the basis for any myth or legends or for that matter folktales and fairy tales. These stories give one a picture of the myths, the ethnicities, religion, heritage, art and traditions of different societies and communities. The

Tea as Food: Tracing the History of Tea   211

idea of cultural identity is the notion of having the same interests, philosophy, culture and heritage culminating in a sense of companionship. Cultural identity can be said to be the relationship of different signifying aspects such as the customs and traditions, the language, location, myths and legends, the religious culture, history and art that forms the general cultural heritage of a place.

Analysing tea as food and associating it with social hierarchy, power relations, social stereotyping and cultural identity, one stumbles upon different habits and patterns across different traditions. Tea is not just a simple beverage. It is a way of life for countries like China, Japan, England and India. Drinking and eating is a patterned activity and the food habits help one to discover social boundaries and cultural differences.

In a world of differences, it is interesting to recognize the remarkable role food plays in differentiating social cultural entities and also acting as a unifying factor, a universal ground for people to identify with. Though food habits differentiate between cultures, food habits had an ordered pattern starting from breakfast to dinner which acts as a unifying factor across cultures. Similarly, tea too acts as a unifying factor across different cultures and, on the other hand, it acts as a distinctive distinction. The example of tea ceremonies across cultures is an ideal way of discovering the similarities and the contrast. A tea ceremony is a ritual of making and drinking tea which is practised extensively in Asian culture, especially by the Chinese, Japanese, Indian and the British. It was a way of life, social status symbol, from the use of expensive tea sets to the fancy food items, the tea culture determines the diverse culture of different regions. For the Chinese, a tea ceremony is the art of making and presenting the tea and often involves a ceremonial preparation. For the Japanese, tea ceremonies are influenced by Chinese tea culture during the medieval times and it often portrays a way of life led by the Japanese, a way of life linked to their historical past. In England and most part of Europe, there is tea culture, but they are not called tea ceremonies; rather they are referred to as 'afternoon tea', 'tea break', or simply 'tea' (which indicate afternoon light meal, consisting of snacks and tea). One of the markers of tea ceremonies is the serving of tea in expensive porcelain tea sets which serves as a demarcation of class.

Kakuzo Okakura talks about different developmental stages in the life growth of tea leaves. In his book, *The Book of Tea* (2014), he explains the features of 'teaism' as an art of life itself, and how tea has transformed from being a medicine to an expensive and highly valued beverage. Kakuzo Okakura also explains how preparation of tea includes choosing the right kind of water too. Okakura further expands on the different stages of evolution of the culture of tea; first stage being the state of making cake tea or boiled tea, where the leaves were steamed then crushed and made into a cake and later boiled with ginger, rice, salt, orange peel, spices, milk and sometimes onions. This method of tea making is almost extinct now and survives only amongst the Mongolian and Tibetan tribes.

Though tea was born in China, it was the Japanese culture which actually built the ways of a proper tea ceremony. There were schools of tea ceremonies which ranged from Monks to Samurai warriors. The tea ceremony defined to them the essence of their life. For the Japanese, a tea ceremony is built with humility and respect both from the host and the guests. The Japanese tea houses have low doors so that one had to bow and humble themselves before entering, and the tea house itself is very simply furnished with simple flower arrangement and a scroll of poetic calligraphy or some artwork adorning the walls. In a Japanese tea ceremony, the expensive porcelain tea sets are never used rather they use humble earthen cups and pots. Kakuzo Okakura explains how significant tea was to the Japanese, that tea with them 'became more than an idealization of the form of drinking; it is a religion of the art of life' (2014, 20).

In China, tea was first used solely for medicinal properties, a health tonic, and treatment for diseases. The green teas and pu'ers (fermented tea) are prescribed for different health complaints and still being used. Later when tea became more widely available to all sections of people, it developed as a drink for pleasure. In China as well as in India, tea is an important part of daily meals, besides mealtime tea is served as a welcoming gesture to guests.

Tea as Food: Tracing the History of Tea   213

In India, tea had a late beginning, which is why there are no elaborate tea rituals and tea ceremonies in India. But tea is very much part of the everyday life. In India tea is known for its uniqueness. It has created a name for itself in today's tea culture. India 'tea-time' can range from high-class tea party served in expensive tea sets to humble streetside stalls, and tea often served in small clay-pots. 'Chai', as known to the western world, can be drunk alone but is enjoyed with snacks. 'Chai-time' is an important part of Indian daily food habit, and the snacks often turn the simple tea time into a proper meal. India has its own varieties of teas, among which Masala Chai, ginger tea (drunk both black and with milk) is most famous. Masala Chai is milk tea spiked with Indian spices like cardamom, cloves, and ginger and sweetened with sugar.

The history of sweet tea is again interesting as the Chinese used a bit of salt in their tea in the ancient times, the way Japanese used to drink it. It was Europe which introduced the custom of having 'sweet-tea' which was later adopted by the other cultures (Smith 1992, 262).

According to the article 'Complications of the Commonplace: Tea, Sugar and Imperialism' by Woodruff D. Smith, in the early European society, sugar was used to enhance the taste of food and was considered a fashionable food item. The love for sugary items is seen in the food items of European civilization which was extensively used during tea time. In England, the afternoon tea is often enjoyed with scones, muffins, biscuits, cakes and pastries. The English even add cream to their coffee to give it a rich, milky, and thick texture. 'Tea' is now, also a social event, a party. For the British, having a 'cuppa' means having tea with biscuits. The nineteenth century saw the creation of tea gardens which was initiated by Queen Victoria for her immense love for tea with cakes and strawberry jam. This act of putting sugar into tea may seem small and insignificant but as Smith points out,

> This custom, which has mistakenly been viewed as insignificant, had important historical effects. Its widespread adoption in Britain and elsewhere in northern Europe eighteenth century greatly reinforced demand for both products, thus helping to foster British imperialism in Asia, plantation slavery in the West Indies, and economic growth in Europe and America.

There are these two American novelties, which have actually revolutionized how tea is consumed, which is iced tea and the other is the tea bag. Iced tea is a popular summer thirst quencher which is flavoured with lemon or mint. The tea bag is more convenient for use and discarding, but it is looked down upon by true tea aficionados and who dismisses it as a shadow of the real thing.

What is fascinating is that, even though there are a lot of different variety of teas, but there is only one species of the tea plant, the *Camellia sinesis*. The different types of tea that one gets today are a result of differences in cultivation, treatment, climate, soil and the growing environment. There are six key divisions of tea: black, green, white, yellow, oolong and pu'er. The contemporary world offers a variation of herbal teas infused with myriads of flavours like Chamomile, earl grey, basil, lavender, hibiscus, jasmine butterfly pea tea and such. Among all the countries and their variations of tea, there is the butter tea 'po cha' as it is called in Ladakh which taste like salty, melted butter and made mostly with yak's milk.

New cultures of tea consumption have been gathering momentum and continue to do so in the contemporary global scenario.

READING THE HISTORY OF TEA THROUGH FAIRYTALES AND FOLK TALES

Apart from having an immense cultural impact, the presence of tea can be found throughout the literature of Asia and Europe. History and culture offer the elemental basis for any myth or legends or for that matter folktales and fairy tales. Fairy tales are mostly considered synonymous with folktales as they are familiar stories rooted in the past, in the culture and are usually attributed to oral tradition originating from the masses. The folklore of a region gives birth to various stories which take forms of myths, legends, and fairy tales. These stories give one a picture of the ethnicities, the culture, heritage, and the food habits of different societies and communities. Through these stories, tea is recognized as an imperative marker of certain ancient societies signifying social hierarchy, power, and formation of cultural identities.

Tea as Food: Tracing the History of Tea

William H. Ukhars, one of the pioneers of tea tales, talks in his book *All about Tea* (1935) about the history of tea being shrouded in mystery and that so many myths, rituals, and stories surround no other industry or product. W.H. Ukhars' book, which can be called a 'Tea Thesaurus' reader, one of the first ever detailed history of tea, where he talks about the beginning of tea and various legends attached to it in different cultures. Ukhars mentions that, according to a Chinese legend, tea drinking in China goes back many centuries. It was said that an old lady used to brew tea and distribute the hot beverage to people in her society freely. She was arrested by the then Chinese King and thrown into a dungeon. That night the door of the dungeon opened automatically and the old lady was found distributing tea among her people. On the other hand, Ukhars ascribes the Japanese to Bodhi dharma and narrates the Japanese legend that talks about a Buddhist monk who visited China between the fifth and the sixth centuries and how the monk, to overcome his sleep during his meditations, cut off his eyelids and threw them on the ground, where they took root and grew up as tea plants.

Tea stories are fascinating historical facts, some are imaginative, some are considered facts, but they are very much part of history. Chinese and Japanese traditions hold a treasure trove of folklore and fairy tales revolving around tea, discovery of tea and how tea established itself as such a powerful beverage today. The Chinese tradition has a huge collection of tea-tales where different kinds of teas are related to in different folktales and fairy tales. The early legends speak about how monkeys were used to gather the tea leaves from inaccessible places. By then, the Chinese had learnt to differentiate between good quality and poor quality tea. Sometimes, the monkeys were trained to bring fine tea leaves from unreachable places where the tea bushes grew. The Chinese men would throw stones at them which would make the monkeys angry and they would break off branches of the tea bushes and throw them down at their tormentors.

One of the most common Chinese folktales is 'The Ancestor of Tea', which talks about an isolated village nestled in the high mountains where, in the poorest part of the village, lived a very old widow without any children. In her humble garden, she would tend to her scrawny tea bushes which she kept as a memory to her late husband. The tea from this plant would be bitter for which she was made fun of by the villagers. They called it the 'old wife's tea' and which is still used in present China for poor quality tea. During one winter, she got a visit from a mysterious stranger who wanted to buy her old millstone mortar which was very dirty and old and caked with years of cooking scraps and rubbish at a very high price. The old woman was surprised, so in an attempt to make the mortar presentable she cleaned it and buried the rubbish under her tea plans. The next evening when the stranger came, she was surprised to find that it was not the mortar he was after, he left her with a strange message that 'it wasn't the treasure at all'. The following spring, the tea bushes grew lush foliage, so fragrant and tender which made very fine tea. Her tea became famous through the land and began to be known as 'the ancestor of tea' instead of 'old wife's tea'.

The Chinese folklore and also some of Japanese folktales speak of the historical significance of different kinds of tea through different stories. The common themes among these stories are the rich quality of teas, which have high medicinal values. Though the authenticities of these tales are not known, it does make an interesting read. The legend of the white tea talks about a special white tea tree whose young buds were covered with silvery hair during the spring and was known to have medicinal values. The legend of Mao Jian Green Tea speaks about the art of tea making and the medicinal value of green tea. The legend of Jasmine Dragon Pearl Green Tea narrates a beautiful story of a brother and a sister, and how the sister went to seek out a magical dragon which would help the sister cure her brother. The dragon decided to help her, he gave her a pearl which appeared from his neck as he made an ominous cry. From the pearl fell a small drop, and a beautiful tea bush sprouted on that spot. The dragon asked the sister to take proper care of the tea bush. When tender leaves appeared, the sister gathered few of the leaves and dried them next to some jasmine flowers. When she brewed some tea from the magical leaves a wonderful aroma of jasmine filled the house. This is the earliest illustration of the historical linkage of flavoured teas.

Though there are few legends of tea from England, other parts of Europe and India, almost all are from nineteenth century onwards. Since this article looks only at the fairy tales and folktales of a region to find the historical significance of tea, only the earliest form of folktales and fairy tales are mentioned. The historical significance of tea is best kept in the myths, folklore and fairy tales of China and Japan.

Fairy tales are mostly confused or are considered synonymous with folktales as they are familiar stories rooted in the past, in the culture and are usually attributed to oral tradition as they are considered popular and originating from the masses. Both fairy tales and fantasy literature are hugely popular, especially among children, which have led to the categorization of these literatures by the critics as children's literature. And in the perspective of children's literature, the concepts of fairy tales and fantasy are used in an arbitrary manner to denote anything that is not realistic, thereby marginalizing both the genres in respect to critical attention. However, not all fairy tales and definitely most of the fantasy literature cannot be dismissed merely as children's literature.

Exploring the evolution of tea through fairy tales and folktales, one knows how stories interpret; articulate the issues, cultural identities, tradition and heritage. Arthur W. Frank, in his book, *Letting Stories Breathe: A Social Narratology* (2010), talks about stories being animate. He speaks about stories working with people, on people and affecting what people see as real stories creating social relation-ship and which helps us form our narrative selves.

Journeys are a major part of the storylines in folktales and fairy tales. The stories of tea tell us about the journeys the humble tea leaf undertook which became one of the biggest trade items in the age of colonization. They are metaphorical and symbolic and deal with common problems people identify with. They are a major part of forming cultural identities; they are preservers of history through stories, whether imaginative or real. Though the historical origins of fairy tales and folktales are hard to trace, it is believed that human beings began the art of storytelling as soon as they developed the way of communicating through speech. People used the stories to communicate experiences, history and exchange knowledge.

There is a notable presence of tea spread throughout literature, especially in the literature of Europe and Asia. Eileen Raynolds, in her article 'Tea: A Literary Tour', talks about the impactful role of tea in some classics like *Alice in Wonderland* by Lewis Carroll and gives instances from the Mad Hatters party and presents the exchange between Alice and Mad Hatter as a parody of British tea parties. She also presents instances from Jane Austen and Charles Dickens where tea time led to some important development in the plot.

J.R.R. Tolkien, in his book *The Hobbit*, talks about the elaborate tea parties of the Hobbits which emphasized their nature as fun loving and merry-making folks. In J.K. Rowling's *Harry Potter*, one finds several instances like Madam Trelawney's tea drinking prediction, the characters being offered tea when in distress or weak of health to the overly sweet tea Umbridge drinks when offering punishments. These instances not only offer a customary relief to the characters but marks the development of the story too and also gives one a view of the customs of the European tea ceremonies. These are only a few of the European texts which shows the impact of tea during various times.

Beyond the literary presences, tea had a significant standing within the religious and political rituals across East Asia, which made its way across the European continent steadily with the colonization of Asian countries, before establishing an empire of its own. Tea has a long, rich, and tempestuous history which captures the imagination of all. It is astonishing how a mere beverage can have, continues to have a massive influence on the cultures and traditions of the past, present and future.

REFERENCES

Anderson, J., 1987, Japanese Tea Ritual: Religion in Practice. *Man, 22*(3), new series, pp. 475-98. doi:10.2307/2802501.

All Things Tea (n.d.). Retrieved on 20 November 2016 from http://www.itoen.com/cultural-tea-traditions.

Douglas, M., 1972, Deciphering a Meal. *Daedalus, 101*(1), pp. 61-81. Retrieved from http://www.jstor.org.vlib.interchange.at/stable/20024058.

Kondo, D., 1985, The Way of Tea: A Symbolic Analysis. *Man, 20*(2), new series, pp. 287-306. doi:10.2307/2802386.

Miles, J., 2011, *The Canadian Journal of Sociology/Cahiers Canadiens De Sociologie, 36*(4), pp. 401-3. Retrieved from http://www.jstor.org.vlib.interchange.at/stable/canajsocicahican.36.4.401.

Okakura, Kakuzo, 2014, *The Book of Tea*. Edited by Everett F. Bleiler, Dover Publications.

Parker, Janet and Julie Stanton (eds.), 2003, *Mythology: Myths, Legends, & Fantasies*, Grange Books.

Paul, E. Jaiwant, 2013, *The Story of Tea*. Lotus.

Raynolds, Eileen, 2010, 'Tea: A Literary Tour.' *New Yorker*, 10 November, https://www.newyorker.com/books/page-turner/tea-a-literary-tour, Accessed on 3 December 2020.

Rowling, J.K., 1999, *Harry Potter and the Prisoner of Azkaban*. London, Bloomsbury.

———, 2003, *Harry Potter and the Order of the Phoenix*. London, Bloomsbury.

Saberi, Helen, 2010, *Tea: A Global History*. Reaktion.

Smith, W., 1992, Complications of the Commonplace: Tea, Sugar, and Imperialism. *The Journal of Interdisciplinary History, 23*(2), pp. 259-78. doi:10.2307/205276.

Taylor, A., 1940, Some Trends and Problems in Studies of the Folk-Tale. *Studies in Philology, 37*(1), pp. 1-25. Retrieved from http://www.jstor.org.vlib.interchange.at/stable/4172470.

Tolkien, J.R.R., 2012, *The Hobbit*. Hammersmith, London, Harper Collins.

SECTION IV

FOOD AND FAMINE: MEMORIES OF LOSS AND SURVIVAL

CHAPTER 13

Cultural Construction of Famine Food

SUCHETA SEN CHAUDHURI

THE PROBLEM OF STUDY

This article aims to understand cultural practices associated with famine in indigenous communities. Mainstream literature locates famine and correlates this with hunger to death. Synonymous words for famine are available in different languages. Those are a testimony of occurrence of famine as a phenomenon, historically. Literature of famine records occurrences of famine globally since 3500 BC (Alamgir 1981, 22). Causes of famines are identified as historical, political, economic, environmental, ecological or otherwise. In sub-Saharan context, Baro, Mamadou and Deubel Tara (2006, 521-38) find out that famine occurrences are linked to contemporary historical, socioeconomic processes and that made African households vulnerable over time. Famine is linked to economic shocks, political conflicts, HIV/AIDS in African situation. Russian famines over one millennium is referred by Dando as political construction (1981, 139-54). Famine occurrence in recent time identifies famine as a phenomenon to consolidate people for ethnic movement. The 'Motum' (-famine) of Lusai Hills happened before the beginning of Mizo movement and transformation of Mizo Famine Front (MFF) to Mizo Nationalist Front (MNF) in 1963-4 (Chaube 1975). The Biafran war for state formation (1967-70) of the Ebo of Nigeria also correlate famine as a phenomenon, which had controlled as well as consolidated the protestors (Mayer 1981, vii). The novel *Half of a Yellow Sun* (2006), written by Chimamanda

Ngozie Adichie, discusses political relation of famine starvation and death.[1] Bengal famine, which resulted in 2 million deaths (1943-4), left a permanent scar on the minds of people. Oral narratives find this as political. The British colonial rulers are accused for the Bengal Famine. It is still believed by commoners that the rulers created artificial crisis by throwing rice in the sea and the river to compel youths to join the Second World War.[2] Tarun Sen Deka,[3] a political activist, said in a personal communication that if the people who died in Bengal Famine had protested against hunger, and starvation to death, India might have received independence early. Early medieval history on Kashmir textile workers identifies economic reasons of famine occurrences, starvation and death. Low wages, excessive workloads were identified as reasons (Kax 1979). The root cause of hunger is not always famine. People suffer from hunger due to unequal distribution of food. Sometimes social problem of inequality leads to hunger and death (Shiva 2012). Mayer (1981, vii) said,

... relation of famine to a single event is very largely delusion except in the case of famine caused by war. What one is usually coping with is indeed a major natural catastrophe, but one that would not normally cause a famine if one were dealing with a well-organized, prosperous society with strong administrative and medical structures and good transportation.

The present article finds a scope to understand famine as an occurrence in the life of different communities of Arunachal Pradesh. The communities belonging to the Tani group like the Nyshi, Galo, Adi and non-Tani groups like the Mishmi and Wancho usually maintained an age-old tradition and are rice and maize eaters. Shifting hill cultivation fill up their food baskets with leafy vegetables, fruits, roots and tubers, ginger chilli, which are grown at home kitchen gardens. Among all these communities in the Seppa region, there is a community—the Puroik (earlier known as Sulung), who consumed Rangbang as staple diet. This is a source of carbohydrate which is collected from a particular tree type similar to the Sago plant. Neighbouring communities of the Puroik refer to it as Tasse/tacheh, which is available from horticultural plantation sources. Except the Puroik, the others consider this source of food as famine/fodder/delicacy/reserve food. The present article aims to discuss the culturally constructed ideas of famine and food relations. Globally, famine is the symbol of starvation, hunger and death. Usually, it is perceived as an outcome of organic, political, catastrophic disorder in nature which disturbs food supply and therefore, death of people and livestock is inevitable.

FAMINE IN LITERATURE

Cox (1981, 3-18), in his article 'Ecology of Famine: An Overview', discusses probable environmental reasons, history of immediate causes and underlying causes of famine. This article mentions famine belts of the world and specifically mentions then geographical areas of erstwhile Soviet Union and Russia, which has a record of famine in every five years for the last one thousand years. The author correlated famine with social system, production patterns. He has selected parameters like effects of social changes, migrations, adaptation of new crops to analyse occurrences of famine. All such analysis focusses on data that famine may occur because of drought too much rain, flood, moist atmosphere, war, disease of plants as well as human and cattle, due to crop failure, but it does not affect all communities equally. Cox says that disruption of cultural integrity, unbalanced cultural changes, and changes of cultural institutions are the decisive parameters of famine and famine-related hunger leading to death. He discusses the relation between famine and disease and how in the long run, famine ecology is responsible for fatal diseases, malnutrition and death. Last but not least, this author identifies famine environment, which in the long run develops food procurement technologies serving specifically in time of famine (as the author quoted Bhandari 1974). Cox (ibid.) identifies two types of social expressions to famine, those who are not prepared to combat famine; secondly, societies who constructed mechanisms culturally to combat famine.

Parrack (1981, 41-8), in his article 'Ecosystem and Famine', selects the following features to discuss ecosystem of famine. Those are: (1) structurally primary producer and primary consumers, secondary, tertiary consumers, as per the rules of Eltonian pyramid (as the author refers); (2) flow of energy through tropic levels; (3) carrying capacity of the ecosystem (seasonal variation); (4) fluctuation of population within a species; and (5) reserve of energy in animals, plants, land, truncated (agricultural) ecosystem, draught and farm animals, poultry birds, plant/animal (producer/consumer) ratio of biomass, and forest. This author correlates famine with carrying capacity of ecosystem and says that disequilibrium in carrying capacity may cause famine. He summarizes that there are several biological reasons that disturb agro or natural ecosystems leading to famine, inclusive of flood drought and war. Parreck's analysis didn't incorporate the concept of famine food which can be considered as a source of energy to be utilized during the situation of disequilibrium in ecosystem. Cox (1981, 7) refers to Bhandari (1974) to discuss the comprehensive use of wild plants and animal food in the Rajasthan desert as procurement of food during famine.

Literature of food supply during famine is most focussed area of study. Developed nations and private food industries paid a lot of attention to this disaster. Huge grants were released. But Rojer and W. Hay (1981, 81-8) concentrated on the problem of food supply during famine and suggested procuring food from both market (international) as well as from local subsistence cropping agriculturists in the neighbourhood. They perceived that food at subsistence level matched with staple diet. This author identifies the importance of collection of food available from subsistence economy, if it is available as cash crops. Staple food is directly linked to environmental resource. This concept underscores the contention that food is not an economic commodity but an essential resource for survival to which all persons have equal access. Cuny (1981, 89-94) discussed issues in the provision of 'food aid' following disasters. This author claims that sufficient food is there on the earth but crisis revolved around planning of distribution and in relation to natural disaster, or war. He cites an example of a cyclone and its aftermath in Andhra Pradesh in India in relation to food aid. He raises a few points to give future direction to international food aid programmes. He suggests, first and foremost, the impact of food aid programmes must be studied. More importantly, he highlights the unequal positions of victims, donor agencies, and food producers of industrialized nations. Cuny (ibid.) classified experts' opinion on food aids and suggests long-term programmes, which may be helpful in eradicating famine from life. Thomas J. Manetsch (1981, 95-104) has discussed strategies and programmes for coping with large-scale food shortages. This author worked with two variables: those are 'Enough' and 'Nothing'. Independent parameters like million tons of foodgrains in stock were compared with millions of deaths. Dependent parameters were rationing, and price control systems, nutritional situation related suffering of people. This author suggested combining different development programmes to get rid of the problem of food shortage. The former author may have referred to subsistence economic source of food and the latter suggests taking multiple programmes to minimize food shortage, but none of the authors highlights strength of culturally constructed local resources, which can be alternative supplement of nutrition. William I. Torry (1986, 11-23) examines benefits of government food supply programmes by comparing between normal distribution system and emergency reliefs. Allan Hoben (1997, 55-62) investigated reasons for the failure of long-term food for work programme by examining impact of environmental degradation in Ethiopia. He criticized agricultural reform programme and civil strife of 1970s. Vandana Shiva (2001, 53-4) believes that India needs more market control to minimize problems of famine. In the above writings, indigenous knowledge and famine food relations are not highlighted except by Cox who referred to Bhandari and Hay. Kalhon's *Rajatarangini*, a historical chronicle of Kashmir from the twelfth century, refers to frequent famine occurrences, which affected life and living of the skilled labourers of famous carpet and shawl industry of Kashmir. The long distance trade of these textile products suffered due to incidents of famines. Famine occurrences in Russia (1601-3) killed one-third of its population (https://military-history.fandom.com [accessed on 23 January 2022]).

In India, since the sixteenth century, Bengal suffered from famine occurrences almost in every century. The most surprising aspect is the Bengal plains is largely a riverine flood plain. The people depended on both agriculture and fish resources. The neighbouring communities of the Bengalis on all the sides depended on similar food habits. Despite abundant food resources in nature, famine occurrences killed people in large numbers. Rahman (2020) refers to the Great Bengal Famine of 1770 as an outcome of taxation policies of the East India Company. Both Rahman (ibid.) and Damodaran (2007) discuss the links of colonization with the happenings of the Great Bengal Famine (1770) and the Famine of Chotanagpur (1897).

H. Lalramnghinglova (2002, 23-3) says that wild edible plants play a significant role in the sustenance of rural life in Mizoram. This author enumerated the knowledge of local people of Mizoram on 78 wild edible and famine food plants. Sudhanshu and Vandana (2007, 62-6) listed knowledge of people on more than 51 indigenous leafy vegetables of Panch-Pargania of Jharkhand, among which some are consumed as famine food. They suggested the government to encourage people to grow those plants to avoid food scarcity and famine. Md. Arif Khan et al. (2012, 387-97), documented the indigenous knowledge of famine food of the Hajong of Bangladesh.[4] Manju Singhi and Ramesh Joshi (2010, 121-4) documented the culturally constructed perceptions of the people of desert on famine food and medicinal plants. They refer to these social practices as the 'Bio-resolutions'. Okoduwa (2007, 133-8) has documented the indigenous understanding of famine, where it is believed that surplus gives way to scarcity. Furthermore, Stoner (1952, 137) says,

The staple food of the Sulung (presently known as Puroik) community is a perfect example of adaptation to the nature from the perspectives of natural calamities like famine those used to occur following the bamboo flowering was reality in every century in the past in this region. The staple food 'Rangbang' is a paste of carbohydrate collected from the stem of a particular species of Palm and Tree-Fern through a laborious technique, in which both men and women get involved at the production at the family level.

Stoner (ibid.) further states the following on the Tree-Fern source of food,

I made enquiries whether tree ferns are used in this region. I was informed that their use is well known, both to the Daflas (Nyishi) and to the obscure Sulung (Puroik) tribe which inhabits the same area. As among the Abors (the Adi), three types are recognized, and one only is eaten; it is known by the same name Tacheh. The plants are not, however, cultivated, but are cut straight out of the forest when wanted; ... (A)mong the Daflas (presently known as the Nyishi), Tacheh is entirely a reserve food, for times of famine, but among the Sulungs (Puroik) ... it is said to be fairly frequently used under normal circumstances, although Sago made from wild palms is preferred.

Stoner discusses the use of Tree-Fern, which is known along the whole length of Assam Himalayas; and quite unknown in any hill areas of this region lying to the south of the Brahmaputra. The author could not locate this food habit among the Naga, Lushai (the Mizo), Khasi, and Garo. Kohli (2001, 169-71) states,

Tasheh, Tache, and Tabe are some of the natural food items used by Arunachal tribes, during natural calamities when sufficient paddy is not available. Tashe (*Wallichiadensiflora* Mart. Syn. *W. caryoloides* Wall. Roxb.) is a tree palm used for its pith. The stem is peeled, crushed and converted into dry powder. This dry powder is taken in a Chepa (cane made cylinder) and water is poured. The collected filtrate is allowed to stand for a few hours. As a result of slow evaporation it solidifies. The solid substance (known as Tashe) is boiled and taken as substitute for food along with salt and chilly.

Sago plant family (arecaceaepalme) is found only in the North East of India. Modi (2008), as quoted by Blench (2016), traces wild sago trees of south China and Arunachal Pradesh of the northeastern part of India. While the former author identifies sago as fodder for pig in the Milan community and still considered as famine food use of which is declining, Blench traces the lost world of sago (metroxylonsagu) of New Guinea, a few eastern Indonesian Islands, Malaysia, Thailand, and Philippines. Bhattacharjee (1983, 57) says that the Idu Mishmi also remember the processing of sago in the recent past. Phytolith analysis of samples obtained during systematic excavations at the site Xincun on the southern coast of China, during 3350-2470 BC people exploited sago palms, bananas, roots and tubers, fern roots, acorns, Job's tears as well as wild rice. A dominance of starch in the phytolith tests indicates use of sago plants in that region three thousand years back (www.geocurrent information).

OBJECTIVES

With this background, the present study aims:

1. To understand correlation of culturally constructed idea of food and famine food.
2. To understand cultural ecology of famine food.
3. To underscore famine food culture complex.

METHODS OF STUDY

This article discusses data from both primary and secondary sources. A field tour to village Sanchu, Cheyeng Tajo, East Kameng, Arunachal Pradesh with students of AITS, Rajiv Gandhi University in 2008, had created an opportunity to learn the horticulturist livelihood activities of the Sulung (Puroik). Students documented steps of Rangbang collection. They further documented the edible and medicinal flora of the people. These exercises enquire more on livelihood of the people and revealed their deep knowledge on forest resources. Thus horticulturist people practise hunting and gathering to supplement food, medicine and other necessities.

SAGO: THE SAGA OF HORTICULTURE-AGRICULTURE CONTINUUM

The Puroik consume Rangbang as staple food. During fieldwork, Taram Soja, the then Panchayat member of the Sancho village told this writer that if one gives a choice to select the staple food between rice and rangbang to Puroik men and women, villagers will prefer the rangbang. The staple food 'rangbang' of the Puroik is collected through horticultural practices. The sago trees (tree fern/palm) are grown through vegetative reproduction. Each Puroik family possesses sago plants in private plots. This plant is considered as mature after ten years. As the Puroik villages are forest villages, those private plots of sago are situated in forests. One mature sago tree can provide carbohydrate to a family of 4-5 members for 3-4 days and more. The collection of pith of the plant is very laborious and needs team work. It needs at least three days to prepare the required quantity of carbohydrate. Men assist to procure this food but turning it into edible food is done mainly by women. Tools used in collection of rangbang are *dao*, wooden hammer, cane strainer, mat for drying and running water stream is required. The process of collection of the Sago is as follows: first the tree trunk is cut into pieces. The innermost portion of the stem is taken out. These portions are hammered to separate fibres from starch. This is done on the mat. The starch is strained, which separates fine particles. The accumulated fine particles are dried on the mat for some time and brought home in the form of yellow dough. Review of literature identifies that people of Malaysia, some part of Indonesia, Thailand and other places collect food from similar types of plants. Such a practice is not found in other parts of India. People of south China consumed similar sources of food two millenni back. This a source of food is maintained by neighbouring communities of the Puroik either as fodder or famine food. The Galo people use this as fodder like Adi (Milan). Professor Tomo Riba[5] said this fodder of pig is believed to invite misfortune to humans if consumed. The age of maturity of this plant vary from community to community. In the Adi community it is considered as matured after thirty years. This plant is available in the habitat of the Wanchos. They maintain this on the boundary of the village. All the above mentioned communities cultivate rice. Among them, the Adi and Galo produce paddy as cash crops and the others at substantive level. Therefore, the sago food as horticulture source is means of support if required, which are further supplemented by gathering, hunting, fishing, trapping of food sources.

Despite being of very ancient origin, Rangbang/Tache remained as an alternative source of food to the people of Arunachal Pradesh. It may be due to ecological reason, which will be discussed in the next paragraphs. Shifting hill cultivation produce paddy, maize, chilli, arum, beans, cotton, ginger and leafy vegetables but didn't exclude horticultural practices among the Adi, Galo, Wancho, Mishmi and Nyishi. This is defined as a continuum of knowledge system that is maintained on food. Hajong, Mishing, who are neighbours of the above-mentioned communities in plains of Assam and Bangladesh identify tubers as famine food.

CULTURAL ECOLOGY OF THE TACHE-FAMINE FOOD

North East India is a seat of rice-eaters. Eastern Himalaya, where it meets south China and the northern border of Myanmar is a land of wild origin of rice (ICIMOD). North East India is home to many species of bamboo. Both rice and bamboo have close relation with all cultures of this region. People adapted to both these essential flora which are source of food, shelter and more. Bamboo is life support for people. Every part of bamboo plant is essential in the life of the people. Bamboo shoots are consumed as spices. Bamboo is used for carrying water, storing food, drinking water and beverages, cooking in natural setting, for construction of houses, basketry, fencing, and carrying loads. Water stored inside bamboo is considered as pure as coconut water and people drink that during the stay in forests. Many wild green leaves, roots, tubers, mushroom, nourishes people. Moreover, there are foods which are of pre-agricultural or horticultural source. One such food is sago. Literature on sago identified it as a food of the people of South China of 3000 BC. Agricultural scientists analysed this horticultural source of food and say that this source of food was an impediment for the growth of labour-intensive agriculture in south China in the past. They further say, the sago tree is available in all corners of Arunachal Pradesh. People of this state are connected with this tree in different ways. This is the source of staple food for Puroik. This is occasional food or delicacy for the Nyishi, and this is fodder for Milan. Among the Galo, there is a saying that this food invites misfortune if it is eaten by human beings. This was food in the past among the Idu Mishmi. These palm trees are planted on the borders of village of the Wancho and the common belief is that this is famine food. The wild variety of Sago (Tasse) is found in Tirap district of Arunachal Pradesh (http://books. Google. co.in, accessed on 17 March 2016). Shibotosh Das mentions that

Cultural Construction of Famine Food 233

some northern tribes have grown groves of Tasse or wild sago plant as individual ownership. In case of the Puroik these individual ownerships are inherited. Communities of Arunachal Pradesh were practising agriculture at subsistence level, collected essential food from forests and water resource. Seasonal food sources supplied nutrients. Cropping, gathering, hunting fulfils hunger and famine and were part of life experiences. People were not solely dependent on the cultivation of rice to generate carbohydrate-containing sources of food. They have been practising ancient knowledge for generation. The habit of extracting sago is one such age-old practice. Artifacts that are used to extract this food stuff are made up of wood, bamboo and cane. People maintain their private ownership of horticultural food sources, which are inherited from ancestors. These lands are located apart and therefore the Puroik families move from one village to another to extract this source of food, while those trees mature. In the Galo and Adi areas people consider thirty years as time for maturity. Despite the fact that scientists have identified the sago as a very good source of carbohydrate, its social status is perceived to be lower than rice. Development initiatives intended to introduce rice cultivation is an economic practice among the Puroik.

Sharma (1987) reported that there are 136 species of bamboos found in India. North Eastern India is home to 58 bamboo species which belong to 10 genera.[6] Bamboo is an essential flora in the life of people. Its tender roots are eaten. Bamboo is used in the construction of houses, fencing, sheds, platforms; bamboo is used to collect water. This plant is essential for the livelihood of people of Arunachal Pradesh. But bamboo flowering is detrimental for rice (Singleton et al. 2010). Bamboo flowering has direct connection with rodent outbreaks (ibid.). Season of bamboo flowering vary from species to species as well as the gap between flowering season of single species vary between 40 and 50 years. Scientists explain that the flowers of bamboo are consumed by rodents, which shoot up fertility of rodents and rodent population increases not following Malthusian rules. Very soon, rodents attack paddy fields, granaries, which cause famine. Therefore, bamboo and paddy in the same ecology are causes of famine. The most important point is that the people adopted both bamboo and paddy. Therefore, famine is a part of social history of the agriculturist societies, which is correlated with ecological systematics (Robson 1981, 3-4; Cox 1981, 5-18; Parrack 1981, 41-8).

Horticultural food, and foraging practices are source of alternative food during famine for both human and domestic animal like pigs. The other most important animal, that is the Mithun (Bosfrontalis) is semi-domesticated animal. It eats salt only from its owner. This is considered as food treasure by people. This animal is found in the altitude between 150 and 3,000 metres, hilly terrains, high slopes, and dense forests. It is used neither for ploughing nor for mulching. This animal is found in northeastern India and hill tracts of Bangladesh. People of Arunachal Pradesh are depended on all the organic resources as mentioned above within their cultural habitat and use them. Therefore, preservation of indigenous knowledge of 'famine food' is age old practice of people and people could maintain rich knowledge of different sources of food in respective communities. As a whole, it maintains an equilibrium with environment due to eco-friendly activities.

FAMINE FOOD CULTURE COMPLEX WITH SPECIAL REFERENCE TO BAMBOO, SAGO, RICE AND MITHUN

Beliefs of bamboo flowering at intercommunity levels of eastern and North Eastern India is associated with 'misfortune'. The Mizo movement of 1964 (Chaube 1975, Goswami 1985) traced famine as immediate reason of that movement as it happened in 1963, which was an outcome of the bamboo flowering. Chaube writes on the transformation of Mizo Famine Front—an NGO established in 1963 which was re-named as Mizo National Front (1964)— the very prominent organization which led the Mizo movement. Laldenga, the pioneer leader, had led both the organizations. This phenomenon is a testimony of relation of food with ecology and politics. The North East India is home of several bamboo species, and therefore, bamboo flowering is a common phenomenon. They are an essential part of cultural diversity. Every community has a cultural meaning associated with bamboo, bamboo flowering and own adaptive mechanisms. Among all communities, the Apatani bamboos are falling apart. Proverb is that the Apatani bamboo never flowers. Such cultural adaptation denotes importance of the indigenous knowledge system. Scientific interventions proved relations between bamboo flowering and famine. It explains that hundreds of communities of North Eastern India adapted to hundreds of bamboo species, and culture traits like rice as staple food, in the culture complexes, maintained rich social history of sustainable ecological adaptation. Against this background, the people classified food as 'staple' as well as 'food to meet up crisis'.

GENDER AND FAMINE RELATION

At the end, the roles of men and women in controlling the sources of energy are very important. Women of Arunachal Pradesh are carriers of knowledge system related to horticulture, shifting hill cultivation, gathering and weaving. Women technologies never allow women to overuse resources. Men are protectors from sudden attack, hunter and warriors. Subsistence economic practices are also not destroying equilibrium between source of food and consumer. Food is collected through gathering, hunting, fishing and trapping and the indigenous process of drying of food resources maintain food store at home. Therefore, natural calamities like landslides or other disasters may disconnect villages but that usually does not lead to immediate food crisis. Low population size, community based natural resource management, institutionally stabilized customs and practices related to food production, distribution and consumption, and women's role in food custodianship may have maintained equilibrium.

CONCLUSION

Famine is not a symbol of hunger and starvation to death in above indigenous societies but a natural occurrence in cultural ecology of indigenous communities. Indigenous knowledge supplements food during famine and that represents people's knowledge on the environment. In fact, 'Rangbang' is an age old example of food from horticulture source as an outcome of adaptation and time tested indigenous knowledge in practice over a period of time. Presence of this age old food tradition signifies that people carried knowledge of the horticulture stage and combat famine in a later era, in the agricultural tradition of rice farming. Further, famine as a natural calamity is not always considered as catastrophe rather part of an environmental occurrence. The bamboo flowering is contrary to rice farming in the same ecological situation. This article ends with the following observations:

1. The cultural adaptation of the rice farming in the bamboo growing environment in the communities of Arunachal Pradesh, despite incompatible relationship of bamboo flower and rice co-existed, due to innovative indigenous knowledge practices of storing food sources from the horticultural practices. Consumption of horticultural food resources kept the food supply steady. The food habit of the Puroik is the missing link to understand the realty.
2. The concept of alternative food in indigenous and traditional knowledge systems regulate temporary problems related to natural disasters of food crisis and save life.
3. This knowledge must be celebrated and acknowledged so that contributions of indigenous and traditional knowledge system to humanity are formally acknowledged for progress.
4. Community-specific cultural practices of such alternative food sources from traditional horticultural tradition do not allow community members to starve to death.
5. Therefore, this tradition of alternative food in a given cultural ecological space indicates that the concept of famine is a political construct that control human labour in the famine situation. Review of literature indicates that at least frequent occurrences of famine in Russia and Kashmir in the previous millennium are testimony of man made famine. The famines happen due to political reasons that detached people from their self-reliant subsistence livelihood and diverted them towards other

occupation. The vibrant industrial growth of the Kashmiri carpet and shawl industry during mediaeval period might have brought about a kind of frequent famine in the region. The works of textile of carpet and shawl industry were labour-intensive. The industrial set-up and 'karkhana'-oriented life and living might have gradually disconnected labourers from food security related indigenous knowledge practices.

NOTES

1. Dr. Shreya Bhattacharji, Dean, School of Languages, CUJ, informed the author while she was searching literature on famine and indigenous experience of people.
2. Narratives of the author's mother on Bengal famine, which she has heard since childhood
3. Communicated to the writer during the 33rd Bodo Sahitya Sabha, Gorchuk, Guwahati, Assam, 1993.
4. N.A.
5. Professor of Geography, Rajiv Gandhi University and a Galo man.
6. Bambusaarundinacea, bambusabalcooa, bambusapallidatulda, denorocalamushamiltonii, etc.

REFERENCES

Alamgir, Mohiuddin, 1981, 'An Approach Towards a Theory of Famine', in John R.K. Robson (ed.), *Famine: Its Causes Effects and Management*, vol. 2, New York: Gordon and Breach Science Publishers, pp. 19-40.

Bang, Frederik B., 1981, 'The Role Of Disease In Ecology Of Famine', in John R.K. Robson (ed.), *Famine: Its Causes Effects and Management*, vol. 2, New York: Gordon and Breach Science Publishers, pp. 61-78.

Baro, Mamandou and Tara F. Deubel, 2006, 'Persistent Hunger: Perspectives on Vulnerability, Famine and Food Security in Sub-Saharan Africa', *Annual Review of Anthropology*, 35, pp. 521-38.

Bhattacharjee, T.K., 1983, *The Idu Mishmi* of Dri Valley, Shillong Directorate of Research.

Blench, Robert, 2015, 'The Lost World of Sago Eaters' submitted by Marlin W. Lewis in www.*Geocurrents.Info*, 4 November.

Cahill Jr. and F. Jeorge, 1981, 'The Role of Disease in the Ecology of Famine', in John J. Robson (ed.), *Famine: Its Causes Effects and Managements*, Gordon and Breach, New York: Science Publishers, pp. 51-60.

Chaube, Shibani Kinkar, 1975, *Hill Politics in Northeast India*, New Delhi: Orient BlackSwan.

Cox, George W., 1981, 'The Ecology of Famine: an Overview', in John R.K. Robson (ed.), *Famine: Its Causes Effects and Management*, vol. 2, New York: Gordon and Breach Science Publishers, pp. 5-18.

Cuny, F.C., 2016, 'Famine and Counter-Famine Operations', *INTERTECT* www.http://oaktrust.library.edu.temu/bitstream/handle, accessed on 13 June 2019.

Damodaran, Vinita, 2007, 'Famine in Bengal: A comparison of the 1770 Famine in Bengal and the 1897 Famine in Chotanagpur', *The Medieval History Journal*, 10(1&2), pp. 143-81.

Dando, William A., 1981, *The Geography of Famine*, New York: John Wiley and Sons.

Goswami, B.B., 1985, 'Mizo Unrest' in K.S. Singh (ed.), *Tribal Movement in Northeast India*, vol. II, New Delhi: Manohar.

Hoben, Allan, 1997, The Cultural Construction of Environmental Policy: Paradigms and Politics in Ethiopia, *The Ecologist*, 27(2) March-April, pp. 55-62.

Kohli, Y.P., 2016, 'Non-Traditional Foods and Ethno-botanical Plants of Lower Subansiri District, Arunachal Pradesh', *Arunachal Pradesh Forest News*, 19, pp. 169-71.

Kax, Wilson, 1979, *History of Textiles*, file. ///C/ Users/ Roselima/ Desktop/ Indian/ History.html, time of accessed on 8 November 2016.

Lalramnghinglova, H., 2002, 'Ethnobotanical Study on the Edible Plants of Mizoram', *Ethnobotany*, 14(1-2), pp. 23-33.

Mayer, Jean, 1981, *Preface*, in John R.K. Robson (ed.), *Famine: Its Causes Effects and Management*, vol. 2, New York: Gordon and Breach Science Publishers, 1981, pp. vii-x.

Manetsch, Thomas J., 1981, 'On Strategies and Programmes for Coping with Largescale Food Shortages', in John J. Robson (ed.), *Famine: Its Causes Effects and Management*, New York: Gordon and Breach Science Publishers, pp. 90-5.

Parrack, Dwain W., 1981, 'Ecosystem and famine', in John R.K. Robson (ed.), *Famine: Its Causes Effects and Management*, vol. 2, New York: Gordon and Breach Science Publishers, pp. 41-8.

Rahman, Aklakh Ur, 2020, 'Reason behind the Great Bengal Famine in 1770 British Claim Vs. Realty' (pdf), Researchgate, December 2020, DOI.13140/RG 2.2.20500.32644; www.researchgate.net.

Rojer, W. Hay, 1981, 'The Concept of Food Supply System with Special Reference to the Management of Famine', in John J. Robson (ed.), *Famine: Its Causes Effects and Management*, New York: Gordon and Breach Science Publishers, pp. 81-8.

Shiva, Vandana, 2001, 'Self-Imposed Sanctions', *The Ecologist*, *31*(9), November, pp. 53-4.

Singhi, Manju and Ramesh Joshi, 2010, 'Famine food of arid Rajasthan: Utilization, perceptions and need to integrate social practices by bio-resolutions', *Studies on Ethno-Medicine*, *4*(2), August, pp. 121-4.

Sudhanshu and Vandana, 2007, 'Some less-known "sags" (leafy vetetables) utilized by the tribals and others of Panch Pargana area in Jharkhand', *Ethnobotany*, *19*(1-2), pp. 62-6.

Stoner, C.R., 1952, 'The Sulung Tribe of the Assam Himalaya', *Anthropos* *47*, pp. 947-62.

Robson, John R.K., ed. 1981, *Famine Its Causes Effects and Management*, vol. 2, New York: Gordon and Breach Science Publishers.

Torry, William I., 1984, 'Social Science Research on Famine: A Critical Evalvation', *Human Ecology*, *12*(3), pp. 227-52.

CHAPTER 14

Scarcity, Survival, and Memories

KANCHAN MUKHOPADHYAY

CHRONICLES OF SCARCITY

Accounts of scarcity and famine are often top down, discourses created and circulated by state and section of academia look at the phenomenon from a distance and present an overview. Such accounts stay away from stating how famine looks like when one is at the receiving end. Only occasionally, experiences and memories of people actually affected by conditions of famine are discussed and their perspectives are brought to the articulate space. This article has attempted to present the latter perspective; Santal residents of a village in West Bengal have remembered what their ancestors experienced back in time. The article also tries to evaluate the reasons for their still remembering the experiences in detail after so many years when there is no apparent threat of acute widespread food scarcity immediately.

FAMINES DURING COLONIAL PERIOD

Protracted scarcity of food in a region can be described as famine. To identify reasons responsible for large scale food scarcity in India, two approaches have been followed. Some looked for the root causes of scarcity in physical environmental factors like failure of monsoon, scarcity of water, poor quality of soil, unproductive livestock, obsolete cultivation practices and techniques. In the nineteenth century, Florence Nightingale presented a more critical view on the subject. She noted how certain administrative policies of the then British colonial government were causing a series of famines in India. It was not the lack of food in a particular geographical area; rather famines were caused by certain political and social conditions that led to inadequate transportation of food from one area to other. She identified two kinds of famine taking place in India: *grain* famine and *money* famine. While the first kind of famine was caused by low production of grain caused by unfavourable natural conditions, famine of the second kind was caused by artificial food scarcity triggered by drainage of money from the peasant to the authorities as land revenue or as repayment of debt. Drainage of money also affected procurement of food by the peasants (Meena 2015, 36).

Economic history of colonial India is replete with instances of famine in different parts of the country. The East India Company was granted *diwani* of Bengal, Bihar, and Odisha in 1765 and immediately afterwards Bengal experienced a famine condition in 1769-70. Other parts of India were brought under control of the Company between early to mid-nineteenth century and northern part of India experienced a famine condition in 1830s. The economic condition of the country during this period can be linked to certain issues, which were 'drain of wealth', de-industrialization in small towns and villages, and reorganization of land tenure systems and agrarian relations. All those factors contributed towards impoverishment of the people of India.

A famine in the Northwest Provinces in 1860-1 resulted in a revolt. The event was followed by the 1865-6 Deccan famine, which was extended from western districts of the Bombay Presidency to eastern districts of Madras Presidency and to the north of the country affecting districts across banks of the Ganga in Bihar and Bengal. Following this massive famine, the colonial government felt the necessity of active state intervention to prevent recurrence of such calamities. With some minimal intervention, intensity of famines lessened to some extent, but occurrence of such events did not stop. There was a famine in 1868-70 in Northern India; in 1873-4, there was a famine in Bengal; and then there was a protracted three-year famine from 1876 to 1878 across a large part of the country. Though there was a 'famine policy' in place, the colonial government abandoned implementation of the policy during this period due to what they described as 'financial hardship'.

In 1880, a commission recommended implementation of the famine policy proactively. Before the recommendations could be executed, there was a famine in 1900 preceded by a condition of drought. After this, the state finally adopted certain proactive roles to prevent famines or to organize relief programmes; once that was done no major nation wide famine took place in India. However, famines of smaller scale that were restricted to local areas continued to take place. There were localized famines in Bombay Presidency in 1905-6 and United Provinces in 1907-8. In 1918, there was a compound situation when drought, rise in food price and a flu epidemic affected several parts of the country. The Next major event was the Great Bengal famine of 1943 which was catalyzed by sudden rise in demand of grains for consumption of the army and also due to drop in import of rice from Myanmar.

Independent India has not faced any famine in the true sense of the term though it has seen several instances of food scarcity, which were confined to smaller areas.

SANTALS AND MARGINALITY

As has been stated, this article has reviewed the famine related experiences of Santals of a village and of the adjacent area. The reason for choosing them for the present study needs to be explained.

The Santals are the third numerically large Scheduled Tribe population in India, they are distributed in the states of Jharkhand, West Bengal, Odisha, Bihar, Tripura, Assam and also in different parts of Bangladesh. From the spatial distribution of the Santal in Indian states, one can delineate a core area, which consists of parts of the districts of Santal Parganas, Dumka, Dhanbad, Hazaribagh and Singbhum in Jharkhand, Puruliya, Medinipur, Bankura, Barddhaman and Birbhum in West Bengal, Mayurbhanj, Keonjhar and Balasore in Odisha. This area has experienced food scarcity time and again during colonial period; it has seen periods of not-so-severe scarcity of food after India became independent.

The indigenous communities in India, most of whom belong to the category of Scheduled Tribe, are often placed in a marginal location in Indian society. The contemporary view of the indigenous groups of people by others has its root in perspective adopted by scholars and administrators during the colonial period. Such a viewpoint conceived of two kinds of people in ancient India, the 'primitive' aborigines and the 'culturally superior' migrants. An attentive reading of Hunter (1897, 88-117) reveals that the Europeans were identifying themselves with the Aryan conquerors of India. The Aryans have been described to be superior to the conquered people in all conceivable ways; physically (or racially) more able, fairer, culturally refined, and linguistically more capable of philosophical thinking.

In independent India, anthropologists and social scientists acknowledged that 'tribe' was a colonial construct; the postcolonial shift from the colonial conceptualization of tribes can be understood if one considers how the tribes were being defined in independent India. Some anthropologists tried to develop a theoretical framework to accommodate groups already identified as tribes through administrative practices (Xaxa 2003, 378). However, unlike the theorists of the colonial era, no social scientist in the postcolonial period was taking recourse to race biology to identify the tribes.

The colonial viewpoint that looked at 'tribes' as disparate social categories has been challenged. Beteille has argued that the Oraon, Munda, Ho and Santal villagers fulfil the criteria for peasants, as proposed by Shanin, more than people inhabiting the Tanjore village that he studied as a peasant community. Among the so-called tribes, especially among the Santals, it is the family that is the principal unit of production and consumption, land husbandry is their main means of livelihood and provides for major part of their consumption needs, they have their specific traditional culture related to the way of life involving conformity to age old habits, practices and subordination of the individual to the community and finally they conform to the 'underdog position' for the dominant outsiders (Beteille 1974, 59, 62, 65).

Once the Santals are viewed as peasants, there is no reason to believe that they represent a marginal and small section of Indian society. The 2011 Census reported that 69 per cent of India's total population live in rural areas and more than 70 per cent of rural Indians are engaged in agriculture and allied sectors like forestry, logging, and fishing. If livelihood practices are given primacy over differences in social organization, language, religious beliefs and practices, Santals stand at par with almost half the Indian population. Their experiences of starvation and efforts for survival are common with many communities in the country.

MEMORIES OF FOOD SCARCITY

A village in the western part of Bankura district of West Bengal is located in a low rainfall area where water retaining capacity of the rocky and porous soil is small. The village has been irrigated sometime in mid-1970s; canal irrigation changed economic profile of Saraspur remarkably, now they can produce two to three crops a year. This has pulled them out of the days of starvation to a large extent. Still, it was revealed that scarcity of food has become part of the collective memory of Santals of the area. They narrate history of their village in terms of famines, which they consider to be the timeline of history. Asked when the village was established, elderly Santal persons recollected immediately that, after its establishment, Saraspur experienced a famine that took place in the Bengali year 1280 (i.e. 1786 AD). They narrated that there was a prolonged drought around that time and a large number of cattle and humans perished. There was none to dispose of the dead; a belief current among the people at that time also prevented them to do so. It was believed that whoever would dispose of the dead would also die. So, the corpses were left to rot.

In those days, people used to eat lots of non-cultivated food largely grown in wild. Such items included tender leaves of *aswattha* or *pipal* tree, leaves of *kundol* plant, fruits of *bhalai, kend, shimul,* and *dumur* (fig) trees. Tender tamarind leaves were dried and mixed with broth to add some taste. *Mahua* flower, tamarind seeds, locally available beans and whatever cereal was available were roasted in an open pan and made into *latha* or balls. The forest provided them another kind of food—they trapped and hunted birds and animals. In addition to certain wild birds, pigeons nesting in villages were eaten. Animals that were hunted mostly included small games like squirrel, porcupine or civet.

As cereals were scarce during periods of famine, rarely any cereal was directly boiled in water and eaten. Tying whatever grains could be obtained in a piece of cloth, it was dipped in boiling water till the water turned into a thin broth. The broth was consumed and the sack of grain was kept aside for future use. The above items became part of regular diet of the Santals of this area since then; they continued to gather, hunt and eat those foods when there was relative abundance of sustenance.

Rice was just one of the cereals consumed in those days; some of the other cereals grown and eaten by the people were *kodo*, *bhutta*, *gundlu*, *marua*, *erba*, and *junur*. In the Bengali year 1300 (i.e. 1806 AD), some *baandh* or dykes were erected on slopes to store a part of the runoff rainwater, which resulted in increased supply of water to the fields. However, it should be noted that the *baandh*s could store a small part of the runoff. If there was a period of drought the system of rainwater harvesting failed.

Even after the *baandh*s were erected, the area experienced several famines, a major one took place in the Bengali year 1322 (1828 AD). Elderly Santal persons of Saraspur recollected, around the Bengali year 1330 (1836 AD) when some *baandh*s were constructed, rice became staple for their community. The villagers knew that in the drought prone area where Saraspur is located, proper cultivation of rice was not possible without adequate artificial irrigation. But no large irrigation project was taken up either by the British government; in independent India no such scheme was implemented for almost three decades after independence.

COLONIAL RULE AND THE VILLAGE COMMUNITY

The economic system, especially the organization of food production prevalent in Santal villages in precolonial times, was interfered with by colonial governance. The major tool of intervention on their part was the land tenure system. The land tenure system of the Santals was largely community-oriented, all land of a village belonged to the village community. Land was broadly divided into two types: homestead or *bari* land and cultivable or *dhani* land. To ensure that some villagers do not enjoy advantage over others by holding good quality *dhani* land permanently, land of good and bad types was redistributed among the households annually. Such a system is commonly found among shifting cultivators; it can be assumed that the Santals continued the system of landholding that they had when they practised *dahi* or shifting cultivation.

In the absence of a tax collection system, Santals had no indigenous system of measuring land; holding of one household was known as *rekh*. When the colonial government parcelled out all land among *zamindar*s or landlords through permanent settlement, the Santals used to seek verbal consent of the concerned *zamindar* before settling down and tilling land within his jurisdiction. However, they disliked the system of paying tax to the *zamindar* who had neither reclaimed the land nor tilled the soil. Still, they were ready to pay tax at the rate of a fixed amount per plough, because they were familiar with that unit. Calculation of tax per *bigha*, a unit hitherto unknown to them, was not at all appreciated.

The revenue collection system of colonial government damaged the agrarian system of the Santals in more than one way. The system protected interests of tax collecting *zamindar*s and *mahajan*s or moneylenders. Those two groups of people exploited the Santal cultivators to such an extent that many of them migrated to other parts of the country and took up non-agricultural occupations. The village society of the Santals revolved round a village council headed by *manjhi*. This important position of *manjhi* was reduced to that of a mere tax collector. In the interest of revenue collection sometimes non-Santal headmen were imposed upon Santal villages (Mallik 1993, 35-6).

The precolonial land management system of the Santals could not survive the onslaught of the new system. As each individual landholder was supposed to pay tax for his or her individual holding, the system of community holding or of annual redistribution of land withered away. In the changed situation, those who were holding good quality land were allowed to retain such land permanently; similarly, poor quality land was not rotated. In matters of ownership of land, lineages acted as corporate groups in place of village societies for some more time and continued to do so till a few years back. More recently, individual ownership has replaced all other modes of land tenure because revenue or administrative or judicial authorities understand that form well.

WADING THROUGH HARDSHIP

Imposition of tax was only a part of misery for the Santals, entry of *zamindar*s and *mahajan*s into their country paved the way for market forces in their lives. Dependent on a subsistence economy, they had little means to purchase industrial products, but they entered the market as sellers. Their produces from land and from forest were sold, their land was put in the market as a commodity and finally the people were taken to other parts of the subcontinent as cheap labour.

In spite of all the hardships, the Santals showed remarkable resilience while facing food scarcities and other forms of adversities. This was reflected in ways they conducted agricultural activities or managed produces from land.

Till date, the Santals prefer to till their land themselves. Generally, a Santal household would not get the work done by appointing others as wage workers or as sharecroppers, unless there is dearth of working hands in the household. Members of the household, both men and women, sometimes even the children, can be seen to carry out all the agricultural work. If a cultivator family felt that the workload was heavy and time available was too short for the members of the family to manage the job, close relations like brothers or cousins or neighbours were asked to help them. Rarely the Santal cultivator families had large landholdings; therefore, their demand for additional helping hands was limited. It was expected that the help in forms of labour, draught animals or agricultural implements would be reciprocated. Labour undoubtedly was a saleable item for the Santals since long; for many of them, wage work remained the major means of subsistence.

However, labour could not be sold to brother or cousin living next door.

In years immediately before the introduction of irrigation, reciprocal exchange of labour was partially replaced by purchase of labour. Reciprocal exchange was possible between very close relatives and friends, others expected payment of wage. Even in such situation, some exercise of choice could be noticed; when in need of appointing wage workers to get a job done, Santal cultivators preferred to appoint their neighbours, whether related or not. If such persons were not available, non-Santal persons were appointed. Wage of agricultural labourers was paid in form of paddy, which was measured in volume in metal bowls. In this area male daily wage workers are called *manish* and their female counterparts are *kamin*. The wage rate was same for both the sexes.

In the drought-prone area where Saraspur is located, Santal cultivators with their smallholdings of land could not produce surplus food crop when there was no canal irrigation. Barring a few families, the produce from the land was not enough to sustain the tiller families through the year; they had to fall upon other means of income like working for daily wage to make both ends meet. Even in such a situation, a part of the produce was sold to the market because the people required cash to pay for groceries, clothing and such other items. A limited amount of barter was also done on a miniscule scale. Households having little or no cash in their possession often gave the village grocer a couple of handfuls of rice for some mustard oil or salt. Travelling potters selling earthen pots or oil-press selling edible oil often accepted price of their ware in the form of paddy or rice.

There was another group of small scale village based traders of food crop called *bhachati*. They were women from the same village, who visited households to buy paddy against cash. The *bhachati*s soaked the paddy in water, parboiled and husked it before selling the rice at weekly markets.

The yield of paddy they got from their land was much less than their consumption requirement. Those grains were cultivated in such a way that the crop could provide them some food during monsoon, when they had to work hard with little or no food.

Some maize, pulses and beans were also grown and the stalks were used as fodder.

Another memory from yesteryears is related to visiting the eastern districts of Hugli or Bardhaman as wage workers. In those parts, the soil is suitable for cultivation of rice and vegetables; there was enough water above or below the ground for growing multiple crops a year. In those areas, there was so much work to be done that the visiting Santal wage workers were welcome; they were offered higher wage than what was available in the western part of Bankura.

Senior persons of Saraspur recounted that Santal people of the area used to walk in large groups all the way to those eastern districts. Those days the men had no banyan, shirt, or shoes to wear; their garments were restricted to two pieces of handwoven cloth. One was the *panchi*, a five-cubit long cloth to cover the loin, and the other one was *chhaita*, it was six cubit long and used as wrapper. The women carried two pieces of cloth, ten cubits each; those are called *dhuni* or *khandi*. Members of a family carried their belongings in bamboo boxes called *pedi*. It contained the essential metal utensils like *bati* or large bowls, *thara* or plate, *mali* or smaller bowl; *kantha* or quilts, *talai* or mat made of palm leaves, tobacco leaves, garments and some money. The women used to carry *pedi* on their head, the men carried it suspended from their stick.

WORTH OF THE MEMORIES

Canal irrigation was followed by new varieties of seeds, fertilizers, and pesticides into Saraspur, which gave a boost to agricultural activities of the village. With the impetus, more land was brought under cultivation and production per unit of land area increased. However, technological inputs like seeds, fertilizers, and pesticides could not make inroad into all households of the village. Some of them had little or no capital to invest in those items and could not move out of a subsistence level of existence. However, they benefitted indirectly from irrigation because there was a higher demand of wage workers in the area, thanks to agricultural activities for a longer part of the year.

Another boon came in the form of an emerging urban centre in the area; in pre-irrigation years, Khatra was a sleepy village that suddenly became a hub of constructional, administrative and trading activities once the irrigation project took off. This nascent township offered various job opportunities to the wage workers. A number of seasonal migrant workers from Saraspur and other villages to eastern districts trickled down to almost nil. All residents of the village were not of similar economic means; still nearly none of them was starving or travelling hundreds of miles to earn two square meals a day.

Why then were they remembering the days of acute food scarcity in so much detail, was an enigma. Not only were they preserving the memories through narratives, they were practising what their forefathers used to do when there was shortage of food. They were keeping the food practices alive by keeping various cultivated and non-cultivated items of food in their regular diet. This way they were keeping multiple food options open to themselves. In times when the state has elaborate arrangement to counter disasters including acute deficiency of food, why a people should keep them ready for calamities, one may ask.

During the colonial rule and in early postcolonial period, the Santals of this area seldom received any help from the state when they were in distress. It was the affected people themselves who tried to counter the scarcity through diversity of cultivated crop, through use of non-cultivated edible biodiversity of the area, by storing whatever rainwater they could, by shifting to areas where there was no imminent threat of their produces being taxed and by occasionally migrating to places where wage work was available. It can be argued that, for them, it was a situation of 'statelessness', they had nobody to look at and seek help from. Perhaps this notion of existing in a void has become a part of their collective consciousness, or possibly 'sub'-consciousness.

What other options were available to the people to keep them out of the recurrent misery? What other resources were there in their possession that could be used to get at least partial relief from hardship? It has been noted that the ability of a person to avoid starvation will depend on two factors: ownership of the person and his exchange entitlement mapping. When there is shortage of food supply, he will be exposed to the possibility of hunger as price of foodstuff will rise and this will have an unfavourable impact on his exchange entitlement. Entitlement relations accepted in a private ownership market economy can be trade based, production based, own labour entitlement, inheritance and transfer entitlement (Sen 1981, 2-4).

The exchange entitlements the Santals of the studied area could make use of to prevent starvation need to be looked into. In the first place, the essential differences between a 'private ownership market economy' and a 'peasant economy' have to be identified. Even when the environmental factors were favourable, the Santal cultivators were producing less than what was required for subsistence. So, the first two categories of entitlement, trade based and production based, can be ruled out from the list of what could be exchanged. The option of inheritance and transfer entitlement, which in this case would involve land, was unavailable to them as ownership of all land of a village was vested with the village community and at a later date with lineages. When village land was parcelled among households after introduction of colonial land tenure system, most of the holdings were so small and less productive that those were not viable for exchange.

So, the only option available to them was own labour entitlement, which was exchanged as much as was possible for them. The Santals often shifted or migrated in search of places where their labour could be sold for food.

State and market economy were either too weak to respond or were too indifferent towards the Santals when they were experiencing scarcity of food. This was not happening to all their neighbours. From the Santal perspective, their neighbours are of two types: one group is considered 'friendly' and the other 'hostile' (Gautam 1977, 37; Sachchidananda 2001, 169). Artisan groups like Tantubay, Karmakar, and Kumbhakar and groups of cultivators and wage workers like the Bagdi and Bauri fall in the friendly group. The Santals often take active part in their festivals and maintain economic relations with some of them. The higher caste Hindus, on the other hand, who once represented the *zamindar*s and *mahajan*s in the area and still own large tracts of land of good quality, are loathed for their exploitative and coercive roles. Such people are referred to as *diku* by the Santals; their relation with the *diku* people is always tense and sometimes hostile. For obvious reasons it was the 'friendly' people who were badly affected by famine. O'Malley (1908) categorically noted it was the 'landless' Santals, Bauris, and Samantas who suffered most, while the *diku*s were least affected. Santals and other affected people knew from experience that the *zamindar*s and *mahajan*s would not come to their help in bad times, they would rather take advantage of the crisis and alienate the impoverished from whatever entitlement was still there in their possession.

Under the above circumstances, the Santals had almost no other option but to keep themselves perennially prepared against scarcity. Memories of famine are repositories of knowledge that their forefathers gained through struggle against many odds. State and market forces have betrayed them in earlier days; in present times, those agencies are controlled by the *diku*s. Even when most people of Saraspur can grow enough food for them, they are not ready to lower their guard entirely against eventualities.

The memories of food scarcity are of enormous value on another count. Knowledge and experience of many generations about biodiversity, which have been retained through narratives and practices, can be used for the benefit of a large section of humanity in the event of changed climatic conditions.

REFERENCES

Beteille, Andre, 1974, *Six Essays in Comparative Sociology*, Delhi: Oxford University Press.

Gautam, M.K., 1977, *In Search of an Identity: A Case Study of the Santal of Northern India*, The Hague: Leiden.

Hunter, W.W., 1897, *Annals of Rural Bengal*, London: Smith, Elder and Co.

Mallik, S.K., 1993, *Transformation of Santal Society: Prelude to Jharkhand*, Calcutta: Minerva Associates (Publications) Pvt. Ltd.

Meena, H.K., 2015, 'Famine in Late 19th Century India: Natural or Man-Made', *Journal of Human and Social Science Research*, 6(1), pp. 35-44.

O'Malley, L.S.S., 1908 (reprint 1995), *Bengal District Gazetteers: Bankura.* Calcutta, State Editor, West Bengal District Gazetteers, Education Department, Government of West Bengal.

Sachchidananda, 2001, 'Change and Continuity in Santal Worldview', in *Santhal Worldview,* ed. Nita Mathur. New Delhi: Indira Gandhi National Centre for the Arts, pp. 162-75.

Sen, Amartya, 1981, *Poverty and Famines,* Oxford: Clarendon Press.

Xaxa, Virginius, 2003, 'Tribes in India', in *The Oxford India Companion to Sociology and Social Anthropology,* ed. Veena Das. New York: Oxford University Press, pp. 373-408.

SECTION V

FASHIONING FOOD: REPRESENTATIONS THROUGH FILM AND NEW MEDIA

CHAPTER 15

The Gustatory Metaphor: Decoding Food Images in Indian Films

SWIKRITA DOWERAH

INTRODUCTION

Post-structuralism posits that meaning is never inherent in a sign, that a sign is what it is not, and hence its meaning is always suspended. This view holds that meanings are not limited to one signified, but flow from signifier to signifier so that the signified is always unstable and a sign is never fully pure or meaningful (Eagleton 2015, 111). Reproducibility and repeatability is part of the identity of the sign which is why what it signifies is never stable but rather varies from situation to situation (ibid., 112). Roland Barthes stressed on this second-order of signification of a sign, the connotative meaning where the sign moves more towards the subjective and inter-subjective. In other words, Barthes points at the subtext in every text, the way the same text can come up with second- and third-order meanings, a text within a text, meaning within meanings. Beyond its material existence, food also qualifies as a sign whose meaning is always in a state of constant flux. Because it can take on a number of meanings in various contexts, food can be used as a marker of emotions where the act of eating is constitutive and reflective of the ebb and flow of human sentiments. While bland food may represent a low state of life, spice and sweets may reflect happiness and fulfilment. The significance of food is not limited to nutrition or its connection with social functions alone, but the major significances of food and eating are more symbolic. Food acts as a semiotic system to cover meanings of widely differing kinds like economic, social, political, religious, ethnic and aesthetic (Montanari 2006, 133). Therefore, the activities surrounding food like what we eat, when we eat, how we eat, and where we eat warrant special attention as they provide insights into meanings that are not directly apparent. It is in this sense that food is often used as a strong metaphor in films to negotiate different ideas.

The use of food in films can be broadly divided into two categories: the distinct 'food film' genre where food occupies a central role with most of the activities revolving around acts of eating, food preparation, serving, etc. with the setting being more or less the kitchen or a restaurant. Even the actors in the lead role will be chefs or domestic cooks, food specialists, or sellers and it is through food that the lead characters will negotiate questions of identity, power, class, or relationships (Bower 2004, 6). Apart from this distinct food film genre, food also finds space in non-food films where it can be used in a more symbolic sense broaching ideas of domination, power, control or distinction from others. In many films, food and its related practices can be taken as reaction against existing stereotypes in the society; while in other films, food preparation and consumption function as reassuring signifiers of cultural continuity.

Beyond its material aspect, the symbolism of food embraces the most intimate aspects of human life. As a giver and nurturer, women's body can be equated to that of food and nature. This association of food to women is not limited to cooking, eating, and serving alone, but is linked to the most primal of desires. Food causes gratification of the senses, and, as such, the control over food is also an indirect control over the body and one's desires. The various regulations on the edible and inedible, the eatable and non-eatable are also indicative of the restraints on the body. This power over the body is exercised by the society through food by means of rituals and traditions. As Sceats (2003, 11) says, 'The symbolic significance of specific foods and eating rituals in particular circumstances are established by various traditions and rituals.' One of the most striking examples of how food functions as a political tool for control of desires is the observance of Hindu widow norms. According to the Hindu tradition, a widow after her husband's death should resign to a life of sacrifice and sorrow. This is ensured by various scriptures that govern over the food that the widow should consume. Food establishes the boundaries that demarcate a widow's life from that of other women in the society. Therefore, it is the food that defines the spaces of inclusion and transgression for women and limits the full expression of her desires.

The aim of this article is to explore how films use food imagery to discuss wider discourses of power and control. In other words, the article will look at how food is used in films to indicate the exercise of power in the society for regulating women and their bodies, and how at the same time, the same food can also be used as a tool to dismantle this domination over one's desires. This is established by the reading of food sequences in three films based on the theme of widowhood—*Adajya* by Santwana Bordoloi (1996), *Water* by Deepa Mehta (2005), and *Goynar Baksho* (2013) by Aparna Sen. All three movies reflect a time period before and just after India's independence when widow norms were strict, and any deviance from the writ and regulations amounted to various forms of purification rituals as well as censure from the society. Although questions of relevance might sometimes emerge when one looks at whether such a selection of films based on a period of rigid social norms is justified for debate on the much widely discussed and recognized idea of body politics through food, the author would like to justify here that the article does not try to emphasize the already established social bindings that women were accustomed to at a certain period of time, but the study looks beyond such periodicity to emphasize how food has emerged as a symbolic marker to be used by filmmakers to talk about the desires of women, where denial or access to food goes beyond simply being reflective of the existing gender norms in society, but can also be used as a sign for creative expression of the gender—power status quo in society. The films use the food metaphor to reflect on how an item of consumption can provide inroads to the deepest of human desires and how the same food can be used to thwart its expression.

FOOD IMAGERY IN *ADAJYA*: DESIRING SOULS, CAGED BODIES

While food emerges as an essential trope in Indian films to establish the distinction between the abject other—the widow and the married women, in Santwana Bordoloi's *Adajya*, food does not remain as a mere item for locating the women in the widow's space, but as an essential pointer towards a widow's desires. *Adajya* is based on Indira Goswami's novel *The Moth Eaten Howdah of a Tusker*, which describes the plight of widows in upper-caste Hindu families in pre-Independence India. The film begins with Giribala, a young widow from a wealthy Brahmanical family being brought to her paternal home after her husband's demise. While Giribala anticipates leading the free life she once enjoyed before her marriage, it becomes more constrained by the social codes dictating a widow's life. The only activity she is allowed to perform is to assist Mark, a British researcher, in translating the old Satra manuscripts. Giribala refuses to follow the dictates of the social norms and had to be chastised on several occasions for her actions. As an act of rebellion, she embraces Mark in view of the elders leading to her purification by fire. In the end, she refuses to emerge after the fire is being lit and is finally burnt down inside the hay hut.

Used as a metaphor, food here is an expression of Giribala's desires. The deprivation of the love and intimacy with her deceased husband and the closed life she led at her in-law's residence, make her crave for love and freedom. The mental image of the food that the film etches out in the minds of the audience as Giribala speaks of her memory of eating monitor lizard at the beginning of the film is a clear indication of her suppressed desires. While her mother weeps over the misfortune that has befallen her daughter and turns down food and water, Giribala rejoices in her release from an unfaithful relationship. On her first night, she confides to her aunt about how confined her life had become after her marriage, and how she now looks forward to live like olden days at her father's residence. As she speaks this, she recalls longingly for meat, the food that is banned for widows. The director here uses a close-up of her face to show the longing that she feels for a life that was more carefree and unrestrained. In this case, meat is used as a metaphor to reflect Giribala's desires.

According to feminist scholarship, meat-eating is the symbol of the male; it signifies dominance, and hence, as an act of rebellion, they associate a vegetarian life with women. The restriction of meat also has sociological roots as meat and spices are considered as food that can increase the libido and as a widow, one must have strict control over the cravings of the body. A widow abstains from mingling too much with men or harbouring any feelings towards them. Out of a religious duty, however, Giribala is allowed to assist the British researcher who takes shelter in their shed in translating the Satra texts. As the story progresses, one can draw strong parallels between Giribala's association with meat and her growing intimacy with Mark. Mark's words of appreciation for her beauty make her realize her self-worth, allowing her to appreciate her own body. This is a point of rediscovery for her, and as she narrates how unfaithful her deceased husband had been, she also unfolds her secret desires of communion with Mark. The craving for meat was also a step towards her primal desires for union with the opposite sex.

Food becomes a strong metaphor in this film with the protagonist's association with meat reflecting her own association with her desires and how by embracing meat she clearly breaks the society's dictates of ruling her body and needs. In one of the strongest images used in the film, Giribala creeps into the kitchen despite her aunt asking her to stay away from it. Giribala rummages through the various pots and pans in the kitchen and, finding meat in one of them, takes mouthful of it. Soon, she is shown taking handfuls of meat again and again. As she enjoys a primal moment of bliss with the meat in the mouth, she is spotted by her aunt who brings in the rest of the family. Shocked at her imprudence and disregard for the Hindu rules, the mother starts beating her in anger. The camera cuts back and forth from the shocked and anguished expression of the mother to that of the rebellious Giribala who continues chewing the meat, unshaken by her mother's fury.

Giribala, here, not just eats the meat, she devours the flesh she was denied. The meat eating was not just an act of rebellion against social norms, but was also an expression of her innermost desires. After her purification, Giribala's closeness with Mark increases. She finds in Mark a friend and a partner who appreciates her beauty. Her closeness with Mark draws her father's attention and he summons her in-laws to take her back. Hearing this, Giribala approaches Mark to take her away. When he refuses, she comes to his hut one night and embraces him in view of elders. Her act of embracing Mark is not an act of love, but like her devouring of the meat she was denied, the act is also a rebellion against the denial of her desires by the patriarchal society of which even Mark is a part. Like the meat-eating sequence, Giribala is not cowered down by punitive measures that she knows would come her way after her embrace. What she does is an open declaration of her longing to embrace life, which social norms and widowhood deny. Just as her meat eating called for purification of her body, her association with Mark also calls for trial by fire. Foucault writes in *Discipline and Punish* (1995, 43),

. . . the body of the condemned man was once again an essential element in the ceremonial of public punishment. It was the task of the guilty man to bear openly his condemnation and the truth of the crime that he had committed. His body, displayed, exhibited in procession, tortured, served as the public support of a procedure that had hitherto remained in the shade; in him, on him, the sentence had to be legible for all.

It is through the expression of Giribala's desires in disregard for the social norms that necessitated her purification and trial. The punishment for flouting the norms had to be borne by the body. However, as a clear mockery of the social norms and traditions, Giribala refuses to come out of the fire and burns herself inside the hay hut, thereby denying anyone the right over her life and body.

In this film, defilement of the body is analogous to eating meat. It also suggests an entry into the world of desires, into the world of men. A vegetarian life is as bland as the food, while meat symbolizes the spices of life, the association with men. By embracing meat, Giribala makes an entry into this world of men and pleasure. In *Adajya*, it is through the imagery of food, that the ideas of sacrilege and defilement were defined. Food not just reflected desires, but also created a separate space for widows. According to Sceats (2003, 2), the cultural pressures in recent years have made women particularly conscious of their body-boundaries in relation to food and eating. While Sceats points to the effects of globalization and the market economy that pressurize women to keep a control over their eating, this statement could also be related to a different kind of control. In this kind, it was for the control of desires that cultural and societal pressures were imposed on the women with regards to their food consumption.

As Angela Carter writes in her book, *The Sadeian Woman and the Ideology of Pornography,* 'flesh comes to us out of history; so does the repression and taboo that governs our experience of flesh' (cited in Sceats 2003, 3). Although she refers to sexuality in the statement, Carter's statement is also relevant to food because, like sexuality, food is also a social and political construct. In *Adajya*, it is by consuming the flesh that Giribala chooses to flout the repressive acts of the social institutions that bars her freedom.

FOOD IMAGERY IN *WATER*: MEMOIRS OF DESIRE

While meat can refer to the innermost desires of the human body, sweets can enable one to relive those moments. *Water* by Deepa Mehta also revolves around the story of widows in pre-independence India. Unlike in Assam, where widows are allowed to live in their houses, *Water* by Deepa Mehta depicts a scenario where they were kept in a separate confinement, where strict widow rules were followed and there was no possibility of mingling with men. The film begins with the eating scene of Chuiyaa, the child protagonist who happily relishes the sugarcane in the bullock cart, while members of her family wear worried looks at her husband's ill-health. A few scenes later, Chuiyya is shown eating plain rice and salt along with other widows in the widow confinement. This transformation of food images from the juicy sweet sugarcane to the rice and salt has been used artistically by Mehta to reveal the blandness of life that surrounds the women in the confinement. While the entire house consumes widow food, the head warden Madhumati quietly consumes spicy food and enjoys liberties like a patriarch. Be it the case of Kalyani, the young widow who she pawns to rich landlords or the other widows whose lives she controls, Madhumati symbolizes a manifestation of the patriarchal society, one who looks over the food and activities of the women. Food here becomes a metaphor of this control. The control Madhumati represents here is symbolic and it is not just the control over a mere item of consumption but the control over the desires of the widows—the desire to bridge the spaces that society has created between them and the other women.

Yet food is also reflective of the memories of our desires. One of the strongest references to the association of food and desire in the film is the sequence where the old widow remembers about her wedding food every time she eats the bland rice. The restriction of food here contrasts most vividly with the freedom of choice 'before', and the old widow wistfully remembers the profligacy of eating food before they were widowed. She tells Chuiyya that day or night she can see the picture of the *jalebis* and *laddoos* that were served during her wedding. Chuiyaa who remembers the old widow's desire for sweets, buys her some one day. In this sequence, Chuiyya, who is disgusted with begging, leaves the temple and starts to walk towards their confinement. On her way, Chuiyya is held back by the aroma of the *jalebis* that are being fried in oil. She stops midway from her trail, takes a few steps back and looks eagerly at the spread that lay before her. The shopowner looks at her suspiciously and reminds her that sweets are not for widows. She says she has money and stands there licking her mouth at the sight of the sweets. Although Chuiyya's face shows no further emotions, the expression was itself a reflection of her inner longings and also a sadistic reflection of the denial that widows were subjected to. The food here is the symbol of that pleasure. Remembering the old lady, Chuiyya controls her urge to taste the *laddoo* and instead brings them to her. She slowly moves the *laddoo* under the nose of the sleeping lady and then keeps it near her bed. On waking up, the old widow's face lights up with joy. She sniffs the *laddoo* and closes her eyes as a volley of emotions fills her soul. As she tastes the *laddoo*, memories of her conjugal life rush back to her mind. The film then includes a flashback to the day of her wedding when she tasted the *laddoo*, and shows the happiness that spread over her face. This scene is replete with a number of connotations. Here, the *laddoo* takes her back to the memories of union with her husband and eating of the sweet thus signifies a fulfilment of desires while the flashback reflects years of denial of her being, the body and the soul after her husband's death. When the old woman tastes the *laddoo*, there is a momentary dissolution of all boundaries that society had created for her; the spaces between the two different worlds of the widows and of the other women collapse into one and, for a moment, she finds a momentary satisfaction of her desires. Widow remarriage was not institutionalized in India till then, and therefore, after the husband's death, a woman had to suppress her needs, both of the soul and of the body. In this film, therefore food emerges as a metaphor for both suppression as well as fulfilment of desires. Food here creates an isolated space for the widows as well as shows how the same food can also obliterate them. The reference to food in *Water* is subtle, yet it establishes the strict confines of a widow's life, the drab reality of their situation and the blandness of their being. In a widow's space, desire is curbed by strict codes of morality and spirituality and food then becomes a medium for that control. The existence of widows is defined as passive and their subjectivity effectively denied by the social norms where they—the widows—become the threatening 'other' in the society, and this 'other' had to be regulated. Food becomes a means of this regulation.

FOOD IMAGERY IN *GOYNAR BAKSHO*: THE UNFULFILLED DESIRE

In Aparna Sen's *Goynar Baksho*, the relationship between food and desires is not explicit. Rashmoni, the aunt of Somlata's husband, is the matriarch of the house. Her main power lies in her jewellery box which came to her as her dowry. After her husband's death, she was taken back to her parent's house, but she had clung on to her jewellery box as means of her survival. In the film, the jewellery box becomes the symbol of her unfulfilled desires, and food becomes a metaphor to describe the lack she feels in all the years of her life. The references to food here are not recurrent, but in the few instances that food is used, it exposes how deprived her life had been of all the pleasures that she sought and held dear. Aparna Sen weaves these desires in the food scenes of the film.

In one sequence, Rashmoni enters the kitchen drawn to the smell of the meat being cooked. She looks longingly at the meat and asks Somlata whether it is dried fish. Somlata says she is cooking mutton, but Rashmoni refuses to pay heed to her. She enquires about the spices that Somlata has put into the preparation and whether she has put adequate amount of onion and garlic. The smell of the preparation takes her back to her days at their ancestral home in Faridpur before the partition of India. She enthusiastically tells Somlata about how the fish was cooked then. She recalls the spices, red hot chilli, onion, and garlic that were used to make dried fish and asks whether Somlata has used the same while cooking the meat.

Like the jewellery box which Rashmoni clings on to, the above memory of food is also reflective of her unfulfilled desires. Married at the age of 11 and widowed at 12, her life has been barren since then. As she narrates in another sequence, that by the time she realizes her bodily needs, she is a widow. Had she been married, she would have been a caring wife and would have enjoyed the sexual life that Somlata now shares with her husband. It is also in the cooking sequence that Rashmoni warns Somlata not to sleep with her husband lest he should die, and if she becomes pregnant, then her child shall die too. The recollection of red chilli, spices and meat stretches out her now dead hopes for a pleasurable conjugal life and how even when she was alive, she could never experience any physical pleasure. As years of bitterness and denial take the better of her, she tries to spoil Somlata's food. By engaging Somlata in her talk and cursing her of widowhood, she cunningly asks her to pour salt in the meat more than once. The above warning indicates that she does not want Somlata to have physical relationship with her husband, and since she was denied, others should also never experience any physical gratification in their conjugal life. The salt she asks Somlata to add to her meat shows her intent to spoil the preparation and in short, the pleasures of a married woman. As one sees that none of the members of the family could eat the meat that Somlata cooked, and this gives Rashmoni a sadistic pleasure.

As a widow, Rashmoni's life was as bland as the food she consumed when alive. Although she craves for the spices, the strict social norms never allowed her the freedom. When Somlata asks her to taste the meat, Rashmoni chides her saying that even if she is a ghost, she is still a widow. Rashmoni's statement reflects that magnitude of power that the society exerts over a woman, that even after death; she is bound by the social norms. What she could not do as a widow when alive, she could never do when dead. That the one instance when she tried to violate the norms and lure a worker to gratify her, she met with ill fate. Not only was her plan squashed but it also led to her lover's death and this broke her determination. Therefore, when Rashmoni refuses to taste the meat, she means that she lived and died a widow and had been deprived throughout her life. What she lost, she could never find now and hence even if dead, she was still a widow and her life would be as bland as before, her desires would remain forever unfulfilled.

CONCLUSION

Food, like the sign, can take up different meanings in different contexts. Like the sign, its meaning is never stable but it is we who attribute meaning to the food we eat, see, and cook. Although there is a long history of food being used as a tool to titillate and lure the senses, the use of the same food as a metaphor to negotiate ideas of control and rebellion is little explored. In all the above films, one sees food being used as a metaphor to reflect the deep seated power within the patriarchal society, where food both reflects and materializes as a symbol of the power that controls the bodies and regulates the desires of women. Michel Foucault writes in *Discipline and Punish: The Birth of the Prison*:

the hold on the body did not entirely disappear in the mid-nineteenth century. Punishment had no doubt ceased to be centred on torture as a technique of pain; it assumed as its principal object loss of wealth or rights. But a punishment like forced labour or even imprisonment—mere loss of liberty—has never functioned without a certain additional element of punishment that certainly concerns the body itself: rationing of food, sexual deprivation, corporal punishment, solitary confinement (Foucault 1995, 15).

He further says,

Disciplinary practices subject bodily activities to a process of constant surveillance and examination that enables a continuous and pervasive control of individual conduct. Thus, discipline produces subjected and practiced bodies, 'docile' bodies (Foucault 1977, 138-9).

It is not, however, only the body that disciplinary techniques target. Foucault presents disciplinary power as productive of certain types of subjects as well. In *Discipline and Punish*, he describes the way in which the central technique of disciplinary power—constant surveillance—which is initially directed toward disciplining the body, takes hold of the mind as well to induce a psychological state of 'conscious and permanent visibility' (Foucault 1977, 201). In other words, perpetual surveillance is internalized by individuals to produce the kind of self-awareness that defines the modern subject. In the films discussed, it is the social norms surrounding widowhood that guards over the women's body and defines ideas of purity and impurity. The norms are then internalized by the women who discipline themselves over time through abstinence. While *Adajya* represents the revolting body which had to be punished, *Water* and *Goynar Baksho* represented the docile body. In all the films, the women and their bodies are imprisoned by the society's codes for acceptable and unacceptable behaviours.

Used metaphorically in all three films, food comes to express the innate needs of the desiring body. In *Adajya*, it was through food that power is exercised, and it was also through food that power is demolished. Food creates binary spaces for the women in the three films. While in *Adajya*, the protagonist Giribala rebels against this binary; in *Water*, Deepa Mehta shows a momentary collapse of the spaces through food. In *Goynar Baksho*, on the other hand, food continues to function as a wall to the desires of a widow. Therefore, in its various ways, food represents the power inherent in the male-dominated society. From a staple dietary requirement, to a sign loaded with meanings, food has also become a metaphor for control as has been reflected in the analysis of the three films. This use of food in films is well summed up by Annie Bower in her article, 'Watching Food', where she points out that when 'food appears in a film it is loaded with much more than calories'.

REFERENCES

Bower, Anne L., ed., 2004, *Reel Food: Essays on Food and Film*. Psychology Press.

———, 2012, 'Watching Food: The Production of Food, Film, and Values', in *Reel Food*, Routledge, pp. 8-20.

Carter, A., 1988, *The Sadeian Woman and the Ideology of Pornography*. Pantheon.

Eagleton, T., 2011, *Literary Theory: An Introduction*, John Wiley & Sons.

Foucault, M., 1977, *Discipline and Punish: The Birth of the Prison*, trans. A. Sheridan. New York.

Montanari, M., 2006, *Food is Culture*, Columbia University Press.

Sceats, Sarah, 2000, *Food, Consumption and the Body in Contemporary Women's Fiction*, Cambridge: Cambridge University Press.

CHAPTER 16

Reconstructing Youth Through Popular Culinary Culture

ANASUYA SREEDHAR

What began as cook books in early twentieth century has reincarnated itself into the food show in the era of cable and satellite television where cooking does not *appear* to be connected with domesticity. Food is a language of communication, and this article examines the transaction of messages in two popular food shows to study culinary culture as a method to critically understand the making of the urban youth set against a culture of consumerism. The world has almost shrunk onto the urban dining platter bringing global culture into the kitchen. However, as the study unfolds, it suggests with the support of empirical findings that this global culture acts more as a glamorous façade behind which reside the constricting norms of patriarchy. The messages provide startling revelations where the urban youth is reconstituted as consumers, women in particular, who are not only sold lessons of domesticity, wrapped in the paper of progress and success but of building the self on *standardized,* prescriptive notions of beauty, perhaps to confine them within a paternalistic frame, devoid of agency.

Foie gras, sushi, and *laksa* are terms not uncommon within the Indian culinary context. Rather, such names have become an intrinsic part of the urban Indian lexicon where food has positioned itself as another facet of popular culture. The world has almost shrunk onto the dining platter and food shows are a reflection of that. In the discipline of food studies, there exists a popular aphorism, 'Tell me what you eat and I will tell you who you are!'

(Caplan 1997, 9). Food, therefore, is inextricably linked to identity, the social, cultural and the political.

Strauss, the structuralist, opined that food needs to be studied because it is an intrinsic part of a cultural system (Caplan 1997, 9). The works of Mary Douglas and cultural studies scholar Lupton reaffirm the belief that food is actually a language that communicates messages that must be decoded to understand culture and society (Lupton 1996). Feminist anthropological scholarship has taken this discourse further to understand gender roles and power-structures (Counihan 1999). The discipline of literature has also been no stranger to the issue of food. Jaber explores ethnic identity as an Arab-American through her memoir of the *baklava* (Abu-Jaber 2006). Even in the world of popular fiction she has resorted to the use of food as a tool to express a myriad of cultural and political issues, emotions and identity. Anita Desai's novel, titled, *Fasting Feasting*, is an elaborate work on sexuality, explored through the twin modes of denial and indulgence in food. Fish acts as a recurring motif in the works of Jhumpa Lahiri, connecting her to her Bengali roots in Bengal and Boston (Lahiri 1999).

Early twentieth century witnessed the emergence of the cook book which soon became a research site to examine sociocultural identities and ideology. From an emasculated Bengali masculinity (Ray 2013), domesticated Malayali femininity (Sreekumar 2011) to the dilemma of the urban housewife (Appudurai 1988), scholars have interpreted the genre of cook books to investigate their research propositions. With the advent of television, especially cable/satellite facilities, the cook book reincarnated itself into the food show.

Women's magazines (beginning around the fifties) were potent sites to document and study not only women's lives, but society, its cultural transitions, socio-political changes and gender relations. It was a time when in an India, free from colonial rule, a new identity was being carved for the Indian woman, in most cases, urban. Apart from Hindi and English, most states had their own circulation of regional magazines. The year 1982 brought in the first rupture in terms of reading population with the launch of television. Further on, a decade down the line, 1992 brought the next big wave in the form of cable and satellite television, breaking the monopoly of the government owned *Doordarshan* (Centre for Advocacy and Research 2003). The private-owned cable and satellite television houses brought with it multiple doors which introduced the urban, metropolitan audience into another world of western consumerism, owing to its largely Americanized programmes and sitcoms.

Beginning with borrowed content from American production houses, soon Indian television shows were replaced by a considerable portion of Indian productions. Over the years, programming for entertainment channels has undergone many changes. Some perished while many survived. Today, the genre of food shows has been repackaged in terms of core-messaging to cater to viewers of varying taste-buds. Food shows happen to be one of those programming wonders that survived but through a different formula. Every show, today, harps on one particular feature which could range from health, fitness, easy-to-prepare, children's meals to Italian spreads and budget dinners, leading to an unending list of ideas that can be sold for ratings and revenues. Once pioneered by Sanjeev Kapoor's *khana khazaana*, catering to housewives, it has today morphed into a phenomenon which no longer associates cooking with domesticity, *apparently*. The messages that are transacted through such shows when studied, become documents of a changing culture, especially in urban society.

This article is a study of food shows, deployed as a methodological tool to explore how the urban youth is constructed by media, against an overarching presence of a culture of consumerism. Two shows were selected for this study. Beginning with method, its challenges and complexities, the article will present the findings for each show, followed by an analysis and concluding comments.

METHOD

Anchored within the framework of feminist research, the field was explored through Standpoint Theory which believes that the standpoints of the marginalized serve as documents of knowledge that help understand power relations of both the marginalized and the dominant (Harding 2004, 2). However, here one is concerned with the standpoint of not the *marginalized* but of the *insider*. As a researcher who had earlier worked in the broadcast entertainment industry, the work experience provided an 'epistemic advantage' (Wylie 2004, 344), which an outsider may not possess. Here the term *outsider* is used in terms of a person who is a viewer of television without knowing about its operational details. This *insider* status and its consequent knowledge became a dual edged sword. While it offered a better understanding of the field; at the same time, it created power issues in terms of interpreting findings. The ethical dilemmas of this positionality of an *insider standpoint* were resolved with Alison Wylie's suggestions. She writes that this epistemic advantage helps garner insights which may otherwise remain hidden, thereby rendering a more insightful study (ibid., 347).

The *insider* knowledge of this writer equipped one with programming information like airtime usage, sponsorship and brand ideology. Most programmes for entertainment channels (food shows are a part) have a target audience as the *youth,* a category understood in terms of an age bracket of 18-25. This information was used to understand the features of this bracket and study the transaction of messages in food shows. Moreover, the apparent shift in target audience for food shows, (housewives to youth) was tapped to account for its reasons. Analysing through the lens of gender, rooted in feminist research, one has empirically supported my view that popular culinary culture, promoted through food-shows have acted as agents of aggressive consumerism where *youth* is reconstructed within a rigid patriarchal framework, held captive by an illusion of progress. The shows selected were:

The Pooja Makhija Show
Mummy Ka Magic

The selection of shows was deliberate. Both shows are aired on FoodFood channel, dedicated entirely to food shows. Both are popular shows due to their re-telecast frequency. Although the content differs, the target audience and core messaging remain similar. The aim was to pick two shows, differing in content but delivering similar messages.

The Pooja Makhija Show

This is a health show aimed at maintaining ideal body weight through right eating habits, hosted by Vishal Malhotra in conversation with Pooja Makhija, a celebrity nutritionist. The show runs for 30 minutes with commercial breaks. There are sections titled, 'This Or That' and 'Eat Delete', where Vishal asks Pooja about wholesome food options, measures to follow while dining at restaurants or parties, diet tips while on a vacation and a host of other food centred queries with weight loss or maintenance as the target. Also there is a call-in section where diet related queries by viewers are answered by Pooja.

The show montage has only Pooja in the frame, mostly dressed in shades of pink/purple and looks like a fashion-model herself. She flips through a diet book written by her; nibbles on a biscuit and plays with a measuring tape to suggest less is good. The montage is followed by a few opening lines by Vishal who sets the theme of the show. What is interesting to note is that while the show harps on *health*, it somehow reduces it to a discourse on weight loss alone. For instance, one episode begins with these words by Vishal: *Friend ki shaadi mein slim dikhne ka sapna, sapna hi reh gaye; aur quick weight-loss ki chakkar mein aise hi jaane kitne deadlines cross ho gaye*, meaning that the dream of becoming 'slim' for a friend's wedding remained a dream and, in the quest for losing weight in a short time, many a deadline has lapsed. Vishal, of course, adds reassuringly that weight loss need not be worrisome since Pooja had taken the responsibility of getting people into shape, the *healthy way*.

Of the eight episodes studied, all begin with this thought. In one single segment, the word *health* features seven times. Surprisingly however, the conversation never proceeds to health issues like cholesterol, blood pressure, diabetes, and a hoard of other ailments that plague urban life. Rather, it revolves around weight reduction methods. Moreover the show, although aimed at the youth, both men and women, the messages however are driven towards women only. Pooja, while speaking about diets, always speaks in terms of the woman. For instance, she says: *Agar aap working mom hain aur strict diet nahin follow kar sakte . . . yaa aapke husband aapse kahe ki aap patle ho jaao . . . .* She displays her concern for the 'working mom' or the wife being coaxed to lose weight by her husband, thereby targeting women alone.

This show translates *health* in the lexicon of weight loss. It acts as a euphemism for weight reduction, promoting an essentially lean body image, simultaneously facilitating sale of her diet book. By positioning herself strategically as a nutritionist, she breaks away from the clutter of countless dieticians, claiming that her way is the *healthy* way of losing weight.

Mummy Ka Magic

This is a recipe based show, hosted by former model, Amrita Raichand. She cooks innovative dishes to satisfy the difficult to please children's taste buds. But the show is not for children. Rather it caters to young urban mothers. It pledges to win the ceaseless battle of adding variety to children's foods. She has, in fact, positioned herself almost as a messiah for mothers with fussy children.

The show opens with a montage where the camera pans across a colourful, aesthetically pleasing but messy kitchen, with a stash of *Real fruit juices* in tetra packs, aligned neatly on a shelf. The utensils are not the boring steel but sport colours like neon green, yellow, and orange. The children's feel is carefully built in the set. The host herself is not the mother as featured in the commercials of yesteryears, like *Lalita Ji* of Surf fame in the 1970s.[1] Raichand looks young, lean, and fashionable.

This show also focuses on *health* but does not count calories. The messages that are delivered tend to emphasize and glorify the role of the mother as the true caretaker of children. For instance, she begins one episode like this: *Moms will be moms. Kitna dhyaan rakhte hain na woh hamara . . .*, voicing that mothers are the ones who constantly care for their children. Further on, stressing the importance of mother's health, she says: *Bachchon ka achha khaas dhyaan dene ke liye, maa ko apni sehat ki bhi utni dhyaan rakhni chahiye, and for that I think it is very important for mothers to feel good, and you can only feel good when you look good and eat good.*

Mother's health, according to Raichand, is important only in terms of improving her capacity to take care of her children and perform her maternal duties competently. Of the eight episodes studied, the *look good* factor comes into play, albeit subtly, most of the times. While the show ostensibly caters to offer mothers solutions in terms of an innovative blend of healthy yet delicious recipes, the messages seem to reinforce the importance of external beauty and bifurcated parental roles where, needless to say, the onus of childcare falls on the mother. The father is conspicuous by his absence.

ANALYSIS

The shows have been analysed through three strains, namely:
Body Image
Gendered Bifurcation of Roles
Consumer Culture

BODY IMAGE

Body image figures as a strong feature in articulating gender identity as revealed in the works of many scholars. Thapan, in her empirical study, exploring gender identity in urban adolescent school-girls, writes that most responses adhered to the notion that a 'good figure' was usually constructed as thin which in turn guaranteed popularity in school (Thapan 2007, 39). The works of Susan Bordo also confirms the importance given to a *lean* body while defining beauty as a feature of gender identity (Bordo 2003).

While the *Makhija Show* is quite blatant in its approach to issues of body weight, *Mummy Ka Magic* is more subtle. As noted earlier, Pooja's show uses health as a tool to sell normative body ideals, targeting women where physical looks supersede all other factors of selfhood and identity. It acts as *Victorian Conduct Manuals* that laid out the do's and don'ts of ideal feminine features which as Bordo asserts, constructed femininity on the principal of denying hunger through self-restraint (Bordo 2003, 130). Controlling hunger became one of the popular and sought after routes for women to maintain an *ideal* body shape and weight. The *Conduct*

Manuals clearly enumerated a list of things that women needed to follow in order to align themselves to the normative standards of beauty and much of the rules had to do with food, its consumption and denial. *The Pooja Makhija Show* appears to be an almost televised, twenty first century adaptation of the *Victorian Conduct Manuals* where food is projected not in terms of denial but restraint. It is this feature of *restraint* which keeps recurring through the episodes that at times border on fear; a fear of extra body weight that is propelled by the notion that *lean is beautiful.* Surprisingly however, such messages are camouflaged by a language where Pooja insists that her book and her show is to dispel the *fear* of food. *Eat Delete ka sirf ek hi maqsad tha, to remove the fear of food.* Yet, once the conversation between Vishal and Pooja gets decoded, the messages seem to reinforce a *fear of food* through the importance on a lean body-image. *Jab aap woh scale har maheene do kilo, teen kilo ghatte dekhenge, aap ko koi vada pav woh khushi nahin dega jitna woh scale aapko dega,* meaning that a drop in the weighing scale would give greater happiness than any delicious food. Here, Pooja replaces food with weight loss as a stimulant for happiness. No wonder, then, according to a study conducted by Bordo suggested that 'ninety per cent of all anorectics are women' (Bordo 2003, 154).

Mummy Ka Magic, by focusing on the logic that feeling good is directly proportional to looking good, reinforces the importance of *good-looks*. The messages confirm the features of the category of *good-looks* which hinges on body weight and youthful disposition. Through the duration of cooking, over eight episodes, while Raichand lists out the health quotient of each recipe, she speaks about calories but with a warning; while mothers can cook healthy yet calorie-laden food for their children, they must observe restraint from eating those dishes themselves. Of course, she adds that mothers can indulge but occasionally. *Restraint,* therefore, is one of the features of this show. The core message in this series also rests on the self being constructed on the aspect of physical features alone. Raichand is primarily a model, not a trained chef. Yet, her selection as a host to conduct a cookery show aimed at urban mothers spells a definitive strategy; a strategy to sell an image of the urban mother who performs one of the major domestic chores, that of cooking but without bearing any mark of drudgery and looking bright, radiant and beautiful at all times.

Quoting Veena Das, Thapan writes that 'the sense of being a woman is internalized' through the twin notions of the body as object and subject (Thapan 2007, 34). This reinstates the dominant norms where body-weight becomes a major feature in determining a woman's identity. Naomi Wolf asserts that certain body images are promoted as ideals of beauty in order to maintain a male dominant culture, reducing beauty to its superficial denominator (Wolf 1990, 59). Both the shows not only conform but propagate such ideals only to be replicated by its viewers, young urban women.

GENDERED BIFURCATION OF ROLES

Bordo, while writing against the naturalized roles of women as cooks, cites the example of Hillary Clinton who when questioned about her 'rabid feminism' at the *cost* of evading maternal duties, had to prove her 'true womanhood' by baking oatmeal chocolate-chip cookies (Bordo 2003, 122). Whether her critics were silenced, remain unknown but this proves, beyond an iota of doubt that the onus of childcare falls on the woman because after all, Bill Clinton never had to prove his paternal love or manhood through his culinary skills!

The messages in the first show indicate that Makhija, while addressing diet difficulties, acknowledges women's burden of managing the kitchen and children. Her assumptions that men go out and work and the women look after the rest reek of gendered stereotyping of roles. In one such episode, Pooja while talking about working women setting 'realistic diet goals' says, *For instance I'm a working mother, mere do bachche hai, mere eight-hour job hain, bachchon ki padhai, plus ghar ka dhyaan*, stressing that working mothers have quite a burden on their shoulders since they have to manage not only work but look after children and do housework as well. In all fairness, it may be assumed that she is not deliberately packing women in one bracket; after all she does speak about working women and their diet issues. Nonetheless, such assumptions, however inadvertent, raise questions about the dangers of *normalizing* the segregation of the public/private domain leading to a regressive society, where especially working women, bear the double responsibility of professional work and house work. Not only do they have to confront the challenges on the professional front but simultaneously carry out their domestic duties as well by virtue of being women.

Raichand, meanwhile, embodies the urban mother where good looks go hand in hand with maternal duties. As the title suggests, it is essentially *mummy* or the mother's *magic*! The frame itself is gendered. The father is hardly ever visible, thereby, subtly, associating and reinforcing culinary *magic* as a metaphor for maternal virtue. It paints an image of the mother as some sort of a fairy godmother who with one swoosh of her magic wand can weave culinary wonders to satiate children's hard to please taste buds. In fact, Raichand usually begins her episodes, echoing this very sentiment. For example, she says, Hello and welcome to my kitchen...aap sabko swagat hain mummy ka magic pe jahaan hum sabko milte hain solutions hamare bachon ki erratic sudden demands ke liye! She voices a collective dilemma through the phrase *hum sabko* (we all) where women are presented as a unit constantly in a quest to innovate and improvise and satisfy the ceaseless food related demands of their children. In another episode, while voicing the range of food issues faced by mothers, she says, *alag alag bachon ki alag alag problems hoti hain; kitne alag alag challenges har maa ko face karna padta hai na?* While she lists out the multiple challenges mothers face in terms of children's food demands, Raichand is quick to come up with a solution where she reassures mothers that they should not worry since her show is all about offering solutions to tackle such challenges, *But not to worry, mummy ka magic after all hai kiske liye. . . inhi challenges ko ache se face karenge and tackle karenge!* Mummy Ka Magic builds a maternal identity where love or maternal care revolves around meeting demands of children, pleasing them and overcoming all food related challenges. Never does Raichand ever mention anywhere that children need to be disciplined; that *fussy children* should not be indulged all the time and perhaps, a little bit of *restraint* would go a long way to-wards inculcating discipline and some manners. In an empirical study by Mallika Das on the representation of men and women in Indian print advertisement, she asserts that the identities of men and women are built around work and emotion (Das 2007, 140). So, while the man takes charge of the public domain by earning a living, the woman is assigned the role of taking care of the home which includes emotional well being also. Raichand reinforces the normative belief that women and only women are most suited for the role of caregivers, expressed of course through innovative culinary skills. Both the shows project the woman only in terms of family, thereby essentializing her. Even when the professional life is mentioned, it is presented along with the responsibility of housework where the load does not appear to be evenly shared between the spouses. Women's roles are circumscribed within the sphere of the domestic, where the family and its needs are placed on a pedestal, to be guarded and executed by women. Veneration of motherhood is packaged through culinary feats and skilful home/work balance. The lives of urban women are translated mostly through housework, like cooking and childcare. In the process, the shows not only push women to the fringes instead of challenging binaries but actively engage in normalizing such bifurcations where women's agency appears redundant.

CONSUMER CULTURE

The shows are a site of 'aggressive globalization of corporate capitalism' (Mohan 2010, 393). This breeds a certain power which is measured in terms of purchase, creating a social space of acute consumerism and the shows exemplify that. Both shows, at a deeper level, serve as selling platforms, where the goods sold range from diets, health, food products to lifestyle and aspiration. In the Makhija Show, she sells a body-image which can be achieved by purchasing gym memberships, diets and a pantry containing exotic food items to facilitate weight-loss. Raichand's show is remarkable in terms of product placement. The '*Real fruit juices*' are strategically placed, obviously for advertising purposes. Her use of exotic herbs and other ingredients focusing on particular brands is carefully projected to entice prospective buyers.

While Pooja promotes global tourism by frequent use of phrases like 'foreign holiday' and 'exotic beaches', Raichand transforms the urban kitchen into a site of global culture. Recipes ranging from Italian, Mexican and Chinese to fusion wonders where she bakes a beetroot *samosa* (an Indian flour-based cookie) with a pasta filling, her show takes the viewers on a global journey which epitomizes the east meets west cliché. This kind of a global concoction with constant references to Italian herbs, Moroccan spices and southeast Asian condiments, renders the urban kitchen into a site of globalization where the term *exotic* defines culinary art. Move away from the mundane *daal-chawal*,[2] cook and savour delicacies from around the world, thereby redefining urban cooking. This reiterates the fact that global culture gets produced *significantly* by media which plays out in different ways in the urban household, one of them being the culture of consumerism (Thapan 2007, 31).

Another feature in both the shows is the use of English as a language of communication, interrupted with a dash of Hindi and phrases borrowed from French and Espanol which reconfirm that global imprints have shaped urban living. Greetings and goodbyes in both the shows are done in multiple languages. Raichand usually begins her shows in this manner, *Namaste, welcome back to mummy ka magic, before we go back into our magical cooking, chaliye lete hain some of your questions at our mother's corner.* In an episode on festival food, Pooja while talking about restraint says, *hamaare palette ko khush rakhne ke liye chhoti si bite le lijiye to make your mind happy and everybody happy.* What is interesting to note is that the transition from one language to another hardly seems jarring. It appears seamless; in fact, it almost appears as a language all by itself, encapsulated in the word *hinglish.* It is neither pure English nor pure Hindi. It is an adulterated mix of both the tongues, often with additions from several foreign languages as well. It could be interpreted as the language of the urban or the urban tongue where language becomes a site of cultural amalgamation. The shows, therefore, function as promoting the sale of goods, cultural goods to be precise and language is an intrinsic part of such an inventory. Any discussion on consumerism would be incomplete without a mention of the consumer. As stated earlier, although the shows technically cater to the urban youth, the messages seem to be directed at women alone. Pooja occasionally refers to men while imparting lessons on right eating habits; Raichand, on the other hand, delivers her messages to women, mothers in particular. The consumer emerges to be the woman, urban in particular who is inclined towards purchasing a lifestyle defined through a lean, glamorous physical disposition, indulgence in world cuisine and speaking a tongue that displays global travel. The focus on the 'woman' as the consumer seems to reiterate a statement, written after conducting a study on Indian television serials by The Centre for Advocacy and Research, where it categorically suggests that 'television is essentially a female bastion' (Centre for Advocacy and Research 2003). The study confirms the understanding that women form the bulk of television's target-audience, making them *heavy consumers* of satellite television viewed in comparison to men. This particular study on food shows, also tends to have similar conclusions where even the ones that are supposedly meant to cater to both men and women as target audience, a deeper analysis of the messages, reaffirms women as the broader consumer base.

CONCLUSION

With the liberalization of markets, came the onslaught of consumerism hinging on the power of purchase where lifestyles were *standardized* and sold as *successful*, promoted by the media and consumed by the people (Mohan 2010, 394). Bordo accounts for the impact of television on human lives by studying notions of body image in Fijian women. Fiji, due to its remote location, was introduced to cable television quite late. Bordo discovered that Fijian women were comfortable with their body weight till 1995, before satellite television reached its shores. Surprisingly, post the advent of satellite television which mostly aired American shows, in 1998, three years later to be precise, cases of eating disorders rose unexpectedly. Eleven per cent girls resorted to vomiting to reduce weight. Bordo traced it to the heavy dose of *standardized* and *normative* body images that were sold as *ideal*, through cable television (Bordo 2003, xvi). Television does impact lives.

This particular study revealed that the target audience is a concept focusing on women as consumers who were sold lifestyle products to epitomize the features of the age bracket. It would be fair to conclude, therefore, that the shift in target audience is a superficial one. Housewives were replaced with housewives, or in the urban language, homemakers but in a different *avatar* where they embodied the features of the youth bracket projecting a *standardized* version of body image, essentially lean, leading to a flourishing health, beauty and fitness industry. So, the *new* woman is young, fitting the 18-25 age bracket (in physical disposition, not human age), fashionable, a global traveller, prepares exotic meals but is confined to the domestic sphere, nonetheless. She is the *traditionally modern* woman who upholds all the features of a patriarchal society but camouflaged by the glamour of urban living. Her progress is an illusion where her biology determines her destiny (Beauvoir 2011) reinforcing gender stereotypes, helped by the medium of television, a strong arm, framing and perpetuating consumer culture. The decoded messages indicate how media, guided by economic interests, repackages patriarchy and sells it in the name of success and progress to the *urban youth* which is more of a concept, described by attributes and not age, constantly being manufactured and reconstructed to meet consumer goals of a global economy. There has been a long standing debate on whether it is art that imitates life or is it the other way around. One may argue in favour of the shows by stating that the shows are but a reflection of urban living. If such is the argument, then it would be all the more important to point out the manner in which the image of the urban woman is being perpetuated. It is perhaps time to question such formulas and make attempts to change the frame so as to inform consumers that there cannot be a *homogenized ideal of femininity* (Bordo 2003, 166) either in terms of physical disposition or roles.

NOTES

1. *Lalita Ji* wore a blue bordered simple but clean saree with a big *bindi*, matured, and maternal, promoting not just a detergent brand but maternal ideals like thrift, intelligence and care. She became not only the face of a detergent brand called *Surf*, but the face of the ideal married woman who employed thrift and care while taking care of her domestic responsibilities.
2. It's a popular and common Indian dish, mostly in northern India which consists of boiled rice, served with a lentil curry/soup. It's a simple and nutritious dish, a part of everyday food.

REFERENCES

Abu-Jaber, Diana, 2006, *The Language of Baklava: A Memoir*, New York: Penguin Random House.

Appudurai, A., 1988, 'How to Make a National Cuisine: Cookbooks In Contemporary India', *Comparative Studies in Societies and Histories*, Cambridge University Press, 30(1), pp. 14-21.

Beauvoir, S de., 2011, *The Second Sex*. Translated by Constance Borde and Sheila Malovany-Chevallier. London: Vintage Books.

Bordo, S., 2003, *Unbearable Weight: Feminism, Western Culture and the Body*, Berkeley: University of California Press.

Caplan, P.,1997, 'Approaches to the Study of Food, Health and Identity', in P. Caplan (ed.), *Food, Health and Identity*. London: Routledge, pp. 1-31.

Counihan, C., 1999, *The Anthropology of Food and Body*, New York: The Feminist Press.

Das, M., 2007, 'Men and Women in Indian Magazine Advertisements: A Preliminary Report', in R. Ghadially (ed.), *Urban Women in Contemporary India: A Reader*. New Delhi: Sage Publications, pp. 139-51.

Desai, Anita, 1999, *Fasting, Feasting*, London: Chatto and Windus.

Harding, S., 2004, 'Introduction: Standpoint Theory As a Site of Political, Philosophic and Scientific Debate', in S. Harding (ed.), *The Feminist Standpoint Theory Reader: Intellectual and Political Controversies*. New York: Routledge, pp. 1-15.

Lahiri, Jhumpa, 1999, *Interpreter of Maladies: Stories of Bengal, Boston and Beyond*, New York: Harper Collins.

Lupton, D., 1996, *Food, the Body and the Self*, United Kingdom: Sage Publications.

Mohan, K., 2010, 'Learning Consumerist Culture: Indian Middle Class' Experience in the Periphery', in D.K. Singharoy (ed.), *Surviving Against the Odds: The Marginalized in a Globalizing World*. New Delhi: Manohar Publishers & Distributors, pp. 385-410.

Ray, U., 2013, 'The Body and Its Purity: Dietary Politics in Colonial Bengal,' *The Indian Economic and Social History Review*, 50(4), pp. 395-421.

Sreekumar, S., 2011, 'Writing the Culinary in Early 20th Century Malayalam', in S. Chaudhari and R. Chatterjee (eds.), *The Writer's Feast: Food and the Cultures of Representation*. New Delhi: Orient BlackSwan, pp. 63-80.

Thapan, M., 2007, 'Adolescence, Embodiment and Gender Identity: Elite Women in a Changing Society', in R. Ghadially (ed.), *Urban Women in Contemporary India: A Reader*. New Delhi: Sage Publications, pp. 31-44.

Wolf, N., 1990, *The Beauty Myth*, London: Vintage Books.

Wylie, A., 2004, 'Why Standpoint Matters,' in S. Harding (ed.), *The Feminist Standpoint Theory Reader: Intellectual and Political Controversies*, New York: Routledge, pp. 339-51.

TV Shows *in order of appearance*

http://youtu.be/uH1Es3Yjew
https://youtu.be/TI98PYVPoj4
https://youtu.be/LRekfAuSKOc

CHAPTER 17

The Nostalgic Foodie: Food Photography and the Representation of Assamese Cuisine on Social Media

GAURAV RAJKHOWA

INTRODUCTION

Smells, flavours, textures—our most spontaneous associations of food often evoke embodied, sensory pleasure (or in many cases, revulsion). Culinary skill in preparing food is often elevated to an almost mystical art. Such is the intensity of our emotional associations with food that at times particular smells or flavours may evoke specific memories. Its connotations of tradition, community and spontaneous embodied knowledge have also meant that food is often seen as an aspect of one's ethnic culture and identity. Correspondingly, public food culture has become an important site of struggle for the recognition of and respect for, the cultural specificity of ethnic communities.

Yet, despite this spontaneous connotation of food as embodied culture, the virtual world of the internet and social media has today emerged, somewhat surprisingly, as one of the most prominent spaces for the public expression and exchange of culinary culture. Photographs, instructional videos, blogs, restaurant reviews, food tours—the internet has opened up many new ways of experiencing food. One might legitimately argue that alongside food flavour, one must now also talk about food image as an important dimension of our culinary experiences.

The question one wishes to explore in this article may be framed as follows: 'what are the implications of this visual turn in culinary culture for food as an expression of ethnic culture and identity?' To this end, this article has been divided in four sections. In the first section, the trajectory of this article will be framed in more concrete terms by mapping some contemporary debates on the politics of Assamese culinary culture. Thereafter, one will explore in the subsequent sections three modes of existence of food in cyberspace—as signifying image, as intersubjective relation, and as commodity. First, one will discuss some of the salient aspects of the 'foodie aesthetic' to argue that it posits a new relationship in the production and consumption of food images on the social media platforms. Second, one will approach this aesthetic problematic as a paradigmatic reconstitution of ethnic identity as such. One suggests that the new forms of social media interactivity that have emerged around food photography have precipitated a reconstitution of ethnic subjectivity in cyberspace. Finally, one will look at how these photographs are embedded in new forms of monetization of image as code; and are implicated in the transformation of ethnicity into ethno-commodity.

FOOD, NATION, AND ETHNICITY

Arjun Appadurai has shown how the construction of an 'Indian' cuisine went hand in hand with the postcolonial project of nation building. Indeed, as Appadurai has suggested, in India the construction of an Indian cuisine has essentially been a post-industrial, postcolonial process (Appadurai 1988, 5). Like so many other endeavours to create a national culture for postcolonial India, the notion of an Indian cuisine was a gastrocultural enterprise that sought, on the one hand, to give form to a distinctive national identity in the culinary world, unique in its flavours and equalling the best in its sophistication of technique and etiquette. On the other hand, it was an effort to encapsulate the true Indian essence that could be distilled from the mind boggling variety of food cultures that were prevalent across the country. Over a period of time, this has led to many notions about Indian culinary habits becoming naturalized—for instance, that Indian food uses a large variety of spices, or that most Indians are vegetarian. In keeping with the statist project of a developmental-reformist reconstruction of Indian culture, 'Indian cuisine' came to represent a standard of refinement against which all other ethnic and regional cuisines were to be judged. At the same time, these local cuisines became the repository of authenticity and culinary tradition, the basis of the uniqueness of Indian culinary culture.

Over the years, this idea of a national cuisine has overshadowed the emergence of cookbooks of ethnic and regional cuisine. Rooted in the distinctive ingredients, techniques and flavours of regional recipes, these notions of regional cuisine also created a set of generalized gastroethnic images of Bengalis, Tamils and so on (Appadurai 1988, 16). Regional cuisines found themselves caught in a dilemma—between staging their authenticity with all its localized peculiarities, and their refinement that reflected the sophistication of Indian cuisine and thus justified its place in the latter. Moreover, in the jostling of the various local and regional traditions for appreciation and mutual recognition, certain linguistic and regional traditions with greater access to urban resources, institutions, and media have pushed others out of the cosmopolitan view (Appadurai 1988, 18). In her discussion of cookbooks related to Assamese cuisine, Zilkia Janer has shown how it came to be situated within this new hierarchy of national and regional cuisines. In keeping with its historically peripheral place in the imaginary of the Indian nation, it has been quite a marginal feature of so-called 'Indian cuisine'. Assamese cuisine remains outside the image of 'Indian cuisine' and rather finds its place in the more condescending 'cuisines of India' category. It has been patronized as a rustic and primitive cuisine that is derivative of the core ideas of Indian refinement, with regard to methods of preparation, use of spices and choice of ingredients. It has often been represented as a (literally) watered down, simplified version of Indian cuisine—a not-yet-Indian cuisine. Ultimately, as Janer suggests, 'the idea that Assamese cuisine uses few spices comes from the presupposition that other Indian cuisines that use more spices are the desirable norm; difference is transformed into simplicity and simplicity is transformed into primitiveness/inferiority' (Janer). Cookbooks, whether national or regional, uniformly contain positive ethnic stereotypes; but the orally communicated images of the culinary. Other are often less than complimentary (Appadurai 1988, 18). All those from the north-east region living in Indian metros have more than a few anecdotes about the confusion, curiosity, disparagement and humiliation that they have faced trying to find fermented dry fish or bamboo shoot or pork around the city. Some years ago, Delhi Police even notoriously issued an 'advisory' to students from the northeastern states living on rent in the city to avoid cooking 'foul-smelling' foodstuff like axone, bamboo shoot, etc. As such, this is but an institutionalized manifestation of a popular sentiment towards such unfamiliar food and cultural habits.

Having said that, one must concede that in the recent years, there has also been a new interest in ethnic and regional cuisines like Assamese. All the major metros have a number of popular Assamese restaurants with a clientele that extends beyond the expatriate Assamese pining for a taste of home. With increasing numbers travelling to these metros to study or work, it is not impossible to find ingredients like bamboo shoot, bhut jolokia, etc. in select shops. Cuisines from the northeastern region, such as Naga, Manipuri and Assamese, have enmeshed themselves in contemporary restaurant dining culture with a range of offerings that cater to an upmarket clientele as well as those on a tight budget. Many bloggers and reviewers have donned the role of urban ethnic food connoisseurs, giving legitimacy to an unfamiliar cuisine and providing an introduction as well as guidance to people on what to eat (Kakati 2015, 116). It has even been suggested that the upscale restaurant culture in big cities seems to have become a liminal site of encounter (Kakati 2015, 114). In the last two decades or so, ethnic food festivals have also been important sites where such encounters have often taken place. With their characteristic focus on specific ethnic cuisines, they have played a crucial role in foregrounding their uniqueness. In addition to the sale and consumption of the food itself, such festivals often also feature panel discussions, live demonstrations and documentary screenings, all of which provide an opportunity to confront misrepresentations, critique dominant predispositions and elaborate on one's distinctive food cultural practices. Indeed, even as purists bemoan the steady erosion of cultural authenticity before the demands of the market, food festivals and eateries have today come to be recognized as expressions of pride in one's ethnic culture and identity. Alongside handlooms and handicrafts, ethnic food in the metropolis is best understood as a form of what Comaroff and Comaroff have referred to as 'ethno-commodities'. Comaroff and Comaroff argue that, in the last three decades or so, ethnicity has been gradually transformed by two concurrent processes: the commodification of ethnic culture in the form of marketable 'authentic' objects and experiences and the reconfiguration of ethnic groups themselves as fledgling business corporations. As such, the present moment constitutes a shift in how ethnicity comes to be recognized in modernity. Often situated alongside the ideas of nationality, indigeneity and citizenship, the modern nation state has historically been the site of recognition of ethnic identity. The present moment, however, marks a departure in that it is now the market that is becoming the predominant space for the articulation of ethnic identity. Ethnic identity is thus increasingly caught up in the consumerist consumption of ethnic products as a form contemporary self-fashioning and expression. At the same time, ethnocommodities are also different from the mass-produced commodity in that the process of commodification does not deplete their raw material—ethnic identity. Rather, the aura of otherness attaching to these identities is paradoxically restored through replication and mass circulation. This transformation of ethnic food culture into ethnocommodities has received an added impetus with the rising popularity of e-commerce and social media platforms. The former opens up new pathways of circulation and consumption, while the latter accelerates the diffusion and transformation of cultural trends and ideas.

It is even more interesting to note that the ethnic restaurant trend has caught on outside the metros as well. A number of popular restaurants have come up across Guwahati, serving up delicacies from ethnic communities across Assam and other northeastern states. As in Delhi and Bangalore, these restaurants cater to a primarily middle class clientele, ranging from budget restaurants catering to students and young professionals, to more upmarket offerings patronized by business executives and families. Indeed, many of these new food entrepreneurs have themselves spent varying lengths of time in one or another of the major metros as students and/or young professionals, and have experienced firsthand the evolving culinary trends among the middle class in these cities. Many have also returned to set up part time, internet based 'cloud kitchens' as they experiment with turning their love for cooking into a profitable business. The popularity of food delivery apps has also contributed in no small measure to the popularity of such endeavours. Similarly, e-commerce opportunities have created a new market for traditional pickles and seasonal preparations like pithas, courtesy a network of self-help groups and small businesses that have taken up the production of such products. While the better connected ones among them sell online and cater to long-distance orders, most of them sell to local shops and supermarkets.

No doubt, the web of linkages connecting the metropolis to the periphery has become all the more complex and entangled in the present moment. But the opening of such ethnic food enterprises outside the metropolis and catering to a non-metropolitan clientele, is more than simply a variation on the old theme of 'the peripheries catching up with the metropolis'. In the course of this article, it is argued that this moment introduces a new theoretical problematic—this present turn in food culture in places such as Guwahati is an instance of ethnic subjects consuming their *own* culture in the form of ethnocommodities, be it in the form of food, handicrafts, weaves, etc. As such, this represents a curious aspect of the ethnocommodity that is often missed in discussions of cultural appropriation—namely, the 'ability' of the ethnocommodity to ambiguate the distinction between producer and consumer, performer and audience. The ethnocommodity marks a conjuncture where the producers of ethnic goods are also its consumers, seeing and sensing and listening to themselves enact their identity—in the process, objectifying their own subjectivity (Comaroff 2009, 26). Indeed, this work of objectifying one's own subjectivity is always a perilous endeavour, fraught with moments of euphoria and liberation, but also doubt and delusion. The subsequent sections of this article will discuss some of the implications of this transformation of Assamese food culture into culinary ethnocommodity.

THE FOODIE AESTHETIC

To the extent that social media platforms such as Facebook and Instagram tend to be strongly influential, food photography has caught on among users in a big way. With the ubiquity of social media, food photographs, food tours, reviews and recipe videos have become new ways in which we think and talk about food. This exponential increase in food related content has much to do with the easy accessibility of technology. No longer a device dedicated to making phone calls, the smartphone has evolved in the last two decades or so into a fully networked digital device that enables one to one communication as well as access to internet based social media platforms, and a whole range of other digital applications. Alongside these developments, the convergence of digital camera technology with that of the mobile phone has resulted in radical changes in the uses and potential of the device (Chopra-Gant 2016, 121). The affordability of these devices and associated mobile-based internet services, has meant that their use is no longer restricted to the affluent sections of society. For the ordinary user, the social media environment has also increased their exposure to the commercial food photography aesthetic, through advertising images, and the work of professional and 'serious' amateur photographers. With a proliferation of paid as well as free instructional video content, it is relatively easy today to acquire a basic working knowledge of the technical-aesthetic aspects of photography. Finally, the digital format offers the advantage of taking photographs at virtually no additional cost. All of this has led to a rapid dissemination of the conventions and sensibility of professional food photography among amateurs. Coincident with this enormous growth in the popularity of photography has been the development, and increasingly widespread use, of mobile-based applications designed to change the appearance of photographs taken with smartphone cameras (Chopra-Gant 2016, 123). These aesthetic preferences are evident in food photography as well, as users look touch up their photos with a variety of post-processing filters look to emphasize particular colours, tints and saturation levels as they try to achieve the 'right look'.

These post-processing techniques are mobilized in a new 'foodie' aesthetic to produce the photo itself as an object of sensory delight rather than strictly documentary value. Food photographs on social media promise a new sensory experience altogether, premised on the dominance of the visual over the textual, the aural, and the gustatory. The foodie aesthetic is not naturalist, rather characterized by a certain stylized excess. Some of the most recognizable features of this new aesthetic are the emphasis on the food's vibrant colours, with soft lighting and high contrast to foreground the same. Often, the photos feature close ups of the food, providing the viewer an intimate visual–sensory experience of the food itself—the freshness of the ingredients and their richness, juiciness and texture. The vibrancy of the colours is intended to convey a sense of what the food tastes like, but also an evocation of mood and emotion. Often, they are also staged against props and backgrounds that look to emphasize the meanings associated with the food in the frame. This includes, for instance, the use of greenery and vegetable produce to signify freshness, health and abundance. Unique ingredients are presented alongside the prepared dish in a visually striking composition. For instance, an image of a soothing fish *tenga* suitable for a simple lunch on a sweltering summer afternoon might be served in a simple white bowl alongside a fistful of the *dhekia* herbs that constitute one of the seasonal ingredients in the dish. When presenting ethnic or regional preparations, photographers often use as props recognizable cultural artefacts such as traditional wooden or bell metal utensils to signify tradition and heritage, and ethnic cultural markers such as weaving patterns on napkins and table runners.

This foodie aesthetic evokes, through its scintillating visual excess, an ideology of 'good food', where food is simply about great taste. The realm of food becomes taste here as a pleasure of the senses that is fundamentally natural and uncorrupted by the artificial barriers of culture. It stands for an embodied authenticity unmediated by the deceptions of representation and the barriers of cultural difference. This new aesthetic of sensory delight claims to capture in a visual idiom a culinary universal of taste that transcends cultures. Thus ethnic-cultural difference acquires a dual valence within the terms of the foodie aesthetic—on the one hand, it is the multiplicity and uniqueness of food cultures that affirms the universality of taste; while on the other, cultures also seen to set up artificial prejudices and taboos that subvert the universal enjoyment of 'good food'. The foodie aesthetic then becomes one of the modes of representation through which hitherto excluded ethnic identities become visible to a public of gastronomic enthusiasts. Correspondingly, these images now constitute one of the ways in which ethnic food cultures become available for consumption as ethnocommodities.

Assamese cuisine, too, has emerged from its relative obscurity, as a number of food bloggers, home cooks and photographers have taken to popularizing it through regular posting of images that are accompanied by nuggets of information that celebrate the uniqueness of Assamese food culture. In recent years, a number of Instagram handles, such as Assamese cuisine, gitika'spakghar, onmyplatee, geeta_4_u have garnered significant followings. Describing themselves as 'foodies', most of them are not professional chefs, rather seeing their food photography as an extension of their love for food and cooking. Their posts usually—but not exclusively—feature traditional Assamese preparations presented in a contemporary visual aesthetic. Affirming the cultural uniqueness of the region, the posts feature many distinctive ingredients and preparation techniques through which they mark their difference from other Indian cuisines. Others post images of dishes made from locally available seasonal herbs and vegetables. Vibrantly coloured chutneys and mashes are presented in vibrant visual arrangements, while relatively uncommon fermented, smoked, and roasted ingredients are imbued with an exotic significance. For instance, the description on the Facebook page for the popular page, Assamese Cuisine & Recipes, states,

Assamese cuisine places emphasis on lightly-prepared dishes which are rich in taste and flavour. The cuisine is largely driven by local ingredients and seasonal variations. Most Assamese dishes are steamed (bhapot-diya), grilled (pura) or in the form of light stew (anja). Assamese food varies by region due to the ethnic differences among the indigenous inhabitants, traditions and culture.

These posts stage the seamless integration of Assamese cuisine within the foodie aesthetic. However, this is possible to the extent that they represent their cultural specificity as an exotic new experience. Embracing a multiculturalist notion of diversity, social media platforms promise a space that is hospitable towards marginalized food cultures; where cultural difference is not just tolerated but valued and encouraged. At the same time, this affirmation of cultural difference also becomes a condition for recognition as such, whereby an ethnicity must assert its distinctiveness not only from the mainstream but other ethnicities as well. The use of ingredients like bamboo shoot, bhut jolokia is claimed and celebrated as part of one's own culture, even as the prevalence of such practices across various communities in the region is momentarily suspended. The transcendence into the realm of good food thus entails an exoticizing of ethnic cuisines, often through the invocation of existing stereotypes. Indeed, the description of Assamese cuisine quoted above reinforces the dominant cultural stereotypes of Assamese cuisine identified by Janer, but with one important difference—they are now being affirmed as the cultural specificity of Assamese food culture and its formerly 'primitive' simplicity is now rehabilitated as nutritious and ecologically sustainable cooking practices. These disparate concerns about nutrition, ecological diversity and ethnic identity are brought together in interesting new ways. For instance, Geeta Dutta, a Guwahati based doctor and foodie not only runs a popular Assamese food related Instagram handle, but also gives public lectures about the health benefits of indigenous cooking methods and locally available vegetables. Accordingly, Assamese cuisine now also tends to elicit curiosity and appreciation rather than just disgust and condescension.

This inversion imbues Assamese cuisine with an abiding sense of nostalgia, which constitutes the dominant thematic in these visual representations, and imbues them with an affective content. Even as the posts celebrate the simplicity and wholesomeness of Assamese food as a reflection of the robustness of the rustic way of life, they are also keenly aware that this is a world that is fast disappearing. And the images themselves become efforts to recapture that perfect world in the present. In this nostalgic idiom, the family becomes a crucial site where this fleeting image of bygone times can be brought to life. The act of cooking traditional Assamese dishes for one's family becomes a way to keep alive the spirit of that way of life amid the humdrum of modern urban life—it is an experience of authentic being. The family, as a social unit wrought of natural bonds of love and caring, thus comes to stand in for a world that is inevitably slipping away. The family is also evoked as the repository of culinary knowledge and tradition—many posts feature special preparations learned from mothers, grandmothers and mothers-in-law, often accompanied by humorous or poignant anecdotes about these encounters across generations and cultures. Ultimately, the family also becomes the site for the staging of the nationalist imaginary of ethnic harmony and cultural assimilation and festivals offer an excellent opportunity to do the same. Influencers usually post images of home-cooked traditional fare during festivals of various communities. Eid is celebrated with culinary delights from Assamese Muslim homes, Bihu through pithas, and Ali Ai Ligang with a traditional Mising platter. Through food, it becomes possible to evoke the festive atmosphere of festivals without their community specific connotations, and communities come to be represented within this family as nation through their cuisine. As such, this marks a subtle shift, in that the earlier emphasis on visiting others' homes during festivals has given way to celebrating various festivals within the home through food. Similarly, another popular user contextualizes the wide range of influences in her own cooking through her upbringing in Kokrajhar in a close knit locality where she was widely exposed to the culinary tastes of her Bodo, Assamese, Bengali and Nepali neighbours.

Fredric Jameson has argued that such nostalgic constructions of the past in popular culture are not about historical accuracy, witnessing, and memory. Rather as a postmodern aesthetic, this 'nostalgia for the present' draws on de-historicized popular cultural representations of that utopian past (Jameson 2005, 281). In doing so, such nostalgic construction of historical periods is an effort to historicize contemporary social experience. As nostalgic construction of Assamese culinary culture and tradition, these images have become 'a mode of reflection, of self-construction, of producing and feeling cultural authenticity' (Comaroff 2009, 9). A recurrent theme in these images of food inspired nostalgia is the idea of dislocation from home, and its subsequent rediscovery within the space of the single family household. Indeed, many of the influencers discussed above are actually living outside Assam. However, this pervasive sense of dislocation is relevant for us not as a matter of biographical details, but a characteristic trope of this aesthetic of nostalgia. This sense of dislocation is palpable in the form of anxieties that constitute the background against which the nostalgia comes to bear its affective significance. To understand this, one might begin by asking what is the loss that these nostalgic reconstructions are trying to represent.

Historically, the Assamese middle class has been largely semi-feudal and petty official in composition, its rank constituted predominantly from among the caste Hindu social and cultural elites (Gohain 1985, 152-3). Even as they inhabited the modern space of the state, their cultural capital and social authority as traditional social elites remained intact, and the two spaces of power supplemented each other. However, the Assamese middle class of today is quite unlike that of just two decades ago. The integration of Assam into the neoliberal market has brought about increased social mobility, urbanization and a burgeoning professional middle class. Moreover, its social composition is somewhat more diverse and the former dominance of caste Hindu elites has been challenged and undone change in many ways. The ethnic identity movements of the 1980s and 1990s challenged the dominant cultural representations of Assamese identity and the attempt of the Assamese middle class's to establish control over the political-bureaucratic apparatus of state administration in the wake of Assam Movement (1979-85) (Choudhury 2007, 237-83; Deuri 2007, 284-98).

These changes have been a doubtless source of anxiety for entrenched Assamese elites who find their dominance in the middle class under threat. Concurrently, against their predecessors who enjoyed traditional social distinction and authority alongside mobility in modern spaces, they now see themselves as becoming increasingly faceless, indistinguishable because without social distinction. The rediscovery of the ethnic self is a figure of ideological inversion through which this anxiety appears in displaced form. In this light, the sense of dislocation that speaks through the nostalgic mode of the foodie aesthetic seems to articulate the anxieties of this specific section of the Assamese middle class as they are faced with the far-reaching transformations set in motion by the forces of neoliberal capital.

Seen in this light, it becomes clear why it is the pre-Assam movement notion of Assamese culture that provides the visual and narrative elements through which the posts above are able to construct the 'past' that is the object of their nostalgia. This discursive operation of representing the past as nostalgia allows one to refurbish the culturalist discourse of Assamese nationalism, without having to contend with the troubling critiques that challenged the same in the two decades that followed. This ideological manoeuvre becomes invisible behind the new elaboration of family and home as metaphor of the Assamese nation, such that after the challenges of the 1990s, the nation returns as a space of the familiar. The elevation of the family as metaphor of the nation implicitly produces an idea of a non-antagonistic, secure and familiar nation. The ideal of the Assamese middle-class family becomes the metaphor of the nation, the paradigmatic form of imagining collective existence.

Thus, these posts are not idealized snapshots of ethnic food culture, nor do they pretend to be. Not so much documentations of 'traditional cuisine', rather they stage the seamless inclusion of Assamese ethnic identity in the mainstream of a multiculturalist public. The images trace the anxieties that accompany this inclusion, even as they make the social underpinnings of this specific form of gastronomic nostalgia clear.

ENJOY YOUR ETHNICITY!

Having discussed in some detail how the conventions of the foodie aesthetic are mobilized to articulate a nostalgic representation of Assamese cuisine, these images must now be taken up as concrete moments of cultural production and consumption. Social media platforms, as enterprises that depend on user generated content, are deeply invested in making interactivity a key aspect of user experience. They offer the user an unprecedented degree of personalization in the consumption of media content and a space for personal expression. Posts on social media are seen as a spontaneous expression of one's personality and individuality. Users are encouraged to explore one's cultural eccentricities in a quest to 'be yourself'. As networked virtual spaces that claim a sense of community, social media platforms encourage users to give up their apprehensions and share freely with the world, with the promise of finding appreciation and enthusiasm from new, unexpected quarters.

This interactive environment has also led to the popularity of 'influencers' as a new form of social media celebrity. As people who claim expertise in a particular subject, they draw a large number of 'followers', and are able to catalyze new online cultural trends. At the same time, the persona of the social media 'influencer' is somewhat different from that adopted by the expert author of a cookbook. Whereas the expert chef offers authentic culinary knowledge, the influencer also promises an interaction with a personality behind the food. Most draw their popularity from the interactive relationship with their 'followers'. Influencers promoting Assamese cuisine talk about food practices with some degree of authority on the subject, even as they share with their 'followers' snippets of their everyday life—personal family photos, weekend trips, and musings on subjects unrelated to food. One's ethnic identity also becomes part of this seemingly unrehearsed persona. On the one hand, it stands as the ultimate proof of their unrehearsed authenticity, as someone who lives the particular ethnic food experience that they post about; while on the other, the food itself comes to acquire a dual signification—not just 'good food', it now becomes food that affirms the person's culture and identity.

This new dimension of interactive celebrity has had an effect on how influencers perform their Assamese identity. First, in their role as experts, they provide information about the food in the accompanying photograph, with details about ingredients and cooking methods involved. Often, these posts are bilingual, being targeted to Assamese and English language users. Many influencers do not restrict themselves to such descriptive or explanatory texts about the food itself. Users like geeta_4u and oneteaspoonof not only post images but also their extended musings alongside, with the intention conveying the emotional significance of the particular food for the person posting the image. Often, this is indelibly tied up with the more mundane aspects of the present—a particular turn of the weather (hot, cold, rainy), the availability of certain seasonal vegetables, or simply one's mood. The association of these aspects of the everyday with specific foods and flavours peculiarly permeates these moments with a vividly embodied sense of nostalgic presence. Often, photos of seasonal fruits, berries, melons, etc. are posted with long reveries that evoke childhood memories of enjoying them on lazy winter afternoons and in the mid-morning swelter of the monsoons. Through these associations, Assamese cuisine is mapped through the body, in the form of the sensory pleasure of flavour and the deeper rhythms of mood, emotional state and physical environment. Thus, even as these posts draw upon an already established repertoire of conventionalized representations, they are encoded here through the register of a deeply embodied sense of Assamese-ness. Even as the childhood experience of enjoying robab tenga in the sun on a winter afternoon is considered quintessentially Assamese, it exists as an embodied memory of a sensory experience of taste.

Thus, it is evident that the new forms of social media interactivity, exemplified by the influencer persona, have given a new inflection to the most abiding tropes of the culturalist discourse of Assamese nationalism. That being said, interactivity on social media is characterized by a fundamental asymmetry. While on the one hand, the influencer is involved in regularly generating new food related content, most people do not actually post on social media. Rather, users participate 'interactively' in this celebration of ethnic food and cultural identity through structured forms of interactivity such as liking, sharing and commenting on posts. Social media users 'like' posts as they scroll through an endless succession of posts on their feeds in a distracted manner. Engaging the user for no more than a few seconds, these images (and their accompanying text) are not seen as objects of extended aesthetic contemplation. Here, users encounter food-related images posted by the influencers they follow as part of this endless succession of posts. Followers interact with the foodie influencers' posts, featuring immaculate photography and elaborate musings, usually by just clicking the 'like', aside from a few innocuous comments about how delicious the food looks and half-serious requests for recipes.

Alongside the foodie images, one also comes across occasional food related posts by friends, say from a restaurant they might have recently visited or something they have cooked at home. Often, these images bear none of the niceties of the foodie aesthetic—the stylized props, or the suggestive lighting and decor, or the subtleties of plating. One is liable to find photos shot in poor lighting, sometimes with the beaming cook beside their creation dressed in a faded T-shirt and pyjamas. On occasion, one might come across blurry images from a fast food stall during an outing of a group of friends, or the same group busy at work cooking up a sumptuous dinner in someone's kitchen. Even as they photograph the same dish, there is a notable difference in that unlike the influencer's post that emphasize an individual, embodied experience of food, these images rather look to capture the effervescence of the moment when a group of friends or relatives come together to enjoy a meal. Indeed, it is through the unrehearsed spontaneity and disregard for the conventions of the foodie aesthetic that these images represent the authentic 'good times' that everyone is ostensibly partaking in. It is curious to note that while the influencers' posts mostly draw likes, posts with similar content by a friend receive enthusiastic comments. While these photographs might not be quite as appealing visually, they nevertheless attract comments expressing effusive reactions, jokingly asking to be invited at the next such gathering of friends.

This contrast is symptomatic of how the followers' 'like' is not a transparent gesture that reflects the influencer's message in the form of approval or disapproval. Rather, the gesture of 'liking' an influencer's post may also have a distracted, ritualistic dimension to it—it is more an expression of convention than of enthusiasm. One might even argue that the stylized excess of the influencers' posts actually has the effect of a waning rather than intensification of enthusiasm. How do we understand this seemingly paradoxical effect and what does this mean for our reading of the aesthetic of nostalgia in the posts of Assamese food influencers? In other words, what is the cultural significance of this lukewarm enthusiasm for the new idiom of nationalist nostalgia?

As a counterpoint to the valorization of social media interactivity, Slavoj Žižek has suggested that the experience of cyberspace may be understood instead as a form of 'interpassivity'. A concept initially developed by Robert Pfaller and Žižek in an effort to understand interactive artworks, it has since been extended to theorize the many forms of interactivity that shape digital culture. In his critique of contemporary aesthetics, Pfaller (quoted in Jagodzinski 2018, 271) suggests that many artworks today are 'self-fulfilling' and require no interaction from the viewer—the artwork takes away performative necessity or effort by its onlookers. Such artworks are thus said to relieve the spectator of the burden of interactivity. Žižek articulates the term within a Lacanian framework to designate an essential feature of subjectivity, namely to 'enjoy through the other' (Žižek 1997 113). According to Žižek, enjoyment itself is not an immediate, spontaneous state but is sustained by a superego-imperative—the injunction to 'Enjoy!' (Žižek). Distinguishing between the order of the public symbolic Law and the superego, Žižek states, 'The public Law "between the lines" silently tolerates, incites even, what its explicit text prohibits, while the superego injunction that ordains *jouissance*, through the very directness of its order, hinders the subject's access to it much more effectively than any prohibition' (Žižek). Interpassivity, as enjoying through the other, allows the subjects to relieve themselves of the superego injunction to enjoy, of the burden of passivity. Thus, such delegation simultaneously acts as a 'defence mechanism' against the demands of the symbolic order (Žižek 1997, 115).

This act of delegation to the 'subject supposed to enjoy' takes place in a wide range of cultural practices—from canned laughter in television sitcoms, to the opera, to Tibetan prayer wheels. On social media, the 'like' may be said to function as the virtual equivalent of the Tibetan prayer wheel. The seamless inclusion of Assamese identity in the new multiculturalist public evinces an ambivalent response from the subject. For even as this new multiculturalism celebrates inclusiveness and ethnic diversity, this also operates as a more sinister superego-injunction to 'enjoy your ethnicity!' One is encouraged to share their unique culture with others, but at the same time one can only become part of this symbolic public on the condition that they perform their ethnicity in ways that are amenable to consumption as cultural commodities. In the influencers' posts, the nostalgic excess that renders these images as authentic is also the trace of its artifice. Thus, even as these images interpellate the subject within a new symbolic register of Assamese nationalism, their staged artifice also prompts the question, 'if Assamese cuisine is indeed rustic, why does it need to be staged as rustic?' This impasse comes to be resolved through the figure of the influencer who relishes the flavours of Assamese cuisine and reminisces about good times. The influencer occupies the position of the subject supposed to enjoy to whom the viewer may delegate superego-injunction to 'enjoy your ethnicity'; and it is the gesture of the 'like' that instantiates this interpassive relation. The 'like' as a gesture of subscribing to the nostalgic content of the image is thus rather an attempt to find respite from the insistent demands of the new symbolic regime of neoliberal multiculturalism. By participating in the ritualized act of liking Assamese foodie influencers' photos, the subjects frees themselves to indulge in the pleasure of reacting enthusiastically to their friends' food photographs.

Thus, the demands of the symbolic order produce an ethnic subject that is constitutively split and mediated, with the interpassive subject of the foodie aesthetic on the one hand and the real 'authentic' subject of spontaneous enjoyment on the other. It is important to note here that the hermeneutics of the Assamese nation is not altogether new. At various times, the social has been imagined as split along ethnic or class lines, between town and country and between the elite and the popular. In the present moment, these antagonisms within the social body of Assamese nation are telescoped into the subject, who comes to embody both terms in these binaries. The foodie aesthetic comes to be signified as sophisticated, elite and middle class and entails an interpassive relation; while the friends' photographs become the rustic/popular where one can be their 'true self' without middle class artifice or pretence.

This split subject is as precarious as it is complex, for even as it embodies both halves of this split subject, they must nevertheless be kept apart. This shows up in curious ways—for instance, in the workings of various virtual communities that have come together around people's shared interest in food. With the growing popularity of food photography, a number of online groups have come up as spaces where foodies may share photos and ideas to indulge their shared love of good food. Guwahati Foodies is one such popular group that announces itself as a space for like-minded people to share their love of food in various ways—recipes, photographs, restaurant reviews, convenient do-it-yourself hacks, and hidden eateries around town. The group was intended to bring together in a single space the culinary knowledge of the 'experts' and crowd sourced information about recipes, restaurants, etc. Regular contributors included not just food writers and critics, but also amateur cooks and food enthusiasts, making the group an inclusive space where not just the experts could talk about food. Participation in the group entailed two caveats. First, the group administrators are quite strict regarding proper attribution of credit for photographs, and warn users against posting restaurant dishes as their own. Second, the group claims a strict 'no politics' policy, whereby discussion on 'political issues' is restricted, with the exception of social activities like blood donation camps and food related charitable initiatives.

For many, the group was an opportunity to show off their culinary skills, but also their experiments in the foodie aesthetic. As expected, such images drew wide appreciation among group members. Buoyed by the enthusiasm many self-confessed novices also posted images of their first attempts at new dishes. On that occasion, they did not turn out very well and may not have made for the most appetizing images. Nevertheless, they marked a gesture of sharing their efforts with fellow food enthusiasts. Such posts soon became subjected to intense trolling and abuse. The food was disparaged, the presentation scoffed at and many bemoaned the appalling culinary taste of someone who could deem such images as worthy of the attentions of self avowed foodies. Eventually, the group administrators had to intervene with a warning and a reiteration of the group's objective of being a hospitable space for all food lovers. Things eventually cooled off but the group also saw a drop in overall user participation and interaction.

This adverse reaction, is symptomatic of the split within the subject, discussed above. Where the food image is an ideological support for the interpassive subject, the virtual community of 'likeminded people' effectively functions as a space for the concentration of such images. Each image posted in the group affords one an opportunity to once again enjoy through the other and the group itself becomes a regular source of images that offer such ritualized moments of relief from the 'burden' of enjoyment. As the above controversy made amply clear, this interpassive relation is sustained by maintaining a strict separation between the foodie aesthetic and the rest. Against the temptation to regard such groups as anticipatory forms of virtual democracy, it is argued that their popularity in the present moment rather points towards the limits of neoliberal multiculturalism as hegemonic ideology. The new forms of interactivity that shape the social media experience are closely implicated in the ongoing reconstitution of the ethnic subject.

BETWEEN IMAGE AND CODE

Jonathan Beller has sought to remind us that in the time of computational capital the digital image is no longer just a visual text to be interpreted for its meaning. It is as much digital data that is subject to manipulation as code. Image and code, semiotics and political economy, are inextricably tied together (Beller) in the images of food that one views, post, and like on social media every day. A 'like' on a nostalgic post about eating robab tenga outdoors on sunny winter afternoons no doubt, entails an act of ideological identification. But it also activates similar posts from friends (or friends' friends), as well as sponsored ads about bhut jolokia sauce, Schezwan peppercorns and amla based health supplements that begin to pop up on one's feed. The food image appears to the subject as interpassive relation, even as it circulates objectively as commodity.

The foodie aesthetic has an important part to play in turning ethnic food practices into commodified cuisines. Food images have been instrumental in popularizing particular dishes as representative of particular ethnic cuisines. The like, share and hashtag have subsequently carried these typical representations far and wide. The new found enthusiasm for ethnic cuisines has also meant that some of the unique ingredients of these iconic dishes have also found their way into people's kitchens, aided in no small measure by automated algorithms that bring together foodie images, food reviews and recipes seamlessly with vendors for the ingredients on e-commerce websites. The ubiquity of the foodie aesthetic is symptomatic of another sort of convergence and integration that is taking place, not just across digital platforms but also among different businesses—the foodie aesthetic is today shared by influencers, restaurants, rural eco-tourism homestays, adventure tourism operators and organic food brands.

Influencers are also invested in this commodification of ethnic culture in various ways. Some use their social media handles to promote their home kitchen/satellite kitchen businesses that offer customers a selection of dishes on a pre-order basis. Another common trend among influencers is the promotion and endorsement of new organic food brands. Indeed, 'organic food' has been a buzzword in urban middle class households for some time now. Growing public knowledge about the overuse of pesticides and ripening agents has fuelled a deepening scepticism towards the nutritional value of not just processed 'junk' food but 'fresh' vegetable and meat produce as well, to say nothing of their long-term effects on health and disease risk. Ostensibly, 'organic' is taken to mean non-GM vegetables and grain grown without the use of artificial chemical fertilizers and pesticides, but for all but the keenest eye, it would be difficult to discern the organic from the non-organic. Rather, it is the supplement of 'culture' that affords the organic product an aura of authenticity. This usually takes the form of either ethnic identification (for instance, Naga King Chilli) or geographical indicators (such as GI-tagged Karbi Anglong ginger).

Organic produce is seen as a more wholesome alternative and not just for the nutritional value of the foods themselves. The relationship of buying and selling organic products somehow comes to be seen to be one of trust and built on a spirit of non-exploitative fair exchange. It evokes a notion of community. A cue is offered up by a sort of image particularly popular among foodies. Users often post images of produce purchased from sellers along highways and in local *haat* markets. The descriptions accompanying the photos invariably mention the produce on sale as being either from the sellers' own gardens or wild herbs, tubers and fruits that have been collected from the forest. This implicitly becomes a guarantee for the freshness of the produce and an assurance of their 'organic' origins. They also make sure to remark that these are not commodities sold for profit but merely a way to make a few extra rupees for an impoverished household. The fresh produce here emerges as a curious amalgam—it is not a product that is being grown and sold for profit, but can nevertheless be bought like any other commodity. Correspondingly, the sellers who appear in these images come to be represented as good, simple, honest rural folk who have not been subsumed within the logic of capital and the temptations of profit-making.

In such instances, nostalgia and nationalism go hand in hand. No doubt, the Assamese middle class subject carries their rustic culture deep within themselves in the form of nostalgia yearning, it nevertheless becomes possible to access this only through the availability of the right ingredients, which are not usually available in vegetable markets in the city. The Assamese subject's own nostalgic sojourn to the past is made possible through the trace of that past in the living present—here, the body of the seller and the rustic rural existence that body signifies. The highway transports the foodie not just across space but also time. And the car trunk full of fresh, 'organic' vegetables allows them to take a souvenir of that world back with them into the here and now of their citybound existence. The foodie subject is able to keep alive their culinary traditions through the guarantee of authenticity signified by the rustic seller.

It is important to note that even as the tropes of rustic Assamese culture are here revived, the site of its elaboration is no longer the state but the market. The imaginary of the Assamese nation is no longer a utopian form of political existence but as a community of buyers and sellers. Indeed, as Comaroff and Comaroff have observed, ethnic groups, which were defined earlier through political classification, are beginning to perceive themselves increasingly also as natural economic groups (2009, 45). An important idea in the political debates in the 1990s that symbolized an alternative to the imperialist exploitation of Assam's people and resources by the Indian ruling class, the notion of indigenous political economy has periodically resurfaced in public discourse in the last few years. Articulating the contours of the ongoing neoliberal transformation of rural Assam, it now coalesces popular sentiment about unremunerative agricultural prices, the migration of Assamese youth to industrial centres outside Assam in search of work, and the workings of syndicates and cartels that control the procurements and pricing of local rural produce, including foodgrains, vegetables, livestock. and fish. The popular discourse of indigenous political economy is an inchoate, often conflicting articulation of contemporary anxieties about the new forms of economic exploitation, ecological degradation and ethnic conflict that have accompanied the neoliberal reconstitution of all aspects of social life.

But, within the terms of the foodie aesthetic, the notion of indigenous political economy is invoked through a curious ideological displacement—the seller beside the highway appears not as a subject of neoliberal capitalist development but as a representation of a simple, traditional, subsistence bound existence. The emerging relation between the metropolis and the countryside is here represented as an encounter between the modern and the pre-modern. And the many forms of conflict that have come to shape this relation mingle within the diffuse sense of nostalgia—they become part of the nameless, noble struggles of the rustic peasant who upholds the traditional Assamese way of life in the face of the relentless march of modernity. This nostalgic fantasy then takes concrete form, as the relation between this authentic subject who lives the rustic life and the subject who yearns nostalgically for it is secured through the exchange of money and commodity.

Unsurprisingly, the staging of this fantasy is no longer restricted to the highway-side or the rural *haats*. It now plays out in urban marketplace as well, in the form of a niche market for 'organic produce' that caters to a relatively upmarket clientele. A number of entrepreneurs have jumped in on the organic produce boom, procuring fresh produce and traditional varieties of rice to sell the same to urban middle-class customers. Ethnic food restaurants in Guwahati have started stocking products like rice, bamboo shoot, bhoot jolokia pickle and powder. Alternatively, there has also been a growth in the number of smaller internet and mobile-based enterprises that provide home delivery of 'farm-fresh produce'. These products are marketed as 'indigenous produce by indigenous farmers', as the rustic peasant authenticates the 'organic' produce and becomes the measure of its value as it enters a marketplace alongside other food commodities. The farmer is able to enter this niche market to the extent that he (or even better, she) can adequately perform their cultural primitiveness.

This has opened up opportunities for a small number of farmers, especially those with enough capital to invest in food processing equipment to produce products such as packaged rice, oven-dried chillies and pickles. This has become a part of state policy as well, with various schemes for self-help groups and farmer producer organizations to provide financial support and skills training for such initiatives for the processing and marketing of local varieties of fruits, spices, rice, etc. The cultural representation of the rustic indigenous peasant—in which the foodie aesthetic is complicit—is thus inextricably linked to the neoliberal transformation of rural political-economy and social relations in Assam today. On the one hand, the small farmer in an emerging neoliberal context is fetishised as a rustic embodiment of authentic Assamese culture; while on the other, this representation itself becomes a key element in the new niche market for 'organic' produce and the neoliberal reconstitution of agriculture that has sought to meet this demand.

CONCLUSION

In the course of this article, one has looked at how food images on social media come to be implicated in the consumption of ethnocommodities by ethnic subjects themselves. The conventions of the foodie aesthetic have enabled a recuperation of the dominant cultural stereotypes about Assamese cuisine, returning this time as positive affirmations of ethnic identity. The recent popularity of these representations of Assamese culinary culture is closely related to the social media platforms emerging as spaces committed to a neoliberal multiculturalist rhetoric of diversity and inclusion. However, these platforms have proved to be hospitable to marginalized identities to the extent that their marginality may be fetishized as diversity and the food cultures of ethnic communities may be commoditized as 'ethnic cuisine'.

Nostalgia emerges as the dominant mode in which Assamese cuisine comes to be represented within the foodie aesthetic. Drawing on a repository of dehistoricized cultural meanings and representations, these images attest to the apparent wholesomeness and rusticity of Assamese cuisine. In the process, Assamese culinary practices simultaneously inhabit the modern present as well as the traditional past—its unpretentious simplicity attests to its origins in a rural, agrarian way of life, even as its emphasis on fresh, nutritious ingredients renders it suitable as an alternative to unhealthy modern cooking practices. At the same time, this nostalgia for the present articulates a specifically middle class social experience. The thematic of dislocation that dominates these expressions of nostalgia, one argues, may be traced to the deep anxieties about the social distinction and status for entrenched middle class Assamese elite. Further, the privileging of the family as metaphor of the nation is but an idealized representation that seeks to disavow the contradictions and contestations that have shaped the historical elaboration of the Assamese nation as a form of political existence.

The production, consumption and dissemination of these images is embedded in the new forms of interactivity that constitute the social media experience. This has, in turn, precipitated new ways in which subjects relate to food images—both as influencers producing such images, and as 'followers' consuming such content. Against the tendency to interpret the recent visibility of ethnic cuisines as a resurgence of ethnic identity, I argue that the representations of Assamese cuisine on social media platforms have set in motion a reconstitution of ethnic identity, as the Assamese subject comes to terms with the new symbolic demands of the regime of neoliberal multiculturalism.

Finally, one saw that this representation of Assamese cuisine as simple, wholesome and rustic has also made possible its monetization as 'organic' food produce. Nostalgia establishes not only a symbolic connection between past and present, but also a material economic relation between the urban middle class and the rural countryside. In more ways than one, the foodie aesthetic is implicated in the subsumption of ethnic identity as ethno-capital. These changes in the representation of Assamese food culture are symptomatic of a broader shift in the cultural, political, and economic terrain upon which the Assamese subject is constituted. They are indicative of the reconstitution of ethnicity in the time of flexible accumulation.

REFERENCES

Appadurai, Arjun, 1988, 'How to Make a National Cuisine: Cookbooks in Contemporary India' *Comparative Studies in History and Society*, 30(1), pp. 3-24.

Beller, Jonathan, 2016, 'Informatic Labor in the Age of Computational Capital', *Lateral*, 5(1), http://csalateral.org/wp/issue/5-1/informatic-laborcomputational-capitalbeller/.

Chopra-Gant, Mike, 2016, 'Pictures or It Didn't Happen: Photo-nostalgia, iPhoneography and the Representation of Everyday Life'. *Photography and Culture*, 9(2), pp. 121-33.

Choudhury, Medini, 2007, 'Asom Andolan aru Janagosthigata Samay', in *Asom Andolan: Pratisruti aru Phalasruti*, (eds.), Hiren Gohain and Dilip Bora, Guwahati: Banalata, pp. 237-83.

Comaroff, Jean and John Comaroff, 2009, *Ethnicity, Inc.* Chicago: University of Chicago Press.

Deuri, Indibor, 2007, 'Asom Andolan aru Jangosthiya Prosno', in *Asom Andolan: Pratisruti aru Phalasruti*, ed. Hiren Gohain and Dilip Bora. Guwahati: Banalata, pp. 284-98.

Gohain, Hiren, 1985, *Assam: A Burning Question*. Guwahati: Spectrum Publications.

Jagodzinski, Jan, 2018, 'Interrogating Interpassivity', *Continental Thought and Theory*, 2(1), pp. 270-97.

Jameson, Fredric, 2005, *Postmodernism or, the Cultural Logic of Late Capitalism*. Durham NC: Duke University Press.

Kakati, Aditya Kiran, 2015, 'For the Love of Pork', in *Odysseys of Plates and Palates: Food, Society and Sociality*, (ed.), Simeon S. Magliveras and Catherine Gatlin. Oxford: Inter-disciplinary Press, pp. 113-25.

Zilkia, Janer, 2012, 'Assamese Food and the Politics of Taste', Seminar 640, December, https://www.india-seminar.com/2012/640/640_zilkia_janer.htm.

Žižek, Slavoj, 1997, *Plague of Fantasies*. London: Verso.

——, 1998, 'The Interpassive Subject', *Traverses*, https://www.lacan.com/zizek-pompidou.htm.

Contributors

SARIT K. CHAUDHURI was the Founder Head, Department of Anthropology, Rajiv Gandhi University (RGU), Rono Hills, Arunachal Pradesh. Currently working as the Dean, FSS. He was the former Director of Indira Gandhi Rashtriya Manav Sangrahalaya, Bhopal (under MoC, Government of India). He had a postdoctoral fellowship in SOAS, University of London, while working on a five-year collaborative project between British Museum, SOAS and Rajiv Gandhi University. He has published over 30 books and 62 papers across various journals and books. His prime research engagements are with the issues concerning indigenous religion, art, identity, cultural heritage, dynamics of India's North East borderlands, and ethnographic museums.

DEBARSHI PRASAD NATH engages in teaching, research, and his outreach is spread over translation, culture, films, media, literature, and cultural theory. He has published eight books so far, and articles in various reputed journals such as *Economic and Political Weekly*, *Comparative Literature and Culture* (Purdue University), *Critical Arts: South-North Cultural and Media Studies*, and *Ethnicities*. He was one of the editors/translators of the volume titled, *The Call of the Pherengadao: Translation of Select Writings of Bishnuprasad Rava*, the English translation of the writings of one of the most revered cultural icons of Assam. He was the course coordinator of an online course (ePG-*pathshala* on 'Comparative Literature and Culture') as part of a general programme on comparative literature. He has co-edited a book published in 2023 with academics from the University of Auckland, New Zealand, titled, *Reflections of Dance along the Brahmaputra: Celebrating Dance in North East India*. He headed a partnership with UNICEF, India, to work on the empowerment of adolescents using folklone as a medium of communication, primarily focussing on folk music and dance.

DHURJJATI SARMA is an Assistant Professor in the Department of Modern Indian Languages and Literary Studies, Gauhati University, Assam. Previously, he was a Production Editor at SAGE Publications, New Delhi, and before that, a Research Fellow in North East India Studies at the Indira Gandhi National Centre for the Arts (IGNCA), New Delhi. He is presently engaged in studying the early and modern literatures of Assamese, Bengali, Hindi, and Urdu from a comparative-cultural perspective. As a student and teacher of comparative literature, he is also trying to develop new insights and perspectives on the composite area of comparative literary history. His writings have been published by various reputed publishing houses, and in journals such as *English Forum*, *Rupkatha Journal*, *Dibrugarh University Journal of English Studies* (DUJES), *Space and Culture India*, and *Margins: A Journal of Literature and Culture*. Currently, he is working on a critical history of Assamese literature.

ANASUYA SREEDHAR is a research scholar who works in the area of food, women's work, and gender. She has completed her MPhil and PhD in women's and gender studies from Ambedkar University, Delhi. Anchored within the domain of women and work, within a theoretical framework of gender, and guided by feminist epistemology, her PhD thesis explored the culinary terrain of women chefs in India's industrial kitchens, from the 90s to the present. She is curious about tracing and navigating through the myriad linkages that exist between food and women's lives, which intersect at many junctions such as caste, class, and gender. She is also a food writer having contributed for several years to an magazine published in Netherlands.

BIJAY K. DANTA is a Professor in the Department of English, Tezpur University. He has a PhD on 'Frames for Reading Meta-fiction: The Example of Kurt Vonnegut' from Utkal University, Odisha. He has also taught at Dibrugarh University. His present research interests, include postcolonial self-fashioning in life and travel writing in Indian and American contexts. He writes in English and translates from Assamese and Odia into English.

CAITLYN D. PLACEK is a biocultural medical anthropologist, global health scholar, and program evaluator specializing in mixed methods research that tests biological and cultural theories of psychoactive substance use and eating behaviours. She earned a PhD in Anthropology from Washington State University in 2016, and served as a postdoctoral research fellow in Epidemiology with the Global Health Equity Scholars program (2016-17), a consortium sponsored by the National Institutes of Health and Fogarty International Center, where she led a year-long collaborative study on substance use among reproductive aged women in India. She is now an Associate Professor of Biological and Medical Anthropology at Ball State University. Her current research investigates how cultural models impact drug use and indicators of health, treatment, and recovery among women in a cross-cultural setting. In her applied work, she relies on a multi-scalar, social-ecological approach to underst and women's challenges in receiving drug treatment during pregnancy and the postpartum period, and applies knowledge of these challenges to improve program outcomes. In addition, she has worked on numerous projects in India with collaborative teams that focus on substance use, the food-medicine-drug continuum, health, and community education.

CHANDAMITA GOSWAMI has an MA in Anthropology and MPhil on Folklore from Gauhati University, Assam. She is currently doing research on the physical folklife, and the impact of modernization on the Garos of South Kamrupa tribal belt of Assam. Shehas attended and presented several research papers in national seminars organised under UGC and ICHR.

CHARISMA K. LEPCHA teaches anthropology in Sikkim University, Gangtok. Her research interests include religion, ethnicity, identity, indigeneity, environment, material culture and visual anthropology of Sikkim and Darjeeling Himalaya. She has published numerous articles and co-edited two books, *The Cultural Heritage of Sikkim* (2019) and *Communities, Institutions and Histories of India's Northeast* (2022). She was a Fellow at the Indian Institute of Advanced Studies (IIAS), Shimla (2018-19), and a Visiting Scholar at the Harvard-Yenching Institute, Harvard University, Cambridge, Massachusetts.

GAURAV RAJKHOWA is an independent cultural studies researcher based in Guwahati, Assam. His doctoral research was on Bhupen Hazarika and the cultural politics of Assamese nationalism, where he sought to bring together his interests in cultural policy, popular culture, ethnic identity, and populism and democracy. Subsequently, as a postdoctoral research fellow in the Departmentof Cultural Studies, Tezpur University, Assam he was involved in the archiving of folk and popular music practices in Assam. His articles have been published in peer-reviewed journals, including the *Economic and Political Weekly* and *Bio Scope: South Asian Screen Studies*.

HASHIK N.K. is an Assistant Professor in the Department of Cultural Studies, Tezpur University, Assam. His research interests are cultural theory, community studies, media and communication, and performance studies.

JAYANTA SENGUPTA is the former Director of Victoria Memorial Hall, Kolkata. He also served as Director-in-Charge of the Indian Museum, Kolkata, and of the Anthropological Survey of India. Educated at Presidency College, Kolkata, and at the Universities of Calcutta and Cambridge, he taught History at Jadavpur University, Kolkata, and the University of Notre Dame, Indiana, previously. His current research focuses on cultural practices in modern India, and transnational and comparative intellectual history. He is the author of four books, including *At the Margins: Discourses of Development, Democracy and Regionalism in Orissa* (2015), and *Those Noble Edifices: The Raj Bhavans of Bengal* (2019). His latest book, in Bengali, is on the culture and politics of food and eating in Bengal, titled *Hensheldarpan: Bangalir Hanrir Khobor* ['Through the Kitchen's Looking Glass: The Alimentary Aspects of Bengal's History'] (2023).

KANCHAN MUKHOPADHYAY has worked for the Anthropological Survey of India for more than three decades. Areas of his research interest include construction and maintenance of identity among migrants and refugees, relationship between small communities and nation-state, impact of exogenous changes on small-scale communities, methodological and ethical issues in social science research, visual anthropology, and anthropology of food. He has some publications on the above-mentioned subjects. He was Tagore National Fellow from 2019 to 2021 and has worked on the society and foodways in Rarh Bengal.

MIHIR RANJAN BHATTACHARYA joined Department of English, Jadavpur University in 1965, and did research work at University College, Cambridge, between 1971 and 1975. He was founder-professor of Department of Film Studies, Jadavpur University after 1991. He retired from Jadavpur University in 2002. He has published articles and papers in the areas of seventeenth century English Literature, Bengali fiction, narrative theory, film and television studies, mass communication, cultural studies, and folklore both in English and Bengali. He has edited three scholarly anthologies, including *Lokasruti Prabandha Sankalan* (1999) and *Bangiya Shilpa Parichay* (2004), and has produced various documentary videos.

SRAVANI BISWAS is currently teaching at Tezpur University, Assam as Professor in the Department of English. Her area of interest has been in Indian Literature in English, British romantic literature and critical theory. She has published a monograph on R.K. Narayan where she uses Bakhtin's theory of carnival to interpret the Malgudi novels. She has several papers published in journals including RMMLA Review of the US. Currently, she is working on partition and migration narratives of eastern India. She is interested in creative writing and translation and is translating Atin Bandyopadhyay's *Nilkontho Pakhir Khonje* into English

SUCHETA SEN CHAUDHURI is an Associate Professor in the Department of Anthropology and Tribal Studies, Central University of Jharkhand, Ranchi, and presently, the Head of the Department and Dean School for the Study of Culture. She was also faculty member in the Centre for Indigenous Culture Studies at CUJ, and Arunachal Institute of Tribal Studies, RGU. She was the founder Director of the Women Studies Research Centre, RGU. She has published monographs and jointly edited books. Her areas of interest are women's participation in social movements, relationship between gender and work, indigenous knowledge systems.

SUKALPA BHATTACHARJEE teaches English at North-Eastern Hill University, Shillong. Her major publications include *Human Rights and Insurgency: The North-East India, Ethno-Narratives: Identity and Experience in NE-India, Postcolonial Literature: Essays on Gender, Theory and Genres* and *Society, Representations and Textuality: The Critical Interface*. Her review articles and research papers have been published in national and international journals and anthologies in the areas of critical theory, gender studies and translation. She has also written popular articles in newspapers such as *The Statesman, The Eastern Chronicle,*and in *The Shillong Times* on gender issues.

SURANJANA BARUA is an Associate Professor of Linguistics at the Department of Humanities and Social Sciences, Indian Institute of Information Technology, Guwahati, Assam. She is a member of the Editorial Committee for the journal *Language and Language Teaching*; an accredited Language Specialist and Aviation English Trainer under the Airports Authority of India (AAI), Ministry of Civil Aviation, Government of India, and has served as a language consultant for many organizations across India.She has published research articles and chapters in various research journals and books; and has translated into English important works of key literary figures of Assam, such as Rajanikanta Bordoloi, Bishnu Prasad Rabha, Chandraprabha Saikiani, Bhupen Hazarika, Arun Sarma and Golap Khound. Sociolinguistics (Discourse/Conversation Analysis), English language teaching, translation studies, gender studies and the socio-cultural history of Assam are her current areas of academic interest. Her latest translation into English is a collection of Assamese short stories by Golap Khound titled, *Girmit* (2023) and her recent published book is titled *Revelation of Self in Language: Narrative Identity as Emergent in Conversation* (2023).

SWIKRITA DOWERAH is an Assistant Professor in the Department of Journalism and Mass Communication at Manipal University Jaipur (MUJ). She completed her Ph.D. from the Department of Cultural Studies at Tezpur University, Assam. Her doctoral thesis focused on tracing the changing phases of Indian nationalism by analyzing war themed films. She has contributed to the field of academia through her publications in esteemed Q1 and Q2 Scopus-indexed journals. Some of the journals she has published in include, *Feminist Media Studies, Studies in South Asian Film and Media, Quarterly Review of Film and Video, Asian Cinema, Journal of Creative Communications*, and *Media Asia*. In addition to her publications, she also serves as a reviewer for reputed Scopus-indexed journals such as *Women's Studies in Communication, Feminist Media Studies*, and *Kritika Kultura*, among others. Her research interests primarily revolve around visual culture, film studies, and media and memory studies. Further information regarding her research work is available at https://orcid.org/0000-0003-2136-9934.

UTTAM LAL is a faculty in the Department of Geography, Sikkim University, Gangtok. Having acquired his doctorate from JNU, New Delhi, while working on Environmental Constraints in the Western Himalaya, he joined Sikkim University as a founding member of the Department of Geography. He headed the Department from 2015-18, and in 2022. He was also the Nodal Person from Sikkim University in the Inter-University Consortium on Cryosphere and Climate Change (IUCCCC). This consortium studied the Himalayan Cryosphere and its effects on society, their adaptive measures. He led the team of Sikkim University. His area of academic interest covers the Himalayan ecology, highland social-economic dynamics, rangeland studies, and borderland studies.

YASHOMANA CHOUDHURY has submitted her PhD thesis on 'Language and the Construction of Alternate Worlds: A Select Study of Modern Fantasy' to the North-Eastern Hill University, Shillong. Her study explores fantasy Literature and its aspects. She holds an MA and BA in English from Gauhati University. Prior to starting her doctorate, she taught courses in communicative English at the National Education Foundation Law College, Guwahati. She is a freelance creative writer, volunteers for local-societal NGO work, and aspires to be a creative writer.

Index

abundance of food: uncontrollable hunger in the midst of 192-3
academic discourses 11
academic interest 11
activities surrounding food 258
acute consumerism 281
alternative food in indigenous and traditional knowledge systems 236
alternative food sources, community-specific cultural practices 236
American Anthropologist 94
Anglo-Indian cuisine 30
Aparna Sen's *Goynar Baksho:* relationship between food and desires 263
Apatani bamboo 102-3
Apatanis 97-8, 103, 104, 105: advanced irrigated rice fields 97-8; festivities linked with production of foodgrains 98; *Kine Nane* 98; *Kombi* festival 98; *Nyanyi Mete* 98; *Pinneng* or *Dorung* festivals 98; rice powder, use as sacred object 98; Solung festival 98; *Unying* or *Aran* 98
Apatanis *Murung* 98
Arabian cuisine 122
Archaeologists/prehistorians 11
Art of Eating 164-5: biblical story of Esau and Jacob, twin sons of Rebecca and Isaac 164-5; Fisher sees Jacob as the father of all *restaurateurs* and Esau of *gastronomers* 165; Jameson's symbolic act 166; Fisher, Mary Frances 164-5

Arunachal Pradesh, spices 102-3: bamboo shoot, distinct aroma of 102; pickled, cooked or fresh, bamboo shoot 102; Upper Siang district 102
Arunachal Pradesh, women: knowledge system related to horticulture, shifting hill cultivation, gathering and weaving 235
Arunachal Pradesh: famine as an occurrence in life of different communities of 224-5; food preparation 104-5; food stuff or food linked ceremonies or festivities 106; foodstuff or the food habits of the tribal population 95; remoteness and the insularity of the area 94; spices 102-3
famine as an occurrence in life of different communities of 224-5: Rangbang as staple diet 224; Tasse/tacheh 224-5
Arunachal tribes, food preparation 104-5: agriculturally advanced tribes, prepare paste or sometimes bake 104; Apatanis preserved pork, 'Ya-acho' 104; bamboo rice (*Khau-Laam*) 105; basic consumption patterns 104; *Khaumouning* (steamed rice cookie) 105; *Khaupuk* (steamed sticky rice) 105; *Khautek* (roasted sticky rice mixed with molasses and made into balls) 105; *Paa-Ping*—fish roasted using bamboo

skewer 104; roasted beef (*Sihi yo sangkho*) of Lower Subansiri district 104; roasted pork (*Waak ngam*) of Changlang district 104; Sulung (Puroik), depend on *Tache*, prepare porridge 104; *Tongtep* (steamed pancake wrapped in leaf) 105

Assamese, cuisine 289, 295-6, 299-301, 304, 311, 312: cookbooks related to 289; cultural stereotypes of 296; emerged from its relative obscurity 295; influencers talk about food practices 300; Instagram handles 295; mapped through the body 301; nostalgia 311; nostalgic representation of 299; seamless integration within the foodie aesthetic 296; vibrantly coloured chutneys and mashes 295; wholesomeness and rusticity of 311

Assamese, culinary culture 288: culinary practices – modern present as well as the traditional past 311; modes of existence of food in cyberspace 288; nostalgic construction of 297; politics of 288; popularity of 311

Atin Bandhyopadhyay's *Nilkontho Pakhir Khonje* (In Search of the Indian Roller) 187-5: abundance of food, uncontrollable hunger in the midst of 192-3; folk imagination thrives on paradoxes 188; frequent descriptions of nature's bounty 191; Jalali 193; Malati, young and beautiful widow who lost her husband in the Dhaka riot 187; Malati's life remained connected to that of Shamu 190; partition of Bengal, own structured logistics 188; Shamu was a Muslim youth 187; Shamu's frustrated love for Malati 190-1

authentic culinary heritage 12
authentic Indian meals 33

Baklava 272
Balarama Dasa's *Jagamohana Ramayana* 179
Bamboo 100-3, 232-4: Aenee and Aejoo 101; Apatani tribe 102-3; Dibang 102; *Ikun* (fermented bamboo shoot which is sour in taste) 101; *Ip* (dried bamboo shoot) 101; *Iting* (green bamboo shoot used as vegetables) 101; preserving shoots, ways of 101; *Talam-lamnam* 103
bamboo flowering 103, 228, 233-6
bamboo shoot (Eeku) 57, 100-2, 104, 156, 232, 290, 296, 310: eyom 101; smell of 57
Bandhyopadhyay, Atin 187
Bangla partition literature, pain and fracture in 187-95: Atin Bandhyopadhyay's *Nilkontho Pakhir Khonje* (In Search of the Indian Roller) 187; food as remembered by partition victims 194; Madeleine acted as a stimulus, connection between body and mind 194; memory as a complex process of the body and emotions associated with it 195; Mnemonic in the sense that history is functionalized 194; partition literature, aim of 188-9; Proust's example and the writing of partition, difference between 194; Sunil Gangopadhyay's *Arjun* 194-5; tragedy of partition, underplaying these grey areas of human reality 189

Index

Bangla partition novels: absence of gory descriptions 189; nature of procuring food as refugees in India 191; focus on the mind of the affected rather than the violence itself 189
Bengal famine 48, 224
Bengal, India, famine occurrences 227-30: bio-resolutions 228; neighbouring communities of the Bengalis 228; Phytolith analysis of samples 229-30; Sago plant family 229; Tree-Fern, use of 229; wild edible plants 228
Bengali cooking: basic and distinctive mode 43
Bengali cuisine 45; food 41, 45
Biocultural approach 66-7: biocultural anthropological framework 66
Biocultural research 67
bland food 257
body and mind 194
Bordo, Susan 59
Bordoloi, Santwana 260
British and tea culture, relation between 209
British colonialism and evolution of food habits in India 27-30: concept of the 'curry' 30; cunning of foxy cooks or *bawarchis* 30; food habits of Bengal's jute mills 29; gastronomic habits of the British in Bengal 29-30; hybrid world of cooking ingredients and styles 30; native kitchen or 'cookhouse' 29; ostentatious and unhealthy dining habits 28; refinement of the eating etiquette 28-9

Camellia sinesis 214
Chai-time 213
Chattopadhyay, Bankimchandra 48
Chaudhurani, Renuka Devi 46: recalls her mentor, Muslim *bawarchi* 46
Chhena Guda vs. branded rasogolla 174-6: *chhena* 175; *guda* 175; Odia cultural historian and satirist Govinda Triapthy makes fun of the people of Odisha 174-5
Chicana and Native American women: ethnic and gender identities through writing about food 62
China, tea use: first used solely for medicinal properties 212
Chinese cuisine 158
Christianity 95, 146, 148, 150, 157: conversion to 158
Coca Colization 40
Colonial rule and hunger 47-50: Bankimchandra Chattopadhyay's *Anandamath* (1882) 48; food culture 50; Fullara and Kalaketu in *chandimangal* 48; Haraprasad Shastri 48-49; story about Ishwarchandra Vidyasagar 48-9; stranglehold of unenlightened cooking 47; waste food 50; women of upper income households 47; distribution of food 50; unreformed hospitality 47-8
commodified cuisines 307
community-based cultural identity formation 124
Consumables, proliferation of 40
Consumer culture 281-3, 284: culinary art 282; frequent use of phrases like 'foreign holiday' and 'exotic beaches' 282; greetings and goodbyes in food shows, done in multiple languages 282; Moroccan spices and southeast Asian condiments 282; *Real fruit juices* 281-2

Index

consumerism 17, 40, 271, 273, 282, 283
consuming uncooked rice 68
contextual belief systems 105
cook book, emergence of 272
Cookbooks and recipe books 62
cookbooks related to Assamese cuisine: Zilkia Janer 289
Cooking, Cuisine, and Class: A Study of Comparative Sociology 94
Cooking, food, and middle classes in India and abroad 30-3: culinary nostalgia 33; export of Indian food abroad 31-2; first Indian restaurants, or 'curry houses' 31-2; food *per se* than about cooking and eating as cultural practice 31; growth of a global Indian diaspora 31-2; Indian food history, burgeoning field of 32-3; modern Indian cookbooks as cultural texts 31; precooked and packaged ready-to-eat single-serving meals 32; regional diversity in Indian cuisine 31; restaurants in both Britain and the United States 32; ubiquitous budget restaurants 32
Cordon Bleu cookery 40
Cuisine 21, 26-7, 34, 50, 53, 111, 118, 139, 142, 143
culinary history, traditional field of 11
culinary skill in preparing food 287
cultural adaptation 235
cultural identity 31, 210-11, 301: idea of 210-11
Culture and Heritage 169
culture of consumerism 273

Dandi Ramayana 178
Dasa, Balarama 176
Dasa, Jagannath 163
Desh-bhager Smriti (Memories of Partition) 191

Devi, Rasa Sundari 43: *amar jiban* 43
Dhasal, Namdeo 56
Diet, socio-cultural determinants of 94
dietary behavior 62
Dietary patterns in pregnancy 65-66
dining platter 271
Discipline and Punish: The Birth of the Prison 267-8: psychological state of 'conscious and permanent visibility' 268
domesticated Malayali femininity 272
Douglass, Frederick 55-6
Dree 98

Early India and the origins of Vegetarianism 23-5: and abstinence 24; animal flesh were consumed by Indo-Aryans in the Vedic period 24; Buddhist *Jataka* tales, practice of consuming the meat 24; Buddhists and Jains, campaign to put an end to Vedic animal sacrifices 25; *Charaka-samhita* (*c.* first century AD) 24; concept of *ahimsa* or non-killing 25; *Dharma Sutras* 25; Francis Zimmerman's work on the concepts of ecology and traditional medicine (*ayurveda*) 24; Harappan civilization, consumption of milk and dairy products 24; Harappan civilization, excessive meat eating and the consumption of fish 23; *Manu Smriti* 25; sacrificial meat, use of 24; *Shatapatha Brahmana* 25; *Sushruta-samhita* 24
ease delivery model 79-80: emic explanation 79
eastern food chains 57
eating vegetarian food or non-vegetarian food 60

'Ecology of Famine: An Overview'
225: ecosystem of famine 225-6;
famine and disease, relation
between 225; famine belts of the
world 225; Rajasthan desert,
comprehensive use of wild plants
and animal food 226
Enjoy your ethnicity 299-306:
Amateur cooks 305; artworks of
today, 'self-fulfilling' 303;
Assamese identity, new
multiculturalist public, seamless
inclusion of 304; authentic
culinary knowledge 300;
consumption of media content
and a space for personal
expression 300; enjoyment,
sustained by a superego-
imperative, the injunction to
'Enjoy!' 303; ethnic food and
cultural identity, celebration of,
users participate 'interactively'
301; ethnic subject, demands of
the symbolic order 304; extended
aesthetic contemplation 301-2;
food enthusiasts 305; food
photography, growing popularity
of 305; foodie influencers' posts,
followers' interact with 302;
group administrators 305; group
claims a strict 'no politics' policy
305; influencer's post, gesture of
'liking' 302-3; influencers,
popularity of 300; interactive
celebrity, influencers perform
Assamese identity, effect on how
to 300-1; occasional food related
posts by friends 302; one's ethnic
identity 300; ritualized moments
of relief from the 'burden' of
enjoyment 306; self avowed
foodies 306; self-confessed
novices 305; social media
interactivity, valorization of 303;
superego-injunction to 304
Enlightened kitchen 43-7: Bengali
Hindu *bhadralok*'s investment,
idea of the sanctity of women 47;
inner world of women in their
particular interior space in the
household 47; *outré* dietary
innovations, derived from
Muslim and European cuisine 46
ethnic and caste-based food 53
ethnic cuisine 197, 198, 290, 307,
311, 312
ethnic food practices 307
ethno-commodities 291
etiologies of dietary shifts: community
education 81
exclusive privatized identity and
foodways 118-24: *Adaminte
Chayakada* (teashop of Adam)
121; apprehension of
marginalization and
discrimination with the symbolic
display of belief and practice
124; Arabian dining experience
122; Araya Samajam 119;
Avathan Muthappan Kavu (sacred
grove) dedicated to God
Muthappan 119; caste-based
Kerala society, eating food
prepared by a lower caste
person/family, considered as
taboo 123; *Chaayakkada*
(teashop) 121; Christianizing
eateries in vernacular names 120-
1; communal ideologues nourish
their ferocity with the making of
the 'good believer' 124; crossing
over from vegetarian to non-
vegetarian in the home 118;
curiosity and comfort of
familiarity among the people
121; entrenched process of

'othering' 123; *Eruvum Puliyum* (spicy and sour) 121; food and food practices in the twenty-first century, changing and evolving meanings 119; food and its authenticity, idea of 121; food habits of other community, transgression to 118; food memory, extraordinary power of 119; individualized/privatized identity 125; 'intercommunity' relationship, lack of 119; interfaith food practices 125; *kudumbasangamam* (family get together) functions 122-3; *kudumbasangamam* (family get-together) venture 122; *Maapilakkada* (shop of Mappila) 121; Malabar Muslims, sociality in the everyday life 120; Malabar people, non-vegetarian food 118; Malabar, 'caste-centred' segregation, deviated into a 'religion-centric' difference 123; Marad region of Kozhikode district the pre- and post-riot situation, sociality of food 118-19; *Milad-i-Sherif* and the *Mandala vratam* 119; Muslim migration to Gulf countries from Malabar 122; Muslims reciprocate with *pathiri* 118; *nadan* (traditional food from the region) 120; *nadan* food (native food) 121; *nadan sadhya* (traditional meal) 121; newly-wedded couples in the community 122; offers and exchanges of food 119; Onam and Vishu festival 118; paranoia of Kerala Muslims and Hindu community, mass media under the ownership of different organizations 120; *pathayoram* (highway) 121; people of Malabar, food menu 121; public and familial spaces, destruction of 124; *puthuma* (novelty) 121; *puttu* (cylinders of ground rice layered with coconut) and fish curry 121; *Qaum/sammudaym* (community) within the cultural landscape of Malabar 120; rejection of cumulative weight of historical baggage 123-4; *Shaapukari thattukada* (toddy shop) 121; sociality of Malabar, role of food in 122; socio-economic mobility due to gulf migration 124; socio-political changes post-Babari Masjid effect 120; *thakkaram* and other intercommunity events 124; *thattukadas* 120; *Uppum Mulakum* (salt and chili) 121; *Usthad Hotel* 121

Fairy tales 214
famine as a natural calamity 236
Famine food, cultural construction of 223-37
Famine in literature 225-30: benefits of government food supply programmes 227; dependent parameters 227; 'Ecology of Famine: An Overview' 225; experts' opinion on food aids 227; food supply during famine 226; *Rajatarangini* 227
Famines during colonial period 241-3: 1880, Commission recommended implementation of the famine policy proactively 243; certain political and social conditions, inadequate transportation of food from one area to other 242; famine in the Northwest Provinces in 1860-1 242;

Index

Florence Nightingale, critical view on the subject 241-2; scarcity in physical environmental factors 241; famines, causes of 223
fasting (*vratas*) 77-80: pathogen-induced anorexia 79
Feeding others 61
Feminist anthropological scholarship 272
feminist food studies 58-9: establish that food practices are gendered 59
Feminist food studies 59
Fijian women: body image in 282
Foie gras, sushi, and *laksa* 271
Folk cookery 145
Folklore 12, 15, 102: and food 95-6; food production and consumption patterns 15; of a region 214; tradition 95
food advertisements 61
food advertisers 62
food and cooking 38
Food and Cultural Studies 13
'Food film' genre 258: actors in the lead role will be chefs or domestic cooks 258; food causes gratification of the senses 258; symbolic significance of specific foods and eating rituals 258
Food and folklore 95-107: association with the Sulungs 95; Buddhist tribes 96; high altitude tribes, maize as staple food 95-6; rice 95; *tacheh* 95
Food cravings 70-2: categories of craved foods and the timing 71; craving sweet foods 71; cravings for mangoes 71; hot foods in pregnancy 71; 'hot' foods can increase *pitta* (fire) in the body 71; spontaneous miscarriage 71-2; unripe mango and unripe tamarind, ample amounts of Vitamin C 72
Food fiction 16, 164, 177
FoodFood channel 274
Food image and code 306-10: buying and selling organic products, relationship of 308; emerging relation between the metropolis and the countryside 309; enough capital to invest in food processing equipment 310; ethnic food restaurants in Guwahati 310; ethnic identification (for instance, Naga King Chilli) or geographical indicators 307; food image appears to the subject as interpassive relation 306-7; foodie aesthetic, turning ethnic food practices into commodified cuisines 307; foodie aesthetic, ubiquity of 307; guarantee for the freshness of the produce and an assurance of their 'organic' origins 308; indigenous political economy, popular discourse of 309; influencers are invested in the commodification of ethnic culture 307; new organic food brands, promotion and endorsement of 307; niche market for 'organic produce' that caters to a relatively upmarket clientele 310; non-GM vegetables 307; nostalgia and nationalism go hand in hand 308; organic food 307; organic produce, wholesome alternative 308; popular sentiment about unremunerative agricultural prices 309; rustic indigenous peasant, cultural representation of 310; social media handles to promote their home kitchen/

satellite kitchen businesses 307; tropes of rustic Assamese culture are revived 309
Food images 12-13: production, consumption and dissemination of 311-12
Food in films, use of 258: films use food imagery to discuss wider discourses of power and control 259; food sequences in films based on the theme of widowhood 259; power status quo in society 259
Food Mnemonics and identity construction 197-207: academic discourses involving food 197; concept of *food voice* introduced by Hauck-Lawson 200; deep psychological and socioeconomic bonds existing between food, culture and societies 197-8; food habits, linked to the manner in which humans have come to use food 198; quotidian experience of food consumption for survival and nourishment 198; role of *memory about* food in conversation 197; social and personal identity 199-200; today's food conscious world 197; today's food conscious world, how one eats tied to identity issues 198
Food paintings 12-13
food photography 288, 293, 295, 305
Food plays 93, 125, 210, 211: discipline of anthropology 93-4
Food politics 55
Food practices 22, 54, 59, 62, 115, 116, 119, 121, 251, 300: women's relationship to 62
Food proscriptions, or avoidances 75, 76
Food regulations 114

Food science 13
Food scientists 13
food shows 17, 271-4, 283
Food stories 168-70
Food Studies 13-14, 53, 56, 58, 62, 106, 197: basis of who eats 'raw' and who eats 'cooked' food 53; cultural dislocation, forced assimilation, or other aspects of political violence 57; *dhal* 56; dietary perspective on food 56; food 'ethnographic in nature' 55; food justice, notions of 56; food, eating habits and the sociology of hunger, descriptions of 55; gender and ideologies 53-63; gender and indigeneity and food, relationship between 56-7; gender relations, social value of the male and female and the constructions of their identities 58; insecurity among the ultra-poor Garo women in Bangladesh 57; politics of othering that operates through food 54-5; relationship between food and people from the variety of perspectives 14; trajectory of development of 14; transition from raw to cooked food 54
Food taboo or food and inequality 105-6: Digaru and Miju Mishmi girls, not allowed to consume meat 105; drinking milk 105; during menstruation period, a woman is not allowed to take roasted meat of wild animals 105; during menstruation, women not even allowed to dine with other members of the family 105-6; Idu Mishmi girls of Dibang valley district 105; Khampti and Singhpho 105; killing of tiger is regarded as a bad sign 106; Pailibo girls 105; person while

going for fishing should not eat any variety of meat 106; social realities or contextual belief systems 105; Wancho clans, like *Joham*, never eat *Nya-me* fish 106

Food tours 287, 293

Food variety: and cultures of consumption, contemporary perspectives on 53

Food, linkages with: ecology, rituals, and symbolism 94

Food, nation and ethnicity 288-92: bloggers and reviewers 290; e-commerce opportunities 292; ethnic food in the metropolis 291; ethnic restaurant trend, caught on outside the metros as well 291; ethnic subjects consuming their *own* culture in form of ethnocommodities 292; food delivery apps, popularity of 292; new food entrepreneurs 291-2; one's distinctive food cultural practices 290-1; regional cuisines 289; upscale restaurant culture in big cities 290

Food: and the act of eating 53; and women's relationship with it 12; as a collective/community activity, preparation and consumption of 14; as a cultural trope 14; as an aspect of material culture 22; as an entity endowed with cultural and moral characteristics 22; as embodied culture, spontaneous connotation of 287; as an intrinsic part of a cultural system 272; availability and agricultural techniques 22; consumption 13, 60; discourse 54; during famine 235-6; flavor 287; habits 11; historically and culturally 11; human relationship to 60; management of 13; materiality of 60-1; nation and ethnicity 288-92; society, symbolic function of 61; sociology of 12

Foodie aesthetic 293-9: act of cooking traditional Assamese dishes for one's family 297; Assamese cuisine 295; Assamese culinary culture and tradition, nostalgic construction of 297-8; Assamese culture, pre-Assam movement notion of 299; Assamese food, simplicity and wholesomeness of 296; Assamese middle class, semi-feudal and petty official in composition 298; Assamese nationalism, culturalist discourse of 299; dislocation, pervasive sense of 298; diversity, multiculturalist notion of 296; ethnic self, rediscovery of 299; ethnic-cultural difference 294-5; food photographs on social media 294; food related content, exponential increase in 293; food's vibrant colours 294; good food, ideology of 294; good food, transcendence into the realm of 296; nostalgia for the present draws on de-historicized popular cultural representations of that utopian past 297; nostalgic constructions of the past in popular culture 297; photography, technical-aesthetic aspects of 293; post-processing techniques 294; social media platforms 293; unrehearsed spontaneity and disregard for the conventions 302; vibrantly coloured chutneys and mashes 295

Food-memories 16

Index

Foods and foodways, stories of 166-8: American slave trade and the antebellum plantation economy 168; Dilsey's kitchen offers a fragmented narrative of African cooking 167; Faulkner's *The Sound and the Fury* 167; growing and enhancing food resources through animal husbandry, pisciculture and agriculture 166-7; *The Autobiography of Miss Jane Pittman* 167; predatory economic practices seen in colonialism and plantation slavery 167; Toni Morrison's *Beloved* (1987) 167-8
food-writing 62
'foul-smelling' foodstuff 290

Gangopadhyay, Sunil 194-5
Garo family 148, 157
Garo food habits and ethnicity 145-9: Christmas festivities, feast arranged for all the villagers 157; diffusion 158; *Do.O.Eching* 157; drinks 149; during festivals, male members engage in cooking 157; eating habits depend on the geographical settings and climatic conditions 148-9; folk cookery 148; horticultural products 146; Jhum cultivators 146; primary and secondary data on the Garos living in Assam 146-7; pressure cooker and LPG gas 158; rice as the staple food 145; *Sonserek* customs and festivals 158; traditional domestic cooking process and preparation 148
Garo food habits and ethnicity, ethnographic studies 149-51: *Garos and the English, The* 150; *Garos in Transition, The* 150-1; *Garos, The* 151; *History and Culture of the Garos* 151; patterns of family and kinship system 150; *Rengsanggri, Family and Kinship in a Garo Village* 150; reports on Garo people, their physical appearances, their way of living 149-50; *Social Institution of the Garos of Meghalaya: An Analytical Study* 150; *Society and Economy of the South Kamrup Tribal Belt* 151; *Some Cultural and Linguistic Aspects of the Garos* 150; *Study of Culture Change in Two Garo Villages of Meghalaya, A* 150; *Tribes of Assam* 150
Garo food habits and ethnicity, material culture 151-2: *Dhowa Chang* 152; different food items have permeated in different cultures 151; ethnic food 152; ethnic food festivals and annual festivals 152; folk cookery in a community, function of 152; religious performances 151; ritualistic purposes 151
Garos 147-9: cooking is associated with the women 157; cooking styles of 15; food culture 145; food habits and recipes 153-6; groups of 147-8; living in Assam and plain areas do plough cultivation 146; living in Guwahati 146-7; living in hilly areas do jhum cultivation 146; of South Kamrup 147; rice as main staple food 145; social and cultural life of 150; social changes among 150
Garos cuisine 159
Garos, food habits and recipes 153-6: Betel nut 157; *Kaldah Nakham Bitchi* 153; *Kharchi Phura* 153; *Nakham Jagua* 153; occasional food 153; *Panikhaity Area* 153;

Index

rice 153; *Sakham Kata* 153; Soda (*Karchi*) 153
'gastro-semantics' 22-3
Gastronomic unconscious 168-70: African spiderman, story of 169; Crosby shows what makes food an ideological apparatus 169; culinary productions 168; *Food and Foodways in African Narratives: Community, Culture and Heritage* 169; food narratives, fasting and feasting help create structures 168-9
Gender and famine relation 235
Geophagy in pregnancy 67-8
Goswami, Indira 260
Goynar Baksho, food imagery in 265-7: Rashmoni is the matriarch of the house 265-6; recollection of red chilli, spices and meat stretches out her now dead hopes for a pleasurable conjugal life 266
Great Bengal Famine of 1770 228; 1943 243
Guwahati Foodies 305

Half of a Yellow Sun (2006) 223-4
Hemendranath Tagore, Prajna's father 41
Hindu caste widows in India: vegetarian food to be consumed 60
Hindu women: sometimes fast to elicit emotional support from others 78
Hindu–Muslim dichotomy, habitual participants of 188
home kitchen gardens 224
home kitchen/satellite kitchen businesses 307
Hospitality and feasting 114-17: food customs and habits 115; food production and consumption 117; food rules and practices, ethical ideals about meaningful human social activity 117; love for cooking constructs alternative narratives 116; Malabar Muslims 115; Muslim food practices 117; non-family members and neighbours, invitation to 115; offering of food 115; 'proper' way of eating food among the Muslims during rituals 116; style of eating, replicated in the Muslim domestic sphere 117; *sulaimani* (a brew of black tea with cardamom) 117; *thakkaram* (hearty welcome) 115; *thakkaram* guests 115; *thakkaram* to other community acts 116
Household kitchens 142
hunger strike 61

In Search of Our Mothers' Gardens: Womanist Prose 60
inclusivity, language of 125
India, pregnancy aversions 74-5: dietary changes in pregnancy 75; dietary diversity hypothesis 74-5; food aversions between the *Jenu Kurubas* 74; *Jenu Kurubas* and the mixed caste farmers, common aversion among 74; maternal-fetal protection, lens of 74; maternal-foetal protection hypothesis 74
India, pregnant women, food avoidances 75-7: 'hot' foods 76; *Jenu Kurubas* of Mysore district 75; potentially harmful substances, ingestion of 76
India: food ingredients and cooking styles 22; northeastern region cuisines 290; regional cuisines 289

India's northeast: women in the cultivation or production of rice 59
Indian cuisine 31, 32, 34, 288-90, 295
Indian culinary habits 288-9
Indian food: as a temporal narrative of various dishes 22; habits through cultural encounters with the Islamicate and the European world 14
Indian kitchen 30
Indian pregnant women, dietary patterns among 65-81: aversions toward specific food and smells 66; cross-cultural similarities and differences 66; culturally transmitted dietary rules 66; dietary changes along with nausea and vomiting 65
Indian society, untouchability in: leftover of food 57-8
Indian television shows: replaced by a considerable portion of Indian productions 273
Indian women during pregnancy: dietary behaviours of 14-15
Indian women's dietary preferences 66
individual consumerism 125, 126
Indological emphasis on India's exceptionalism 23
infants after birth, intrauterine growth or anthropometric measurements of 80
insider standpoint, ethical dilemmas of positionality of 274
interfaith activism 125-6
interfaith food practices 125
internet based 'cloud kitchens' 292
Irom Sharmila: act of fasting 61-2; decade long hunger strike 61
Iron deficiency anemia 79
iron-rich foods 81
Islamic and early European influences 25-7: Bengal, Portuguese generated a significant demand for cottage cheese 27; contact with Europe and through it with the New World 26; culinary style influenced by the nomadic lifestyle of the steppes 25; Humayun, brought with him an entourage of Persian cooks 25-6; Mughals gave shape to the concept of an Indian cuisine 26; Muslims imported dining etiquette into Hindu society 25; Portuguese introduced a wide range of new foods 27; the Biryani, combining Indian spices and Persian arts into a rich fusion 26

Jagannath Dasa's *Odia Bhagavata* 163
Janer, Zilkia 289
Japanese culture, tea ceremony 212

Kapoor, Sanjeev 273: *khana khazaana* 273
Kashmir textile workers, early medieval history 224
Kerala cuisine 114, 119, 121
Kerala, foodways in 111
Khatra village: colonial rule and in early postcolonial period 251; constructional, administrative and trading activities due to irrigation project 251; *dikus* 253; entitlement relations accepted in a private ownership market economy 252; exchange entitlements of Santals 252; friendly neighbours 252; hostile neigbours 252; inheritance and transfer entitlement, option of 252; Santal cultivators 252; Santals, perennially prepared against scarcity 253; State and market economy, too weak to

respond or too indifferent towards the Santals 252

kitchen 31, 41, 43, 46, 59-60, 62, 114, 116, 158, 261, 266, 271, 276, 279, 302: as a space of domesticating women 59-60; infrastructure of 152; modern kitchen, amenities of 158; of a household 137; of Bihari and Marwari families 142; of Malabar 121; ritualized purity of 118; tools 152

kitchen culture 62

Lakshminath 42-3: accomplished and innovative cook 42

Language in food 200-1: analysis 206-7; Extract I 201-4; Extract II 204-6

Lebanese Muslim women: fasted in Ramadan 80

Leftovers 58

legacy of food and the associated memories 18

Lepchas 130

Malabar and its people 111-12: Arab Muslim traders 112; Kerala, social structure of 111-12; Mappillas or Moplahs 111; pre-Islamic trade relationship of Arabians with Kerala 111; Thiyyas, Parayas and Cherumans who came forward to embrace Islam 112; Zamorins of Calicut 111

Malabar cuisine 119

Malabar food practices 111, 112-14: Biryani 113-14; culture based meaning of food 112; dishes of the Mappillas, mostly meat based 113; Islam instructs no food should be wasted 113; Kerala cooking style and dietary habits 113; Malabar Muslims follow their dietary habits based on the *Quran* and the *Sunnah* 113; Malabar Muslims, differentiating Halal (permissible) from Haram (forbidden) 113; Malabar Muslims, food culture of 113; Mappillas, rich culinary tradition of 114; *Muttamala* (egg garland) 114; social groups express their distinctive 'social habitus' through material practices 112

Malabar women: crafted with unique food preparation of the family 116

Malati 187-8, 190-1, 193: life remained connected to that of Shamu 190

Mapilla cuisine 121

Masala Chai 213

McDonaldization 40

meal 28-9, 44, 61, 77, 94, 114, 115: in the restaurants 117

Meanings of Food and Cooking 60

Mithun 99-100: Abang (Limir Libom) 99; Adis of Siang 99; Akas of Kameng district 99; Dadi Karki Bote 100; Dadi Komi Yomko 100; Donying Ang 100; Engo Takar 100; Khowas (Bugun) 99; meat of 99; Mishmis of Lohit district 99; 'Tapum' or worm 100

Mizo Famine Front/ Mizo National Front (1964) 223, 234

Mizo movement of 1964 234

mnemophobia 53

Mohanty, Asit 176-9

Mopin 96-7: Abo Tani and his brother Taki, born out of Earth (Sisi) 97; Abo Tani, myth of 97; Apatanis 97-8; Galo tribe 97; most popular festivals of Arunachal 96-7; paddy crop, cultivation of 97-8

'Motum' (-famine) of Lusai Hills 223
Mummy ka Magic 276-7: body image 278-9; focuses on *health* but does not count calories 276; *Lalita Ji* of Surf fame in the 1970s 276; mother's health 276-7; Muslim kitchens 114
Muslim cuisine 46, 121
My Bondage and My Freedom 55

Narrative of the Life of Frederick Douglass 55
native kitchen or 'cookhouse' 29
Neo-imperialism 40
neoliberal structural adjustment programme 39
Nepali kitchen: Tibetan delicacies 142
Nilkontho Pakhir Khonje 16
Non-dominant food preferences and practices 53
non-food films 258
Non-vegetarian cuisine 54
North East India 232, 234: home of several bamboo species 234

Oriya Hindu women fasting: ways to garner moral authority 79

Padams 101-2: long oral narratives 102
partition literature 188-9: fictionalized history 194
partition narrative, food in 192: Prafulla Roy's *Keya Patar Nouko* (The Keya Leaf Boat) 192; *Subarnarekha* 192
pathogen and toxin avoidance 80
pathogen response hypothesis 79
people's kitchen 307
Persian cooks 25-6
Pica 67-70: Ayurvedic tooth powder as a replacement for clay for fear of retribution 68-9; community members and participants 68; earth-eating 67; Geophagy 67, 70; hiding substances from peers 69; human behavior, *etic* explanations for 69; in India, social stigma 68; pregnant Indian women, cravings for ash 69; protective benefits of 70; stigma towards clay consumption 69
Political Unconscious: Narrative as a Socially Symbolically Act, The 165
Pooja Makhija show 275-6: body image 278; 'Eat Delete' 275; show translates *health* in the lexicon of weight loss 276; 'This or That' 275
poor food 47
popular food 38
postcolonial societies: food as a metaphor and reminder of one's own roots or belonging 57
Post-structuralism posits 257
poverty and hunger 47
Prajnasundari Devi 41-3: daughters and wives of the Tagores, pioneering role in enlightening enterprises 42; Loreto School run by Christian missionaries 42
Prajnasundari's cookbook 43-7: Chefs from outside Hindu caste society 46; entries under plain rice 44; everyday labour of the woman is a theoretical practice as well 45; first volume, devoted to vegetarian food 43-4; frequent engagements of Muslim *bawarchis* (chefs) in affluent Hindu households 46; Indian component of the colonial bureaucracy 45; *orthograde* 44; recipes come mainly from Bengal, Assam, and Orissa 44; second volume, non-vegetarian cooking 44; third volume, preserves and

Index

chutneys from various parts of the country 44; total number of entries in the vegetarian volume 44

Prajnasundari's recipes 41-3: *amish o niramish aahar* 41; apprentice at first and then moved towards being something of a 'master chef' 41; Bengali food 41

pregnancy fasting 77: adverse pregnancy outcomes, risk of 77; cascade effect 77; gender inequality model 78; Indian households, gender discrimination in 78; normal pregnancy circumstances 78; physiological costs of 78; reduces pregnancy complications 79; women, devaluation of 78

pregnancy fasting centres: ethnophysiological perceptions of pregnancy 79-80

pregnancy: cross-cultural dietary shifts 81; dietary behaviours 62

pregnancy-related food and drug aversions 72-5: cross-cultural aversion 73; focused on western populations 73; Nicotine exposure *in utero* 73; spicy foods, aversions to 73; substances were those that could have teratogenic effects 73; to both meat and plant based toxins 74; vegetarianism, higher rates of 74

pregnant Indian women: craving sweet foods 71; dietary patterns among 65-81; food avoidances 75-7

pregnant women in Karnataka: food consumption influences size of the baby 80

pregnant women: crave non-food items 69; learned about avoidances from their maternal relatives 76; might fast in response to pathogenic infection 79; require additional antioxidants 72; representing diverse religions and cultural settings 76

problematic food, refraining from consumption 114

production prevalent in Santal villages in precolonial times 246-7

public food culture 287

pure vegetarian restaurants 139

Puroik 224

Purushottam Deva 179

Rajatarangini 227

Ramayana/ Dandi Ramayana/ Jagamohana Ramayana 176-180

Rangbang 224, 228, 230, 231, 236: as staple food 230; as an alternative source of food 231; food from horticulture 236

Rasa Aswadate: Rasogolla-eater's essay on cognitive logic 171-3: ancient poetic text, saying *rasa asvadate iti rasa* 172; different reasons to justify the rasogollaeater's unhappiness *after* eating it 172; *The Prajatantra* 171

Rasogolla, nationalism, *and Vakrokti* 173-4: one's relationship to national artefacts and assets 174

Rasogolla: debate between Odisha and West Bengal, in-depth criticalhistorical analysis 16; origin and literary-cultural journey of 164; rasogolla war between Odisha and Bengal 163-4

Rasogolla-Kokakola fights in Western Odisha 170-1: 1977, satirical song about rasogolla and Coca Cola 170-1

Raw and the Cooked, The 131-2

ready-to-eat single-serving meals 32

Reconstructing youth through popular culinary culture 271-84: associating and reinforcing culinary *magic* as a metaphor for maternal virtue 280; body image 277-9; gender identity in urban adolescent school-girls 277; gendered bifurcation of roles 279-81; *insider standpoint,* ethical dilemmas of positionality of 274; Mummy ka Magic 276-7; *mummy* or the mother's *magic* 281; Pooja Makhija show 275-6; representation of men and women in Indian print advertisement 281; *Victorian Conduct Manuals* 277-8; women's roles are circumscribed within the sphere of the domestic 281
religious purists 124
reproductive-aged women 80: iron deficiency anemia 80
Republic of Hunger, The 38
research protocols 81
Rice 23, 25-6, 28-30, 44-6, 49, 59, 68, 95-8, 103-5, 114, 118-19, 141-2, 145-6, 149, 153-7, 169, 187, 192-3, 201-5, 207, 212, 216, 224, 227, 229-36, 243, 246, 249-50, 252, 263-4, 285, 309-10: important source of folklore materials in Arunachal Pradesh 96; Khamptis of Lohit district 96
Rice farming: cultural adaptation of 236
Rice-eaters 201, 203, 232
Right to rasogolla 176-8: aspects of the 'bittersweet war' 176; Balarama Dasa's *Dandi Ramayana* 176; biosocial markers 178; *chhena* or cottage cheese, indispensable part of ritual temple offerings 177; *chhena*-based foods and sweets in medieval and precolonial texts 177; *Dandi Ramayana* 178; food cultures and food rights, materiality of neighbourhood 177; iconic rasogolla migrated to other parts of India, especially Bengal 177; shelf life of food items and issues of body and health 178; *kora rasogolla je amruta rasaabali* 178
Roy, Prafulla 192
Russian famines 223

Sadeian Woman and the Ideology of Pornography, The 263
Sago trees 230-2: Puroik villages 230-1
Santal residents of a village in West Bengal 241
Santal villages in precolonial times, colonial rule and the village community 246-8: calculation of tax per *bigha* 247; homestead or *bari* land 247; organization of food production in Santal villages, precolonial times 246-7; precolonial land management system of the Santals 247; *rekh* 247; revenue collection system of colonial government 247
Santals 17
Santals of Saraspur, famine related experiences of 243-5: Europeans identifying themselves with the Aryan conquerors of India 244; food scarcity during colonial period 243; 'tribes' as disparate social categories 244; viewed as peasants 244-5
Santals of Saraspur, food scarcity, memories of 245-6: *baandh*s were erected 246; canal irrigation

changed economic profile of Saraspur 245; cereals were scarce during periods of famine 246; lots of non-cultivated food 245
Santals, wading through hardship 248-50: *bhachati* 249; imposition of tax 248; prefer to till their land themselves 248; reciprocal exchange was possible between very close relatives and friends 249; remarkable resilience while facing food scarcities and other forms of adversities 248; Santal wage workers 249; Saraspur, drought-prone area 249
Santwana Bordoloi's *Adajya*, food imagery in 260-263: based on Indira Goswami's novel *The Moth Eaten Howdah of a Tusker* 260; defilement of the body is analogous to eating meat 262-3; food here is an expression of Giribala's desires 260-1; meat-eating is the symbol of the male 261; meat-eating sequence, Giribala is not cowered down by punitive measures 262; protagonist's association with meat reflecting her own association with her desires 261
Sarala Dasa's *Mahabharata* 180
Saraspur, canal irrigation 250-3: agricultural activities of the village 250
scarcity and famine, accounts of 241
Selling food/telling food 178-80: Balarama Dasa completed *Jagamohana Ramayana* during the reign of Purushottam Deva 179; Balarama Dasa's *Jagamohana Ramayana* 180; global food market, food is made famous by packaging companies 180; Portuguese tradition of cheese-making 179; Sarala Dasa's *Mahabharata* 180; Sri Chaitanya's arrival in Odisha in 1509 179; sweet- and cheese-making tradition of Bengal 179
Sen, Aparna 263
Serve it Forth (1937) 164
Sikkim Himalaya, gastronomic terrain of 129-43: culinary preferences 129; material culture 129; Nepalis, largest ethnic group of Sikkim 130; nutritional value of a food item 129
Sikkim kitchens 131, 135, 137, 138, 142
Sikkim, as melting pot of cultural geographies 131: *bhakthuk* 131; *Bhat-dal* and *roti* 131; culinary experience 131; *dhindo* 131; *gundruk* 131; *gyathuk* 131; *momo* 131; people's adaptability from subtropical climate type to cold-arid conditions 131; *sha-phale* 131; *sinki* 131; *thenthuk* 131; *thukpa* 131
Sikkim, food culture in 15
Sikkim, food, categorization of 131-2: binary oppositions as food 132; processed food 132
Sikkim, organic food 137-8: 1993, prohibiting grazing 138; 2003, banning import of chemical fertilizers, pest-controlling chemicals 138; gastronomic terrain, noteworthy developments 138; till 2002, Sikkim practised regular agriculture 137-8
Sikkim, perceived gastronomic landscape 138-9: several travellers try to stick to pure vegetarian restaurants 139

Sikkim, street food vs. eating out 139-41: limited number of street food options 140; mobile vendors regulated by issuing permits 141; nascent street food, food preferred by students 141; prefers to eat at 'decent' eating joints 140; street food culture 140

Sikkim, traditional food processing 132-7: brewing 136-7; cold-arid trans-Himalayan landscape 135; dairy processing 132-5; *Dried meat* 135-6; milk, processing of 135; pickling 136

Sikkimese food 130-1, 142-3

Single Malts 40

Slavoj Žižek: experience of cyberspace may be understood as a form of 'interpassivity' 303; order of the public symbolic Law and the superego, distinguishing between 303

Social and cultural diversity 22

social change and continuity, practices of 12

Social etiquettes 61

social media 'influencer' 300

social media interactivity 301

South Kamrup Tribal Belt 153-6: *An chi Kapa* (Blood Fry) 156; Bamboo shoot pickle 156; *Bona Bhat* 154; *Bora rice* 154; Christmas, beef or pork as main food 155; coconut sweets 154; *Do.o Modipol* (Chicken with Raw Papaya) 154; *Do.o. with Gal'da* leaf (Roselle or red sorrel leaves) 155; *Do.O.Eching* 154-5; Dried fish (*Nakam Jagua*) 153; fish cooked with bamboo shoot (*Me.a*) or small tapioca 155; *Galdah Nakam* 156; *Janko* (Wild cat) curry 155; *Keda* or *Resu* (Banana stem) with *Wak* (Pork) or *MatchuBe'n* (Beef) 155; Maize 153-4; *Nakam Jagua* (Dried Fish) 156; Rice (*Mi*) 153; *Rongchu* or Chira 156; Tapioca with dry fish 156; *Wanthi* (Rice cake) 154

Standpoint theory 273-4: *insider* 274; *outsider* 274

Street food 39

subsistence economic practices 235

Tache-famine food, cultural ecology of 232-4: bamboo shoots consumed as spices 232; communities of Arunachal Pradesh, practising agriculture at subsistence level 233; Eastern Himalaya 232; habit of extracting sago 233; horticultural food, and foraging practices alternative food during famine 234; North East India, rice-eaters 232; Sago (Tasse), wild variety of 232-3

Tagore, Rabindranath 42

taken-for-granted-aspects of culture 11

Tani group 224

Tapioca 155-6

taqwa (consciousness and fear of God) 125

target audience 283

Tarun Sen Deka 224

Tea as food 209-18: associating it with social hierarchy, power relations, social stereotyping and cultural identity 211; food habits differentiate between cultures 211; tea ceremony 211; tea ceremony for Chinese 211; tea ceremony for Japanese 211

Tea bag 214

Tea break or an afternoon tea 209

Tea culture 209

Tea history, through fairy tales and folk tales 214-18: *Alice in Wonderland* by Lewis Carroll

218; *All about Tea* 215; Chinese and Japanese traditions 215; Chinese legend, tea drinking in China 215; Chinese tradition, huge collection of tea-tales 215; fairy tales and fantasy literature 217; *Harry Potter,* several instances like Madam Trelawney's tea drinking prediction 218; journeys as major part of the storylines 217; legend of Jasmine Dragon Pearl Green Tea 216; *Letting Stories Breathe: A Social Narratology* 217; 'old wife's tea' 216; presence of tea spread throughout literature 218; rich quality of teas, high medicinal values 216; 'The Ancestor of Tea' 215-16; *The Hobbit* 218

Tea leaves: developmental stages in the life growth 212

Tea: being served with other food items 209-10; in different folktales and fairy tales, historical significance of 210; mealtime tea 212; origin and use in India 213; trade 210

Teaching food history in India 33-4: course on Indian food history 34; India's evolving material culture 34; Indian food history courses 33

Thakkaram 115-16, 124, 125: interfaith relations, practices of 125

thakurbarir andarmahal 41

The Prajatantra 171-2

thematic of dislocation 311

Through the Kitchen Window: Women Writers Explore the Intimate

Tiffin 39

Train to Pakistan: habitual and instinctive life of everyday materiality 189

unhappiness *after* eating it 172

upward social mobility 12

urban kitchen 282

Vegetarianism 22-5, 54, 74, 81, 145

Vidyasagar, Ishwarchandra 48-9

Water, food imagery in 263-5: Chuiyya controls her urge to taste the *laddoo* and instead brings them to her 264; food is also reflective of the memories of our desires 264; old widow remembers about her wedding food every time she eats the bland rice 264; story of widows in pre-independence India 263; Western consumerism 271

Wild vegetables 103: Akas of West Kameng district 103; Nyishis habituated in taking wild roots 103; Wanchos of Tirap district 103; wild fruits used by the Adis of Jomo village 103

woman's food work 60

Women: as consumers who were sold lifestyle products to epitomize the features of the age bracket 284; assert their gendered caste or class identities 54; association of food, linked to the most primal of desires 258; burden of managing the kitchen and children 279; confined to the interior parts 43; conscious of their body-boundaries in relation to food and eating 263; creativity and appropriation of patriarchal ideology 60; devaluation of 78; domestic work of 61; increasing involvement in leadership roles in the food system, neglected 59; nutritional demands 74-5; of upper income households 47-8;

position in the nineteenth century 47; pregnancy food avoidances among Indian women 75; relationships to food 60-2; reported aversions to spicy foods 74; roles circumscribed within the sphere of the domestic 281; spicy food aversions 74

women's body: equated to that of food and nature 258

Women's magazines (beginning around the fifties) 272

women's relationship to food: myriad narratives on the lives of women 60; stereotyping of 61

Women's Studies scholars: food practices and their representations 59

World cuisine 283

Zimmerman, Francis 24